Aid for Elites

Current foreign aid programs are failing because they are based upon flawed assumptions about how countries develop. They attempt to achieve development without first achieving good governance and security, which are essential prerequisites for sustainable development. In focusing on the poorer members of society, they neglect the elites upon whose leadership the quality of governance and security depends. By downplaying the relevance of cultural factors to development, they avoid altering cultural characteristics that account for most of the weaknesses of elites in poor nations. Foreign aid can be made much more effective by focusing it on human capital development, especially in the governance and security sectors. Training, education, and other forms of assistance can confer both skills and cultural attributes on current and future leaders.

MARK MOYAR is the author of numerous books and articles on national security and capacity building, including *Triumph Forsaken: The Vietnam War, 1954–1965*, *A Question of Command: Counterinsurgency from the Civil War to Iraq*, and *Strategic Failure: How President Obama's Drone Warfare, Defense Cuts, and Military Amateurism Have Imperiled America*. He is a Visiting Scholar at the Foreign Policy Initiative, and has served as a professor at the U.S. Marine Corps University, where he held the Kim T. Adamson Chair of Insurgency and Terrorism, and the Joint Special Operations University. A frequent visitor to foreign conflict zones, he has served as a consultant to the senior leadership of several U.S. military commands.

Aid for Elites

Building Partner Nations and Ending Poverty through Human Capital

MARK MOYAR
The Foreign Policy Initiative

CAMBRIDGE
UNIVERSITY PRESS

CAMBRIDGE
UNIVERSITY PRESS

32 Avenue of the Americas, New York, NY 10013-2473, USA

Cambridge University Press is part of the University of Cambridge.

It furthers the University's mission by disseminating knowledge in the pursuit of education, learning, and research at the highest international levels of excellence.

www.cambridge.org
Information on this title: www.cambridge.org/9781107565012

First published 2016

Printed in the United States of America by Sheridan Books, Inc.

A catalog record for this publication is available from the British Library.

Library of Congress Cataloging-in-Publication Data
Moyar, Mark.
Aid for elites : building partner nations and ending poverty through human capital / Mark Moyar.
    pages   cm
Includes bibliographical references.
ISBN 978-1-107-12548-3 (Hardback) – ISBN 978-1-107-56501-2 (Paperback.)   1. Human capital–Developing countries.   2. National security–United States–Planning.   3. Military assistance, American–Developing countries.   4. National security–International cooperation.   I. Title.
HD4904.7.M693 2015
338.91'73–dc23   2015013322

ISBN 978-1-107-12548-3 Hardback
ISBN 978-1-107-56501-2 Paperback

Contents

Preface

On September 11, 2001, four suicide airplane attacks ended a decade of optimism about global progress and showed that events in the third world had a more direct bearing on first world security and prosperity than ever before. Energized by the specter of international terrorism, the United States invaded Afghanistan and Iraq to nullify perceived threats to U.S. security and international peace. But the unexpected duration and costs of those wars, along with the passage of a dozen years with few terrorist-related casualties inside the United States, eroded American enthusiasm for large overseas commitments. American politicians began to slash defense spending and downsize America's military presence across the world while urging other nations to take on greater roles in international security.

In justifying American retrenchment, the administration of Barack Obama asserted that the attrition of Al Qaeda, the training of Afghanistan's security forces, and various other developments had made the world a safer place. Some tactical victories had indeed been scored in recent years. Yet the situation in the third world does not, in general, look much better today than it did on September 11, 2001, and is in some respects worse. Political upheaval, war, and the persistence of Islamic extremism have woven a belt of instability from Pakistan in the east through Afghanistan, Iran, Iraq, Syria, the Palestinian territories, Egypt, and Libya in the west. Pockets of danger lurk not far afield in Yemen, Somalia, Mali, and Nigeria. In these countries, the tremors of international terrorism, war, and humanitarian catastrophe continue to be felt with disturbing frequency and at times shake entire lands. Terrorist organizations also retain strength in Asia, especially in Indonesia, and the rogue regime in North Korea menaces the world with nuclear weapons, conventional military power, illicit financing, and cyberwarfare. In the Western hemisphere, the destabilization of Mexico and most of Central

America by large narcotraffickers has caused large flows of illicit immigrants, drugs, and drug-related violence into the United States.

During the past five years, in various official and unofficial capacities, I have visited many of the countries buffeted by the tide of instability. During most of this travel, my primary purpose was to find ways for the United States to help these countries and, in the process, to protect its own interests. Without exception, the American civilian officials and military officers in these nations recognize that developing indigenous capabilities to contend with instability is becoming ever more important in light of America's military and diplomatic retrenchment. In fact, this mission has become so much accepted as an overarching objective that it has acquired its own buzz phrase, "building partner capacity," and an accompanying acronym, "BPC."

Despite all the current emphasis on BPC, little has been written on what can be called HBPC, or "how to build partner capacity." Popular and scholarly books on global affairs continue to focus on large trends, themes, and theories, such as globalization, the decline of American influence, or the nature of international power. As I have often heard generals and diplomats complain, such books have their uses in formulating grand strategy but are considerably less useful in putting strategic principles into practice, which today is the most daunting challenge. It is easy to determine that strengthening third world governments should be a key component of U.S. grand strategy but much more difficult to figure out how those governments can be strengthened.

Specialists at think tanks, academic institutions, government agencies, and the World Bank have written valuable studies on specific areas of contemporary U.S. foreign assistance, many of which are published by the sponsoring organization and read mainly within specialist communities. Most of today's experts on foreign assistance specialize in one of the three basic sectors – development, governance, and security – and spend little time on the other two. This division is unfortunate, because the three sectors are interrelated, and an optimal foreign assistance strategy requires an understanding of the interrelationships as well as the relative importance of each sector. One of the principal purposes of this book is to bring together the disparate strands of thinking on foreign assistance for the benefit of the parts and the creation of a coherent whole.

This book argues that misperceptions of the nature of human societies have resulted in flawed foreign assistance strategies. Too much of the foreign aid pie has been allocated to social and economic development and not enough to governance and security. While development is vital to the welfare of a country and to the self-sufficiency that diminishes the need for foreign assistance, it cannot be achieved under the conditions of poor governance and insecurity that prevail in much of the third world today. If foreign donors wish to alleviate poverty and make lives better in the third world, they should shift aid resources from development to governance and security.

Fundamental misperceptions have also caused donors to neglect the development of the third world's human capital, the most important ingredient in governance and security, as well as in social and economic development. Because of egalitarian developmental theories, current foreign assistance programs are overwhelmingly focused on helping the poorer members of societies, to the neglect of the elites. But a nation's ultimate viability depends on the elites, the persons of highest authority or influence, so to neglect them is to leave the country in perpetual dependency. During the 1950s and 1960s, the first world spent heavily on human capital development in order to provide poor nations with the leaders required for all critical sectors of society. It needs to do so again.

Training and education are the cornerstones of human capital development. They are critical not only because they confer skills but also because they confer culture, another aspect of building partner capacity that has been neglected because of flawed theories of development. Foreign aid should support advanced training and education for the individuals best suited to leadership positions. In addition, the military organizations of both recipient and donor countries can and should play critical roles in human capital development.

As the book's endnotes attest, I made extensive use of publicly available sources on contemporary foreign assistance programs. Those sources are, however, often incomplete or out of date. I therefore devoted considerable time to interviewing the people designing, implementing, and evaluating those programs, at overseas embassies, military outposts, donor conferences, and Beltway office buildings. This book is much the richer for their willingness to talk about current activities and events. One hears much at the U.S. embassy in Addis Ababa or the headquarters of the Colombian Special Forces that one would never learn from newspapers or think-tank reports.

For the most part, the individuals interviewed on the front lines of foreign assistance go unnamed in the pages that follow. Some asked that I not mention them by name. I omitted the names of a number of others because of the possibility that mention of their names could adversely affect them.

The research for this book also included extensive historical investigation, based on a belief that the ideas of the current generation are not necessarily superior to those of its predecessors. I have endeavored to probe history for what has been tried and how it worked in the past, and held it up against the backdrop of today to assess whether it will work now. As shall be seen, this methodology brought me to the conclusion that many American foreign assistance programs of the 1950s and 1960s should be resurrected. At the same time, I looked for approaches that had not been tried, especially with regard to newly emergent problems, and identified some that are deserving of pilot testing or immediate application.

The future of U.S. foreign assistance is bound to the future of the United States in the world more broadly. In the past few years, American politicians from across the political spectrum have advocated a reduced role for the United

States in world affairs, in which the United States spends much less on foreign assistance and defense, defers to regional powers in solving localized problems, and concentrates on "nation building at home." The sources of this new isolationism range from feelings of guilt over past national transgressions to perceptions that U.S. involvement in the world has been ineffective or counterproductive. This book employs facts to correct misperceptions of the past and to show why the real mistakes of the past need not determine future behavior. With the security of wealthy and poor countries linked as never before, promoting human capital development in the third world will result in greater security and higher quality of life for the people of all nations.

Acknowledgments

This book was made possible by the Smith Richardson Foundation, which provided a generous research grant. I would like to thank Nadia Schadlow and the anonymous peer reviewers commissioned by the foundation for their help in guiding the project through the foundation's wickets. The peer reviewers who read the manuscript for Cambridge University Press also offered many useful comments.

Former USAID administrator Andrew Natsios, Dr. Mark Ahles of the Defense Institute of Security Assistance Management, Dr. Melissa Thomas of Johns Hopkins University, and Lieutenant Colonel Adam Strickland read chapters of the manuscript and provided valuable feedback. Juan Zarate, the former deputy national security adviser for counterterrorism, and Chip Poncy, director of the Treasury Department's Office of Strategic Policy for Terrorist Financing and Financial Crimes, were invaluable sounding boards and sources of information and insight. Brigadier General Hector Pagan has done much to broaden my comprehension of Latin America and the activities of U.S. special operations forces around the world.

Tina Malone, Dean E. Cheves, and Stephen Fitzpatrick arranged meetings with U.S. and foreign officials in various countries. Other individuals who provided similar assistance or agreed to be interviewed must remain anonymous, but they are no less deserving of thanks. Jerre Wilson of the Marine Corps University and John Hales and Brigadier General Thomas V. Draude USMC (Ret.) of the Marine Corps University Foundation permitted me to work as a research fellow while completing the book.

Neither these individuals nor anyone else interviewed for this book or cited herein bears responsibility for the book's content. Any and all criticisms should be directed at the author alone. Although I have spent much of the past decade working for the U.S. government, the views expressed in the book are solely those of the author and do not represent the views, policies, or positions of the U.S. government.

Last but not least, I must thank my family for their loving support. My wife, Kelli, and children, Greta, Trent, and Luke, weathered my prolonged trips to distant lands with patience and good cheer. My parents, Bert and Marjorie Moyar, and my in-laws, Ralph and Barbara Meilander, lent much-needed hands during the period in which the book was written.

Pathways to Development

Sitting in his executive office at Mali's Ministry of Defense, Sadio Gassama received word early in the morning of unrest at the Kati barracks. Soldiers were preparing to march the twenty kilometers from the barracks to the center of the capital, he was told, in protest against the government's mishandling of the northern rebellion. The previous month, widows of troops killed in northern Mali had attracted international media attention by setting up barricades and burning tires in the Malian capital of Bamako, but until now the soldiers themselves had stayed on the political sidelines. Gassama and other Malian leaders were acutely conscious that the participation of uniformed military personnel in a political protest would amplify the national discord to a dangerous new level. It would threaten the separation of the military from politics that had prevailed since 1991, when the military had deposed President Moussa Traoré and set up the nation's first democratic government.[1]

The long-simmering Tuareg rebellion in northern Mali had boiled over three months earlier, at the start of 2012. Tuareg separatists and Islamists who had fought in Libya's civil war were at the front of the action, wielding heavy weapons they had brought back from Muammar Ghadaffi's arsenals. Their newfound firepower enabled them to overrun towns and military outposts that had withstood assaults for years. The most prominent rebel victory took place at the town of Aguelhok, where the rebels killed nearly one hundred people, including both soldiers and their families. News of the violence and mayhem spread fear across the civilian population of the northern provinces, causing two hundred thousand to flee their homes.

Malian soldiers blamed President Amadou Toumani Touré for the defeats in the north, seeing in them the same inertia, incompetence, and corruption that had characterized his government's past efforts against drug traffickers and terrorists. Reports of corruption in the supply pipeline were particularly galling to the military. Supply shortages in the north had spelled death for soldiers at isolated outposts, including the one at Aguelhok, where the defenders had fought effectively until running out of ammunition.

Gassama, in his capacity as Mali's Minister of Defense, decided to travel to Kati himself in order to head off the protest march. His chauffeur drove him through Bamako's streets to the barracks compound, a collection of ramshackle cement buildings with tin roofs. Arriving at 1 P.M., Gassama succeeded in reaching the malcontents before they had set their plans in motion. Had he possessed a disarming personality or a keen understanding of human psychology, Gassama might have averted calamity, and hence the fate of an entire nation would have turned out very differently.

Gassama's speech was, by all accounts, a debacle. Evidencing no concern for the frustrations of the soldiers, he talked down to them like a curmudgeonly schoolmaster who has caught young boys plotting to skip class. "You want to march?" Gassama said dismissively. "You're a bunch of uneducated people. I'll educate you."

The soldiers responded with howling denunciations of the government for failing to resupply the military units in the north. One soldier flatly accused the government of betrayal. Then they started throwing stones at the minister. Gassama's nervous bodyguard fired a shot into the air in an attempt to drive the crowd back, which prompted members of the crowd to fetch weapons from the armory and fire them into the air. Outgunned, the minister and his bodyguard scrambled into their car, and the chauffeur sped away under a hail of stones.

Had the officers at Kati been intent on keeping their soldiers under control, as the officers of most highly professional military organizations would have been, they most probably could have gathered them up, settled them down with stern words, and dispersed them in a manner that would have prevented the tempers of hotheads from reinforcing one another. But they attempted no such actions, which reflected both a lack of professionalism and a degree of agreement with the complaints of the mob. In the wake of the defense minister's ignominious departure, most of the senior officers fled the scene. Their absence cleared the way for junior officers to steer the frenzied mass of enlisted soldiers.

The man who took charge was Captain Amadou Haya Sanogo. The mere fact of Sanogo's presence at Kati was testament to the deficiencies of Mali's military. During officer training, he had failed several exams, which would have prevented him from becoming an officer in a more professional military organization. He had advanced up the ranks more slowly than most of his peers; as a man of thirty-nine years, he was only a captain. Most militaries would not have selected such an individual to receive American military training, as they reserve the coveted slots for the best and the brightest, but for some reason the Malian military repeatedly sent him to the United States to attend training courses.

During the fall of 2011, Sanogo had been removed from his job at a military college as the result of a hazing scandal in which five soldiers had died. Although his superiors had been right to relieve him, their next action constituted yet another momentous misstep. Reassigning Sanogo to the Kati barracks, they neither imposed restrictions on him nor gave him any job or other responsibilities, leaving him free to spread dissension and stir up trouble all day long. Sanogo quickly gained popularity among the enlisted soldiers by socializing with them regularly, something else that professional militaries do not permit their officers to do.

In the aftermath of Minister of Defense Gassama's inglorious departure, Sanogo decided to lead the throng of soldiers to the presidential palace. According to those close to him, he did not intend to overthrow the president, but merely planned to "dress him down." How he expected the president's bodyguards to react to a junior officer attempting to dress the president down is unclear.

Meanwhile, officers loyal to President Touré alerted him that soldiers had staged a mutiny at Kati. Touré used his personal Twitter account to notify the Malian citizenry that the country faced a mutiny, not a coup, a message that presumably was intended to shore up confidence in the government. To protect the palace, the presidential security staff summoned the elite paratroopers of the 33rd Parachute Regiment, who were known as the "Red Berets" because of their resplendent headgear.

When Sanogo and his followers arrived at the palace, they fired their automatic weapons in the air and shouted threats. The Red Berets responded in kind. This posturing went on for some time, neither side being so bold as to fire their weapons horizontally. The standoff allowed time for security personnel to whisk the president to safety. Once he had been evacuated, the Red Berets abandoned the defense of the palace, leaving Sanogo's troops to enter unopposed.

Unruly soldiers availed themselves of the opportunity to steal chandeliers, vases, and other valuables. As Sanogo surveyed the scene, he mulled things over. President Touré's decision to flee and the absence of presidential authority in the palace reportedly made a strong impression on him, triggering a reconsideration of his objectives. Within a couple of hours, Captain Sanogo decided that if the president could be driven out of the palace, then he might as well be driven out of office.

The mutineers next headed for the studios of the state TV and radio stations. Firing their weapons in the air in their customary style, they chased the guards away. Once inside, they compelled the studio technicians to replace the regularly scheduled TV programming with videos of traditional dancing and music, which ran in a loop for several hours while Sanogo and his coconspirators worked out what they would announce.

Late in the evening, the dancing videos went off the air, and viewers found themselves looking at twenty men in military uniforms and green berets. Beneath them was superimposed a caption that read "Committee for the Re-establishment of Democracy and the Restoration of the State." Sanogo and others explained that they had ousted the government for its failure to provide the army with the resources to defeat the northern rebellion. Lieutenant Amadou Konare, said to be the group's spokesman, averred, "We promise to hand power back to a democratically elected president as soon as the country is reunified and its integrity is no longer threatened."

The coup of March 21 proved highly popular with Mali's citizenry and armed forces. The country's two decades of democracy had been marred by widespread corruption and incompetence, robbing Malians of whatever affection they might once have had for democratic principles like the subordination of the military to civilian authority. "Our democracy needed this coup so that it could right itself," fifty-four-year-old Soumara Kalapo told Associated Press correspondent Rukmini Callimachi. "It was a democracy run by, and benefiting, a mafia."[2]

Reactions were far less favorable in the international community, dominated as it was by officials who viewed military coups as unmitigated disasters. The United States, the World Bank, and other national and international donors issued statements of condemnation and suspended their aid to Mali, except for certain types of humanitarian aid. Their pressure ensured that Sanogo would act quickly on his promise to restore civilian rule; just a few weeks after the coup, Sanogo transferred power to a transitional government led by Dioncounda Traoré, a seasoned civilian politician.

The formation of the interim government appeased some international donors, but not the United States. Democratic elections had to be held, American spokesmen said, before aid could be restored. The continued suspension of American military aid undermined the already weak capabilities of the Malian army in the north. Lack of external assistance to the army, together with bureaucratic turmoil resulting from the coup, enabled rebel groups to gobble up huge chunks of territory in April.

At this juncture, the Tuareg separatists who had dominated the rebellion in 2011 and early 2012 gave way to fanatical Islamists. Several Islamist groups, including Al Qaeda's North African branch, Al Qaeda in the Islamic Maghreb (AQIM), established dominion over northern Mali in the middle of the year. Bent on imposing sharia law with draconian purity, the Islamists whipped, beat, dismembered, stoned, and shot individuals for alleged violations of the code. They destroyed UNESCO-listed ancient shrines of local saints in the fabled trading town of Timbuktu, and they ransacked Christian churches, provoking a mass exodus of Christians.[3]

Extremists in neighboring countries who were under pressure from counterterrorist forces flocked to northern Mali and used it as a sanctuary and staging ground for cross-border attacks. The governments of Mali's neighbors sent despondent pleas for help to foreign nations and multilateral organizations. During the summer, the Economic Community of West African States laid plans to deploy three thousand African soldiers into northern Mali to drive out the rebels, and the organization's member nations asked France and the United States to provide support. The French were agreeable, but the Americans balked, arguing that the problem should be solved politically rather than militarily. Political stability had to be restored in the south through elections, they said, and then the parties could negotiate a political solution in the north.[4] Johnnie Carson, the U.S. Assistant Secretary of State for African Affairs, explained to American congressmen on June 29 that the United States would enhance the prospects for negotiation by providing assistance that would "increase economic development and provide economic opportunities to disaffected youth populations in northern Mali."[5] In September, Secretary of State Hillary Clinton rebuffed mounting international pressure for military action with the assertion that "only a democratically elected government will have the legitimacy to achieve a negotiated political settlement in northern Mali, end the rebellion, and restore the rule of law."[6]

But then, out of nowhere, Mali became a matter of national security for the United States. On September 11, the eleventh anniversary of the 9/11 attacks, militants assailed U.S. government facilities in Benghazi, Libya, killing American Ambassador Chris Stevens and three other Americans. For a week, the U.S. administration attributed the killings to a spontaneous mass demonstration, but soon it became clear that the operation had been a premeditated terrorist operation, carried out by Al Qaeda in the Islamic Maghreb and other extremist organizations. At a press conference on September 26, Secretary of State Clinton acknowledged that Al Qaeda might have been behind the attack, and she mentioned that the organization was using Mali as a springboard for operations into Libya.[7]

Just four days later, Carson announced a reversal of the American position on military intervention. He explained that the world was facing terrorists in Mali, "and the response to that must be a security, military response."[8] The evaporation of formal U.S. opposition to a military solution opened the door to a United Nations resolution for the use of force in Mali. The United States, however, continued to insist on democratic elections as a precondition for an African military expedition, which prevented the dispatch of any foreign troops in the near term. The Islamists strengthened their grip on northern Mali in the ensuing months.

Extremist forces advanced toward Bamoko in January 2013, intent on establishing an Islamist government with control over all of Mali. The Malian government issued desperate pleas for military intervention, concentrating on the most likely saviors, the United States and France. The U.S. government, which had little appetite for military intervention at this time, avoided making military commitments and instead continued talking about the need for elections and negotiations. The French government, on the other hand, rapidly deployed its ground and air forces. French troops saved the Malian capital and then drove the extremists from northern Mali. Afterward, the French sought to hand over security to forces from Mali and its West African neighbors, but the French military would end up remaining for years afterward, owing to the ineffectiveness of the African forces.

The most obvious lesson of the Mali crisis of 2012 is that security problems in seemingly remote countries can endanger the security of other nations, near and far. That lesson will be explored in Chapter 5. This chapter is concerned with a subtler aspect of events in Mali, the internal dynamics of impoverished countries and their relevance to foreign assistance programs. While personality and chance dominated many of the coup's events, the susceptibility of Mali to this sort of cataclysm was a product of those dynamics. The same is true across the third world.

In the years leading up to the coup, the United States had concentrated its considerable assistance to Mali in select sectors of government and society. With Mali, as with every other country in the world, policymakers and congressmen in Washington allocated funds to the primary sectors of assistance – governance, development, and security – and their various subsectors, based on their personal views about the relative importance of each. In the foreign assistance world, governance is generally understood as the exercise of political authority, and its leading subsectors of assistance are administration, justice, human rights, political competition, and civil society. Development is most commonly defined as the advancement of social and economic conditions, and its subsectors include health, education, infrastructure, agriculture, economic growth, and women's rights. Security is the protection of state and society from physical harm and intimidation, with the military, police, courts, and corrections the primary subsectors.[9]

Reasonable and knowledgeable people often have very different views on how much each of these sectors and subsectors contributes to national betterment and how much each can be improved by foreign aid. In 2011, the U.S. government concentrated its aid to Mali on development, based on a particular interpretation of foreign assistance that has both strong supporters and strong detractors. Out of the $221 million allocated to development, $79.8 million went to roads and irrigation infrastructure, $46.5 million to the improvement of Bamako's airport, $24.5 million to malaria prevention and treatment, and $16.0 million to basic education.[10]

That same year, the U.S. government spent less than $4 million on what it characterized as security, which also reflected a view of foreign assistance that is controversial. Most of that total, some $3.2 million, went toward the Trans-Sahara Counter-Terrorism Partnership, a program that funded not only security forces but also development programs intended to curb the popular appeal of AQIM and other terrorist groups long known to be active in Mali.[11] A USAID document explained, "The Trans-Sahara Counter-Terrorism Partnership aims to provide Malians with the means to overcome the acute poverty and weak institutional capacity exploited by extremist groups," with primary emphasis on "enhancing civic engagement and economic opportunities among Malian youth."[12]

The security budget included only $350,000 for International Military Education and Training, which was the principal funding line for the education of military officers, and $200,000 for Foreign Military Financing, which paid for the acquisition of U.S. military equipment and training. "We provided training and equip support for many years, but in relatively modest quantities," Deputy Assistant Secretary of Defense for Africa Amanda Dory acknowledged to a Senate subcommittee in December 2012. She added, "I don't think that level of resourcing was commensurate with the threat."[13]

It should be noted that Mali was not among those nations that pour large amounts of their national income into defense and hence have little need for foreign military aid. In 2011, at which time the country already faced serious security problems in the vast north, Mali spent a modest 1.9 percent of its small GDP on defense. Foreign observers were struck by the dearth of resources available to the Malian army. "In Mali, they barely have AKs that have butt stocks," an American officer remarked in 2011. "They have old Chinese ammo where one of every three rounds work." The forty-two vehicles that the Americans had provided sat idle in motor pools because of a lack of fuel to run them.[14]

While low internal and external funding ensured that Mali's military would have too few resources to vanquish the rebels, the resource shortages were exacerbated by corruption. Considered less corrupt than many of its neighbors, Mali was nonetheless rife with corruption, ranking 118 out of 182 countries on Transparency International's Corruption Perceptions Index.[15] The impact of corruption and the ability of foreign donors to influence corruption levels are also the subject of much dispute, which helps explain why the U.S. government spent so little in 2011 on programs aimed at improving Malian governance. Expenditures on governance programs targeted directly at the Malian government amounted to just $114,000 for the year, with another $724,100 spent on other governance subsectors such as civil society and political competition.

In Mali's case, low U.S. spending on security and governance facilitated the further deterioration of security and governance. High spending on development did not improve security or governance, in part because the risks posed by armed Islamists and separatists in the north caused many aid donors to concentrate aid projects near the capital and other areas in the south.[16] Once security and governance crumbled in the north, the development projects that had been implemented there crumbled, too, unable to withstand rebel bullets and knives.[17] Subsequent efforts to regain the north with development and governance measures came to naught, necessitating recourse to a military solution.

In hindsight, it is safe to say that the U.S. government did not accurately perceive which types of human activity were most important to Mali's national betterment. Consequently, it did not concentrate assistance in the sectors where it could have been most effective. As we shall see, Mali was far from unique in this regard.

What accounts for these misperceptions? The answer is to be found in the theories on national prosperity that guided American decision makers. Since the days of Thucydides, bright minds have tried to figure out why some nations are rich and others are poor, in order, among other things, to help the poor countries become rich, or at least less poor. As with most controversies on the fundamental nature of politics, no consensus opinion has ever emerged, compelling those engaged in the business of prioritizing foreign assistance to select from a range of opinions. In the recent history of the United States, a few schools of thought have dominated the policy choices of foreign assistance organizations and third world governments.

FOREIGN EXPLOITATION

During the Cold War, large numbers of intellectuals subscribed to the view that wealthy nations acquired their riches by exploiting poor nations. European colonial powers, followed by the neocolonial United States and its multinational corporations, pilfered natural resources from the world's poor countries, employed their people at low wages, and compelled them to buy manufactured goods at inflated prices. This interpretation was to be found not only in the Marxism–Leninism of the Communist bloc but also in a number of left-wing offshoot theories that enjoyed currency in the intelligentsia of the free world, of which the most prominent were dependency theory and world systems theory.

Political leaders in a variety of newly independent countries embraced the view that foreign exploitation accounted for the inequality of nations, and they enacted measures to stop the alleged exploitation, such as the expulsion of foreign businesses, the banning of foreign investment, and the imposition of high tariffs. But they achieved only economic stagnation and continuing poverty, while some of the third world leaders who adopted free-market capitalism saw their countries soar to prosperity. By the end of the Cold War, all but the most ideologically rigid national leaders had abandoned economic isolationism in favor of open international commerce. Consequently, the theory that foreign exploitation is the principal cause of national inequality has fallen out of favor with most serious theorists and development practitioners.

General agreement now exists that the wealth of nations is largely dependent on economic growth, and that economic growth is a function of a nation's own economic productivity, not of how much wealth it takes away from other nations. The settling of that dispute has been a huge step forward for international development, but it has not settled the larger question of national prosperity, only shifted the debate to a new battleground. The debate has moved from the question of whether economic weakness is the result of external or internal factors to the question of why some nations have been less capable than others of achieving economic growth.

THE ANNALES SCHOOL

This shift has induced a large-scale migration from the dependency theory and world systems theory of the Cold War to *Annaliste* theory, which explains the inequality of nations as the consequence of geographic and environmental variations. The theory began with Fernand Braudel, a French historian born at the start of the twentieth century. Braudel was blossoming into a promising young scholar when World War II erupted and he was called up for active service in the French army. Captured by the Germans in 1940, Braudel spent the remainder of the war in captivity, where he took advantage of the solitude to write his seminal work, *The Mediterranean and the Mediterranean World in the Age of Philip II*. After returning to France at war's end, Braudel became the leading figure of the *Annales* school of historians, named after its journal *Annales d'Histoire Économique et Sociale*.

Braudel and the other *Annalistes*, as the school's disciples were called, asserted that the truly important factors in history were geography and environment. The *Annalistes* found the greatest profundity in the access to commercial activity and foreign ideas afforded by the Mediterranean and in the prevention of interaction by the desert sands of the Sahara. In comparison with lasting facts like soil fertility or the steam engine, they said, the wars, artists, and kings of mankind were fleeting trifles. Individuals and peoples were creatures of their environment, not altogether different from other species, their choices meaningless except when the same choice was made a million times over during a period of centuries or millennia, in response to geographic or environmental conditions. Such behavioral patterns produced economic and technological trends that accounted for the disparities in economic output from one region to another.

The *Annales* school quickly accumulated adherents in the United States and other Western countries, becoming the most influential historical school in the world during the 1950s. In the latter decades of the twentieth century, its influence waned in academic history departments as postmodernism and other abstractions took hold. Then suddenly, near the end of the century, it vaulted back to prominence, with the help of a few authors whose eloquence captured the minds of politicians and publics.

Foremost among these authors was Jared Diamond, a career physiologist who became a professor of geography later in life. In his bestselling *Guns, Germs, and Steel: The Fates of Human Societies*, Diamond looked through the *Annaliste* lenses of geography and environment to explain why certain peoples had achieved higher levels of prosperity than others. A few years later, the economist Jeffrey Sachs employed *Annaliste* principles to formulate global poverty solutions in his blockbuster *The End of Poverty: Economic Possibilities for Our Time*.[18] Sachs, who had already been established as a towering figure in academia, became a worldwide celebrity, making *Time* magazine's list of the one hundred most influential people on the planet.

Diamond and Sachs repackaged Braudel's ponderously expressed ideas into terms more accessible to the average reader. Inequalities among nations, they wrote, resulted from the presence or absence of various natural "curses" and "traps" that were consequences of humankind's surroundings rather than of humans themselves. One was the curse of being landlocked, a feature of many impoverished sub-Saharan African countries, which deprived societies of access to maritime commerce and the technological knowledge that boosts economic productivity. Another was the "disease curse," whereby climates conducive to debilitating diseases like malaria depleted the work force. Countries afflicted by the so-called resource curse, such as Saudi Arabia and Nigeria, failed to develop politically and economically because their elites could enjoy lives of luxury merely by selling abundant natural resources to foreigners. Poverty itself made the list of curses, because the poorest nations lacked the levels of income required for the personal saving that led to economic investment.[19]

According to Diamond and Sachs, rich countries could eliminate severe poverty in poor countries through large expenditures on social and economic measures that exorcised the curses of geography and environment. Building roads to landlocked states would mitigate commercial disadvantages. Administering vaccines would remove the scourge of disease. Large infusions of external funding would facilitate personal saving. Once these measures were taken, poverty would recede, education would increase, and the population would make use of the technologies that had enabled other countries to thrive. Because spending on social and economic development held such promise, foreign donors needed to concentrate their aid resources on the development sector.

Another group of writers, emerging a few years after the publication of *Guns, Germs, and Steel,* focused more narrowly on the *Annaliste* theme of geographic and environmental influences on the flow of information. Among the leading lights of this group was Thomas P. Barnett, author of *The Pentagon's New Map.* Barnett depicted a world divided into two camps, which were differentiated by their degree of "connectedness" to information. The "disconnected" countries, which together comprised the "Non-Integrating Gap," were the countries in Africa, the Middle East, Central Asia, East Asia, and Latin America that were generally considered to be the members of the third world. The other countries, which were called the "Functioning Core," had to "connect" the "Non-Integrating Gap" countries through information technology and commerce. Once they had been connected to the rest of the world, the "Non-Integrating Gap" countries would prosper, and the problems of international terrorism and political instability would wither away.[20]

The impact of Barnett's work would be felt for years to come, particularly within the U.S. defense establishment. In Iraq and Afghanistan, commanders made life-and-death decisions on the basis of the theories presented in *The Pentagon's New Map.* During a visit to an insurgency-plagued Afghan district in 2008, I was told by an American military officer that the United States was helping the Afghan government build a new road from the district's largest town to "disconnected" villages in order to "connect" them to the outside world. The villagers would stop supporting the Taliban once they could visit the town, the officer explained, because the town had the internet, television, and other information portals that would expose them to new political ideas and new information.

During another trip to Afghanistan, two years later, I heard from a NATO media expert in Kabul that the Afghans were losing interest in the Taliban as the result of two recent developments: the growth in the number of Afghans with television sets, and the airing of progressive soap operas on Afghan television stations. In these soap operas, he said, Afghan women performed tasks that had traditionally been performed by Afghan men. He was convinced, as were many of the other Westerners in Kabul, that as soon as Afghans received access to information about gender equality, they would cast off their ancient traditions of male dominance and renounce the Taliban for clinging to those backward ways.

THE ANNALES SCHOOL ON GOVERNANCE

The modern-day apostles of the *Annales* school, like their forbearers, explicitly downplayed the influence of governance on the inequality of nations. In their view, variation in the quality of governance was not very pronounced from one country to the next. Western reports on widespread corruption in poor countries were myopic at best, and ethnocentric at worst. Therefore, the first world ought not waste its time or resources on altering third world governance.

Sachs was especially vociferous in arguing that corruption was not a central factor in the economic weakness of Africa, the continent most often cited by those positing a link between governmental corruption and low national income. As proof, he said that African countries tended to be significantly weaker economically than Asian countries with comparable levels of perceived corruption. He attributed these disparities between Africa and Asia to geography and diseases, particularly AIDS and malaria, which in his view demonstrated that geographic and environmental disadvantages were the true cause of African poverty. As further evidence that governance was not crucial, he noted that Ghana, Malawi, Senegal, and Mali were "relatively well-governed" but were nonetheless still poor.[21]

THE WEIGHT OF EVIDENCE

The theory that geography and environment dictate national outcomes does not measure up well against the facts. First of all, a substantial number of nations confound the theory's principal generalizations. While Africa's landlocked countries may rank among the world's poorest countries, the landlocked nations of Austria and Switzerland rank among the wealthiest, and they stand far ahead of countries with long coastlines like Myanmar and Mozambique. Canada and Norway have an abundance of fossil fuels, but their governments and economies look much more like those of fuel-importing countries like the United States and Germany than those of Saudi Arabia or Nigeria.

Were geography overwhelming in its power, one would expect that the economic output of particular pieces of terrain would not depend upon who inhabited them. In actuality, however, changes in inhabitants have altered output levels with stunning regularity. The Westerners who settled in Australasia, North America, and Africa consistently accumulated wealth at rates far exceeding those of the indigenous populations. The settlers introduced advanced agricultural methods and technologies, enabling them to produce more crops per acre of soil. To overcome geographic obstacles to commerce, they erected steel bridges and built oceangoing ships. Their factories churned out trucks that could carry goods in far greater quantities than mules, and mass produced machine guns that could kill people in far greater quantities than spears.

Such differences were not merely the result of knowledge differentials. Indigenous populations that were exposed to the advanced technological knowledge of the settlers often failed to make effective use of that knowledge. In places where immigrant groups coexisted with indigenous groups, they often differed widely in economic productivity many generations after the immigration occurred.[22] Numerous other societies with access to advanced knowledge, moreover, have not made productive use of it. History shows that information is certain to yield higher economic productivity only when the recipients already possess certain capabilities and motives, which are much more abundant in some societies than in others.

The inadequacy of geographic and environmental determinism can also be seen in the persistence of economic stagnation in many third world countries after a sixty-year period in which wealthy nations transferred more than $2.5 trillion in aid to poor ones, much of it aimed directly at mitigating natural barriers. If we look closely, we will find that a large fraction of the aid was squandered because of human factors that trumped geography and environment. When Western development organizations have provided radios and cellular telephones to remote communities for the exchange of commercial data or the summoning of emergency assistance, some recipients have used the devices in the intended ways, while others have used them only to chat with relatives or to notify their criminal friends of an approaching police patrol. When the West has distributed bed nets to third world populations to protect them from malarial mosquitoes, some recipients have used the nets, while others have sold theirs on the black market. In certain countries, infusions of foreign aid have led to higher personal saving and economic growth, while in others they have led only to fleets of German luxury cars and excursions to the French Riviera for the families of top government officials. Afghan television programs depicting rising incomes for families with fewer children may have inspired some watchers to change their behavior, but the average Afghan woman is still having close to six children.

GOVERNANCE AND NATIONAL PROSPERITY

The flaw in *Annaliste* reasoning that has garnered the most attention from experts and donors is its downplaying of governance. Over the past decade, numerous experts at the World Bank, USAID, OECD, and various universities have assailed the view that governance has little to do with economic development. Their research shows that badly governed nations cannot achieve broad and sustained economic growth no matter how much foreign aid they receive.[23]

For most of these experts, corruption is the dominant feature on the visage of bad governance, as it undermines nearly every activity that contributes to economic growth. Corrupt officials steal funds and materials earmarked for economic development programs. Demanding exorbitant bribes from private businesses, they enervate existing firms and discourage investment in new ventures. Corruption deprives states of the resources to perform the governmental functions that facilitate economic growth, and it reinforces the impoverishment of the government by spurring indignant private citizens to vote against tax levies or to engage in tax evasion. Recent estimates put the costs of corruption for developing countries at close to $1 trillion per year, dwarfing the official development assistance annual total of $141 billion.[24]

Corrupt government leaders devise all manner of ingenious schemes to steer revenue from state taxation, natural resources, and foreign aid into their offshore bank accounts or into the pockets of political supporters or protection forces. International researchers with access to the financial records of third world countries have uncovered remarkably efficient corruption within governments that are normally considered grossly inefficient. Chad, for instance, ranks in the bottom 10 percent of the world's countries in governance effectiveness, according to the World Bank's Worldwide Governance Indicators.[25] Yet a 2004 study found that more than 99 percent of the money released by the Ministry of Finance for rural health clinics was pilfered before it reached the clinics.[26]

Geography and disease help account for the fact that African countries are less prosperous than Asian countries with comparable levels of corruption, but it does not necessarily follow that only geography and disease matter. Corruption can cause serious harm to a nation's economy in concert with AIDS. It often does.

With the exception of Botswana, every country in modern sub-Saharan Africa has experienced bouts of massive corruption that have stifled development. Countries like Ghana and Senegal are well governed relative to most other African countries and some Asian countries, but in absolute terms their governments are corrupt and only marginally effectual, and their economies have suffered as a result. A recent study on Ghana commissioned by USAID stated that the principal hindrance to economic growth was the president's appointment of political supporters to key positions in the civil administration and state-owned enterprises, for these individuals routinely awarded state contracts and jobs to their cronies. "The main beneficiaries of Ghana's economic development," the report's authors lamented, "are increasingly the privileged few who have the capacity to gain access to the political elite."[27]

A study on Senegal by Management Systems International observed, "It is widely acknowledged that a lack of transparency in public affairs and financial transactions, as well as chronic corruption, plague Senegal today." This corruption "increases chronic poverty and the gap between citizens and their state." The report added that foreign donors "are increasingly recognizing the importance of good governance and citizen participation at the local level as essential for effectively implementing anti-poverty and local development programs."[28]

While the nasty effects of corruption form a critical part of the explanation for why good governance is a prerequisite for social and economic development, they are not the only critical part. When political meddling prevents law enforcement from keeping criminal activity in check, criminals routinely steal or extort from businesses and aid organizations. Incompetent governance hinders the administration of government-sponsored development projects and governmental organizations engaged in social or economic work.

Foreign development agencies frequently build facilities and then hand them over to the indigenous government, whether because the government demands it or the development organization prefers it. When the recipient government is ineffective or predatory, the school classrooms sit empty and health clinics have no nurses. According to a U.S. development official with decades of experience in Latin America, 50 percent of the facilities built by the U.S. government in the region during recent years have ceased operations within two years of project completion.[29]

Perhaps the most appalling example I have personally encountered was a court house in rural Afghanistan that had been built at the behest of the West a few years earlier and then had been thrust into the hands of the Afghan government. The Western donors had expected the Afghan government to use the court house to bring the "rule of law" to a district that had known only the traditional justice of the tribes, in which the judgment of tribal elders ruled supreme. The introduction of modern justice, it was believed, would increase the popularity of the Afghan government at the expense of the Taliban. The court house had been built to Western standards and was extraordinarily large in comparison with other Afghan governmental buildings. But the Kabul government had been unable to convince any judges or lawyers to leave the comfort and safety of the cities to work in this rough-and-tumble area. The local population, having no particular desire to replace their traditional justice system with a foreign one, undertook no effort to pressure the national government, the Western donors, or anyone else to come up with judges or lawyers. Quickly discerning that the fancy new building had no tenants, some enterprising Afghans convinced the local authorities to let them use it for business purposes, in exchange for cash. After stripping out and selling whatever building materials and furnishings they deemed unnecessary, the Afghan entrepreneurs turned the court house into one of Afghanistan's finest sheep stalls.

Even where externally funded facilities remain in operation, they often fail to live up to their potential because of a lack of work ethic among government employees. In 2005, researchers from Harvard and the World Bank paid unannounced visits to educational and health facilities in Bangladesh, Ecuador, India, Indonesia, Peru, and Uganda to measure actual staffing levels and staff productivity. They found that 19 percent of all teachers and 35 percent of all health workers had skipped work on the day of the visit.

Development theorists often attribute lower work hours in poor countries to inferior salaries, which compel individuals to divert some of their official work time to supplementing their income through other activities. But that argument could not be made with regard to the facilities in question, the Harvard and World Bank researchers pointed out, because workers in the education and health sectors in these low-income nations received much higher salaries than their fellow citizens. Teachers earned on average four times the per capita GDP of their country, due to strong public employee unions.

Even more compelling evidence of the influence of work ethic was to be found in the project's discovery that many of the employees present were not performing their assigned tasks. In India, for example, only half of the teachers were found to be teaching during the periods of scheduled instruction. The others were drinking tea, reading the newspaper, or gabbing with colleagues. Not surprisingly, a separate study conducted in India during the same period found that of all the students in grades two through nine, only 40 percent could read at a second-grade level, and only 30 percent were capable of performing second-grade-level mathematics.[30]

Since the start of the twenty-first century, the international aid community's attentiveness to governance has risen sharply as a result of the research demonstrating the influence of governance on economic development. The World Bank, which in the past had shown little concern, now makes governance a major part of its assistance programs, incorporating good governance measures into grants and loans and underwriting stand-alone governance initiatives.[31] Other aid agencies have followed suit.[32] In 2004, the desire to promote good governance and work with able partners led the U.S. government to create the Millennium Challenge Corporation, which provides aid only to countries that have achieved certain standards of governance.

Nevertheless, those who share the view of Diamond and Sachs that governance is relatively unimportant remain highly influential in the development world. In Mali and many other countries, governance still receives paltry funding from the U.S. government and other donors in comparison with development. Most foreign assistance continues to fund traditional development programs, many of which seek to negate unfavorable geographic and environmental factors, like bridge construction and treatment of infectious diseases. Some of what is characterized as donor spending on security or governance is really development, as in the case of the Trans-Sahara Counter-Terrorism Partnership. As we shall see, the *Annaliste* worldview undergirds the

UN's Millennium Development Goals, which have exerted and continue to exert enormous influence on the dispensation of foreign aid.

THE SECURITY FACTOR

While awareness of the importance of governance has risen in recent years, the same cannot be said of the importance of security, or of the relationships among governance, development, and security. Foreign donors frequently address governance and development in isolation from security, which obscures the symbiotic relationships among them and discourages adoption of a unified strategy addressing all three. As World Bank president Robert B. Zoellick has observed, helping countries threatened or beset by insecurity requires a much better understanding of "the linkages and overlaps among weak governance, poverty, and conflict."[33]

Governance and development experts are often located in the same organization, which helps explain why they tend to work more with each other than either of them works with security experts. More often than not, the security experts serve or have served in military organizations that are very different in character and purpose from civilian organizations. Cultural differences divide the governance, development, and security tribes, with the gulf greatest between the development and security tribesmen. Some development workers consider military personnel and other security professionals to be coarse brutes whose only solution to any problem is the sledgehammer. Some security specialists deride development experts as sandal-wearing hippies who care more about showing how enlightened and generous they are than about protecting the interests of their own country.

There is a grain of truth in these stereotypes, because a minority in each group has conformed to them to one degree or another. But most members of both groups are better than the stereotypes would imply, and some have crossed the dividing line to work together. Sharing a willingness to spend months or years in impoverished countries, which distinguishes them from nearly all of their countrymen, they often develop an unanticipated respect for one another. Nevertheless, the governance, development, and security tribes still tend to operate according to very different interpretations of the world.

For many academics and practitioners who specialize in governance or development, insecurity is simply a by-product of bad governance or under-development. Therefore, the remedies to insecurity are to be found in governance or development programs, rather than in security programs, which are liable to make the situation worse by giving more power to unsavory military officers.[34] "Too often, the development community has treated states affected by fragility and conflict simply as harder cases of development," notes Zoellick.[35]

Theories that designate governance and development as determinants of security have been disproven repeatedly by the failure of governance and development to engender security where the government's security apparatus is grossly abusive or inept, as it very often is in the third world. The abuses of security forces exacerbate the problems of violence or rebellion that they are supposed to quell, while their ineptitude permits insurgents and criminals to use violence and intimidation on a scale that makes governance and development very difficult if not impossible. Tax collectors seldom collect taxes in areas where people are regularly raped and murdered. Teachers do not show up for work when terrorists threaten their families at gunpoint. Foreign companies stop doing business in a country if rising criminality imposes high costs and risks on commercial enterprises.[36]

Security deficiencies also prevent aid agencies from carrying out governance and development programs. The bombing of the UN office in Baghdad's Canal Hotel in August 2003 led to the prompt withdrawal of all six hundred members of the UN staff from Iraq. In January 2012, the U.S. Peace Corps pulled all of its personnel out of Honduras after one of its members was shot and another was raped. Peace Corps Director Aaron S. Williams explained that the agency was withdrawing because "the safety and security of all Peace Corps volunteers is the agency's highest priority."[37]

Some of the misunderstanding about the relationships among governance, development, and security stems from the publication of Greg Mortenson's enormously popular book *Three Cups of Tea: One Man's Mission to Fight Terrorism and Build Nations ... One School at a Time.* In the book, Mortenson related that the Taliban kidnapped him in Pakistan in 1996 and held him for eight days before letting him go in return for a promise to build schools for Pakistani children. The coeducational schools Mortenson subsequently built in rural Pakistan and then Afghanistan did not come under Taliban attack, which he attributed to respect for education of both boys and girls on the part of the Taliban and the rest of the population. According to Mortenson, the schools strengthened communities and provided moderate coeducation as an alternative to the extremist, male-only education offered in many Islamist schools. Therefore, building more coeducational schools could solve the problem of extremism across Pakistan and Afghanistan.

Key sections of Mortenson's narrative unraveled in April 2011, due in large part to the sleuthing of author Jon Krakauer, a former Mortenson supporter who discovered glaring factual inaccuracies in various claims by Mortenson. Inspired by Krakauer, producers at CBS News tracked down Mortenson's supposed Taliban kidnappers for a *60 Minutes* segment and learned that they had belonged not to the Taliban, but to Mortenson's own personal protection detail. Neither the Taliban nor anyone else had kidnapped Mortenson. It turned out that the Taliban hadn't left the schools alone because of a grandeur of spirit or an ardor for the education of girls, but because of an absence of Taliban fighters in the areas where the schools had been built.

Regrettably, the fraud was detected several years too late. Between the publication of *Three Cups of Tea* in 2006 and Mortenson's fall from grace, the book fueled a school construction spree in Afghanistan under the auspices of the U.S. military and a host of governmental and nongovernmental development agencies. In areas controlled by the Afghan government, the schools educated large numbers of children, but rarely did they cause individuals to fight against the Taliban or other insurgent groups, for Afghans picked sides based on whichever side could provide them long-term security and justice, not whichever could spend the most on development or teach the most about gender issues.

In areas where the Taliban were strong, school building was, with few exceptions, an unalloyed failure. Like most insurgents, the Taliban saw government-sanctioned schools as symbols of governmental power and prestige, so they torched schools, threatened and assassinated teachers, and chopped off the fingers of pupils and parents. A report by the UN Special Representative for Children and Armed Conflict in 2010 found that insurgent intimidation and violence had closed between 50 and 80 percent of schools in the provinces where the Taliban had a presence in at least a few areas. Given that the Taliban did not have complete control of any of these provinces, the percentage of schools closed in villages where the Taliban had a substantial presence was probably closer to 100 percent. In further contradiction of Mortenson's depiction of liberal-minded Taliban warriors, the report noted that female students and the schools they attended had been "particularly hard-hit" by insurgent attacks.[38] Unfortunately, these developments largely escaped the notice of the West, as evidenced by the fact that Mortenson's fall from grace was accompanied by numerous statements that his personal foibles should not detract from his splendid achievements in the field of education.

Because of Mortenson and a number of other influential individuals who advocated nonviolent measures as the sole solutions to insurgency, some of the NATO commanders in Afghanistan based their entire counterinsurgency campaigns on the premise that insurgencies could be defused by redressing grievances and fulfilling unmet needs. They ordered their troops to steer clear of enemy strongholds, avoid discharging their weapons except in self-defense, and limit their fire to warning shots aimed at frightening the enemy away. Violence, they said, would only enrage the relatives of the victims and eliminate leaders who were needed as peacemakers. "We're at risk of killing the Gerry Adams or Martin McGuinness of the Taliban," the senior British officer in Helmand explained to his troops in 2008.[39]

The renunciation of aggressive military operations was a flop wherever it was tried. The population, desperate for security, lost confidence in NATO forces upon seeing them run away when the Taliban ignored their warning shots. By avoiding confrontations with Taliban fighters, NATO units ceded the military initiative along with control of much of the population, allowing the insurgents to recruit new members and tax farmers at will. NATO forces ended up confined to a few towns, which became the only places safe enough for the implementation of governance and development activities, and even there the activities generated little enthusiasm among citizens who knew that such pro-government pockets were surrounded by a countryside seething with hateful Taliban.

Most districts in Helmand province remained highly insecure until 2010, when U.S. Marine battalions arrived with a more hard-headed approach, involving aggressive military patrolling throughout the province. Inflicting heavy casualties on the insurgents and pushing them out of towns and villages, the Marines permitted the expansion of governance and development activities and induced the defection of tribes that believed the military tide had turned against the Taliban. Because the Marines could move anywhere they wished, they were able to visit NATO-funded development projects and see whether the Afghans were using the aid money to operate health clinics or line their pockets. They discarded the dubious theory that indiscriminate development spending would shift the population's behavior by creating gratitude and reducing poverty, and instead they provided money only to local elites who provided tangible benefits to security in return, such as identifying the location of improvised explosive devices or preventing attacks on Marine patrols in their areas. Using development money to buy short-term security improvements did not ensure long-term development, but it was necessary to make long-term development possible.[40]

The failed efforts at "winning without fighting" in Afghanistan might have been avoided had the attention given to *Three Cups of Tea* been devoted instead to American experiences in Colombia just a few years earlier. In 2000, the United States began a $500 million development program aimed at convincing Colombian farmers to stop growing the coca plant, the leaves of which are used by international narcotraffickers to produce cocaine and are chewed by locals for a milder and less addictive stimulation. American planners believed that financial incentives and legal pressures would cause the peasant farmers of the Andean nation to switch from the lucrative coca to more benign crops.

During the program's first two years, it did little to curb coca cultivation in areas where security and governance were lacking, which meant most of the areas under coca cultivation. Vanda Felbab-Brown, who authored an assessment of the program for USAID, determined that implementation of the program was often frustrated by the inability of local governments to handle the financial and administrative requirements.[41] Another study, by the Washington-based Center for Strategic and International Studies, noted that the program's financial remuneration and legal strictures failed to alter the behavior of the farmers when fighters from the Marxist-Leninist Fuerzas Armadas Revolucionarias de Colombia (FARC) and other insurgent groups operated regularly in their area, as these fighters would employ persuasion or intimidation to get them to continue growing coca.[42]

In recognition of these realities, USAID discontinued program implementation in Colombia's insecure areas after 2002 and shifted focus from coca elimination to poverty reduction and economic growth. Planners hoped that the prosperity generated by these initiatives would draw people from the areas of illicit cultivation to areas held by the government.[43] But most of the coca-producing farmers were content to stay where they were, enjoying the profits from the leaves they sold, the pleasant chewing of the leaves they kept, and the smiles of gun-toting insurgents who would be certain to frown at the first sign of an intention to depart.

Ultimately, the Colombian government gained the upper hand in its struggle against coca cultivation by pursuing security first, governance second, and development third. Álvaro Uribe, elected president in 2002, disputed the conventional wisdom of Colombian and American experts who viewed security as the result of governance and development initiatives, rather than as a precursor to them. "Security will not be the only concern of the National Government, but it will be the first," Uribe pronounced. Security was essential to governance and development, he asserted, as well as to the safety of the citizenry, particularly the poorest citizens since they had the least protection from violence. "Economic development and job opportunities," Uribe said, "are equally dependent on the existence of a security environment that encourages investment, business, and public spending on behalf of the community that is the objective of permanent depredation by the armed illegal groups."[44]

Uribe expanded the security forces and directed them to attack the insurgents relentlessly. After the military drove the insurgents from an area, soldiers and policemen established a permanent security presence. Next, the central government built up the local governance capabilities required to administer official programs and enforce laws. Finally, the government implemented programs to replace coca with other crops. The authors from the Center for Strategic and International Studies noted, "Improvements on the security side – above all, those related to the ability of the government to control territory and impose the rule of law – have been fundamental to furthering other objectives such as economic development, protection of human rights, and improved governance."[45]

The success of Colombia in improving governance and development via security operations confounds the theory, popular in civilian governance and development circles, that large investments in security are a recipe for military domination of the government, tyrannical rule, and underdevelopment.[46] Plenty of other countries have similarly spent heavily on security without succumbing to such ill effects, including South Korea, the United Arab Emirates, Taiwan, Oman, and India. Countries like North Korea and Chad that have poured large sums into their security forces and are devoid of political rights, civil liberties, and economic prosperity owe their troubles not to defense spending, but to bad governance. Security forces seldom operate independently of the political authorities – even the militaries of Nazi Germany and the Soviet Union bowed to the will of their civilian masters. When military officers stage a coup or otherwise intervene in politics, they usually seek to return power to civilian authorities as quickly as possible because they prefer orchestrating combat operations and flying aircraft to formulating fiscal policies and managing the postal service.[47]

Governments that have skimped on security have often fallen victim to insecurity or worse. As shown at the beginning of this chapter, Mali's low expenditures on security facilitated rebel gains that precipitated a coup by a military that was too ineffectual to wage war but more than capable of overthrowing the government. The shrinkage of Côte d'Ivoire's military at the start of the twenty-first century enabled militias to engage in ethnic violence and foment a civil war that raged for four years.

The radical downsizing of Guatemala's national security forces after the civil war of 1960–1996, a measure intended to prevent a recurrence of violence, permitted domestic criminals and Mexican drug traffickers to operate with impunity in much of the country. A report published by the Brussels-based International Crisis Group in 2010, at which time the rate of violence in Guatemala exceeded that during the civil war, stated that "citizens from all walks of life increasingly face the threat of murder, kidnapping, extortion, gang violence and shootouts between rival drug trafficking organisations." It also noted that criminals were sabotaging governance by buying off officials or driving them away, and stunting economic development by coercing businesses into paying them "protection" money.[48]

In some countries, chiefs of state have purposefully kept the armed forces weak to keep them from interfering with the government's corrupt and predatory behavior. Such has been the case in the Democratic Republic of Congo. According to a recent study by a conglomeration of nongovernmental organizations, Congolese President Joseph Kabila has striven to prevent the emergence of a strong military for fear that it "would constitute a threat to the entrenched political and financial interests of the Congolese elite, especially those around the Congolese President."[49]

The idea that the military can guard the citizenry's interests better than the political leadership can is an alien concept to most Westerners, conditioned as they have been by the absolute subordination of the military to political authorities in their own countries and by caricatures of foreign military coups. But that idea resides in many minds in countries where tyrannical civil regimes know no judicial or legislative restraints. The downtrodden often welcome the intervention of the military into the political sphere, especially since military officers are often more competent and trustworthy than the civilian political elites.[50] Americans tend to forget that they themselves have elected more than a few presidents based on their successes as military officers and their reputations for integrity. And they lose sight of the fact that in the late eighteenth century, thirteen colonies employed an army to overthrow an unpopular civil government, and then installed the commanding general of that army as their first president.

Underestimation of the power that security can wield over the human mind is a common foible of those who live in safety. When the first world feels secure, it has the luxury of looking after its political rights, civil liberties, and economic prosperity without thinking about its security, and it fails to appreciate that billions of other people do not have the same luxury. The peoples of the first world occasionally receive a shock like 9/11 or the Benghazi attack that brings them to their senses, but then lapse back into the myopia of luxury afterward. Had someone suggested on September 10, 2001, that the U.S. government should receive expansive powers of surveillance and information gathering, or that it invade Afghanistan to neutralize anti-American terrorists, that person would have been widely denounced by Americans of all stripes as a dangerous menace to individual and collective freedoms. Yet later that same month, the U.S. Congress authorized those very measures in the form of the Patriot Act, which passed by a vote of 98 to 1 in the Senate, and Public Law 107–40, which passed 98 to 0. A few years later, when threats to American security had receded, earlier concerns about rights and material prosperity resurfaced, and some Americans denounced the supporters of the stern measures of 2001 while forgetting that they themselves had concurred at the time.

Although convincing Western development experts of the preeminence of security can be a formidable challenge, convincing foreign partners who live in conditions of insecurity is easy. In fact, assigning primary emphasis to security is an exceptionally good way of advancing meaningful partnerships with foreign countries. As George Washington University professor Amitai Etzioni noted in his ground-breaking book *Security First*, security is a universally recognized good: Every society wants its people to be able to walk down the street without risk of kidnapping or murder. The democracy and capitalism that many in the West would like to export are, on the other hand, viewed with suspicion on much of the planet. In numerous countries, especially Islamic ones, overzealous efforts to push liberal democracy alienate large numbers of "illiberal moderates" – individuals who oppose both liberal democracy and violent extremism and are often the only viable allies of the West since they command a much larger following than the liberal democrats. Encouraging and helping them to improve security first will make possible future improvements in governance and development. Pushing democracy or economic liberalization first, before security has been firmly established, will yield only resentment if it fails to yield democracy, while if it succeeds in yielding a liberal democracy, the government will likely be incapable of providing the security required for good governance and development.[51]

CONCLUSION

The causes of the inequality of nations are to be found not in vast, impersonal forces, but in the functioning of societies in the economic sector and the related activities of security and governance. Economies cannot thrive until a society is governed reasonably well, and societies cannot experience economic growth or good governance unless they are secure. In other words, security is a prerequisite for effective governance, and security and effective governance are both prerequisites for development. Among international development agencies and donor governments, awareness of the importance of governance to development has risen sharply, but awareness of the relevance of security remains weak. Much current development assistance is still dispensed on the assumption that development can proceed independently of security and governance.

While economic development depends on security and governance, security and governance also depend to some extent on development. Economic development increases the wealth that can be taxed to pay for security and governance. Given the considerable costs of security and governance, the most difficult challenge for poor countries is paying for security and governance before they achieve the economic take off that generates large tax revenues. Consequently, foreign assistance concentrated on security and governance can be highly valuable to these countries, more valuable than any other type of assistance.

2

How Governments Work

Although the experts who view good governance as essential to economic prosperity have been gaining ground, they are divided among themselves on another fundamental question: What exactly accounts for good governance? One major reason for the lack of consensus is that only a small minority of these experts has delved into the details of governance in the real world. The remainder prefer to operate at a higher, more abstract level, from which they purport to have the best view of the forest. But this chapter, and several that follow it, shows that we cannot fully comprehend the governance forest until we walk into it and look closely at the trees.

THE INSTITUTION SCHOOL

One leading academic school of thought attributes the quality of governance to the quality of a country's political institutions, including its political organizations, laws, and practices. Within this school, a subgroup views the quality of institutions as primarily a matter of resources and hence concludes that bad governance is the result of geographic disadvantages or acts of foreign oppression that have prevented the economic growth required to provide a sufficient tax base. "Many well-intentioned governments simply lack the fiscal resources to invest in the infrastructure, social services, and even the public administration necessary to improve governance or to lay the foundations for economic development and private sector-led growth," asserted a 2006 report of the United Nations Millennium Project.[1]

Achieving good governance does require substantial financial resources, to pay for salaries, facilities, and other essentials, and thus is more difficult for poor nations than for rich nations. But it is still very possible for poor nations to attain reasonably good governance; were it otherwise, then most of the world would still be mired in bad governance and poverty. Many of the recent success stories – countries such as Botswana, Singapore, and South Korea – achieved good governance before becoming wealthy. These countries benefited from considerable foreign assistance – which provides strong evidence that foreign assistance in the realm of governance can reap large rewards.

At the same time, large transfers of resources to poor countries for the purpose of governance have often failed to yield improvements. Bad governments have a penchant for absorbing foreign aid without becoming any less bad. Because so many of these failures have accumulated over the decades, the view that good governance is merely a matter of resources does not have many adherents these days.

The more common view in the institutional school is that the effectiveness of governance depends on the character of political institutions.[2] Within this group, a minority maintains that authoritarian as well as democratic governments can maintain institutions of the type necessary for good governance. Most prominent among this minority are MIT professor of economics Daron Acemoglu and Harvard professor of government James A. Robinson. In their book *Why Nations Fail: The Origins of Power, Prosperity, and Poverty*, Acemoglu and Robinson assert that national success requires "inclusive" institutions, meaning institutions that permit broad popular participation and provide individuals with incentives to succeed. Acemoglu and Robinson blame national failures on "extractive" institutions, which exploit the masses for the benefit of a few. Authoritarian governments, they say, can have "inclusive" institutions, particularly of the economic sort, though such institutions tend to generate pressure for democratization, which they acknowledge to be the best generator of "inclusive" institutions.[3]

Among those who see the character of institutions as the key to effective governance, the majority believes that good governance requires democratic institutions. According to the majority position, moreover, these institutions must be liberal, meaning that they abide by the rule of law, encourage broad civic participation, employ impartial standards of merit in selecting their members, and respect the rights of minority groups. The institutions must, in addition, operate within a liberal system of governance, in which checks and balances ensure that no single institution dominates the others.[4]

DEMOCRACY

Those who view democratic institutions as inherently superior emphasize that elections compel public officials to perform well. A chief of state is more likely to ensure that the trains run on time and the garbage is collected if citizens can vote him out of office than if he is a dictator for life. A democratically elected mayor is more likely than an autocratically appointed mayor to discourage abuses by city officials because only the former will lose votes in the event of misbehavior. In addition, elected officials are more likely to solicit and heed the population's views on how to use government resources, and to allow citizens to monitor government finances for signs of impropriety.

Although democracies frequently elect mediocrities and sometimes elect charlatans, they seldom empower lunatics as has occurred at times with autocracies in which leaders held their jobs merely because they were better at outmaneuvering or killing their opponents, or because they happened to be the offspring of such individuals. The Roman emperor Caligula, who murdered most of his relatives and many members of the Senate, in addition to appointing his horse as a political official, would not have been elected in a country with a free press and fair elections. Nor do democracies normally tolerate extravagant foreign adventurism of the sort practiced by monarchs such as King Louis-Philippe of France, who in 1838 invaded Mexico in the so-called Pastry War after unruly Mexican soldiers ravaged a French pastry shop.

Liberal democracies have proven more effective than other types of governments in curbing abuses of power by their leaders. Their legal codes enshrine principles that are critical to good governance, such as due process and equal treatment before the law. With judicial bodies independent of other branches of government, they can punish government officials for bad behavior. Liberal democratic governments tend to afford greater freedom to private enterprise than do illiberal authoritarian governments, encouraging economic growth. The ability of all members of society to participate in the political process reduces the likelihood that they will resort to political violence or other extralegal measures.

Some of the most significant recent analyses of democratization have found that low-income democracies enjoy better economic growth and governance than low-income autocracies. Productivity and foreign investment are higher in these countries than in other countries, and poverty and corruption lower. These democracies are less likely to go to war and less susceptible to repression than their autocratic counterparts.[5]

Yet history shows that democracy does not necessarily lead to good governance. Democratically elected leaders have proven capable of tyranny and corruption on as grand a scale as autocrats. Some of these leaders took charge of "illiberal democracies" that had few checks on executive powers, but others came to power in what were considered liberal democracies by most definitions. Elected leaders have tampered with elections and used state money to buy votes. They have violated democratic laws and put cronies in charge of democratic institutions as means of making themselves dictators in perpetuity.[6]

Adolf Hitler came to power by gaining a top position in an illiberal democracy, which itself had been converted from a liberal democracy three years earlier by Paul von Hindenburg and his political allies. In 1997, elections that were intended to fill a liberal democratic government in Liberia produced the presidency of Charles Taylor, who in April 2012 was convicted by a UN court on eleven counts of crimes against humanity, including mass murder, the use of amputation as a terrorist weapon, employment of child soldiers, and sexual slavery. In many of the third world countries that have been democratized in recent years, the failure of democracy to provide security, governance, and economic development has engendered widespread yearning for a return to autocracy.[7] In some nations, such as Mali during 2012, this yearning has precipitated antidemocratic coups.

Autocracies, moreover, do not necessarily govern badly. The ubiquity of liberal democracy in Western countries today has created a misperception that liberal democracy's virtues are the sole reason for effective governance and development in the West. In reality, liberal democracy did not predominate until long after the West had risen to political, economic, and military greatness. Autocrats ruled throughout Western Europe during the initial ascent of the modern Western world from 1000 to 1500, and monarchy remained the norm in most Western European countries through the nineteenth century. The Portuguese and Spanish rolled back Islam, circumnavigated the globe, and settled vast new lands in the Americas under the leadership of hereditary kings. France amassed the military strength to overrun most of Europe under Napoleon, and Germany became the world's greatest land power and built a navy second only to England's during the reign of the Hohenzollern dynasty. Much of the Western world was not converted to liberal democracy until the aftermath of World War II, and, in the cases of Germany and Italy, the conversion required massive external military intervention and occupation. The powers of most of the Western European autocrats were constrained by representative bodies, laws, and property rights, in a way that the powers of Chinese or Mongol emperors were not, but they were still autocrats. Westerners would do well to keep these facts in mind before browbeating developing countries for their autocratic ways.

In today's non-Western world, some autocracies govern as well as or better than many democracies. During the Arab Spring of 2011, certain Arab autocracies easily weathered the storm of popular protest because of the conviction of their subjects that the autocrats were governing well, which for most Arabs mattered more than whether their leaders were governing democratically.[8] In Qatar, which saw no significant protests, a student explained to a British journalist, "If you have everything you need, who needs democracy?"[9] The Arab Spring similarly bypassed the United Arab Emirates. Jordan witnessed small protests that ended as soon as King Abdullah II fired the prime minister and appointed a new one.[10] In Oman, a small number of individuals held demonstrations while pointedly emphasizing their "undying loyalty" to the sultan, and they ended their activities when the sultan replaced a few unpopular cabinet ministers and increased the minimum wage.[11]

In a recent study of autocratic governments, Tim Besley and Masayuki Kudamatsu of the London School of Economics concluded that most modern autocracies fall into one of two categories: those that are governed very well and those that are governed very poorly. The difference between the two groups, they found, stems from their ability to get rid of bad leaders. The autocracies characterized by good governance are those possessing a small elite that is willing and able to oust the chief of state for ineffectiveness or abusiveness.[12]

This distinction can be seen clearly in the history of the Arab world during the past half century. Dictators such as Saddam Hussein in Iraq and Muammar Gaddafi in Libya amassed so much power that no one in their countries could oust them by peaceful means, enabling them to remain in office as they moved their countries in disastrous directions. Most of the Arab autocracies that have become stable and prosperous, on the other hand, have been able to replace bad leaders without resort to violence.

During the 1950s, Oman's Sultan Said bin Taimur broke with the traditional division of power between the Sultan on the coast and Imam of Oman in the desert interior, in an effort to get his hands on the interior's newly discovered oil. Stripping the Imam of Oman of his powers, the sultan issued a set of draconian rules and punishments to the desert's nomadic inhabitants, such as a ban on radios and books and a prohibition against unauthorized foreign travel. Unlike the more effective Arab autocrats of the day, Said bin Taimur did not soften the harsh aspects of his rule with expenditures on social services, infrastructure, mosques, or anything else that contributed to the general betterment of the population. His tyranny incited various tribes into an insurgency that was eventually infiltrated and taken over by Marxists. The sultan responded to escalating insurgent violence by shutting the roads leading into the mountains where the nomadic tribes congregated, which alienated tribesmen who had not already joined the rebellion. In the next few years, rebel fighters drove the sultan's forces from the interior and isolated them at a few strongholds on the coast.

By the middle of 1970, the situation had become so dire that the sultan's own son, the twenty-nine-year-old Qaboos bin Said, decided to mount a coup against his father. The coup proved to be a bloodless one, save for the drippings of a single gunshot wound to the foot of the sultan. Irrevocably disgraced, Said bin Taimur was exiled to London, to pass his remaining years in tea houses reminiscing with other exiled chiefs of state.

A graduate of the Royal Military Academy Sandhurst, Qaboos differed vastly from his father in worldview and personality. With an alacrity that stunned Omani royal watchers, the new sultan reversed the travel restrictions and other hated policies of his father. He invited exiled political dissidents into the government and encouraged his subordinates to voice their concerns instead of serving as yes-men. With the financial assistance of the British, who were enthralled by the vigor and virtue of the young monarch, Qaboos spent heavily on schools, wells, roads, and health clinics in the desert. The armed forces reversed the security situation in 1971, which enabled the government to reestablish its presence in the tribal areas and begin development work. Qaboos negotiated with the clans and tribes, winning some of them over through offers of governmental spending and personal magnetism. In 1974, Yemen's Marxist government sent forces into Oman to shore up the rebels, but both they and the rebels were trounced by the sultan's forces. At the end of 1975, the remaining rebels and the Yemeni forces scampered back into Yemen.[13]

After the war, Qaboos continued to improve the public services in Oman's desert interior. He did not engage in bloody witch hunts for oppositionists, as many other Arab rulers were doing at the time, and yet he enjoyed a much safer country than those rulers. Unlike other leaders of oil-rich nations, he did not expend the country's oil wealth on massive palaces and fleets of limousines, but instead used it to fund development projects and national saving accounts.[14] In 2010, a United Nations Development Program study on health, education, and income improvements in 135 developing countries from 1970 to 2010 concluded that Oman ranked number one in the rate of improvement.[15]

Autocracy has often been more effective than democracy in setting the conditions for sustained economic growth and for long-term democratization. Autocrats can push through dramatic political and economic changes that would encounter stiff resistance in a democracy. By providing security and good governance and promoting economic growth, authoritarian leaders such as Park Chung Hee of South Korea, Augusto Pinochet of Chile, and Chiang Kai-shek of Taiwan fostered the growth of the middle classes that would spearhead the development of liberal democratic institutions. Inder Sud of George Washington University's Elliott School of International Affairs notes that most of the countries that have experienced rapid development in recent history were governed by autocrats, and "the experience of successful countries indicates that strong, committed, and sustained leadership is critical to promoting development and to reducing poverty."[16]

As political philosophers such as Edmund Burke and Friedrich Hayek observed, political change is most likely to succeed when undertaken gradually and in concert with cultural change. Being creatures of tradition, humans are reluctant to abandon political and cultural traditions at a rapid pace, even if those traditions are far from perfect. Individuals and societies require time to adjust to new political realities. If radical change is imposed upon them, as with overnight democratization in countries without democratic traditions, they are liable to resist the change by drastic means, even it requires collaboration with fanatics such as the Nazis or Al Qaeda.

INSTITUTIONS AND INCENTIVES

Rational-choice economists and political scientists, who account for a large share of the institutional school, contend that the effectiveness of political institutions depends mainly on the incentives they provide to individuals and corporations. Liberal institutions have been the most successful because they have provided broad segments of society incentives to participate in the political process and engage in economic production. States that deprive most of their people of incentives to participate politically and economically, such as Cuba and North Korea, stifle political and economic development.[17]

This same group of thinkers contends that an institution's character is itself determined by incentives and rules, and that those incentives and rules are created by impersonal political, social, and economic factors, not by moral or cultural factors. Organizations are run by rational, self-interested actors who behave predictably based upon those incentives and rules. Modifying institutions is therefore simply a matter of altering the incentives and rules.[18]

Rational choice theorists attribute the corruption and other misbehavior of third world elites to "perverse incentives" generated by Western politicians, first world consumers, or natural resources. Governmental leaders face no moral decisions between right and wrong, between civic virtue and selfishness, only favorable and unfavorable incentive structures. This avoidance of morality permits circumvention of cross-cultural comparisons, a taboo subject at many Western aid organizations and universities.

A 2010 study by the British government's Department for International Development explained that consumers in prosperous nations had created the "perverse incentives" that caused third world leaders to loot the revenues from their countries' natural resources. "Because wealthy countries are willing to pay such high prices for scarce commodities like oil, gas, diamonds and coltan," the study's authors asserted, "they signal clearly that getting a share in the huge surpluses to be earned from extracting and exporting such products is a good way to get ahead."[19] A report by economists at the OECD blamed the general ineffectiveness of third world leaders on unspecified "incentive structures," asserting that "whether or not an organisation is able to achieve its purposes depends not just on whether it is adequately resourced but on the incentives generated by the way it is resourced under prevailing rules."[20]

THE POLICY SCHOOL

The other leading academic school of thought on governance says that the quality of governance depends primarily on the soundness of governmental policies. The members of this school agree with one another on some of the key criteria of sound policies, such as promotion of the population's material well-being, alleviation of its grievances, and protection of its rights. They differ among themselves on other criteria and engage in continuous modifications as successive ideas fail to pan out. Among the recent policy criteria that have rocketed to fame and then fizzled out are economic liberalization, decentralization of authority, partnership with the private sector, support for civil society, and incorporation of traditional governing institutions.[21] The policy school's adherents include the proponents of the U.S. military's "population-centric" counterinsurgency doctrine, which was widely credited for the defeat of the insurgents in Iraq,[22] as well as rational choice theorists who view policy formulation as the science of finding the policies that will elicit the best behaviors from rational actors.[23]

INSTITUTIONS AND POLICIES ARE NOT SUFFICIENT

Although some of the advice from the institutional and policy schools on how to achieve good governance is unsound because of erroneous philosophical assumptions or lack of appreciation of local realities, much of it would work well if heeded by third world states. Most of this advice has been widely available for several decades, which is one good indicator of its limited utility. Foreign experts have provided third world countries with countless reports on sensible institutional and policy reforms, and yet most of these countries remain poorly governed.

"You can get on the Internet and you will come up finding millions of papers which talk about various 'pillars,'" notes Sergio Jaramillo, Colombia's former vice minister of defense. "You need your justice pillar, and your governance, and your social development, and security. But all those things are obvious." The hard part, he says, is turning those concepts into reality. "It's not a question of the 'what'; it's a question of the 'how,' and the 'how' is the really difficult thing."[24]

The problem with the institution and policy schools is not that institutions or policies do not matter. They do matter a great deal. The problem is that their emphasis on the machinery of government distracts from the more important factor, the machine operators.

ELITES AND LEADERSHIP

The main reason for bad governance in the third world is bad leadership. The political elites of badly governed countries either do not want to or are incapable of pursuing what most people consider to be good governance. In every country of the world, including those where the government has been democratically elected and its leaders profess egalitarianism with the utmost zeal, small groups of political elites form and lead institutions, allocate human and material resources, make policies, and organize the implementation of policies. Their choices and actions are consequently the primary determinants of the quality of governance.

The importance of leaders may seem obvious, particularly to individuals who work in the business world or the military. The point must be established, however, because it is not obvious to many of those who write about organizations in the present age. During the mid-twentieth century, organizational theorists regularly addressed questions of leadership, but their work fell out of style among academics during the latter part of the century with the rise of rational choice theorists and other economists and political scientists preoccupied with elaborate theorizing.[25]

Thomas Schelling, a preeminent rational choice economist whose theories earned him the Nobel Prize in economics and inspired some of the worst strategic decisions of the Vietnam War, played a major role in the downgrading of leadership as a determinant of organizational effectiveness. Schelling contended that universal rationality caused all individuals to respond in the same rational ways to the organization's internal incentives and rules, and therefore the incentives and rules were the deciding factor. An organization's performance, Schelling asserted, "is different from the individual performances of the people in it. An organization can be negligent without any individual's being negligent. To expect an organization to reflect the qualities of the individuals who work for it or to impute to the individuals the qualities one sees in the organization is to commit what logicians call the 'fallacy of composition.'"[26]

The assertion that all individuals behave in the same rational ways based on incentives and rules is not borne out by the historical record. Two individuals have often reacted very differently to the same incentives and rules. What one individual considers rational is frequently different from what another person considers rational, owing to differences in perceptions or thought processes. Within similarly constituted governments, for instance, some executives are highly trusting of subordinates and never second-guess their decisions, whereas others constantly look over their subordinates' shoulders and micromanage. Both groups of executives can come up with rational explanations for their behavior. Both likely have adopted their behavior for less than entirely rational reasons, such as personality.

Leaders often act irrationally, because of cultural, religious, ideological, or emotional influences. At times, they behave in ways that run contrary to the self-interest that guides the actors in rational choice models, often as the result of moral choices. For the head of a central bank in a country with weak anticorruption mechanisms, rational self-interest would dictate transferring large sums of public funds into a private bank account for personal use. Some individuals in this situation have taken that path. Others have taken the path of leaving the public funds in the bank for the benefit of society.[27]

Most of the world's bad governance, in fact, has its origins in decisions to put self-interest before the public good. "Nigerian leaders have the power to educate, inspire, and provide the people with the resources to advocate for the causes they believe in," asserts Lanre Olu-Adeyemi of Nigeria's Adekunle Ajasin University. Instead of making good use of that power, Olu-Adeyemi laments, those leaders have decided that "the primary goal of assuming a leadership position is self-enrichment."[28]

Some rational choice theorists have claimed that a government's effectiveness is determined by how it provides incentives to private citizens. This theory is likewise undermined by the reality that citizens are motivated by more than just rational self-interest. Governmental effectiveness in promoting national prosperity is, however, certainly influenced by the incentives that the government creates for private individuals and corporations. Governments that promote free-market capitalism have achieved greater economic success than socialist, governments by providing greater incentives for talented individuals to engage in economic activity. Yet even in this respect, political leadership plays a vital role. Governmental leaders design political and economic institutions, and they determine the extent to which those institutions can deviate from their original design.

In the creation of governments and governmental institutions, the characteristics of leaders count for a great deal. The formation of the government of the United States was dominated by a handful of individuals of extraordinary brilliance and exceptional command of history and political theory, James Madison and Alexander Hamilton foremost among them. Their ideas met fierce opposition from other men of ability and distinction, such as Patrick Henry and Samuel Adams. Had the small group that wrote the Constitution or the fifty-five-man Constitutional Convention been dominated by individuals of different intellectual abilities or educational backgrounds or opinions, the United States could have adopted fundamentally different governmental institutions, possibly at the cost of the government's existence.

Popular fervor may exert influence on the individuals who create governmental institutions, or it may shift responsibility for creating the institutions from one group of elites to another. But mass fervor is almost invariably organized by members of an elite group, whether it be the governing elite, a dissident political elite, an educational elite, or a military elite. For example, the pro-democracy protests during the Arab Spring of 2011 were led by highly educated students and faculty from prestigious universities. The Islamists who were voted into office after the democratic movements toppled the autocratic governments were highly educated individuals from the ranks of Islamist political parties. The Egyptians who filled the streets in 2013 to protest against the Islamist government took direction from elements of the educational elite and the military elite.

The ultimate success or failure of mass movements, moreover, depends on whether they enjoy the approval of the most powerful elites. The governments of Tunisia and Egypt quickly fell during the Arab Spring because the military elites in those countries sided overwhelmingly with the protesters. Libya and Syria plunged into chaos because the loyalties of the military elites were divided between the autocratic leaders and the protest movements.

It is also left to elites to decide whether institutions function as written on paper or in some other manner. When a chief of state seeks to subvert the constitution, the average civilian on the street is not going to stop him. It will most likely be legislators, judges, or military officers. The ordinary citizen might play a role in motivating legislators, judges, or military officers by participating in public demonstrations, but he or she most likely will do so under the guidance of a highly educated organizer with a megaphone or a Twitter account.

Top government leaders have a large say over the functioning of institutions down to the lowest level, because they can compel compliance by subordinate officials. In countries where governors, mayors, police chiefs, and budget directors are elected by local communities, the national leadership possesses either the power to remove local officials or authority over attorneys general or anticorruption agencies that can prosecute them. In countries where the central government appoints and supervises local officials, which includes most of the world's authoritarian states and some democratic ones, the national leadership can control local affairs without resorting to such instruments.[29]

Corruption levels are determined primarily by the extent to which elites choose to put personal or factional gain before the public good, not by "incentive structures" or other external factors that absolve the leadership of moral responsibility. If local administrative personnel are so underpaid that they cannot provide for their families, or if their superiors threaten to fire them unless they engage in extortion, then they may not have much choice as to whether they are parties to corruption. Leaders in the upper tiers of the government, however, certainly are not forced into corruption by dire need. In every highly corrupt nation, the senior leadership has made a conscious choice to misuse public resources for private gain. As the keepers of the purse strings, they can decide whether to siphon tax revenues into their personal checking accounts or whether to award huge contracts to friends and relatives without an impartial bidding process. When civil servants demand bribes as a condition for issuing driver licenses or collecting the trash, the senior leaders decide whether those officials will be punished or whether they will receive a phone call commending them and instructing them to forward a portion of the proceeds to higher authorities.[30]

No institution, however brilliantly conceived, can stand in the way of corruption if a preponderance of the political elites believe that their private interests should receive priority over the general public welfare. During the 1990s, Peru had all of the liberal institutions lauded by advocates of democratic governance, including open and transparent elections, a written constitution, independent courts and legislatures, and a large private media establishment. Yet President Alberto Fujimori subverted the entire system by buying off the would-be guardians of democratic integrity.

To gain acquiescence to his plans for political and financial self-aggrandizement, Fujimori paid legislators between $5,000 and $20,000 per month. Judges, whose official salaries were lower, received between $5,000 and $10,000 per month. Because of Fujimori's bribery, the Peruvian Congress overturned the statutory presidential term limit, enabling him to run in a third presidential election, which he won under the most dubious of circumstances. Newspapers received payments ranging from $500 for a single article to $60,000 per month for generally favorable coverage. The biggest payoffs went to the TV channels; the channel with the most viewers raked in $1.5 million per month, and the second-ranked channel received a tidy $500,000. Each day at 12:30 P.M., Fujimori met with television producers to plan the evening newscasts.

Over the course of his ten years in office, Fujimori and his associates made off with $600 million in Peruvian public funds. They would have pulled in even more had Fujimori's chief of intelligence not chosen to record the payoffs on video cassettes, one of which fell into the hands of a television station of such a small size that Fujimori had not seen fit to bribe it. Two months after the first airing of the tape, Fujimori wearied of the denunciations from Peruvian and foreign critics and decided that he had made enough money to quit. During a visit to Japan, his country of birth, he sent his letter of resignation to Peru by fax.[31]

The making of policy likewise depends on the attributes of leaders. If all the right institutions are in place but the leadership is uninspired or concerned only with its own interests, the government will make poor policy choices. Good leadership is equally important for the implementation of policy; if the leadership is disorganized or lazy, it will carry out its policies ineffectively.[32] Even where federalism and the separation of powers limit the power of executives, the competence of chiefs of state, governors, and mayors is critical. Incompetent chiefs of state have a propensity for appointing incompetent or corrupt cabinet ministers, and incompetent governors have the same propensity when it comes to appointing police chiefs and judges. On more than one occasion, I have encountered a U.S. ambassador who arrived in an underdeveloped country with a thorough and sensible list of policies that he or she sincerely believed would fix the country's problems immediately, only to have this enthusiasm wrenched away by the unwillingness or inability of the government's leadership to put those policies into practice.

Steven Radelet of the Center for Global Development, in a highly influential study of sub-Saharan Africa, observed that the most successful sub-Saharan African nations had achieved strong economic growth because of more democratic and accountable governments and more sensible economic policies, but he emphasized that the key to better governmental institutions and policies was the coming of age of the so-called "cheetah generation." Whereas recent political, economic, and technological changes had made substantial marks on these African nations, Radelet asserted, the cheetahs "are not so much a thing that is changing as they are the driving force that is bringing about that change. They are the force that brings together these other changes, gives them their power, and brings them to life."[33]

For additional evidence that institutions and policies are subordinate to people, we should look at the transition of the Central Asian states from Soviet control to independence in the 1990s. Turkmenistan, Uzbekistan, and the others adopted the institutions of democracy and announced policies that conformed to Western recommendations but kept the same people in charge. Governance, in practice, did not differ very much from what it had been in the Soviet era. Dictators continued to run the governments and economies and to suppress dissidents without mercy.

By contrast, changing governmental personnel without changing institutions or policies can yield enormous changes in the quality of governance. In Poland, President Aleksander Kwaśniewski and his friends spent the decade from

1995 to 2005 enriching themselves through bribes and kickbacks. The most famous of the scandals involved a Polish polo player who cut sweetheart deals with the state's largest oil company, PKN Orlen. Another scandal had its origins in a media mogul who wanted governmental permission to snatch up other media companies. Kwaśniewski also did injury to Poland's prestige through his frequent episodes of public inebriation. On one occasion, he was so drunk that he attempted to enter his car through the trunk.[34]

The Law and Justice Party of Lech Kaczyński won the national elections of 2005 on an anticorruption platform. To the amazement of those inured to broken electoral promises, Kaczyński and his lieutenants proved as good as their word. Using institutions and policies that already existed, they purged corrupt officials and legislators from the government en masse. In 2007, Kaczyński fired his own deputy for corruption. As a consequence of the government's stern anticorruption measures, Poland became one of the fastest risers on Transparency International's Corruption Perceptions Index, moving from number 70 in 2005 to number 41 in 2010.[35] The reduction in corruption facilitated an economic boom, which enabled Poland to weather the recession of 2009 better than any other country in the European Union. In January 2010, a few months before President Kaczyński and other Polish leaders died in a plane crash near Smolensk, the *Economist* declared that "Poland has never been more secure, richer or better-run."[36]

LEADERSHIP DEPTH

A modern state requires decisions and actions far more numerous than a single person can handle, necessitating that top executives delegate authority to leaders at lower echelons. If the top leadership is good but most subordinate leaders are short on talent or character, then local governance will suffer. In today's third world countries, one frequently finds a good slate of leaders at the cabinet level who are unable to make much headway because of a lack of people to execute the government's policies at the local level. An incompetent local police chief cannot be made competent by the decrees of a cabinet minister in the capital. He can perhaps be replaced, but if the country is short on capable police officers, then the replacement is not likely to be much better.

In Yemen, prior to the overthrow of the government in January 2015, the governmental ministries and nongovernmental organizations (NGOs) had some highly skilled and talented individuals in the national capital of Sanaa, yet the government did very little outside of the capital because the quality of leadership fell off rapidly as one moved from the densely populated city limits into the surrounding valleys. Yemeni officials in the rest of the country lacked training and held their jobs simply because they were friends or relatives of government leaders. "The technocratic talent at the top of agencies and in NGOs is stymied by the lack of local implementers," Barbara K. Bodine, former

U.S. ambassador in Yemen, observed. The ineffectuality of the government beyond the capital allowed multiple rebel groups to flourish, including the highly dangerous Al Qaeda in the Arabian Peninsula.[37]

SECURITY LEADERSHIP

Leadership is as essential to security as it is to governance. The leadership quality of the security forces responsible for counterinsurgency and other internal security activities is far and away the most important factor in the effectiveness of those activities, no matter where on the planet they happen to be located. Well-led security forces possess the tactical competence to defeat the enemy and the discipline and sense of purpose to refrain from abuses of power. The same is never true of poorly led security forces. The characteristics of leaders in other parts of the security sector are also critical; judiciaries that lack honest judges and prisons that lack honest wardens let insurgents and criminals go free.[38]

A good current example of the insecurity arising from poor leadership in the security sector is Honduras. As I saw during a recent trip to that country, the population's fears of criminal activity have risen to the point that one sees more security guards than pedestrians on the city streets, even in the most secure areas of the capital. Nearly every shop, restaurant, and apartment building has a uniformed guard with a holstered pistol, some of them standing on sidewalks or driveways, others peering into the street from behind grated doors that they unlock when the appropriate persons present themselves. Citizens avoid walking even a block if they can help it, so as to minimize the risk that street thugs will accost them with a weapon or swipe their possessions from the seat of a speeding motorbike. Visitors are told to avoid wearing watches and jewelry to reduce their attractiveness to thieves, and are advised not to carry their passports or sizable amounts of cash because anything in their possession might soon be in someone else's.

Many of the thieves are not poor, Hondurans told me, but steal simply because they can get away with it, owing to dysfunctional law enforcement. The Honduran police apprehend few criminals because their leaders do not order them to patrol the streets or respond to reports of crime, out of either laziness or bribes received from criminals. The crooks who do get caught frequently evade prolonged incarceration by paying off judges or prison officials.

Honduran policemen are themselves perpetrators of much of the criminal activity. Honduran military officers, who increasingly work alongside the police because of the latter's ineffectiveness, observe that policemen routinely shake citizens down. "They will ask the citizens to provide the 'registration paper' for their cell phone, which is something that does not actually exist," one military officer explained to me. "The people get nervous and say they must have forgotten the paper at home. The cops then threaten to take the cell phone away, so the citizens hand over some cash in order to keep the phone."

Accustomed to constant supervision of junior troops, Honduran military officers are scathing in their critiques of the police leadership for leaving corrupt policemen to their own devices. "The police commanders never leave their desks to supervise the police," one military officer remarked. "Therefore, the policemen do whatever they want." When the military notifies the police leadership that patrolmen are stealing from citizens or using cocaine, nothing is done.

Police brutality is also a serious problem in Honduras, as it is most anyplace where the police lack good leadership. Honduran media outlets regularly report cases of police abuses, but their newscasts and articles only occasionally lead to governmental promises of police reform and almost never generate real reform. "We are tired of the police treating us like animals," the head of an international development organization in Honduras told me.[39]

CONCLUSION

The key variable in the effectiveness of governments is not institutions or policies but leaders. Institutions and policies are only as good as the elites in charge of shaping and managing them. Good governance is primarily the product of capable and honest leadership, at multiple levels, and bad governance is primarily the product of incompetent and corrupt leadership. The same holds true in the realm of security, the inevitable partner of governance. No matter what the country, the leadership of governance and security lies in the hands of a small elite. That truth may be difficult for the egalitarian-minded to accept, but acceptance of it is nonetheless vital for those who would seek to influence governance and security, as it demands concentration of effort on the small number of people who determine whether the government wields power for good or for ill.

3

Civilization

Chapter 1 showed that national prosperity is dependent on the quality of governance and security, and Chapter 2 showed that the quality of governance and security hinges on the quality of leaders. This chapter addresses the most fundamental level of causation, showing that national differences in prosperity, governance, security, and leadership are all the result, to a large degree, of differences in civilization. Few of today's development experts have attempted to argue this case, either because they believe it to be erroneous or because they fear that its articulation will elicit condemnation from their peers. "It is much more comfortable for the experts to cite geographic constraints, insufficient resources, bad policies, and weak institutions," Lawrence Harrison has noted. "That way they avoid invidious comparisons, political sensitivities, and bruised feelings often engendered by cultural explanations of success and failure."[1] In the broader intellectual community, however, can be found some highly persuasive arguments in favor of the proposition that civilization is the root cause of disparities in national performance.

CIVILIZATION AND THE INEQUALITY OF NATIONS

A long and distinguished line of thinkers have argued, with rigor and dispassion, that the inequality of nations is the result of differences in civilization and its core components of religion and culture. The Frenchman Alexis de Tocqueville and the German Max Weber provided what remain the most famous expositions of this view, in the early nineteenth and early twentieth centuries, respectively. During the middle of the twentieth century, renowned intellectuals such as Edward Banfield, David Donald, Will Durant, Gunnar Myrdal, and Lucian Pye spent decades analyzing the influences of civilization, culture, and religion on national strength, with particular interest in why the West had acquired greater wealth and power than the rest of the world.[2]

Since the 1960s, however, this school of thought has been under attack by multiculturalists, *Annalistes,* and other academics, who have seen arrogance or even malevolence in any suggestion that Western civilization might be superior to others. To assert that non-Western peoples are less industrious or caring than Westerners, they have alleged, constitutes "culturism," which in their view is nearly as bad as racism.[3] Some of them argue that all cultures are inherently equal, which is at least consistent with the moral relativism of multiculturalism, while others claim that non-Western cultures are actually superior to Western culture because they are not tainted by racism, greed, colonialism, and other malign characteristics that they consider to be peculiarly Western.

During the 1970s and 1980s, the rise of multiculturalism, postmodernism, poststructuralism, and other new intellectual trends at Western universities led to a sharp decline in rigorous scholarship on Western civilization and culture. The subject began to undergo a limited renaissance in the 1990s, mainly because of the work of a few people at Harvard University. Harvard professor Samuel Huntington's book *The Clash of Civilizations,* which upheld civilization as the principal driver of human achievement, became one of the most influential books of the decade. Huntington underwrote the Culture Matters Research Project, led by Lawrence E. Harrison, who himself produced several important books arguing that culture determined the fate of nations more than did rivers and mountains.[4] In 1998, Harvard professor of government David Landes afforded preeminence to civilization in his incisive book *The Wealth and Poverty of Nations: Why Some Are So Rich and Some So Poor.* More recently, Harvard professor of history Niall Ferguson published a history of civilization that explained Western success by stressing distinctive characteristics of Western civilization.[5]

Among those who have attributed Western strength to the merits of Western civilization, there is general agreement on the cultural, political, social, and religious attributes most important to the rise of the West. The preponderance of these attributes had their origins in ancient Greece and Rome. Among them was individualism, which encouraged restrictions on governmental power and spurred individuals to great achievements in commerce and the arts and sciences. Respect for private property encouraged individuals to take care of what they had and to seek the acquisition of more, while deference to impersonal laws facilitated commercial contracts and transactions. The use of representative bodies provided citizens avenues for advancing their ideas and interests and served as another restraint on the power of central authorities.

Pluralism – the toleration of beliefs and ideas differing from one's own – encouraged the questioning of conventional wisdom and reduced the frequency of conflict. Rationalism encouraged scientific inquiry and the technological development required for rapid gains in economic and military power. Receptivity to change led Westerners to invent economically lucrative technologies and to find practical employment for foreign inventions such as printing and gunpowder that other civilizations had been unable to employ because of cultural or religious aversion to innovation.

The foregoing elements of Western civilization harnessed the power of individual self-interest toward the common good. But the modern West, like its ancient forbearers in Greece and Rome, adhered to the belief that civilization required appeals to the higher nature of man, to the individual's willingness to sacrifice for the benefit of a cause, a community, or other individuals. Western societies cultivated a sense of civic virtue that made citizens willing to pay taxes, to send their sons into military service, and to serve in the government without using their office to ill ends. In the modern West, as in the ancient world, this civic spirit materialized first at the level of the village, then the town or city state, and eventually extended to nations and empires whose people had never met most of their fellow citizens. Civic virtue manifested itself as both nationalism, which encompassed irrational attachments such as race and language, as well as patriotism, which was based on rational arguments about the benefits of loyalty to the nation, although it too harnessed the power of the irrational through flags, songs, and heroes. The extreme European nationalism that produced the two world wars was followed by a sharp decline in nationalism and patriotism in Europe, although patriotism has remained strong in much of North America and Australasia.[6]

By promoting good governance as well as hard work, nationalism and patriotism contributed heavily to the economic growth of the West. Most episodes of explosive economic growth, in the Western world as well as the non-Western world, have been accompanied by popular affection for the national state and society, from France and Britain in the early nineteenth century, to Germany, Japan, Russia, and the United States in the late nineteenth and early twentieth centuries, to Taiwan and South Korea in the second half of the twentieth century, and to China and India in the late twentieth and early twenty-first.

The importance of nationalism and patriotism can be seen as well in the history of nations and empires that rose to greatness through a spirit of national solidarity but subsequently lost that spirit. More often than not, the disappearance of love of country led to economic and military decline, if not destruction. In the last decades of the Roman Empire, evaporation of enthusiasm for Rome made the Romans less willing to sacrifice their wealth and their lives for the good of the state, and more willing to quarrel with one another. As the citizenry's willingness to serve in the military deteriorated, the empire was compelled to rely increasingly for its security on barbarian mercenaries, who eventually turned against Rome and, finding it much weakened, ended its existence.[7]

Germany's swift military defeat of France in 1940 has long been cited as the culmination of a decay in national spirit. In recent years, historians have assailed that interpretation by showing that it overstated the case and disregarded other causes of defeat, but they have at the same time demonstrated that a decline in patriotism was still a major cause of France's downfall.[8] During the 1920s and 1930s, a large number of French citizens and politicians subscribed to strains of pacifism that disdained both patriotism, which was blamed for the disastrous Great War, and the military, which was accused of reactionary elitism and senseless militarism.[9]

In the period between the world wars, a great number of Frenchmen avoided explicit renunciation of national solidarity but manifested their aversion to patriotism and the military through their deeds. French university students refused to take a special training course, the Préparation Militaire Supérieure (PMS), that allowed university students to perform their compulsory military service as officers. Historian Julian Jackson assigns some of the blame for the French Army's poor leadership in 1940 to the shunning of the officer corps by the most educated and most intelligent Frenchmen.[10] Antimilitary sentiments also caused politicians of the Left to curtail the military's training periods and shrink the officer corps, leaving the French Army desperately short on experienced personnel when war came.[11]

Because of inferior leadership and the hidebound military culture that went with it, the French military was unable to develop innovative tactics for employing new military technologies such as the tank and the dive bomber. France's next-door neighbor, Nazi Germany, emphasized patriotism and elite participation in the military, resulting in an officer corps that proved much more creative in devising new tactics and much more effective in applying its innovations on the field of battle.[12] Superior German leadership also accounted for differences in battlefield discipline. "Panic was rare in the German armies on the Western front in the spring of 1940, whereas it became common in the French Ninth and Second Armies," notes Ernest R. May. The French armies experienced high rates of surrender, desertion, and disorganized flight from battle, May asserts, because they "contained the dross of French soldiery and were carelessly commanded from army level on down."[13]

THE GOD FACTOR

Although most of the major elements of modern Western civilization originated with the Greeks or the Romans, such was not the case with the most important element of all – Christianity. Western civilization, like most of the world's other major civilizations, is defined above all by its religion. Since the dawn of the modern West in the fourteenth century, Christianity's effects have been felt on every shore where Westerners planted their flags, touching every sphere of life. Christian concern for forgiveness and humility moderated Western justice, bringing it into sharp contrast with non-Western systems of justice that liberally dispensed amputations and death sentences without concern for the rights of defendants. The promise of an eternal after-life made Christians more willing to undertake dangerous or dreary activities that strengthened the state or economy, such as seafaring and factory labor. Christianity's emphasis on individual responsibility reinforced classical individualism.

Christian faith and Christian ethics promoted civic virtue, charitable giving, and cooperation among different social classes and ethnicities, and often proved a barrier against oppression stronger than the laws and philosophies of the Greeks and Romans. For some, the fear of hell and hope for heaven provided the primary stimulus for heeding Christian teachings. For others, it was the conviction that virtuous behavior was an obligation to be readily accepted by the saved. For both groups, the Biblical admonition that God was always watching led individuals to act virtuously even when no human could detect or punish unethical deeds, a sharp difference from belief systems in which individuals were concerned only about the perceptions of their fellow citizens.

The great Christian theologians and lay thinkers asserted that God was the sole reliable source of morality, the human capacity for sin being too great for mere human reason to restrain it. The Russian novelist Fyodor Dostoyevsky argued in *Crime and Punishment* and *The Brothers Karamazov* that God alone could keep individuals and the state from committing the vilest of crimes. "Without God, everything is permitted," explained Ivan Karamazov. The French philosopher Simone Weil, who enjoyed as much favor on the Left as Dostoyevsky enjoyed on the Right, put it a bit differently in her 1943 Statement of Human Obligation. The only way that individuals would be sure to respect and abet all others, said Weil, was to believe in God, for this belief enabled them to see in all humanity the image of the divine. Although adherents of Christianity have committed plenty of crimes and misdemeanors over the past two millennia, they have been much less prone to capricious violence, torture, and genocide than the adherents of atheistic ideologies such as Communism and Fascism or the pagans of ancient civilizations such as the Aztecs and Fijians.

Christianity has also been a driver of Western economic growth. The most famous analyst of the relationship between Christianity and prosperity, Max Weber, argued that Protestant Christianity was the main catalyst for the meteoric rise of the United States and Western Europe. In his seminal essay *The Protestant Ethic and the Spirit of Capitalism,* Weber contended that Protestantism encouraged private enterprise, hard work, and asceticism, which together resulted in the capital accumulation required for investment and economic growth.

Later analysts found flaws in Weber's argument, such as its disregard for the Protestant promotion of mass literacy, which stimulated scientific inquiry and technological innovation. But his central point that Protestant Christianity contributed to the exceptional economic growth of the West has stood the test of time. Subsequent research has found that during the ascent of the West, Protestants predominated among the leaders of Western industry and among the scientists and technicians who created and operated the industrial machinery.[14] It has also shown that Europe's Protestant countries have consistently outperformed the Catholic ones in economic production.[15]

In making the case for Christianity's unique effects, Weber and other explicators of economic differences among civilizations have shown that other religions have had very different effects on economic output. Islam, which is second only to Christianity in the number of adherents worldwide, contains formidable hindrances to capitalist economic development. Islamic reverence for tradition discourages innovation, and concerns for the economic well-being of fellow Muslims discourages competition among Muslim businessmen.[16] The lack of separation between mosque and state deprives political and economic institutions of the flexibility that has permitted innovation in the West.[17] In pre-Communist China and its many vassal states, the secular religion of Confucianism impeded economic development in similar ways. The Confucian emphasis on maintaining social harmony and the existing order discouraged the innovative thinking and risk taking that stimulate economic development.[18]

Prominent atheists have vehemently disputed the view that religion has benefited public morality or economic prosperity.[19] The most compelling evidence that nations can behave morally and prosper without God is the persistence of good behavior and economic growth in Western Europe following the decline of Christianity in the post–World War II era.[20] But conditions in Europe since 1945 have much to do with the legacy of Christianity. In Western Europe, Christianity shaped cultural, social, and political traditions that, like many other traditions, have endured after the original source of inspiration receded.

Ethics derived from Christianity, and peculiar to Christianity, are still taught in secular European schools. Christian concern for the downtrodden is still preached by secular Europeans in the halls of parliament, it is just not called Christian. The universal literacy of European populations and the absence of slavery in European societies are lasting monuments to the exertions of European Christians in centuries past.

Of especial concern to us, the low levels of corruption in Western Europe's governments are to a considerable extent a legacy of institutional cultures and procedures developed in the nineteenth and early twentieth centuries by Christian Europeans, who denounced corruption in public service on religious as well as patriotic grounds. Western Europe, like every other part of the globe, experienced periods of demographic and political turmoil in which governments employed state power to oppress select members of society or to enrich other select members. Unlike many of the other regions, however, it had enough people with the conviction and wisdom to reform the ethical culture of governance.[21]

"An individual European may not believe that the Christian Faith is true," T. S. Eliot once remarked, "and yet what he says, and makes, and does, will all spring out of his heritage of Christian culture and depend upon that culture for its meaning."[22] Eliot was writing in the mid-twentieth century, when the decline of European Christianity was not so far advanced as it is today, but his observation has been repeated many times since. "Swedes are probably the most unreligious people in Europe," remarked one Swede at the end of the twentieth century, "but you cannot understand this country at all unless you realize that our institutions, social practices, families, politics, and way of life are fundamentally shaped by our Lutheran heritage."[23]

The decline of Christianity and the concomitant decline in patriotism in Europe have, however, had some profound consequences, for European nations and for the rest of the world. One of those consequences is a profound change in work ethic. Most Western Europeans no longer work as hard, whether for themselves or for others, as their forefathers did and instead exhibit a strong preference for leisure. In 2010, the average German worked only 1,419 hours per year, the average Norwegian 1,414, and the average Dutchman 1,377. By contrast, the average American worked 1,778 hours per year, and the average South Korean 2,193.[24] The sociologist Charles Murray explains that Europeans have replaced "the idea of work as a means to self-fulfillment" with "the view of work as a necessary evil, interfering with the higher good of leisure." Murray aptly characterizes declining European work hours as one symptom of a larger continental "syndrome," whose other symptoms include declining rates of marriage and childbirth, expansion of the welfare state, and indifference to great achievement, and whose causes are to be found in loss of belief in anything transcendent.[25] Niall Ferguson links Europe's decline in work hours directly to its decline in religiosity, observing that "the transatlantic divergence in working patterns has coincided almost exactly with a comparable divergence in religiosity."[26]

European welfare states, with their lavish unemployment benefits and work regulations, have contributed heavily to the declining European work hours, but the impact of welfare statism cannot be separated from religion and culture. Europe's welfare politics are primarily an effect of Europe's cultural development, not a cause of it. In most of Europe, there is an overwhelming cultural preference for relying exclusively on the welfare state to help the needy, which is why Europeans consistently approve of high taxation and large welfare programs and why they donate very little to private charities. In the United States, by contrast, cultural preferences for self-reliance, limited government, and private philanthropy have prevented politicians from going as far as Europeans in taxation, welfare spending, and impingement on charitable organizations.[27] In the 1990s, for instance, half of Democratic lawmakers joined Democratic President Bill Clinton and most of the Republicans in approving a restrictive welfare reform law called "The Personal Responsibility and Work Opportunity Reconciliation Act of 1996," a law that would never have been accepted by a European party of the Left. The health care reform act that was passed by the Democratic Congress in 2009 and signed into law by Democratic President Barack Obama in 2010 is considerably less generous than the single-payer system that prevails in Europe, as it does not provide universal coverage and puts the onus on companies and individuals to pay for their own health insurance. And even this limited expansion of the welfare state has provoked strong resistance from Americans who concluded that it expanded the size and reach of the government too far.

Arthur C. Brooks, in a pioneering study of philanthropy, concludes that for both Americans and Europeans, religious belief is a key determinant of opinions on the roles of the state and private philanthropy. According to Brooks, people who are not religious are much more likely to view the state as the sole guardian of the poor, and hence much less likely to donate to philanthropic organizations. Those who are religious are less inclined to favor an all-encompassing welfare state and more likely to donate to charities. Thus, Brooks asserts, the much lower rates of religious belief in Europe help account for Europe's culture of welfare statism and the manifestation of that culture in European political institutions.[28]

The decline of religion and patriotism in Europe has also led to strong aversion to the employment of military force and steep reductions in defense expenditures. If there is no afterlife, and no community worthy of the highest personal sacrifice, then it is exceedingly hard to justify putting individuals in situations where they could suffer death at an early age.[29] Although Western European military organizations still have some troops who are willing to risk life and limb, most of their political leaders do everything possible to spare their military forces from harm. In the war in Afghanistan, European politicians have gone to extraordinary lengths to keep their military forces from sustaining casualties, imposing restrictions on their activities that render them incapable of performing most military functions. Visitors to installations in Afghanistan where Europeans and Americans work together are invariably stuck by the differences between European and American forces in their exposure to danger and the length of their work days.

"The fierce nationalism that once drove millions into the trenches of two world wars has evaporated, and with it has gone the thirst to identify oneself with a glorious national past or with heart-stirring national traditions," observes Josef Joffe, editor of *Die Zeit*. As a consequence, he believes, Europeans have lost their willingness to use military power in the service of the nation, and they instead cling to "civilian power" and international institutions as ineffectual substitutes. Joffre laments, "Individual European armies are no longer repositories of nationalism or career advancement, but organizations with about as much social prestige as the post office."[30]

Of NATO's twenty-eight nations, only two European members – the United Kingdom and Greece – are now spending the minimum of 2 percent of GDP on defense that is specified in NATO guidelines. As a result, the United States now finances nearly 75 percent of NATO's military spending.[31] When today's European nations deem military force absolutely necessary, as for instance during the Balkan crises of the 1990s or the war against Libya in 2011, their military weakness compels them to request help from the U.S. military, which is richer in material resources and is teeming with vigor borne of religious and patriotic conviction.

BORROWING CIVILIZATION

Non-Western nations that have been able to industrialize successfully have done so by borrowing major elements of Western civilization, such as respect for property rights, rationalism, and long work days. Some of what they borrowed reinforced existing aspects of their civilization, while some of it replaced what had existed or filled empty holes.[32] A few non-Western countries achieved rapid economic growth by borrowing from Western culture but not from Western religion, of which Japan and Turkey are the foremost examples. More commonly, Christianity has figured prominently in Western-inspired economic ascents, whether by reinvigorating historically Christian populations as in Latin America's most successful countries, or by proselytizing among previously non-Christian populations as in the economic powerhouses of East Asia.

When the Chinese Communists of Mao Zedong conquered China in 1949, the country had fewer than half a million Protestant Christians. Mao's persecution of Chinese Christians, his expulsion of foreign Christian missionaries, and his closure of Christian churches led his fourth wife, Jiang Qing, to exclaim gleefully that Chinese Christianity would soon exist only in the museum. Yet after Mao's death, Christianity rebounded and grew with stunning speed, despite intermittent suppressive actions by the government. Today, estimates of the number of Chinese Protestant Christians range from 40 million to 110 million. When Catholics are added, China may have as many as 130 million Christians. If current growth trends continue, Christians could make up 30 percent of the Chinese population within the next three decades.

Recent scholarship on Chinese Christianity has found that the Christian worldview has promoted entrepreneurship, hard work, and moral values that enhance economic growth. Some of the most successful Chinese entrepreneurs today are Christians, and workers in predominantly Christian regions are reported to be among the most diligent members of China's work force.[33] Leading figures in the Chinese intelligentsia and even some Communist Party leaders are embracing Christianity because they view it as the source of Western prosperity. A scholar from the Chinese Academy of the Social Sciences explained how Chinese thinking on the sources of the West's dominance has evolved: "At first, we thought it was because you had more powerful guns than we had. Then we thought it was because you had the best political system. But in the past twenty years, we have realized that the heart of your culture is your religion: Christianity."[34]

Within the relatively small circle of Western scholars who today comment on the beneficial effects of civilizational borrowing can be found a smaller circle containing individuals who actively champion the practice, of whom the foremost is Lawrence E. Harrison. Like many Americans who joined USAID during the Cold War, Harrison began his career in international development with the belief that the third world's ills resulted not from indigenous cultural factors but from mistreatment by the West. Over the course of a career that included postings as USAID mission director in five Latin American countries, Harrison came to the realization that the real roots of Latin America's problems were not to be found in the policies of the United States, but in the culture of Latin

American peoples. Throughout the region, Harrison concluded, there was "a limited radius of social identification resulting in lack of concern for the interests and well-being of people outside the family and for the society as a whole," a phenomenon he blamed on the extreme indulgence of boys during their childhoods. The disregard for people beyond the family, he believed, was the principal cause of Latin America's social pathologies, including corruption, tax evasion, the inability of citizens to work together in solving problems, and the absence of philanthropy.[35] This discovery led Harrison to write a series of books and articles and organize research projects aimed at imparting Western values such as civic virtue and hard work as central elements of foreign assistance.

Many more Westerners with long experience in the third world have concluded that non-Western countries would do well to adopt at least some elements of Western civilization, but without referencing the Western origins of those elements. Those who were imbued with multiculturalist relativism in college often learn through experience that those philosophies are considerably less attractive in the real world than in the classroom. Few are the Westerners who can refrain from applying absolute standards of morality when they come into contact with government ministers who plunder the public coffers, police officers who sodomize children, or men who make the women do all the work.

In 2006 a thirty-nine-year-old *Vanity Fair* reporter named Nina Munk came to see the shortcomings of multiculturalism while covering Jeffrey Sachs and his antipoverty crusades in Africa. During their travels, Sachs informed Munk that cultural and religious explanations for the inequality of nations were nothing but a preposterous manifestation of "cultural imperialism." Once the poor had been lifted out of poverty with an influx of foreign money, Sachs maintained, they would "move beyond superstition and outdated rites."[36] Munk recalled later, "Jeff is a charismatic man, and I wanted to believe in him."[37]

African poverty and Sachs's antipoverty campaigns so enthralled Munk that her *Vanity Fair* project, originally scheduled for six months, turned into six years and a book. She concentrated her attention on the Millennium Villages Project, which Sachs had designed as a model for poverty eradication across the world. Raising large amounts of money from celebrity benefactors such as Bono and George Soros, Sachs inundated a small number of African villages with cash over a five-year period to demonstrate the value of large foreign aid infusions. By the end of five years, Sachs predicted, the villages would attain such high rates of economic growth that they could continue their development without further aid.

As Munk followed the program's development, she discovered that it was not achieving its objectives, and that culture was a big reason why. Livestock programs that had been intended to stimulate commerce ran aground because Africans did not sell their livestock at market value as the rational choice theories of Western economists had predicted. They instead chose to hoard the animals, as their cultural traditions dictated, even if it meant economic disaster. When aid workers stocked village dispensaries with free birth control pills and condoms and explained how these gifts would promote prosperity, only a handful of people ever availed themselves of the contraceptives. Meanwhile, banditry and violence arising from historical tribal feuds compelled the diversion of development funds to security.

Munk watched Somali men lounge under the shade of trees while their wives collected wood, fetched water, milked camels, cooked meals, swept homes, nurtured children, and treated the sick. The Millennium Villages Project, she discovered, had to pay Bantu men to do construction work that the Somali men would not do. "Somali men are lazy," lamented Fatuma Shide, a health coordinator for the Millennium Villages Project. Gesturing toward the women, she said, "At the age of thirty-five, they look the age of sixty." One Somali man retorted, "Somali men are not lazy. We are very proud people. We are descendants of Abraham, and if you descend from Abraham, you don't do manual labor. We don't cook. We don't make tea. We don't clean or sweep. We don't do construction or garbage collection. Our only business is animal herding."[38]

Non-Westerners are often willing to acknowledge that their societies would benefit from absorbing Western ways. Their ranks include Hussein Onyango Obama, a Kenyan convert to Islam who was the grandfather of U.S. President Barack Obama. In Onyango's view, differences in the achievements of the European settlers of Kenya and the native Africans were the result of basic cultural differences, particularly in terms of civic virtue and social collaboration. "The white man alone is like an ant," Onyango remarked. "He can be easily crushed. But like an ant, the white man works together. His nation, his business – these things are more important to him than himself. He will follow his leaders and not question orders. Black men are not like this. Even the most foolish black man thinks he knows better than the wise man. That is why the black man will always lose."[39]

Daniel Etounga-Manguelle of Cameroon, the president of the African development organization Société Africaine d'Etude, d'Exploitation et de Gestion, has called upon his fellow Africans to pay more attention to the future and plan ahead as Westerners do. "In traditional African society, which exalts the glorious past of ancestors through tales and fables, nothing is done to prepare for the future," he explains. Because many African societies remain averse to planning ahead, their people find "no more seats on the train, no more money at the end of the month, nothing in the refrigerator for the dinner hour, and nothing in the granary between seasons."[40]

BORROWING LIMITS

In his seminal book *The Clash of Civilizations*, published in 1996, Samuel Huntington predicted that Western influence over non-Western countries would wane in the coming decades as the spread of democracy caused Westernized elites to lose influence to the masses, who were less Westernized than many in the West believed. When everyone in a society owned a telephone and wore machine-manufactured clothing, Huntington observed, Westerners assumed that these features of modernity indicated acceptance of the Western world by the masses, when in reality most people in these countries had accepted modernization without Westernization. The masses in Bahrain and Belarus might be eating Big Macs and watching Hollywood movies, but they had not accepted core Western principles such as representative government or the rule of law.[41]

A number of key countries have since defied Huntington's predictions of growing resistance to Westernization. In countries with high rates of education, such as Japan and South Korea, Western civilization appears to be gaining in influence across all social strata. Protestant Christianity is gaining ground across much of the non-Western world.

But Huntington's warnings about the pressures of non-Westernized masses in democracies have proven prescient in some cases. During the Arab Spring of 2011, Westernized Egyptian elites forced President Hosni Mubarak from power and brought about democratization, but the ensuing elections revealed that the majority of the citizens were less interested in liberal democratic governance than Islamic governance. Wishy-washy elites who wanted to get elected had to distance themselves from the West and embrace the illiberalism of political Islam. When the elected president, Mohammed Morsi, attempted to remove the checks on his power and turn the country into an Islamist autocracy, the Egyptian military overthrew him – a move applauded by all of Egypt's liberal democrats, despite its antidemocratic character.[42] The West must bear such realities in mind the next time it considers democracy promotion as a means of spreading its values.

CIVILIZATION AND GOVERNANCE

Most of what has been written about the influences of civilization, culture, and religion on national inequality has focused on economic development. But the influences on governance are also profound. The relationship of civilization to governance is often subtle and hence poorly understood, with the result that it is often neglected by those who seek to transplant methods of governance across civilizations.

To understand this relationship, let us begin by looking at the first part of governance, state formation. Here again we find a plethora of rival theories purporting to explain why things are the way they are. *Annaliste* disciples attribute the shape of state institutions to geographic considerations: Countries comprising large numbers of islands, for instance, will have more decentralized political systems than countries where the population is concentrated along a single river. But although geography may exert influence on state formation, it has not shown the ability to determine the most salient characteristics of states. As Princeton University professor Jeffrey Herbst has noted in a comprehensive examination of sub-Saharan Africa, countries that are located in the same region and possess similar geographic characteristics have often adopted very different types of institutions.[43]

Some of today's most talented political scientists and economists contend that economic development is the leading determinant of effectiveness in state formation. Economic growth, they contend, creates a middle class that insists on competent and responsive institutions. It is true that the growth of the middle class can and often does facilitate democratization and good governance, yet it does not always do so. People have free will, and they often choose to make decisions that do not conform to the deterministic theories of social scientists. In the 1930s, large middle classes in Germany, Japan, and Italy embraced dictatorial rule. China has not democratized as its middle class has grown, and much of that middle class has embraced a nationalist rejection of democracy similar to that of the Germans, Japanese, and Italians in the 1930s.[44]

Other social scientists have argued that the creation of state institutions is driven by external threats, particularly military threats. When states need to defend against invasion, protect commerce, or fend off marauders, they are compelled to adopt institutions of particular types, characters, and virtues. Through a Darwinian process, governments that cannot create effective institutions are likely to be overthrown by states that can.[45] But this theory also does not hold up well against the broad record of human history. Iran, Rwanda, and Belgium have all been threatened and invaded frequently during their histories, yet their institutions have differed vastly in nature and size from one another historically, and remain vastly different today. External threats, like geographic features and social changes, can constrain and influence how societies choose their political institutions, but they do not reduce the number of choices to one.

Much more persuasive is the argument that civilization is the dominant factor in state formation. Civilizations whose leading thinkers afford primacy to property rights and the rule of law are likely to yield governmental institutions that safeguard property rights and the rule of law. That truth explains why the lands of the West have consistently produced governments that abide by core principles of Western civilization, whereas Islamic and Confucian countries have consistently produced governments that abide by the principles of their civilizations. Countries adopt elements of governance from other civilizations only when their elites have made a concerted effort to borrow from those civilizations, as, for instance, in Turkey or Taiwan.

The most acclaimed book on governmental institutions in recent years, authored by MIT economist Daron Acemoglu and Harvard political scientist James A. Robinson, pointedly dismisses explanations of governance quality that emphasize civilization and culture. The principal evidence marshalled in support of this dismissal is the disparity of economic outcomes in countries with similar cultures but different institutions. Among their examples are the two

Koreas. When the two Koreas were first divided, they say, the two nations had identical cultures. South Korea became wealthy because it adopted liberal political and economic institutions, while North Korea stagnated economically because it adopted illiberal institutions. If there are any cultural differences today, they are the result of the differences in political institutions, not the cause of those differences. Furthermore, according to Acemoglu and Robinson, the adoption of those political institutions was determined not by culture, but by elite perceptions of whether the elites stood to profit more from institutions that allowed broad or narrow participation in politics and economics.[46]

It is not true, however, that the political elites of the two Koreas embraced the same civilization or culture at the time of division. Nor is it true that elite preoccupation with self-aggrandizement outweighed civilization and culture in the selection of political institutions. Before setting up the Democratic People's Republic of Korea, Kim Il Sung had spent decades in exile with the Chinese Communists, who encouraged their comrades to cast off old-fashioned civilizations and adopt the new civilization of international Marxism-Leninism, with its state control of the economy, abjuration of property rights, militant atheism, and other novel answers to issues of central importance to civilization. The tenets of Marxism-Leninism guided Kim Il Sung in his creation of dictatorial institutions in North Korea. His rival in South Korea, Syngman Rhee, spent his decades of exile in the United States, where he was exposed to a very different civilization, elements of which influenced the political and economic institutions he formed. In contrast to Kim Il Sung, though, Rhee was guided more by the traditional Confucian civilization of Korea rather than by a foreign civilization, which explained why his government was autocratic rather than democratic.[47]

Although Rhee and his authoritarian successors established economic institutions conducive to growth, South Korea's liberal democratic political institutions did not take root until 1987, and they came into existence only because of widespread cultural changes that caused the South Korean middle class to throw its weight behind democracy. In the years leading up to 1987, exposure to democratic principles through educational institutions and youth organizations, many of them underwritten by U.S. aid, built support for democracy among the younger members of South Korea's middle class.[48] That this phenomenon reflected profound cultural change could be seen in the fact that South Koreans who supported democracy voiced considerably less attachment to certain Confucian ideals, such as unified governmental power and nonadversarial politics, than South Koreans who preferred authoritarian rule.[49]

In *Why Nations Fail*, Acemoglu and Robinson also cite the United States and Mexico as evidence that differences in the wealth of nations are the result of institutions and not cultures. Residents on the Mexican side of the border earn much less than their northern neighbors and receive much less education and health care, they say, and yet belong to the same culture. Some differences in social norms and values may exist between the two countries, Acemoglu and

Robinson concede, but these are merely a by-product of differences between U.S. and Mexican institutions, which are the real reason why the two countries differ so much economically.[50]

Few people living along the Mexican border would agree that communities north of the border – even those comprising mainly Mexican Americans – have the same culture as those to the south. Recent immigrants to the United States who have not learned English may retain much of their Mexican culture, but to survive they must conform to certain cultural norms that are alien to them, such as consistently showing up to work on time and obeying traffic laws. The school principals, sheriffs, and businessmen who run the towns and cities north of the border most certainly have a different culture than their counterparts to the south, which helps explain why truancy, crime, and corruption rates are much lower in the north. These elites, including those of Mexican descent, have been (North) Americanized by U.S. education, from kindergarten through graduate school, and by interactions with other U.S. elites.

Some of the cultural differences between Mexico and the United States are, as Acemoglu and Robinson contend, influenced by the character of institutions. For instance, low teaching quality and high teacher absenteeism in Mexican schools can be blamed, to some extent, on Mexico's all-powerful teachers' union, which dwarfs U.S. teachers' unions in its ability to prevent the firing of bad teachers. "It's really impossible to fire a teacher, even for horrendous violations like raping a student," remarks Lucrecia Santibanez, an education researcher at the RAND Corporation.[51] One could also blame the union for the practice of teaching school children dubious cultural values, such as fatalism and dependence on the state, since those values serve the union's interests.[52]

But the problems of Mexico's educational institutions and its other political institutions have deeper origins that predate the teacher's union and the state itself. Much of Mexican culture, including the fatalism that is still taught in the nation's schools, originated with the Aztecs. When Spaniards conquered the Aztecs in the sixteenth century, they did not eradicate Aztec culture, but instead infused it with elements of their own culture, creating a mixture that has dominated Mexico until very recently. Among the features of Mexican culture most relevant to Mexico's political development were the concentration of political power, aversion to political and economic competition, disregard for laws, and blurring of the lines between public and private property. Mexico was insulated from the northern European cultural influences that guided the political development of the United States, particularly the Reformation and the Enlightenment. Those cultural sources inculcated in the United States fundamental principles that were antithetical to Mexico's, such as limited government, democratic competition, free market capitalism, the rule of law, and private property rights.

From the outset, the governments of the two countries reflected the cultural values of their respective peoples. For most of its modern history, Mexico has been ruled by authoritarian governments that thwarted or coopted political opposition, sustained economic monopolies, failed to enforce laws, and tolerated private appropriation of public resources. The United States, by contrast, has been ruled by a democratic government that has maintained a separation of powers, encouraged open political and economic competition, enforced the rule of law, and respected private property rights. In the past couple of decades, Mexico has shifted toward liberal democracy, but only because Mexican culture has begun to embrace liberal democratic principles as the result of greater exposure to Europe and the United States; it has liberalized less quickly than some other countries because major elements of Mexico's traditional culture remain.[53]

Civilization, culture, and religion also play dominant roles in the functioning of governments. Governments with constitutions, which include most of the governments in the world today, adhere to their constitutions only if there is a culture that supports adherence. Where the national culture embraces pluralism, limited government, and the rule of law, such as in Denmark or Japan, people are likely to resist efforts to subvert the constitution. In countries lacking such cultures, powerful individuals can and frequently do get away with disregarding the constitution.[54] In Iraq, for instance, the ability of Iraqi Prime Minister Nouri Al-Maliki to grab for himself many of the powers that belonged to other Iraqi institutions has much to do with an Iraqi culture accustomed to authoritarianism rather than to pluralism, limited government, and the rule of law.

Article One of Turkmenistan's constitution states that the country "shall be a democratic, law-based and secular state in which the state rule shall be implemented in the form of a presidential republic." According to Article Four, "The state shall be based on the principle of separation of powers – the legislative, the executive, and the judiciary – which shall exercise their authority independently and interactively, checking and balancing one another."[55] In actuality, however, the hidden hand of President Kurbanguly Berdymukhamedov controls both the judiciary and the legislature, which helps account for Turkmenistan's ranking of 165 out of 167 countries in the *Economist's* Democracy Index.[56] Berdymukhamedov was reelected in February 2012 with 97 percent of the vote, an outcome that the anchor of the state television channel unabashedly called "the clearest evidence of the irreversibility of the democratic process."[57] Berdymukhamedov has spent much of the country's oil and gas revenue on marble palaces and luxury hotels, which he sees as more durable monuments to his presidency than the signature achievements of his predecessor Saparmurat Niyazov, which included renaming the months of the year after his relatives and compelling school children to recite a pledge of allegiance to him each morning.[58]

The extent to which culture and civilization restrain governmental power and stigmatize corruption correlates closely with the extent of governmental corruption. In countries such as Sudan and Venezuela where culture and civilization have attached few restrictions to governmental authority and few stigmas to corruption, no one thinks twice about offering or accepting a bribe. In countries such as Canada and Japan, where culture and civilization have limited the government's power and produced popular animosity toward corruption, individuals are much less likely to participate in bribery.

Astute governance experts have attributed endemic corruption in Asia, Africa, and Latin America to cultural subordination of the public good to the family, tribe, or ethnic group. Oliva Z. Domingo, Professor at the National College of Public Administration and Governance of the University of the Philippines, notes that the corruption that has plagued the Philippine government in recent history can be traced to the fact that her countrymen "value family ties more than they express love for country or promote the public interest." Philippine culture dictates that "when a member of the family becomes a public official, he or she is expected to do something for family and kin because not doing so would constitute betrayal."[59]

As Douglass C. North, John Joseph Wallis, and Barry R. Weingast observed in their book *Violence and Social Orders,* the use of governmental authority and resources to support select groups within society has been the hallmark of most human societies. Elites have used political power in this manner not only to make themselves wealthier but also to sustain patronage networks that promoted stability and security. Revulsion to favoritism in the exercise of governmental power is a peculiarly Western phenomenon, born out of the combination of the classical world's civic virtue with Christianity's morality.[60]

Most of the research on the relationship between civilization and corruption has focused on how corruption levels are influenced by religion, which is a reasonably good proxy for civilization since religion is the defining characteristic of most modern civilizations. Grouping countries together by dominant religion, researchers have compared perceived levels of corruption for each major religious group, making adjustments for differences in national income because corruption tends to be higher when a given country is poor than when it has become economically advanced and can pay decent wages to government employees. They have found that the group of historically Protestant countries ranks substantially better on corruption indices than all other groups. European Catholic countries, most of which were inspired or compelled to institute ethical reforms in church and state in response to the spread of Protestantism, come next. Orthodox Christian, non-European Catholic, Muslim, Hindu, and Buddhist countries are all roughly on par with one another.[61]

Country-level analysis works reasonably well for countries dominated by a single religion but is insufficient for countries with religious minorities that are well represented in elite society. A number of the most virtuous and least corrupt Asian leaders of the twentieth century, including some who led their countries through wars at great risk to themselves, were committed Christians living in religiously diverse nations. Some of them lived in majority Christian countries, such as Ramon Magsaysay of the Philippines, while others resided in countries where Christians were in the minority, such as Kim Young Sam of

South Korea, Ngo Dinh Diem of South Vietnam, and Chiang Kai-Shek of Taiwan. The histories of these individuals suggest that Christianity helped convince them to break with local traditions of using public offices to enrich the families of the officeholders.[62]

A survey of the world political landscape today shows that religion continues to play a large role in combating corruption and other forms of bad governance. In Africa, Christianity accounts for much of the opposition that has been mounted against corruption and ethnic oppression.[63] When Norwegian researchers went to Africa to study the widespread misuse of training "allowances" by government employees, an African health official told them, "It is only those who have integrity who do not abuse these allowances, like maybe those working in Faith-Based organizations. If a reverend or pastor is responsible for approving allowances, I think such abuse is minimized."[64]

In Latin America, Christianity is often the force that motivates government officials to resist the drug traffickers who routinely tempt government officials with bribes and perpetrate violence against those who dare refuse. Among the most celebrated of the resistors is Maria Santos Gorrostieta, mayor of the Mexican town of Tiquicheo, who publicly cited her Catholic faith as the inspiration for her refusal to be bought off. In 2009, drug traffickers made two attempts on her life, killing her husband and striking her with several bullets that forced her to use a colostomy bag. Gorrostieta vowed that she would not surrender, saying, "I will get up however many times God allows me." On November 12, 2012, as she was driving her youngest child to school, gunmen dragged her from her vehicle and murdered her, dumping her corpse on the side of a road a few days later.[65]

Many of the leading corruption fighters in twenty-first century East Asia are Christians who have called upon their countrymen to stop putting their families before God and country. Heidi Mendoza, a relentless anticorruption investigator who was recently appointed the head of the Philippine government's internal audit department, has been vocal in urging politicians to stop engaging in corrupt practices and urging citizens to stop tolerating those practices. "Love for family should be tempered by an even greater love for country and love of God," Mendoza says. She credits "the prayers and support of so many Filipinos" for her persistence in pursuing corruption cases in the face of threats, offers of bribes, and legal countercharges from powerful politicians.[66]

Adherents of other monotheistic religions have been active of late in the discouraging of corruption. Qatar, the United Arab Emirates, and Oman have used Islam effectively in combating corrupt practices, emphasizing Koranic injunctions against corruption and selfishness. Of the top fifty countries on Transparency International's corruption perceptions index, only three – Japan, Singapore, and Bhutan – do not have cultures that were shaped by one or more of the three major monotheistic religions, Christianity, Islam, and Judaism.[67] Katherine Marshall, a former World Bank executive who now directs the World Faiths Development Dialogue at Georgetown University, notes that religious leaders, institutions, and networks of all faiths are well positioned to lead anticorruption efforts today because "they have a particularly keen interest in reflections about values and integrity, and because of their extensive presence and reach."[68]

If religion can impede corruption, why do some countries with high rates of religiosity also have high levels corruption, as is true in much of Latin America and the Arab world? The answer lies in the pervasive failure of professed believers to adhere to basic tenets of their religion, which is most often the result of cultural traits that contradict the religion, such as extreme loyalty to family or obsession with the past. In Latin America, for example, Protestantism has gained much ground during recent decades because of the perception that Latin American Catholics have disregarded the core beliefs of Christianity or are too willing to accept elements of paganism into the faith. Amy L. Sherman, in a detailed study of religion in Guatemala, found sharp distinctions in behavior among devout Protestants and Catholics on the one hand and "Cristo-Pagans" on the other. The former had greater interest in education, higher levels of income, greater openness to change, lower levels of fatalism, and lower propensities to beat or cheat on their spouses.[69]

CONCLUSION

Civilization and its core components of religion and culture are, ultimately, the primary determinants of the prosperity of nations. They guide those engaged in economic production and those committed to the activities of governance and security on which economic development depends. If third world countries wish to become first world countries, they must acknowledge this truth and pursue fundamental changes in culture, if not also in religion and civilization. Their foreign friends can help in this regard, as the coming chapters will demonstrate.

4

Human Capital Development

Because a modern government needs a multiplicity of able leaders and technicians to be effective, a nation must develop and maintain a large pool of individuals with the attributes required for those jobs. In the terminology of human resource experts, the public sector needs "human capital" of substantial quantity and quality. Without this human capital, no nation can provide effective governance and security on a consistent basis. Nevertheless, some nations and foreign donors devote much more attention to human capital development than others.

In the 1950s and 1960s, historians, social scientists, and development professionals placed high value on human capital in the advancement of nations, believing that large-scale social and economic development hinged on the quality of the indigenous elites. First world donors consequently spent heavily on human capital development. This "elite-centric" view of development fell out of favor in the 1970s, in part because of the belief that the persistence of poverty in many countries had discredited it, but mainly because of the proliferation of the view that human capital development benefited only the elites and hence foreign assistance should be funneled exclusively to programs directly benefiting the poor.[1] Ever since, hostility to elite-centric development has been strong in development, governmental, and NGO circles. Of late, only a few prominent thinkers, such as Thomas Sowell, Ashraf Ghani, and Clare Lockhart, have stressed the importance of human capital and advocated reinstatement of human capital development at the top of the foreign assistance priority list.[2]

THE HUMAN CAPITAL UMBRELLA

Some human resource experts define human capital as the accumulated capabilities and motives of individuals, which is how it will be defined in this book.

58

Other experts refer to the culturally and socially influenced aspects of human motivation as components of "social capital," since they are reflective of broad trends within society, whereas they consider human capital to refer exclusively to individual capabilities, particularly those conferred by training, education, and experience.[3] I have opted to include motivation in the definition of human capital for several reasons. First, the cultural factors that determine a person's motivation are not always easy to separate from individual factors such as personality and character, and therefore attempts to differentiate between social capital and human capital can create more confusion than clarity. Second, activities widely viewed as human capital development, such as training and education, can have profound effects on social capital, a subject that later chapters will explore in depth.[4] Third, it makes intuitive sense to keep capabilities and motives together because capabilities are useless in the absence of motivation. A government ministry led by skilled technocrats will fail if those technocrats use their skills to raid the public coffers. In such a ministry, we are inclined to conclude that the organization has a human capital problem, much as we would conclude that a basketball team had personnel problems if the players were highly skilled but played lackadaisically or selfishly.

For some of today's development specialists, the term *human capital* refers only to people at the lower and middle levels of the government, which is where those experts most often have worked when assisting foreign governments. At those levels, there is a natural tendency to view the top leaders as inhabitants of a distant planet, beyond the capability of ordinary mortals to alter. One American expert on Africa told me that human capital was all well and good but it didn't make much difference in countries where corrupt chiefs of state obstructed the building of effective governmental capabilities to protect their personal power and wealth.[5] But chiefs of state are human capital just as police lieutenants are, and although they may be more difficult for an outsider to influence than police lieutenants, they can still be influenced. And one must keep in mind that today's police lieutenant could be tomorrow's chief of state.

THE COMPONENTS OF HUMAN CAPITAL

The first step in developing effective human capital strategies and programs for governments is identification of the individual attributes and skills most important in the public sector. Those attributes and skills vary from activity to activity and from job to job. Advantages can be gained, though, by grouping all of them into a handful of broad categories, as it promotes clear analysis and stimulates thought. Below are the five categories that I have found to be most useful.

1. Natural Talent

Some of the most crucial attributes required for effective service in the public sector are hereditary, either in whole or in part. Mathematical talent, for example, is as an inherited trait – individual scores on mathematical aptitude tests do not vary appreciably over someone's lifetime, however much, or little, effort the individual devotes to mathematics. Physical endurance, on the other hand, is only partially genetic – certain individuals are born with more efficient hearts and more resilient muscles than others, but a woman who runs five miles a day has greater physical endurance than her identical twin sister whose exercise is limited to trips between the couch and the refrigerator.

Some natural attributes, such as intelligence and vigor, are required for most any job in the public sector, whereas others are valuable in select occupations. For instance, sociability is important for a public relations official who interacts constantly with the press, but not so much for a computer programmer who spends most of his time pressing keyboard buttons in a cubicle. The ability to empathize is valuable for a policy planner who seeks to anticipate how foreign leaders will react to new policies, but not for an engineer who designs bridges.

Most of the key natural attributes are relatively easy to assess. Some, such as intelligence, can be determined through testing or school performance. Others, such as sociability or the ability to institute change, are better identified through observation. The most difficult to measure are those that are most subjective and least susceptible to common definition.[6]

A prime example of a subjective and hazily defined attribute is charisma. When a group of people are asked to provide a definition of charisma, few can answer right away, and after thinking it over they will provide a wide range of answers. Academics who have spent years pondering the question disagree sharply with one another, with some claiming that charisma is based purely upon actions, not natural characteristics, and others denying its existence at all. Most individuals who have worked in the boardroom or the map room and not just the classroom, on the other hand, recognize that charisma depends on ingrained features such as personality, as well as on deliberate behaviors. They can readily discern an individual's level of charisma, even though they might not be able to explain in precise terms how they reached that conclusion.[7]

Large numbers of people with natural talent are necessary for a strong public sector. A government whose leaders and technical experts are short on intelligence, creativity, innate charisma, and other natural gifts is certain to fail. But natural talent alone is not enough. Many highly talented people have proven ineffective, corrupt, or even diabolical when placed into governmental leadership positions. The charisma and organizational genius of Robert Mugabe propelled him to the forefront of the independence movement in Zimbabwe and earned him the admiration of Westerners sympathetic to his cause, but once in power he engaged in massive human rights violations and property seizures, along with regular electoral fraud that has enabled him to retain power in the supposedly democratic country since 1980. Queen Elizabeth II, who had earlier bestowed on Mugabe the honorific Knight Grand Cross in the Order of the Bath, became so fed up that she stripped him of the title in 2008 "as a mark of revulsion at the abuse of human rights and abject disregard for the democratic process."[8]

2. Acquired Interpersonal Skills

Central to the success of large organizations, whether governmental finance ministries or industrial corporations, is the capability of their leaders to propel others into actions that achieve the organization's objectives. One of the greatest shortcomings of intelligent and well-educated government leaders of recent times is a lack of the managerial and other interpersonal skills that are fundamental to this capability. Having focused on big ideas and grand strategies at elite universities and in other ethereal environments, they often struggle when trying to get others to transform their abstractions into realities. Benazir Bhutto, to cite one example, excelled as a student at Harvard, but as Pakistan's prime minister she could not organize people into constructive action. "Benazir's a dreamer, a great conceptualist," remarked one Western ambassador. "She says all the right things, but there's no follow-through. She wasn't able to focus, to move things forward, or control things."[9]

Some of the requisite interpersonal skills are influenced by personality and other natural traits; a shy, unassuming youth cannot be turned into a boisterous and domineering leader such as Donald Trump, just as someone with Donald Trump's personality will never spend decades pining away quietly at the bottom rungs of the organizational ladder. Nevertheless, many of the interpersonal skills required to manage and motivate others can be acquired or enhanced through concerted effort. Military officers spend years honing their posture and their manner of speech because military organizations know that how officers stand and how they talk affect the behavior of subordinates, especially when it comes to following orders that put their own lives in jeopardy. Successful businesses routinely spend large sums of money on courses that teach their managers effective interpersonal skills, because they recognize the value of those skills in terms of organizational performance and employee retention.[10]

3. Technical Skills

Effective governance, development, and security all require technical skills. Some are very general, applicable across a wide range of jobs, such as the ability to employ basic software applications on a computer. These are the most worthy of inclusion in broad training or educational programs. Others, such as the ability to monitor elections, are peculiar to a small cluster of jobs and hence more suitable to specialized instruction.

Some technical skills can be learned quickly, with little or no formal training. It takes only a matter of hours to teach someone how to fill out a parking ticket.

But conveying the knowledge required to prosecute a government official for corruption involves several years of advanced legal education and a few more years of on-the-job training. The longer it takes to acquire a technical skill, the scarcer and more valuable is that skill, and the higher the salary premium. Governments or businesses that seek to develop advanced technical capabilities among their employees must make substantial investments in human capital, in the form of training and education, and they must plan to pay employees higher amounts once the skills have been acquired.[11]

4. Experience

Even the most talented and educated individuals require years of experience before they can effectively take on critical leadership or technical jobs. That reality explains why both the public and private sectors in most functioning countries bestow greater authority and higher pay on individuals with more experience. Effective organizations typically require at least ten years of managerial experience for middle management positions, and fifteen or more for senior positions.[12]

When governmental human resource planners overlook experience, as they have on some noteworthy occasions, the results can be catastrophic. During conflicts and other crises in which the government desires a rapid increase in organizational capacity, governments often hire or conscript huge numbers of inexperienced individuals. The fact that junior civil servants or enlisted soldiers can be mass produced in six months fuels the misperception that leaders can be mass produced in a similar time frame. When organizations are flooded with large numbers of new personnel, the need for more lower- and middle-level leaders necessitates reliance on individuals with little or no experience.

Organizations with acute shortages of experienced leadership have been highly prone to ineptitude and criminality. When the Salvadoran Civil War broke out in 1980, the government sought to contain the insurgents by expanding the size of the security forces from 10,000 to 42,000 within a period of three years. Although they were able to get enough young men in uniform and provide them some basic training, the scarcity of experienced officers yielded military forces whose incompetence led to embarrassing military defeats, and whose lack of discipline led to theft, murder, and other crimes against the population. The insurgency ended up stronger than before.[13]

The consequences are not quite so dire for organizations that are short on technical experience, but they can still be serious. Mechanics who have received training but lack experience cannot fix many of the problems that befall helicopters, which means that helicopters will be grounded for months until the few seasoned mechanics can get to them, thereby reducing the access of government officials and security forces to distant areas. A recent graduate of investigative school will have a much lower ability to analyze a crime scene and question witnesses than a criminal investigator with two decades of experience.

5. Motivation

The fifth element, motivation, is the most controversial and the most difficult for an external party to influence. With enough resources and time, large numbers of people can be given the skills and experience required to be supervisors or engineers. But education and experience may not be sufficient to get people to work hard, to treat others with respect, or to keep their hands out of the state's cookie jar. Ensuring such positive behaviors requires overcoming entrenched individual or cultural characteristics, which is daunting for both the leaders inside a government and those who would assist them. One Mexican military officer put it to me this way: "We appreciate the skills that the U.S. military has taught to us, but what we really need help with is figuring out how to make our soldiers honest."

We have seen already that civilization profoundly affects the motives of the members of that civilization. Within a civilization, huge differences among individuals are also to be found, and understanding them is essential to any effort to influence the behavior of the elites. We need to know that the average American governmental official is less likely than the average Iraqi official to demand bribes from ordinary citizens, but we also need to know that some Iraqis are less likely than other Iraqis to demand bribes, and we must be able to tell these Iraqis apart from one another.

Individuals can often rise to positions of prominence in spite of, or because of, motives inimical to good governance and security, such as disregard for the thoughts of others and overwhelming preoccupation with oneself. This problem plagues even highly advanced organizations in the Western world. A survey of 22,000 soldiers conducted by the U.S. Army's Center for Military Leadership in 2010, for instance, found that 80 percent of respondents had observed a "toxic leader" in the past year and that 20 percent had worked directly for one. "Toxic leaders" were defined as "commanders who put their own needs first, micromanaged subordinates, behaved in a mean-spirited manner, or displayed poor decision making."[14]

In countries where executive power is subjected to fewer checks and balances than in the United States – a club that includes most of the third world and many of the countries currently in the transition from third to first – individual differences are all the more important. A comparison of the presidencies of Carlos Salinas and Felipe Calderón in Mexico is instructive. Salinas, Mexico's chief of state from 1988 to 1994, took corruption to a level that made Governor Rod Blagojevich's transgressions in Illinois look like elementary school artwork. Carlos and his brother Raul received humongous bribes from drug traffickers in return for unimpeded transportation of South American cocaine through Mexico into the United States. The Salinas brothers organized the murder of those who resisted them, except for a few prominent drug traffickers whom they arrested with great fanfare to show Mexico's northern neighbors how seriously the Salinas government took counternarcotics. Over the course of the Salinas presidency, Raul's Swiss bank account accumulated more than $100 million in ill-gotten funds. Eventually, after Carlos's term ended, the crimes of the Salinas brothers caught up with them. Raul was imprisoned for murder, and Carlos fled to Ireland to escape the same fate.

Felipe Calderón came from a background very similar to that of Carlos Salinas. Both were the sons of prominent Mexican political figures. Both held graduate degrees from Harvard and came to power with reputations as savvy technocrats. But when Calderón took office in 2006, he rejected collusion with the drug traffickers and instead went to war with them. Facing sophisticated criminal organizations that possessed armored vehicles and automatic weapons that outclassed anything the Mexican police owned, Calderón increased the participation of the Mexican military in the drug war. He gave the most important missions to the Mexican Marines, whose officers were the most aggressive and least corrupt in the Mexican armed forces. Calderón's trusted agents used polygraphs to weed out corrupt police chiefs and judges, of whom there proved to be a great many. Overcoming Mexico's longstanding hostility toward the United States, Calderón obtained over $1 billion in U.S. aid for counternarcotics efforts and stepped up Mexico's own spending on counternarcotics and operations. With U.S. assistance, Calderón captured or killed twenty-five of the thirty-seven most wanted drug traffickers by the end of his term in late 2012. Although he did not put an end to drug trafficking, he undermined the traffickers to an extent that few had thought possible in a single presidential term.[15]

PERSON BUILDING

American politicians of both parties frequently denigrate "nation building," a term that typically encompasses the development of a national identity, the construction of social and economic infrastructure, and the building of governmental institutions. George W. Bush came to office in 2001 saying that he wanted to get away from nation building – but then engaged the United States in massive nation-building projects in Afghanistan and Iraq. The Obama administration repeatedly claimed that it was not engaged in nation building in Afghanistan, while at the same time it was escalating the U.S. government's involvement in nation-building activities there. The failure of large nation-building investments to yield the expected results in Afghanistan, Iraq, and other countries has heightened the skepticism about nation building, with many now maintaining that it works only when it is nation rebuilding – the reconstruction of nations that had already developed strong national identities and states of their own accord, as in Germany and Japan after World War II.[16]

This book argues for nation building of a sort that is both less expensive and more effective than the nation building of the recent past. It is best described as person building, as it is focused more on building people through human capital investment than on building railroads or administrative buildings or legal codes.[17] Person building can succeed in any nation, although it is more difficult in certain cultures than others because of the profound influences of civilization on human motivation.

Much of the rhetoric and reality of recent American nation-building efforts reflects a philosophical desire to remake the world in America's image, which is a leading cause of both support for and opposition to nation building. This book will argue that the United States should help impart certain core elements of Western civilizations to non-Western countries, while acknowledging that efforts to Westernize such countries entirely are likely to be futile or even counterproductive. The United States should participate in this enterprise not because it is more righteous than other nations, but because both the United States and the nations in question stand to gain when elements of Western civilization are transfused.

For nations seeking to escape from poverty, human capital is critical in the private sector as well as in the public sector. Without effective managers and technicians, commercial enterprises will founder.[18] As the engine of economic growth, the private sector is essential to enriching the society and state and hence cannot be excluded from discussions of national welfare. Its pool of human capital is highly relevant to the public sector's pool, because individuals from the private sector can and sometimes do move into the public sector, particularly in higher leadership positions. This book will, however, focus on the governmental side of human capital because it is more readily influenced by foreign assistance and because it determines whether states can provide the security and governance that must be attained before economic development can proceed.

CONCLUSION

Human capital is the lifeblood of the public sector as well as the private sector. Subject to the influences of civilization, culture, and religion, it also varies according to individual talents, skills, experiences, personalities, and free will. The fundamental problems of the third world are all rooted in deficiencies of human capital. Consequently, the fundamental problems of the third world can be solved only through measures that improve the quality of human capital.

The countries of the first world can readily assist the third world in enhancing the skills and experience required for human capital development. They can also help, in a much slower and less obvious way, in altering the motivational side of human capital, by imparting elements of their own civilization. How exactly the first world should provide such assistance will be addressed in subsequent chapters. First, however, we will examine the national security implications of human capital deficiencies in the third world. This examination will bring greater clarity to the problem of human capital development and help convince skeptics of the need for greater first world investment.

5

Human Capital and National Security

Most Americans are repulsed by governments that fail to provide good governance and security to their populations. But most are also reluctant to ask their own governments to take action or spend money to remedy such problems, especially after nation-building efforts in Afghanistan and Iraq failed to live up to expectations. In the current climate of declining budgets and skepticism about the effectiveness of foreign aid, the only way to convince the American people to invest in the third world is to show that it will both enhance American security and save American lives and money. As this and subsequent chapters will show, human capital investments are inexpensive in relation to the threats they mitigate, and they often yield dividends at rates that rapidly recoup the initial outlays.

THE THIRD WORLD AND U.S. NATIONAL SECURITY

At the start of the Cold War, the earth was said to have three worlds. The first world consisted of the United States, the other industrialized democracies of the West, and Japan. The second world encompassed the Soviet Union and the communist nations of Eastern Europe, mortal ideological enemies of the first world. Soviet efforts to convince Western Europe's first world countries to switch sides came to naught, in part because of American infusions of money into Western Europe through the Marshall Plan. America's entreaties to Eastern Europe's second world countries also failed to yield converts, because Soviet tanks showed up whenever the Eastern Europeans tried to break ties with Moscow.

The countries most receptive to first and second world solicitations, and hence the ones that would be most fiercely contested, were the nations lying outside of the first two worlds, termed the third world. Lacking the modern industries of the first and second worlds, the countries of the third world were much weaker economically and militarily. Most of the third world countries in Asia and Africa had been European colonies before World War II and owed their newfound independence to a combination of European debilitation during the war and the rise of indigenous nationalism. Set adrift in a sea of global struggle between the great powers, they found themselves incessantly courted by the emissaries of the United States and the Soviet Union and the smaller nations of the first two worlds.

The first and second worlds invested heavily in the civil administrations and security forces of the third world to build influence and bolster current or potential allies. American and Soviet advisers spent decades of their lives in the countries of Asia, Africa, and Latin America. At elite institutions of higher learning in the United States and the Soviet Union, aspiring politicians and military officers from across the third world acquired technical skills and political ideologies.

The American and Soviet superpowers also extended development aid to the third world as a means of obtaining influence and securing alliances. The irrigation systems of Afghanistan's Helmand River Valley, which would later make possible the opium cultivation that funded the Taliban insurgency of the early twenty-first century, were underwritten and constructed by the United States in the interest of gaining favor with a country on the Soviet Union's southern border. The 360-foot-high Aswan Dam, which allowed Egypt to harness the waters of the Nile for agriculture and hydroelectricity, received its financing from the Soviet Union as part of an effort by Moscow to cement an alliance with Egyptian President Gamal Abdel Nasser.

The success of the Marshall Plan in Europe raised expectations of foreign assistance to levels that proved unattainable in most of the third world. Numerous non-Western countries made poor use of foreign aid, because of corruption or insufficient technical skills. Over the course of the Cold War, only a few non-Western countries, concentrated in East Asia, were able to approach first world status.

With the demise of the Soviet Union in 1991, the second world collapsed and most of its countries scrambled to remake themselves into members of the first world. Many observers, in the United States and elsewhere, declared that major geopolitical conflict had been eradicated for good. International relations theorists sought a new paradigm that would explain the dynamics of the entire world system, just as the paradigm of superpower competition had done during the Cold War. One school of thought, led by Francis Fukuyama, asserted that the whole world was converging toward a consensus on liberal democracy. The fall of Soviet Communism, this school asserted, had shown that dictatorship was a bankrupt form of government and hence liberal democracy was the best possible political system. According to Fukuyama, the world had now completed what Hegel had called the essence of history – the progression toward the highest attainable freedom. Fukuyama wrote, "If we are now at a point where we cannot imagine a world substantially different from our own, in which there is no apparent or obvious way in which the future will represent a fundamental improvement over our current order, then we must also take into consideration the possibility that History itself might be at an end." With this end of history, the great powers would refrain from the violent strife of the past, and poor countries would shun internal wars of ideology. First world military intervention in the third world would be confined to the occasional humanitarian intervention caused by state failure or fiendish leadership in countries that still had a ways to go to the point of convergence, as in Somalia, East Timor, the Balkans, and Sierra Leone.[1]

Some optimists emphasized the spread of Western secularism and capitalism beyond the West as a deterrent to conflict. Fouad Ajami asserted that the religious and ethnic passions that had led to war in the past had been supplanted by desires for economic and social advancement. In his view, nations would "rather scramble for their market shares, learn how to compete in a merciless world economy, provide jobs, and move out of poverty" than fight over old beliefs or principles.[2]

The paradigms of the global optimists came under attack from some sage observers of international relations, Samuel Huntington and Robert D. Kaplan being the most prominent.[3] Much of the non-Western world, the dissenters argued, was rejecting Western civilization and its dreams of universal liberal democracy. Large-scale ethnic violence in the Balkans and Africa during the 1990s showed that conflict, not peace, had become the hallmark of the post–Cold War world. Huntington emphasized that members of one civilization were striving to kill, suppress, or drive out members of another in the former Yugoslavia, Chechnya, Sri Lanka, Sudan, and East Timor, and argued that the clashes among civilizations were likely to grow in number. Kaplan noted that shortages of food and natural resources were rising in prominence as sources of conflict.[4]

These pessimists did not attract a large following during the 1990s. In the intellectual world, the forecasting of civilizational conflict came under attack from numerous directions. Some asserted that it exaggerated differences among civilizations and underestimated growing commonalities among people of different civilizations. Others contended that it overstated the geopolitical importance of civilization, which in their estimation paled in comparison with the persistent power of the nation-state.[5]

In the broader world, the warning bells of the pessimists were drowned out by favorable global political and economic trends. With the end of superpower competition, the United States no longer had to coddle dictators to keep them out of the enemy camp and could instead focus on bettering the lives of the third world's citizens. Wealthy countries sent the governments of poor countries less money for fighter jets and more demands for democratization, respect for human rights, and poverty alleviation. The rise of the internet and the lowering of international trade barriers seemed to portend the dawn of a new era of global cooperation and prosperity. The wars of the 1990s did little to alter perceptions of global progress because they touched few in the first world and several of them came to a quick end through the internationally authorized application of American air power.

A decade of optimism about global political and economic advances was shattered in a single day with the catastrophic attacks of September 11, 2001. The paradigm of civilizational convergence immediately fell out of favor, while prophecies of conflict came into fashion. New theorists arrived in search of a universal paradigm for the post-9/11 world, and in most cases their paradigms involved a protracted conflict between extremism, Islamism, evil, ignorance, and/or poverty on one side, and the West plus at least some of its friends on the other. By making alliances with malign states and taking refuge in failed states, the theorists warned, nonstate extremist groups such as Al Qaeda could strike terror into the hearts of any country, and therefore the United States had to exert its power in the third world to thwart them.

The influential neoconservatives Richard Perle and David Frum, authors of a 2003 book that warned of a struggle between good and evil for world dominance, convinced President George W. Bush to lump Iraq, Iran, and North Korea into a rhetorical "Axis of Evil."[6] The Bush administration would use the paradigm of a global conflict between Islamic extremism and the rest of the world to justify the invasions of Afghanistan and Iraq and aggressive counterterrorist measures everywhere else. Political scientists and politicians who viewed the struggle between extremism and moderation as the defining feature of international politics, but who did not support regime change by invasion, recommended an alternative option of nonmilitary assistance to weak states. That position gained in popularity as the Iraq War went awry. For the decade following the 9/11 attacks, addressing the problems of weak and poorly governed states was the foremost security concern of the U.S. government.[7]

Although the struggle against extremists in the third world was very real and very important, characterizing it as the overriding theme of global affairs unduly diminished other themes that demanded attention from the world's nations. A single paradigm had roughly approximated international realities during the Cold War, but in the twenty-first century no single geopolitical paradigm could embody simultaneously the realities of Africa, the Arab world, Europe, East Asia, South Asia, and the Americas. After 9/11, Al Qaeda and other Islamist extremist groups aspiring to terrorize the West were active in much of Africa, the Middle East, and South Asia. But they were not the sole problem, even in the countries where they acquired the most strength, and they would be eclipsed in some countries by subsequent events.

In recent years, conflict between the supporters of democracy and autocracy has shaped the security environment in much of the Arab world, resulting in regime change in Tunisia, Egypt, Libya, and Yemen and bloody civil wars in Libya, Syria, Iraq, and Yemen. Humanitarian concerns arising from those civil wars prompted Western intervention in Libya and led to the international ostracizing of Syria. Nuclear proliferation is the foremost issue in the cases of

Iran and North Korea, and it is a major concern in the case of Pakistan. Islamic extremism has never been a central problem in Latin America, where illicit narcotics have reigned preeminent since the Cold War, or in East Asia, where competition between China and the United States has been the order of the day. Russian expansionism is the most worrying issue in Europe. In sub-Saharan Africa, one needs a grab bag of paradigms to explain recent developments, as resource exportation, religious and ethnic civil warfare, extremism, democratization, and disease have all been defining features of national and geopolitical landscapes.

As this chapter will show, human capital deficiencies account for many of the world's most dangerous geopolitical problems, primarily because those problems are caused or facilitated by bad governance and inadequate security. It would be too much to declare a new universal paradigm, according to which all the critical problems of international security can be solved by eliminating human capital shortfalls. China's naval expansion and India's trade policies, for instance, are driven primarily by traditional great power competition rather than by major deficiencies in the capabilities or motives of national leaders. Russian nuclear missiles can be deterred more effectively with antiballistic missiles than with human capital advancements.[8] Nevertheless, many of today's geopolitical problems, and most of those that are susceptible to alleviation through U.S. foreign assistance, can best be addressed with assistance targeted at human capital.

ISLAMIC EXTREMISM

More than a decade after the 9/11 attacks, Islamic extremism terrorism remains one of the greatest threats to U.S. security. American operations in Afghanistan and Pakistan have inflicted major losses on Al Qaeda's leadership, but Al Qaeda has retained considerable strength in Pakistan and has gained sanctuary areas in Yemen, Somalia, Syria, Iraq, Libya, and Mali. Within Pakistan, Al Qaeda receives support and protection from the Haqqani Network, Quetta Shura Taliban, the Tehrik-i-Taliban Pakistan, and other extremist groups that continue to flourish with unofficial support from the Pakistani government. American drones no longer threaten these groups as in the past, because international criticism has caused the U.S. government to curtail drone strikes and extremist leaders have moved from the rural areas where the strikes were concentrated to cities that are off limits to the drones.[9]

Al Qaeda in the Arabian Peninsula (AQAP), based in Yemen, is considered among the most likely of the Al Qaeda franchises to attack the American homeland. Terrorism experts blame AQAP leader Anwar al-Awlaki for inciting the shooting spree of U.S. Army psychiatrist Nidal Malik Hasan, which killed thirteen American military personnel and wounded twenty-nine at Fort Hood, Texas, on November 5, 2009.[10] AQAP operative Umar Farouk Abdulmutallab attempted to kill the 289 passengers on Northwest Airlines Flight 253 on

Christmas Day of the same year. Shortly before the plane was scheduled to land in Detroit, Abdulmutallab used a syringe to add a combustible liquid to 80 grams of the highly explosive compound PETN, which had been sewn into his underwear. Fortunately it did not detonate with the anticipated force, causing injury only to the so-called underwear bomber himself.

In May 2010, an ineffectual detonator again spared the lives of hundreds of Americans, this time in Times Square. The would-be bomber, Faisal Shahzad, belonged to the Tehrik-i-Taliban Pakistan, also known as the Pakistani Taliban. A thirty-year-old man of Pakistani birth, he had lived in the United States for more than a decade, becoming a U.S. citizen in 2009. Working by day in the markedly unsuspicious job of financial analyst at Elizabeth Arden Cosmetics, Shahzad spent his vacations traveling to Pakistan, where he took courses in terrorism from the Pakistani Taliban. On May 1, 2010, he loaded three twenty-gallon propane tanks and 250 pounds of fertilizer into a blue Nissan Pathfinder that he had purchased on Craig's List and drove into Times Square, parking in front of the Minskoff Theater. He set the timer and bolted from the scene, in anticipation of a massive fireball that would inscribe his name in the terrorist pantheon and leave New York with another hideous scar. But the SUV bomb produced only smoke and firecracker noises.

The Syrian civil war has created sanctuaries for thousands of Sunni extremists who have flocked to Syria from all continents to fight against the government of Bashar Assad. In January 2014, U.S. intelligence and counterterrorism officials divulged that Al Qaeda's affiliates in Syria were especially welcoming to American and European extremists who had traveled to Syria, urging them to undertake terrorist attacks when they went back to the West.[11] Director of National Intelligence James R. Clapper said that U.S. intelligence had identified "training complexes" in Syria that were intended "to train people to go back to their countries and conduct terrorist acts, so this is a huge concern."[12] Following the conquest of much of Iraq by ISIS in mid-2014, foreigners from around the world traveled to Iraq and Syria in unprecedented numbers, acquiring training and experience that would pave the way for a future terrorist diaspora. Elements of the nascent diaspora have already helped ISIS make inroads in such places as Libya, Egypt, Tunisia, Algeria, Indonesia, Afghanistan, and Pakistan.[13]

Shiite Islam also has its share of militant terrorist groups with international ambitions. Foremost among these is Hezbollah, a quasi-independent organization based in Lebanon that receives an estimated $100 to $200 million in annual subsidies from the government of Iran.[14] Hezbollah fought a short war against Israel in 2006, which resulted in several thousand civilian and combatant deaths and taxed the Israeli armed forces to the extent that they needed large transfers of stockpiled U.S. military equipment.[15] The threat of Hezbollah attacks on the United States and Israel serves as a major deterrent to military strikes on Iran's nuclear program.

Replacing governments for their real or potential support of terrorism, as occurred in Afghanistan and Iraq, has entailed massive costs. The United States and its allies expected to exit those countries quickly after overthrowing their governments, but instead were compelled to fight off insurgencies while engaging in large-scale, long-term nation building. The costs from those two conflicts have discouraged further interventions, compelling the United States to seek alternative counterterrorism approaches.

Some noted analysts contend that the threat of terrorism to the first world has been vastly overblown. They point to the scarcity of casualties inflicted by terrorists since 9/11 and assert that the economic aftershocks of terrorist attacks are unlikely ever to approach the massive proportions attained after 9/11.[16] There is some truth to this argument, but it is not wholly convincing. For one, it understates the impact of the lavish first world counterterrorism expenditures since 9/11; without the operations made possible by those expenditures, terrorists would have killed many more people and they would be much stronger today.

In addition, the idea that the United States can shrug off a few domestic terrorist attacks is anathema to the political psychology of the American people, the existence of which cannot be ignored regardless of how much one finds to criticize in it. The United States has been and remains enormously sensitive to even small numbers of casualties from terrorist attacks. In the fall of 2002, a terrorist duo paralyzed the population of the U.S. capital and several million people in the surrounding suburbs by shooting a few people with a semiautomatic rifle. Western publics are willing to let airport security personnel view images of their naked bodies and frisk their grandmothers to avert another airborne terrorist strike. In recognition of the public's fears, the liberal Obama administration has invested extraordinary amounts of money in counterterrorism and has broken campaign pledges to scale back its predecessor's illiberal counterterrorist measures. So long as terrorist organizations thrive in places such as Pakistan, Yemen, Syria, and Somalia, the United States is going to pour huge sums of treasure into counterterrorism.

The terrorist threat also carries substantial risk of future wars on the order of Afghanistan and Iraq. The popular will, at least in the United States, is unwilling to tolerate states that facilitate major attacks on the homeland, as Afghanistan showed. The United States even invaded Iraq to forestall such an eventuality. Although the costs of Afghanistan and Iraq have eroded America's resolve to launch retaliatory or preventive military expeditions, that resolve would surely be restored by a terrorist attack on the U.S. homeland that killed Americans in the hundreds or thousands.

Those who minimize the terrorist threat have, moreover, given too little heed to the possibility that terrorist organizations will acquire weapons of mass destruction and employ them against Western targets. To date, Western intelligence agencies have thwarted attempts by extremist groups to purchase these weapons on the black market. Those successes, however, are not guaranteed to continue, and even if they do, extremists could still obtain weapons directly from the stockpiles of an unstable state. Among the most serious concerns in this regard is the nuclear arsenal of Pakistan, where extremists have been gaining in influence not only in nonstate organizations but within the elected government and the security forces. Worries about the Pakistani nuclear arsenal contributed to Barack Obama's decision in 2009 to send troops to Afghanistan.[17] Syria's chemical and biological weapons arsenals face more immediate peril, in the form of extremist organizations currently at war with the Syrian government.[18]

The problem of Islamic extremism is a human capital problem for several reasons. First, the terrorists are the products of human capital development gone awry. They are not the products of poverty, as is often said by champions of poverty alleviation while advocating greater spending on development.[19] Most of the terrorist leaders – the individuals who conceive and orchestrate terrorist attacks – come from the middle and upper classes, not from the classes of the destitute, and the same is true of large numbers of their followers. Islamic extremism, in fact, often gains more adherents from countries that are improving economically than from those that are stagnating.[20]

It would also be mistaken to contend that terrorism is the result of a lack of education. Many Islamic extremists have been recipients of advanced educations, as was also true of earlier extremists of fascist and communist persuasion. Rather, it is the content of the education received that has driven these Muslims toward extremist violence. These extremists constitute a variant of what can be called "negative human capital" – people whose education and other forms of acculturation have motivated them to employ their capabilities toward harmful political, social, or economic ends.[21]

The fact that international terrorism has been perpetrated overwhelmingly by Muslims has convinced most experts that it has roots in Islamic religion and culture. Less obvious, however, is whether it reflects mainstream Islam or a perverted offshoot. Samuel Huntington argued that it was the former, blaming the rise of terrorism on mainstream Islamic education funded by surging oil revenues in the Arab world beginning in the 1970s.[22] Others who deem Islamic terrorism reflective of mainstream Islam have attributed terrorism to a cultural and religious backlash sparked by the spread of digital media. Television and the internet have exposed Muslims to images of Madonna dancing in her underwear, pontifications by Bill Maher about the virtues of atheism and homosexuality, and other material offensive to Islamic sensibilities.[23] Still other analysts contend that Islamic terrorism is simply a manifestation of widespread Islamic hostility to America's foreign policies, particularly its occupations of Muslim lands and its support for Israel.[24]

Each of those factors has influenced some Islamist extremists. None, however, can be said to be the dominant factor. None suffices to explain why most Muslims are not terrorists, or why many Muslim governments have cooperated actively with the West in combating terrorism. The most persuasive explanation of the causes of Islamist terrorism comes from scholars such as Bassam Tibi of Syria, Daniel Pipes of the United States, and Malise Ruthven of the United Kingdom, who have probed deeply into the lives of individual terrorists and steered clear of preconceived theories. The sources of terrorism, they conclude, lie primarily in the realm of education and culture.

According to these experts, most Islamic terrorists have been middle class males with university degrees in scientific or technical fields. Most were born in small villages or towns and moved to big cities in their teens or twenties to obtain jobs or to attend state universities built by modernizers who had expected those institutions to promote progressive secularism. Like the rustics of many societies, they were alienated by urban culture, with its dearth of personal interaction and tradition. This alienation was magnified by the wide gulf between traditional Islam and modernity, particularly the Western aspects of modernity that could be found in the cinemas and newsstands of large cities of the Islamic world. Studying Western engineering but not Western politics, they developed a superficial understanding of Western civilization that equated the West with the materialism, promiscuity, and crime to be found in Western pop culture.

Seeking kindred spirits and intellectual silver bullets, these alienated young men were drawn to eloquent purveyors of radical interpretations of Islam, such as the Qutbists and the Wahhabists. Qutbism, Wahhabism, and other radical strains of Islam promised a return to an idealized past, in which Islam dominated world affairs and everyone adhered strictly to Islamic law. They averred that he who sacrificed his life in the service of this cause would gain entry to heaven, where seventy-two virgins and a full cup of wine awaited. The embrace of these theologies put Muslims in opposition not only to the West, but to the majority of their countrymen, including in most cases the political authorities, who deemed these views dangerous distortions of Islam.[25]

Terrorism is also a human capital issue because terrorist organizations have received invaluable support from states ruled by individuals whose intentions are as malevolent as their own. The Taliban leaders who provided Al Qaeda sanctuary in Afghanistan until December 2001 were inspired by Deobandi Islam, a form of Sunni Islam as extreme as the Qtubism of Al Qaeda. The Taliban tortured men for wearing beards of insufficient length, lopped off the heads of women for failing to wear the burqa, sawed off the arms of thieves, and slaughtered entire villages of minority ethnic groups for disregarding their commands.

Today, several Islamic countries continue to support terrorist organizations, and at least some of them suffer from negative human capital at the top.[26] President Omar Al Bashir of Sudan, a country that the U.S. State Department has listed as a state sponsor of terrorism since 1993, has been charged with genocide by the International Criminal Court for his attempts to exterminate the non-Arab population of Darfur. Mahmoud Ahmadinejad, who supported Hezbollah and Hamas as Iran's president from 2005 to 2013, believes that the Holocaust never occurred, and has been mocked by many in his own country for claiming that a halo appeared over his head during a speech to the United Nations.[27]

Human capital is also central to the problem of violent extremism because it is an essential ingredient in indigenous counterterrorism, which is the most cost-effective type of counterterrorism and the only one that is certain to reduce the need for U.S. counterterrorism expenditures in the long run. The primary determinant of a state's effectiveness in combating extremist organizations is its ability to provide security and governance, which is a function of its human capital. Al Qaeda and other international terrorist organizations thrive in countries where the government is too weak to maintain firm control over the entirety of its territory and bring terrorists to justice, countries such as Chad, Mali, and Yemen. By contrast, Muslim countries with well-led security forces and civil administrations, such as Oman, Turkey, and Qatar, are much better at finding and incarcerating terrorists and hence have far fewer terrorists running loose within their borders.[28]

Nowhere is the connection between ineffectual governance and ineffectual counterterrorism more starkly apparent than in Somalia. For two decades, Somalia has lacked a viable national government, owing to the inability of Somalian elites to subordinate clan loyalties and personal aggrandizement to the interests of the country. The absence of central governance and security capabilities has permitted home-grown radical Islamist groups to multiply and has attracted terrorist leaders from other countries who want a place to plot attacks without having to worry about policemen and soldiers pestering them. The Somalian terrorist group Al Shabab, which in February 2012 officially declared itself a franchise of Al Qaeda, has grown into one of the most dangerous organizations on the planet. It has perpetrated vicious attacks against Ethiopians, Kenyans, and Ugandans, in addition to enforcing a draconian form of Islam in areas under its domination, which includes the banning of movies and the whipping of women who are found to be wearing bras that make their breasts look deceptively large.[29] Al Shabab has plotted a host of attacks against first world targets, although to date most of these plots have been thwarted.

Somalia's governance and security voids have triggered avalanches of aid from Western countries that are concerned about Somali terrorism and the abject misery of the Somali people. Over the past twenty years, foreign donors have spent an average of $1 billion annually on development, governance, security, and humanitarian programs in Somalia.[30] The commitments in treasure have been accompanied, at times, by commitments in blood. American forces entered Somalia in 1992 to help stabilize the country but departed in 1994 after the deaths of eighteen Americans during the botched mission immortalized in Mark Bowden's book *Black Hawk Down*. In 2006, provocations from Somalian Islamists led Ethiopian troops to swarm into the country, where they remained until 2009, at which time they handed the country over to a transitional government's UN-trained police forces, who proved ineffective, contemptuous of Western human rights standards, and prone to desertion and defection. Within a year, Al Shabab and foreign fighters from Afghanistan, Yemen, Pakistan, the United States, Canada, United Kingdom, Kenya, and Saudi Arabia seized control of most of Somalia.[31] Once again, international terrorists stampeded to Somalia and used the country as a launching pad for attacks elsewhere.

In 2011, with extensive Western support, African Union forces retook Mogadishu and other major cities. In the absence of a viable government and indigenous security forces, however, it was impossible to secure the whole country, leaving Al Shabab free to operate in rural areas. In November 2013, Erastus Mwencha, the African Union's deputy chairman, reported an alarming rise in the strength of Al Shabaab and recommended that the United Nations Security Council authorize the deployment of more African Union troops to Somalia. The Security Council concurred with the grim appraisal of Al Shabaab's strength but authorized only a small increase in the African Union's forces in Somalia, from 17,731 to 22,126.[32] Those forces were too few in number to hold much additional territory in the short term, and their long-term staying power was in doubt because of the reluctance of the contributing nations to keep troops in harm's way year upon year. Thus, restoration of indigenous governance and security remained essential if the country were to avoid reversion to full Islamist control.

Human capital development can affect the willingness of third world countries to collaborate with the United States on counterterrorism. Few countries outside the West have the personnel or the technology to carry out sophisticated counterterrorist operations, and they are often eager to obtain these assets from the United States. The U.S. government wants help from its third world counterparts in the form of information sharing and permission to operate on or above their territory. The amenability of foreign nations to collaboration on counterterrorism is a human capital issue because it is heavily influenced by the core human capital development activities of training and education, which shape individual perceptions of foreign countries and the advisability of working with them.

Pakistan is a prime example. During the Cold War, numerous Pakistani military officers received American training and education, which in general made them favorably disposed toward the West and desirous of cooperation with the U.S. military. From 1990 to 2001, however, the United States halted its training and education of Pakistan's military officers because of the Pressler Amendment, which barred U.S. military assistance to the Pakistani government in response to Pakistan's illicit development of nuclear weapons. The Pakistani officers who came of age during these years received no direct exposure to the West, and many became virulently anti-Western because of the anti-Western tendencies of the broader Pakistani culture. As these younger officers have risen through the ranks, their anti-Western sentiments have undermined collaboration with the United States on counterterrorism and counterproliferation.[33]

INTRASTATE WARS

Since the late 1990s, conflicts between states and between members of different civilizations have declined, defying the predictions of rising violence across national and civilizational borders that Samuel Huntington made in his epochal *Clash of Civilizations.* Of the twenty-six major armed conflicts in 2010 – those with at least twenty-five combat-related deaths in the preceding year and total accumulated combat deaths of at least 1,000 – twenty-four were clearly conflicts internal to a single country. The other two – the war in Afghanistan and the U.S. war against Al Qaeda – involved a mixture of conflict between opposing residents of a single state and violence between Western expeditionary forces and Muslim nonstate actors. Of the twenty-four purely intrastate wars, only nine were conflicts among groups representing different civilizations. Muslims were party to all nine of those conflicts. They were fighting Christians in six cases, Buddhists in two, and Jews in one.[34]

In contrast to interstate wars such as World War II or the invasion of Iraq in 2003, intrastate wars do not normally conjure up images of massive destruction of property and person. But they can be more destructive than appearances would suggest. Often lasting a decade or more, intrastate wars have inflicted fearsome damage, some of which harms neighbors and trade partners as well as first world countries that are called upon for emergency relief and rehabilitation. For the average civil war, the estimated total cost to the world is $64 billion, with the country victimized by the war incurring costs equivalent to thirty years of economic growth.[35] In addition to full-blown civil wars, which pit large segments of the population against one another, many states have experienced insurgencies in which a smaller segment of the population supports an armed rebellion against the government. These too have been extremely costly. The United States has already paid more than $1 trillion in combating the insurgencies in Afghanistan and Iraq.

The motives of the rebels in intrastate conflicts often differ from those of international terrorists, for these rebels are usually focused more on the government in their own country than on foreign nations. The acquisition of political power or wealth is more often a central motive for rebels, who are more likely than terrorists to obtain these spoils in the near term. On the other hand, some of the factors that attract individuals to international terrorist organizations also bring them into groups engaged in insurgency or civil war. Political ideology and religion are often central factors for both groups.[36]

Intrastate conflict often counts bad governance among its principal causes. Perceptions of governmental incompetence or malice, the inability of the government to maintain law and order, and ideological opposition to the government are common motives of insurgent leaders. In the development community

and in the current White House, it is often said that poverty and other manifestations of underdevelopment are the leading causes of armed rebellion, but in
truth people of all races, creeds, and cultures are much more likely to take up
arms because of dissatisfaction with governance than dissatisfaction with social
and economic development.[37] Governments that fail to renovate dilapidated
schools or stimulate economic activity do not generate the same sense of
outrage as governments that misuse public funds or allow the police to brutalize
innocent civilians. In some instances, poverty and unemployment can facilitate
rebellion by providing manpower that rebels can obtain for a fee, but the hard-
core leadership that is essential for success is seldom motivated primarily by
general economic privation.[38]

Andrew Wilder, a development expert who specializes in Afghanistan and
Pakistan, has risen to prominence during the past few years by challenging the
development community's conventional wisdom that underdevelopment causes
insurgency. By concentrating resources on economic and social development in
Afghanistan and Pakistan, Wilder observes, Western governments have taken
their eyes off of the principal drivers of insurgency, bad governance and
insecurity. "One of the main rationales given for the assumed link between
aid and security is the belief that poverty is a major factor fueling the insurgency," Wilder told a U.S. Congressional committee. "Yet there is little evidence that poverty, inadequate infrastructure, or the lack of social services are
major factors driving the insurgency in either Afghanistan or Pakistan. In fact,
some of the poorest and least developed regions of Afghanistan are actually the
most stable." The Taliban, Wilder notes, recognize that governance and security are the foremost concerns of the population and have gained adherents "by
promising better security, justice and governance rather than more roads,
schools and clinics."[39]

One reason why bad governance is more likely than underdevelopment to
incite rebellion is that governmental abuses are directly traceable to an individual, whereas underdevelopment can be blamed on a variety of people and
external factors, such as large macroeconomic problems, bad weather, feckless
business owners, and the previous government. Political leaders invariably
place the blame for economic hard times on such scapegoats, even as they
attribute all economic successes to their own genius.

Another reason is that humans are prewired to attach a premium to fairness,
which is fundamental to good governance. Scientists have determined that
perceptions of unfairness trigger chemical reactions in the brain, reactions that
appear to be instinctive rather than acquired. Children can discern the unfairness of giving more candy to one child than the other well before they can grasp
intellectual arguments about the need for fairness.[40] Adults typically react to an
unjust court verdict or revelations of nepotism in government hiring with a
sense of indignation that contains a large dose of emotion.

Insecurity is also a leading cause of insurgency and civil warfare. When
security forces cannot prevent violent criminals from raping and murdering

with impunity, or when the security forces are themselves raping and murdering, the populace becomes receptive to the idea of a new political order. Rebels who demonstrate a superior ability to provide security usually attract broad support from the masses, because the masses want to be safe today and on the side of the victors tomorrow. In the 1990s, much of the Afghan population embraced the Taliban despite its many unsavory features because it was able to stifle rampant violent crime through the apprehension and draconian punishment of criminals.[41]

Human capital is even more important in counterinsurgency and civil warfare than in counterterrorism, because the required political and military actions are broader in scope and geographic coverage. Large numbers of good town mayors, district police chiefs, and army battalion commanders are needed to orchestrate the governance and security activities that will weaken the enemy and gain the support of the population. If the government has only a few good mayors or military commanders, the enemy can evade them by moving to the places where the mayors and commanders are weak.

The French writer Bernard Fall once asserted that a government that is losing to an insurgency is not being outfought, it is being outgoverned.[42] The truth is that such a government is losing because it is being both outfought and outgoverned. And the reason why it is being outfought and outgoverned is that it is being outled.

In a previous book, I identified the ten personal attributes most important to effective leadership in counterinsurgency, as a means of helping counterinsurgents identify the individuals best suited to leadership positions. The attributes were initiative, flexibility, creativity, judgment, empathy, charisma, sociability, dedication, integrity, and organization. In addition, leadership effectiveness was heavily influenced by two other factors – experience and identity. To provide the necessary governance and security at the local level, a counterinsurgency must have a significant number of leaders with at least ten years of relevant experience. Identity matters because some individuals are more willing to follow leaders of their own ethnic, tribal, religious, or political group.[43]

Whenever the United States deploys its military forces into foreign insurgencies and civil wars, it faces public pressure to bring the troops home quickly, so it strives from the outset to build indigenous forces that will eventually be able to handle the conflict themselves. The central challenge is developing the human capital required to lead the military, the police, and the civil administration. This challenge has been tackled with widely varying degrees of effectiveness. In Afghanistan, the United States and its NATO allies spent enormous sums on Afghan security forces as part of a strategy to turn the war over to the Afghan government. Some of the money has led to human capital improvements, especially in the military, and some of it has been squandered because of a lack of selectiveness in recruiting, shortages of competent trainers, or abbreviation of training below the duration required to instill the right capabilities and values. As of this writing, it remains unclear whether the United States and

other NATO countries will continue their resource commitments long enough
to ensure that the Afghan police, which achieved little in human capital development prior to 2010, receive the necessary decade of human capital development. If Afghanistan does not have the requisite human capital in place when
foreign security forces withdraw, the Taliban are likely to regain control of
large sections of the country, opening new sanctuaries for the Pakistan-based
terrorist organizations.

During the occupation of Iraq, the United States made more rapid progress
in building up indigenous human capital, partly because the U.S. government
made Iraq a higher priority than Afghanistan, partly because the Iraqi population contained a much larger number of educated and experienced leaders at
the time of the regime change. Initially, the U.S. government expelled Iraq's
most developed human capital from the government through de-Baathification
and the disbandment of the security forces. Disfranchised military and police
officers turned to insurgency and for several years got the better of the Iraqi
security forces, whom the United States had hastily cobbled together with little
regard for the human capital requirements of a massive security apparatus.
Eventually, the ineptitude of the Iraqi security forces and their complicity in
murders of Sunni civilians convinced the Americans to change tack. They
pressed the Iraqi government to fire bad commanders and replace them with
individuals who had been marginalized after the fall of Saddam Hussein, or
with individuals nurtured in recently created training and educational institutions. In Sunni areas of the country, the Americans bypassed the central Iraqi
government, directly empowering handpicked Iraqis to command local counterinsurgent militias. As a result of these changes, the insurgency went from a
seemingly unstoppable force in 2006 to a largely moribund enterprise by the
end of 2008.

DEMOCRATIZATION

During the past two decades, democratization in the third world has been a
central national security issue for the United States, and it will remain so for
decades to come. A number of influential Western social scientists have argued
that democratization should be encouraged throughout the world because of its
numerous virtues. In addition to curing political and social ills within a country,
they argue, it averts conflict, as evidenced by the absence of wars among
democracies in recent history.[44]

For the past two decades, numerous Western politicians have embraced the
positive interpretations of democratization and have consequently employed
military and political power, with widely disparate degrees of subtlety, to
encourage or impose democratic elections and democratic governance. They
have targeted nearly every nondemocratic country in the world and have
caused or influenced the holding of elections in a slew of countries such as
Afghanistan, Azerbaijan, Burundi, Cameroon, Egypt, Indonesia, Iraq, Kosovo,

Libya, Mali, Palestine, Sri Lanka, Tunisia, and Yemen. We do not yet know how all of these democratic experiments will turn out, but the initial returns are not very encouraging. Since the end of the Cold War, liberal democracy has taken root in only a few third world countries, of which Indonesia and Tunisia appear to be the most promising. A large number of countries in Latin America and sub-Saharan Africa have held elections and maintained democratic governments but have not yet developed the institutions of a stable liberal democracy. Many of the recent democratic elections have produced illiberal democracies that proved ripe for reversion to illiberal autocracy, as in Egypt and Sri Lanka, or led directly to illiberal autocracies, as in Azerbaijan and Cameroon. Liberal democracy has lost out in these countries because they have lacked electorates with the educational levels and cultural attitudes necessary to make wise electoral choices, and because they have not possessed sufficient public sector human capital to run a democratic government effectively.

Western interests have suffered as a consequence of these failed democratic experiments. In a ground-breaking study of democratization in the past two centuries, the political scientists Edward D. Mansfield and Jack Snyder have shown that although successful democratization has promoted peace, incomplete and unsuccessful attempts at democratization have promoted conflict. They also note that for every instance of successful democratization, two attempts at democratization have failed.[45]

Democracy has often degenerated into a competition of ethnic or religious groups instead of a competition of political ideas, at times resulting in bloody civil wars or offensive wars against other states. The success of democratization, assert Mansfield and Snyder, hinges on strong institutions that can prevent popular passions from combusting into civil conflict. Like most modern social scientists, Mansfield and Snyder do not characterize popular passions or governmental institutions as human capital issues, but both are. Ethnic and religious passions can be transformed into mass movements only when elites take charge, for elites are required to organize and inspire the masses and, in the case of democracies, to run for office. Every ethnically or religiously defined political movement has readily identifiable leaders, from Serbia's Slobodan Milosevic to Iraq's Muqtada al-Sadr to Rwanda's Hassan Ngeze.

As we have seen in preceding chapters, the weakness of governmental institutions is a function of human capital deficiencies. Among the most important of institutions, as Mansfield and Snyder put it, are "a non-corrupt bureaucracy and a police force that follows the law," along with organizations that regulate political competition impartially. Bureaucracies and police forces are noncorrupt only if their leaders are noncorrupt. The ability of institutions to regulate politics impartially is contingent on whether the leaders of those institutions are more committed to impartiality than to their own religious or ethnic identities, and whether they have the managerial skills to lead an institution effectively.

The case of Kosovo shows what can happen when democratically elected national leaders put religion and ethnicity first. Democratized by NATO air strikes, Kosovo held elections in which the Muslim Albanian majority, comprising 90 percent of the population, voted into office a government that promoted the ethnic cleansing of the Christian Serb minority. Since 2008, Kosovo's democratic government has been led by Hashim Thaçi, who had previously headed the Kosovo Liberation Army at a time when, according to a multiyear investigation by the Council of Europe, the organization was murdering Serbs and harvesting their organs.[46] Under Thaçi's prime ministership, Kosovo has grown into a safe haven for international Islamist terrorists, who find it a particularly auspicious staging ground because of its location inside Europe. Bajram Asllani, one of nine members of a North Carolina–based terrorist ring that the U.S. Department of Justice indicted in 2009 for material support to terrorists and conspiracy to murder, is presently at large in Kosovo after a brief detention by the government.[47]

Ethnic passions proved equally problematic for democratization in Burundi. The national elections of 1993, which were intended to liberalize the country and pave the way for economic development, instead stoked internal conflict between the two main ethnic groups – the Hutu, who made up the majority of the population, and the Tutsi, who had historically dominated the government and armed forces. Political parties sprang up along ethnic lines, and party leaders baldly appealed to ethnic loyalties in their campaign propaganda. Once the electoral results were announced, the vanquished Tutsi parties claimed to be victims of ethnic oppression and began plotting to subvert the government by extralegal means. The government and security forces joined the rest of society in ethnic polarization, with Hutus and Tutsis jockeying for military commands and laying plans for ethnically pure military units in anticipation of an ethnic civil war. A few months after the elections, fears of Hutu ascendancy caused Tutsi military officers to assassinate Hutu President Melchior Ndadaye, sparking a civil war that ultimately claimed 300,000 lives.[48]

POLITICAL TRANSITIONS

Human capital can also play a pivotal role in abrupt political transitions, particularly those from authoritarian to democratic rule. The ability of opposition movements to overthrow governments and start new ones often boils down to the decisions of a few key leaders in the government's security forces. For illustrative cases, we need look no further back than the Arab Spring of 2011.

The Arab Spring began in Tunisia on December 17, 2010, with the attempted suicide of Mohammed Bouazizi, a twenty-six-year-old fruit vendor who had been driven to desperation by the abuse of a female police officer. The woman had slapped him – an unconscionable humiliation for the male recipient in an Arab society – and confiscated his produce because he lacked a permit. Pouring gasoline over his head and lighting himself on fire, Bouazizi suffered ghastly burns that would end his life in a Tunis hospital two weeks later. His suicide attempt sparked street protests that led to escalating clashes between thousands of Tunisian citizens and the police, in which more than one hundred protesters perished.

The inability of the police to quell the dissidents convinced Tunisian President Zine El Abidine Ben Ali to throw the military into the breach. On January 14, he ordered armed forces chief of staff General Rachid Ammar to unleash the might of the Tunisian armed forces on the protesters. Ammar had, over the course of his career, attended three French military schools, and he was considered a "Francophile," both of which may well have contributed to his sympathies for democratic protesters and his aversion to using force against them. At the moment of decision, Ammar refused to obey the president's order and instead forced him to step down. In one fell swoop, a single military officer ended autocracy in Tunisia and opened the door to democratic elections, which in Tunisia's case led to a government that has been relatively successful thus far.[49]

In Egypt, where protests began on January 25, 2011, the military leadership similarly stayed on the sidelines in the first weeks while the police struggled to club and handcuff the opposition into submission. The generals initially favored a plan that allowed President Hosni Mubarak to stay in power until September, but as the protests gained in strength and protesters died at the hands of Mubarak's police, the military's loyalty wavered. On February 11, the military compelled Mubarak to abdicate, ending a reign of thirty years. Although the full details of Mubarak's fall may not emerge for decades, if ever, the available evidence suggests that the Egyptian military was influenced in its ultimate decision by America's military assistance programs, which had built ties that facilitated communication during the crisis and may have made the Egyptian generals more amenable to American advocacy of Mubarak's departure.[50]

In the Arab countries where the military leadership remained loyal to the political leadership after large initial shocks – Libya and Syria – the chief of state stayed in power and bloody civil war ensued. In Libya, 25,000 people perished between the start of the civil war in February and the death of Muammar Gaddafi on October 20. As of this writing, the Syrian conflagration has claimed the lives of more than 200,000 people, and the four-year-old conflict shows few signs of abating. Both conflicts have led the West to provide large amounts of military and humanitarian aid, and the open wounds of Libya and Syria are likely to require expensive Western salves for many years to come.

Military leadership has also proven critical in the aftermath of the Arab Spring's regime changes. In Egypt, the military initially constrained the powers of President Morsi, a maneuver that was offensive to Western sensibilities but beneficial to Western interests because the Egyptian military was much more moderate, secular, and pro-Western than Morsi and Egypt's other newly elected leaders, most of whom hailed from the Muslim Brotherhood and other Islamist groups.[51] A few months into his presidency, Morsi fired the top military leaders and renounced the limitations the military had placed upon the presidency in preparation for democratic rule. He went on to rewrite the constitution to give himself expansive new powers and curtail the authority of the courts over the executive branch. By the end of his first year in office, his power grabs and repressive tactics had so alienated military leaders and other influential Egyptians that a junta of generals ousted him and installed a new government.

NATURAL RESOURCES

Bad governance and insecurity in oil-producing countries have reduced oil production, driving up world oil prices and hence undermining economic growth in nearly every country on the planet. In today's volatile global oil marketplace, where production barely exceeds demand, disruptions in a single country can cause staggering price spikes. The extent of the problem is growing because oil drilling is spreading into regions that already suffered from bad governance and insecurity, an inevitable result of the rising demand for fossil fuels caused by surging automobile ownership and industrial manufacturing in China, India, and other emerging countries.

Among the oil-producing countries suffering the most harm from poor governance and insecurity is Nigeria. Insurgent attacks on drilling facilities and pipelines in Nigeria's oil-rich Niger Delta have disrupted oil production with great frequency, as have insurgent raids on offshore oil platforms. In 2008, the depredations were so numerous that oil production plummeted to 1.2 million barrels per day, down from a recent peak of 2.2 million and far below the maximum capacity of 4 million barrels per day.[52]

Insurgents and Western analysts blame abusive local policemen and corrupt national leadership for the armed rebellion in the Niger Delta. When UN-sponsored survey teams asked delta residents to identify their greatest sources of dissatisfaction, the top three answers were poor leadership, poor governance, and corruption.[53] Chris Newsom of the U.S. Institute of Peace observed in 2011 that governance is "both at the heart of the problem and the place to seek solutions," and all the drivers of the conflict "have poor leadership practices more or less at their core."[54]

Nigeria's oil revenues – which are vast even at reduced levels of production – go mainly into the pockets of Nigerian leaders. Most of the remainder fund high-paying government jobs for the leadership's friends, relatives, and political supporters. Very little makes its way to public services for the masses or to economic development beyond the oil sector. During the first decade of the twenty-first century, the Niger Delta provided Nigeria with $200 billion in oil revenues, and the government raked in untold additional sums from levies and bribes from private businesses, such as "protection fees" of between $500 to $5,000 per day, and charges of $18,000 for a two-vehicle escort from the Port Harcourt airport to a hotel. Yet more than half of the delta's residents earned less than $2 per day.[55]

Corruption and insecurity have discouraged the financial investment required for reviving oil production in Nigeria, as have excessive governmental regulation and lack of technical expertise within the government. For years, reform advocates have pressed for passage of an oil industry bill that would address many of these problems, but the government's leaders have stonewalled because they stand to lose a great deal of money if the problems are solved.[56]

Recent democratic reforms, which were supposed to alleviate Nigeria's governance woes, have only made matters worse, owing to the prevalence of negative human capital. Peter M. Lewis of the Paul Nitze School of Advanced International Studies at Johns Hopkins University notes that the advent of elections, political parties, and a democratic legislature "have fostered oligarchy rather than responsive government."[57] Nigeria's democratic elections have, without exception, been marred by fraud, with the political parties buying votes through the dispensation of patronage. Although well-founded corruption allegations against high elected officials are easy to find, no one has lost an election as a result of complicity in corruption.

HUMANITARIAN INTERVENTION

As NATO's Libyan intervention of 2011 demonstrated, the difficulties encountered in Iraq and Afghanistan have not prevented the West from intervening in foreign countries when their governments slaughter their own citizens in large numbers. Even politicians who entered office professing aversion to military intervention in other countries, such as Barack Obama, have found it hard to stand idly by when civilians are murdered nightly on CNN. Such massacres, being the most extreme manifestation of bad governance, reflect human capital problems of the highest order.

The unexpectedly long duration of the Libyan enterprise has, however, dampened the West's enthusiasm for direct military intervention. The material costs were high – the European powers that led the charge ran out of bombs, compelling their ministers to beg the United States for more. Bombing did not end the bloodshed quickly but was instead followed by months of fighting, and the aftermath has been far messier and far less liberal than forecast.

The Libyan experience is a leading reason for the lack of a Western military response to violent repression in Syria. The United States and some of its allies provided humanitarian aid to Syria and eventually provided aid to select Syrian rebel groups as well. With no end to the conflict in sight, those aid expenditures are likely to continue well into the future and will be followed by many additional expenditures to rebuild the country.

The United States has also felt compelled to send military forces on humanitarian missions under less extreme manifestations of bad governance, such as famine and lawlessness. Western involvement in Somalia began in 1992 as the result of media images of starving Somalis. In 2004 the United Nations sent 6,700 military personnel and 1,600 policemen into Haiti to restore order and reconstitute the government after armed insurgents chased President Jean-Bertrand Aristide from the country. Aristide, a democratically elected chief of state who had been reinstalled by the United States in 1994 following a military coup, left the country in an appalling state of government-sanctioned criminality, having empowered the police and armed groups to prey on Haiti's lower classes.[58]

Political elites who mire their countrymen in poverty through corruption and ineptitude but do not preside over large numbers of fatalities – a description befitting a large fraction of the third world's political elites – are unlikely to find U.S. Marines or UN peacekeepers crossing their borders in armored personnel carriers. But public and private organizations in the United States and other first world countries expend huge sums on humanitarian and developmental assistance to alleviate the poverty resulting from their misrule, diverting resources that could otherwise be used to handle different international problems. Much of that assistance, moreover, never reaches the intended recipients on account of corruption in the governments of the recipient nations. With the populations of poor nations continuing to expand, the first world will be left with ever higher bills for assistance to the third world unless the human capital problems at the heart of the matter can be solved, as they have been solved in countries such as South Korea, Taiwan, and Chile.

PEACEKEEPING

Bad governance and insecurity often necessitate the long-term deployment of international peacekeepers, who are costly to sustain and difficult to manage. Peacekeeping has been a high-growth sector since the end of the Cold War, with the number of UN peacekeepers deployed worldwide reaching 100,000 in 2012, a sevenfold increase since 1999. Because of debacles such as Srebrenica and Rwanda, where the passivity of peacekeepers permitted the wholesale murder of civilians, peacekeeping forces are increasingly taking sides in disputes, thereby heightening the risks and costs of peacekeeping missions. The global annual costs of peacekeeping operations have run to $7.8 billion, of which the United States contributes 27 percent.[59]

Human capital development can contribute in valuable ways to the effectiveness of peacekeeping forces from third world countries, reducing the burden on the United States and other Western countries that provided most of the manpower for the peacekeeping missions of the twentieth century. Improvements in the leadership of non-Western armed forces, to which Western assistance has contributed greatly, have permitted those forces to participate in peacekeeping missions that might otherwise have required U.S. forces. In Africa, one of the most politically and logistically difficult places to send foreign peacekeepers, nations such as Uganda, Ethiopia, Kenya, Burundi, and Rwanda have contributed the bulk of manpower for a host of peace and stability operations. Not all of these missions have been shining successes, but they have prevented the resumption of conflict in such places as Liberia and Sierra Leone.

Much work remains to be done in strengthening the human capital of the third world peacekeeping forces. During the past decade, the world has been inundated with reports of rape, prostitution, and pedophilia committed by international peacekeepers, mostly of third world origin, in Côte d'Ivoire, Sudan, Liberia, and Haiti, among others. The United Nations has organized special training programs and formed "conduct and discipline teams" to stop this criminality, but the crimes have continued.[60] The only way to end the misdeeds is to put peacekeepers under the supervision of officers who are personally committed to stopping it, which requires further human capital improvements in third world armed forces.

DISEASE

In numerous third world countries, shortages of human capital in the health sector have precipitated large U.S. expenditures on health care, which, like expenditures on poverty alleviation, absorb scarce resources that could be put to good use elsewhere. With few exceptions, third world countries lack enough doctors and nurses, whether in the public or the private sectors, with the skills and work ethic to serve the entirety of the population. In some places, decent health care is available only to the wealthiest members of society.

Poor health care capabilities make third world populations exceptionally vulnerable to deadly diseases that American remedies can cure or contain, most notably HIV/AIDS, malaria, and tuberculosis. The U.S. government and private U.S. donors have taken the lead in administering these remedies in countries where the health system cannot or will not administer them. The most recent statistics from the OECD indicate that first world governments spend $10.4 billion per year on health aid, of which the U.S. government accounts for 55 percent. Multilateral institutions such as the Global Fund and the World Health Organization, which obtain much of their funding from first world governments, shell out another $5.1 billion. Of the private foundations and charities, the largest health donor is the Bill and Melinda Gates Foundation, which provides $1.7 billion annually. Unfortunately, huge expenditures will remain necessary so long as human capital problems remain unsolved. Those expenditures themselves serve as a formidable impediment to human capital solutions, as the next chapter will show.[61]

Foreign health assistance has saved millions of people from the ravages of deadly diseases. The numbers of lives saved are, however, considerably smaller than originally promised because of unforeseen problems, many of them pertaining to human capital. The death and debilitation have, moreover, exacerbated the human capital problems, by striking down students and skilled workers in their youth.

At the dawn of the twenty-first century, Merck, Bristol-Myers Squibb, and the Bill and Melinda Gates Foundation launched a program to provide antiretrovirals (ARVs) to the entire HIV-infected population of Botswana. As is often the case in such difficult undertakings, organizers began at the place with the best odds for success to start a positive narrative and build momentum. At the time, Botswana had a population of just 1.5 million, which meant that the number of infected persons was much smaller than in many other African countries, and it was one of the best-governed and most prosperous countries on the continent. Yet even Botswana lacked sufficient health care personnel and infrastructure to implement a major ARV program, a fact that organizers did not fully grasp until they were deeply engaged inside the country. With no medical school, the country had to rely on doctors who were foreign-trained Botswanans or foreign-born immigrants. Botswana had a nursing school, but many of its nurses had emigrated to South Africa or the United Kingdom, lured away by higher salaries. Laurie Garrett, an international health expert at the Council on Foreign Relations, noted that by 2002, "the once-starry-eyed foreigners and their counterparts in Botswana's government had realized that before they could start handing out ARVs, they would have to build laboratories and clinics, recruit doctors from abroad, and train other health-care personnel."[62]

Five years passed before patients began receiving the treatments. From then on, AIDS fatalities declined in Botswana. But other health problems worsened, because the HIV/AIDS program had taken scarce doctors and nurses away from the general health care system.

Following the early struggles in Botswana and several other countries, international donors and recipient governments promised to train more health care workers. Shortages of human capital have nonetheless continued to plague HIV/AIDS programs throughout sub-Saharan Africa. Recent reports have found that indigenous health care workers remain far too few in number and quality to treat all of the HIV positive individuals, and general health care is deteriorating because of the concentration of human capital on the HIV/AIDS problem.[63]

Outside of Botswana, corruption and mismanagement have caused much additional harm to HIV/AIDS efforts in sub-Saharan Africa, in some cases causing donors to withhold funds. Health workers and administrators often steal ARVs and other pharmaceuticals intended for the poor and sell them on the black market.[64] Kwama Ampomah, an official at the Joint UN Programme on HIV/AIDS, notes that the selfishness of national leaders in Kenya has left only the political elites with access to the ARVs. A successful HIV/AIDS program, he says, "requires transparency, and a strong sense of nationalism by leaders, not tribalism. You need leaders who don't build palaces on the Riviera. ... If the government is corrupt, if everyone is stealing money, then it will not work."[65]

DRUG TRAFFICKING

Transnational drug trafficking is among the most pernicious problems facing the world today, imposing staggering economic and social costs on states and peoples. For the United States, which leads the world in illegal drug consumption, the most obvious costs are the $26 billion per year in the National Drug Control Budget and the $3 billion per year for border patrolling.[66] Less visible are the health care costs associated with treating adult addicts and babies who are addicted at birth, estimated at $11 billion per year. The costs of prosecuting and incarcerating individuals for drug-related criminal offenses amount to another $61 billion per year.[67] Illicit drug users are more than twice as likely as the average American to be unemployed, necessitating massive additional governmental expenditures on unemployment benefits. Each year, the U.S. economy loses an estimated $120 billion from drug-related absences, incarceration, and premature death.[68]

Drug trafficking has also harmed the commercial and strategic interests of the United States. The violence and corruption engendered by the narcotics trade in Mexico have undermined the Mexican economy, which in turn hurts the U.S. economy because Mexico ranks among America's largest trading partners. In Afghanistan, the opium trade has provided much of the revenue for the Taliban insurgents who are waging war against NATO and Afghan forces.[69]

The United States and other countries with high rates of illicit drug consumption have sought to fight the drug problem by intercepting drugs at their borders, but drug traffickers have proven highly adept at slipping through the cracks. Even with the most advanced technologies, no government can detect most drug shipments when couriers can move across lengthy borders with numerous entry points and high volumes of vehicular crossings, as is the case with the U.S. border with Mexico. The only viable solution is to combat the narcotics industry at the production stage and every other stage where it is vulnerable, which requires collaborating with foreign governments to combat drugs on their territory, in their airspace, and across their territorial waters. U.S. law enforcement agencies have made some headway in foreign nations through bilateral actions against processing and storage facilities, transportation routes, and bank accounts, but they have not been able to achieve decisive results because the U.S. government has committed relatively few resources, as a result of the wars in Afghanistan and Iraq, and, most importantly, because the countries where narcotraffickers prosper usually suffer from human capital shortfalls and the attendant problems of weak governance and insecurity. No country, no matter how much foreign aid it receives, can suppress drug trafficking if it lacks lengthy rosters of honest policemen, courageous mayors, and skilled criminal investigators.

Recent victories in reducing the flow of South American cocaine into the United States have resulted primarily from human capital improvements in Mexico and Colombia. As discussed in the previous chapter, Mexico's Felipe Calderón prosecuted the drug war aggressively, breaking the tradition of collusion with drug traffickers set by the Salinas brothers and other leaders of Mexico's Institutional Revolutionary Party. He undertook reforms to improve the nation's human capital but was still impeded by shortages of capable and resolute personnel in the army, police, judiciary, and civil administration. His successor, the Institutional Revolutionary Party's Pena Nieto, has promised to continue these reforms; whether he follows through or returns to the old ways of his party remains to be seen.

Colombia obtained good national leadership and robust American support eight years before Mexico did and hence is now further along in human capital development and effective counternarcotics operations. The dramatic improvements in governance and security that Colombia has experienced since the late 1990s were scarcely imaginable on the eve of reform. For most of the 1990s, the Marxist-Leninist Fuerzas Armadas Revolucionarias de Colombia (FARC) and other insurgent groups exploited profits from a rapidly expanding cocaine business to enlarge their forces and seize chunks of territory from a sclerotic government. In rural areas and small towns, the insurgents killed, drove out, or co-opted the local political elites and established shadow governments. By 1995, the insurgents had a presence in 58 percent of Colombia's municipalities, up from 17 percent a decade earlier, and the police no longer had any presence in one-quarter of the municipalities. During 1996, adhering to the Maoist formula of building upon guerrilla successes to launch conventional military attacks, the FARC began overrunning military and police bases. In March 1998, a large FARC force decimated one of the government's elite counterguerrilla battalions for the first time, killing or capturing more than one hundred soldiers. Fearing that the FARC would overthrow the national government, 800,000 people fled the country by the end of the decade.[70]

The Colombian government began overhauling its internal security capabilities in 1998, owing to the convergence of several critical factors. The first was a change in the president. Ernesto Samper, who had been elected in 1994, had taken bribes from drug traffickers in return for tepid prosecution of the counternarcotics campaign, leading the United States to decertify Colombia for aid. The winner of the 1998 election, Andras Pastrana, restored amicable relations with the United States and sought American assistance in bolstering the nation's security forces.

The second key event of 1998 was the appointment of Generals Fernando Tapias, Jorge Enrique Mora, and Carlos Ospina to senior positions in the army. Known as vigorous reformers, they were appointed as the result of widespread alarm at recent military defeats. The three generals increased the length and quality of training, especially in fields requiring advanced skills such as intelligence, logistics, and communications, and purged officers who had shown themselves unwilling or unable to take the fight to the insurgents.

The third key event in 1998, which stemmed in part from the first two, was a change in the attitude of the United States. The setbacks suffered by the Colombian military had bolstered American concern about Colombia, and the changes in Colombia's political and military leadership had assured the Americans that they had Colombian partners who could make effective use of foreign assistance. In September 1999, the Americans agreed to Plan Colombia, a six-year partnership for strengthening the army, police, judiciary, and civil administration for the purposes of subduing the FARC and slashing drug production. The U.S. pledged $3.5 billion to the plan while Colombia ponied up $4 billion of its own money. The number of U.S. personnel in Colombia increased to 500 military and 300 civilians, most of whom engaged in advising and training activities designed to improve the quality of the Colombian government's human capital. Subsequently extended, Plan Colombia was to receive more than $6 billion in U.S. funding by 2008.

Improvements in Colombia's military and civil capabilities were readily apparent by the time Pastrana left office in 2002. The percentage of Colombians who viewed the Colombian armed forces positively increased from 42 percent in 1998 to 79 percent in 2002.[71] But much remained to be done. Pastrana's principal achievement was sharpening the blade; most of the swinging and slashing was left to his successor, Alvaro Uribe.

The son of a wealthy landowner who had been murdered by the FARC, Uribe came to the job with a steely resolve to destroy the enemy, in sharp contrast to Pastrana, who had held out vain hopes of negotiating a peace through gestures of goodwill. "Pastrana was more Latin, more social, more engaged and seemingly more up to enjoying life as it came at him than Uribe," remarked American Under Secretary of State Thomas Pickering. "Uribe gives the impression of being more tightly wound, more business-like, even a little bit more Anglo-Saxon in his quiet demeanor. He is certainly more focused and intense than his predecessor, with little time for humor and the enjoyment of life."[72]

Within months of taking power, Uribe sent the Colombian armed forces into the urban strongholds of the FARC, located in the slums of Medellin, Cali, and Bogota. After clearing those areas, they swept into the countryside and ejected the insurgents from some of the most strategically valuable territory. Over the next few years, the Colombian forces captured and killed huge numbers of insurgents, and thousands more deserted. By 2008, the number of FARC combatants had declined to an estimated 9,000, down from a peak of 17,000 at the turn of the century. The National Liberation Army, the next largest insurgent group, declined in strength from 5,000 to 2,500 in the same period.[73]

Programs to reduce coca cultivation made headway once the government's security forces had rendered the areas of major cultivation safe enough that government personnel could enter them with little risk of kidnapping or death. From 2001 to 2011, annual cocaine production fell by 61 percent. Heightened security also allowed resumption of economic activity. Between 2003 and 2006, highway traffic increased by 64 percent, and thefts and attacks on vehicles decreased by 54 percent.[74]

Although criminals continue to produce large amounts of cocaine in Colombia, the improvements in Colombia's governance and security that resulted from human capital investments ended the threat to the government's survival. They also enabled Colombia to rely more on itself and less on the United States, permitting reductions in U.S. assistance that did not endanger the country. In the past few years, U.S. material assistance to Colombia has subsided toward the levels of the 1990s, and the number of U.S. personnel in the country has fallen.[75]

Improvements to counternarcotics capabilities in Mexico and Colombia have caused the transnational trafficking organizations to shift much of their activity to countries with weaker governments and security forces, particularly Honduras and Guatemala. Further strangulation of the narcotraffickers will therefore require major human capital improvements in those countries as well. In counternarcotics, as in counterterrorism, thwarting the enemy requires human capital assistance across a multitude of countries, not just the countries the United States finds the most convenient to assist.

ILLEGAL IMMIGRATION

Every year, bad governance and insecurity in the third world cause hundreds of thousands of people to migrate to the United States and other first world nations. Violence, political repression, and the accompanying economic stagnation in countries from Afghanistan and Guatemala to Iraq and Somalia have ignited the desperation that inspires individuals and families to leave their homes en masse for a strange country, sometimes without that country's permission. The biggest migrations to the United States in recent decades, both legal and illegal, have come from Latin America, driven by drug-related violence and economic privation resulting from bad governance and insecurity.

The difficulties inherent in measuring illicit activities and the political sensitivities surrounding the immigration question have hindered efforts to estimate the economic impact of illegal immigration. The existing research, however, suggests that the costs greatly outweigh the benefits. The only recent study on the question, conducted by Jack Martin and Eric A. Ruark of the Federation for American Immigration Reform, put the net costs to U.S. taxpayers at $99 billion. Martin and Ruark estimated that illegal immigration costs $113 billion per year, including $52 billion in educational expenses and $17 billion in health care expenses, while the revenues that the U.S. government obtains from the illegal immigrant population total $14 billion.[76]

Drug traffickers and other criminals who are interspersed among the illegal immigrant population have perpetrated crimes on a large scale, compelling the U.S. government to ramp up deportations. In 2011, the United States deported 188,000 persons who had been convicted of crimes in the United States, along with another 204,000 foreign-born persons. Ninety-three percent of the deportees were natives of Mexico, Guatemala, Honduras, or El Salvador.[77] With the U.S. government spending approximately $12,500 to arrest, detain, and deport a single individual, the annual bill for deportation comes to nearly $5 billion.[78]

Latin American immigrants have entered the United States at such a high rate as to preclude the assimilation that has characterized all prior immigration to the United States. In border-state metropolises such as San Diego and Houston and in cities far removed from the border such as Chicago and Philadelphia, unbridled immigration has spawned Latino neighborhoods where Spanish-language signs adorn shops and Spanish-language television stations rule the airwaves. Immigrants can live in the United States without fully adopting its language or its culture, to the detriment of both their economic well-being and U.S. society as a whole, which traditionally has derived its strength from cultural unity rather than cultural separatism.

The rate of illegal immigration into the United States decreased in conjunction with the decline in available jobs since late 2008, but it is likely rebound when the U.S. economy fully recovers. Although American politicians routinely vow to halt the next wave of illegal immigration by "securing the border," there is little evidence that border enforcement of the sort contemplated by the major political parties will prove much more effective than past border enforcement. Mass deportation is out of the question, because of the monetary and political costs involved. The only way to halt illegal immigration is to make safer and more prosperous those nations where the immigrants begin their treks, by bolstering their human capital.

PIRACY

Bad governance and insecurity facilitate piracy on the high seas, at a time when the lowering of international trade barriers and the massive industrial growth of countries such as China and India have put more ships on the seas than ever before. The problem is at its worst in Somalia, where pirates dart from the coast in speedboats to prey on international ships in the Gulf of Aden and the Indian Ocean. Somali piracy costs private shipping companies approximately $5.5 billion per year, and foreign governments pay another $1.5 billion for antipiracy operations.[79] The prevailing view among experts, note Christopher Alessi and Stephanie Hanson of the Council on Foreign Relations, is that "the root of Somalia's piracy problem has been the lack of an effective central government in Mogadishu."[80] Once again, the problem boils down to bad governance, insecurity, and the human capital deficiencies that account for both.

INTELLECTUAL PIRACY AND CYBERCRIME

States with weak law enforcement capabilities are breeding grounds for intellectual property violations, which deprive the property owners and their societies of large revenues and, at times, jeopardize their security. The diffusion of information technology into the third world has led to a surge in the piracy of software, music, and movies. Even in the isolated backwaters of countries that are themselves isolated backwaters, one can now find bootlegged copies of *Harry Potter* movies and Mariah Carey albums. A 2011 report by the U.S.

government's National Intellectual Property Rights Coordination Center notes that there is no reliable estimate of the cash value of intellectual piracy, but it provides estimates for specific sectors in a small number of countries that convey a sense of what is at stake. In 2009, 48 percent of music acquired by Brazilians was pirated, with losses to the music industry estimated at $147 million. The piracy rate in Paraguay was 99 percent, resulting in losses of $128 million. The piracy rate of business software in Brazil was 73 percent, yielding losses of $831 million, while in Paraguay the piracy rate was 82 percent but, owing to the country's digital backwardness, the losses were only $8 million.[81]

Like drug trafficking, intellectual piracy has provided funding to dangerous terrorist organizations. In the triborder area of South America, the piracy of compact discs, software, pharmaceuticals, and other goods has generated mountains of cash for Hezbollah and other extremist organizations. Among the most creative of the Hezbollah pirates were the nineteen men charged by the U.S. government with "trafficking in counterfeit Viagra." Dawood Ibrahim, whom the U.S. Treasury Department has labeled a funder of the Pakistani terrorist organization that killed 164 people in the Mumbai attacks of 2008, has raked in large profits by pirating DVDs in South Asia. Pakistani government forces who raided six of his production facilities in 2005 found 400,000 pirated discs.[82]

The spread of personal computers has facilitated intellectual piracy as well as a host of other criminal activities that are usually less lucrative but, in some cases, more dangerous. Computer hackers steal the identities of individuals and the proprietary data of corporations. Foreign intelligence services steal defense secrets that can be used to create new weapons, and they probe defense networks for vulnerabilities that could be exploited in wartime. A recent study by the Center for Strategic and International Studies estimated global cyber-crime costs at between $80 and $400 billion per year.[83] Individuals in China and other wealthy countries perpetrate a substantial fraction of this crime, but they often owe their successes to weak law enforcement in poorer nations, which permits them to cover their cyber tracks.

MONEY LAUNDERING

Drug traffickers, pirates, terrorists, mobsters, white collar criminals, and rogue regimes engage in money laundering, often on a massive scale. Their objective is to move billions of dollars of ill-gotten cash into the first world financial system, because that system insures deposits, provides interest, and facilitates large investments and purchases. It is not easy to pay cash for an office building in Los Angeles or a new Mercedes S-Class, and attempting to do so will invite the scrutiny of first world law enforcement authorities whom the holders of dirty money would much prefer to avoid.

Putting large sums into U.S. or European bank accounts is a tricky proposition. Western governments monitor large bank deposits and possess mechanisms for tracing their sources, in order to block funds obtained through illicit means as well as funds belonging to states and organizations that have been slapped with sanctions for other misdeeds. The ne'er-do-wells must therefore find ways to clean the dirt from their money before putting it into accounts at Wells Fargo or HSBC.

The holders of dirty money are prepared to pay criminal financiers huge sums to devise ingenious money-laundering schemes. In third world countries with lax regulatory enforcement, the financiers create or manipulate financial institutions to turn suitcases of $100 bills into electronic deposits. They set up webs of shell companies through which financial transactions are routed and concealed. In what is called trade-based money laundering, the perpetrators falsify the value of exported goods to push money through seemingly legitimate transactions.

Current knowledge of money laundering is far too incomplete to permit a valid estimate of the global magnitude of the problem. Certain facts, however, give some idea of its size. For example, Americans consume roughly $65 billion of illegal drugs per year, but only $1 billion of the revenue is captured through seizure of cash or bank deposits; most of the other $64 billion is believed to be laundered.[84] According to UN estimates, global illicit trade totals $870 billion annually, equal to 1.5 percent of global GDP, making the demand for money laundering and the opportunities to reap profits from it extraordinarily high.[85]

Money launderers spin their webs across continents and oceans. The world's most dangerous rogue regimes have been complicit in money-laundering schemes that penetrate Latin America and even the United States and Canada. Iran, which has dedicated some of its smartest minds to money laundering, is widely recognized as the world's leading money-laundering power. Some of its laundered funds wind up in the hands of its terrorist proxies, Hezbollah and Hamas.[86] North Korea holds the number two position on the money-laundering charts. Although North Korean proceeds have not been definitively tied to Hezbollah and Hamas, the lengthy history of collaboration between North Korea and those organizations gives reason to suspect that some of the money reaches them.[87]

Among the biggest obstructions to combating money laundering is a lack of cooperation from third world banks and governments that profit from the money-laundering process. In the Western hemisphere, the biggest culprits are to be found in Panama. The Panamanian government passed stringent anti–money-laundering laws years ago to placate the United States, but it has not enforced those laws in the slightest, because drug traffickers have paid off the people in the government who could interfere with their financial pipeline.[88]

Impeding money laundering depends upon human capital improvements in a host of third world countries. It requires the acquisition of advanced skills in accounting, forensics, and intelligence. Above all, it requires leaders with the integrity and courage to refuse the handsome bribes which money launderers offer them.

CONCLUSION

From the streets of Mogadishu to the mountains of the Hindu Kush, human capital problems give rise to many of the largest threats to global security today. Negative human capital has provided the inspiration and leadership for terrorist groups, rebel movements, and criminal organizations, plus the states that assist those organizations. Human capital deficiencies in the public sector of third world countries deprive them of the governance and security capabilities to contain these blights and often produce misrule severe enough to drive citizens into the arms of the miscreants. Inferior human capital is also to blame for the poverty and disease that spur huge wealth transfers from the United States to the third world, and for the dissipation of much of that aid through waste, fraud, and abuse. The interests of both those countries and the United States demand prioritization of U.S. aid to human capital development.

6

Training

This chapter, and the five that come after it, examine the principal methods by which the United States and the rest of the first world can help the governments of poor countries develop their human capital. They explore and evaluate what has been tried, both in recent years and decades long gone by, and consider new solutions for new problems. Based on those evaluations and consideration of current world conditions, they make recommendations for the way ahead.

We begin with training, in all its forms. Training may include instruction in a classroom, a government office, or a forest. An instructor may train a group of one hundred or ten. In some cases, the instructor works with a single individual, a practice that is variously called training, advising, or mentoring. Generally speaking, training confers specific technical competencies, in contrast to education, which confers information and ideas for the general betterment of the mind.

When it comes to public sector employees, the line between training and education is often blurred. Some facts or concepts contribute to both technical proficiency and general intellectual heft. Some institutions provide a mixture of training and education, particularly institutions dedicated exclusively to employees of the state. Institutions and programs that are more concerned with training than with education are covered in this chapter; the others are addressed in the next chapter.

U.S. TRAINING: AN OVERVIEW

During the first half of the twentieth century, the United States conducted training of foreign personnel in its one major colony – the Philippines – and in Central American and Caribbean countries where it fought the various "banana wars." Its training efforts were small and rudimentary in comparison with what European colonialists had been providing for centuries. The United States did not become a large purveyor of overseas training until the Cold War, when the imperative of containing Communism drove it to seek allies and influence across the third world.

During the 1950s, American training of foreign governmental personnel mushroomed into a massive enterprise, larger than anything ever attempted by any other nation or empire. It has retained its size in ensuing decades, although its shape has changed markedly. Yet the American people know next to nothing about it. Familiarizing Americans with the foreign training that they fund is therefore a major objective of this chapter.

U.S. civil agencies and the U.S. military have taken distinctly different approaches to training, for both philosophical and practical reasons. Those different approaches have led to very different results. Civil and military training usually take place in isolation from one another and are almost always analyzed separately because they fall under different "tribes" of the foreign assistance world. But much can be learned from studying them in tandem, for some of the best methods in one can be used to improve performance in the other, and they can in some cases be merged as a means of better preparing civil and military personnel for working closely with one another.

CIVIL TRAINING

Civilian aid experts use the term "technical assistance" to refer to the provision of first world experts to third world governments for training civil personnel or performing skilled administrative tasks.[1] These experts can be full-time employees who reside in the recipient country or part-timers who come and go for short periods to work on specific projects. In the early years of the Cold War, U.S. aid agencies viewed the performance component of technical assistance as a short-term measure for getting development programs started and expected that it would be used less and less as the training component of technical assistance built up the local human capital. Within a few decades, they believed, the indigenous governments would have enough human capital that they no longer needed foreigners for either performance or training.

Events conformed to this prognostication in only a small minority of third world countries. For most of the others, the number of technical assistance personnel has increased rather than decreased over time. Today, sixty-five years on, technical assistance is a huge global industry, accounting for one-quarter of all foreign aid expenditures. Hundreds of thousands of individuals are engaged in technical assistance in poor countries, most of them employed by private companies or NGOs under contract with USAID and other international aid agencies. The costs of paying, housing, protecting, insuring, and managing a full-time technical assistance employee come out to more than $300,000 per year.[2]

Why has technical assistance failed so spectacularly in meeting the expectations of self-sufficiency? One reason is that the training mission has frequently taken a back seat to the performance mission. Those two missions have often been entrusted to a single individual, which in abstraction seems acceptable, but which in practice has usually resulted in allocation of most of the individual's time to performance.[3] When aid budgets shrink, a common occurrence in the aid business, the training mission is typically cut before the performance mission, to ensure that the sick continue to receive their treatments and the farmers continue to receive their microloans. The aspiring nurses and bankers whose training is cut off are left to find other ways to learn their trade, which is not usually a recipe for success, even with the global proliferation of information on the internet. Individuals whose work is being done by others are often more inclined to devote their energies to recreation or corruption than to online manuals on civil administration. As B. J. Ndulu of the World Bank has observed, the use of technical assistance to fill capacity deficiencies has "tended to engender psychological dependence on expatriate capabilities" and has "often discouraged efforts to build and retain local capacity in government."[4]

SPEED AND EFFICIENCY OF CIVIL TRAINING

The prioritization of performance ahead of training is not the result of decisions by technical assistance personnel in Kathmandu or Monrovia. Rather, it reflects the dictates of funders in Washington and New York. The U.S. Congress and the United Nations, among others, frequently demand rapid and efficient attainment of results in so overwhelming a manner as to crowd out all other priorities, of which human capital development is the most important.

In its zeal to avoid the inefficiency and waste of past aid programs, the U.S. Congress insists on quick and orderly implementation when it funds programs to alleviate poverty, increase literacy, or reduce infant mortality. Few members of Congress recognize that their stance compels USAID and other agencies to assign the work to skilled Westerners instead of training local personnel to do it. First world aid agencies can readily get the job done by using their own personnel or hiring foreign contractors and NGOs with deep experience in development work. The local base of human capital, on the other hand, may be so small that accomplishing the task with local personnel would require years of preparatory training and education. Moreover, large foreign contractors and NGOs have the administrative experience and knowledge to fulfill relatively quickly the Herculean administrative requirements of international donor organizations, whereas indigenous contractors and NGOs often need months or years to meet the requirements, if they can meet them at all.

The first-world donor's abhorrence of idleness, corruption, and other inefficiencies, understandable though it may be, gives further encouragement to aid agencies to rely on first world performers. Western contractors and NGOs are managed by individuals raised in societies with low tolerance for corruption, and they are good at keeping track of funds and documenting their work. Neither can be said of their third world counterparts. Local personnel and organizations are more susceptible to fraud, embezzlement, and other forms of corruption that infuriate donors.[5] Aid officials who employ third world contractors or NGOs risk a corruption scandal that would spark public outrage and ruin their careers, whereas no one will fault them for hiring a U.S. mega-contractor or mega-NGO.

In the twenty-first century, the single most important impetus for elevating speed and efficiency above all else has been the Millennium Development Goals. Approved unanimously by the membership of the United Nations at the Millennium Summit in September 2000, the goals were sweeping in ambition. They called for the achievement by 2015 of numerical targets that included halving the number of people in extreme poverty, halting the spread of HIV/AIDS and malaria, and providing primary education to all children. The intellectuals behind the Millennium Development Goals, of whom Jeffrey Sachs was the preeminent figure, argued that improvements in social and economic conditions were the key to jumpstarting national advancement. If everyone received decent health care and learned how to read, it would create a baseline from which further progress was certain to flow.

The setters of the Millennium Development Goals did not specify how the goals were to be attained, leaving the nations responsible for implementation free to choose their methods. Such wide latitude made a certain amount of sense, as it encouraged local initiative and innovation. But lack of consideration of the ways and means to be employed toward the ends inhibited thinking about feasibility and unintended consequences. The most portentous of those unintended consequences would be the obstruction of human capital development.

Widely embraced by governmental leaders and aid agencies, the Millennium Development Goals multiplied the incentives to use first world contractors and NGOs in performance of development work. In the case of HIV/AIDS, for example, the inability of local health care workers to treat people in the numbers specified by the Millennium Development Goals led Western organizations such as the U.S. President's Emergency Plan for AIDS Relief (PEPFAR) and the independent Global Fund to Fight Aids, Tuberculosis, and Malaria to spend vast sums on foreign health workers to administer antiretroviral treatments.[6] Their programs provided effective medical treatment to millions of afflicted persons in poor countries, they lost relatively little to theft of supplies or funds, and they generated impressive statistics that were presented to donor politicians and the media with much fanfare. But they did little to improve the skills of indigenous nurses, doctors, or health administrators. Without such increases in human capital, the recipient nations have been left dependent indefinitely on foreign personnel and foreign money, both of which are subject to the vagaries of economic conditions in the first world.[7] The global recession that began in 2008 halved donations for third world health care from all private donors except the Gates Foundation.[8]

Deployments of Western military forces to war zones like Afghanistan and Iraq have also generated great pressure for rapid gains in development, governance, and security. Fearing that protracted military deployments and the attendant casualties would alienate voters, Western politicians sought to make swift progress that would enable them to declare victory and withdraw the troops. They did not ignore the matter of the long-term viability of indigenous organizations but usually accorded it a lower priority. Consequently, the United States and its NATO allies hired foreign experts and companies to undertake a broad array of tasks, most of which involved performance rather than training.

For Afghanistan's Ring Road, a three-thousand-kilometer highway linking the country's major cities in a loop, the NATO countries contracted the construction out to large foreign firms, making no effort to train Afghans in construction or maintenance or to promote the development of an Afghan construction industry.[9] The infrastructure projects that accounted for a large fraction of total U.S. assistance to Iraq were likewise built with predominantly foreign manpower and minimal concern about the development of indigenous capabilities to construct or maintain them. When American soldiers and infrastructure experts went back to the United States, few Iraqis had both the desire and the capability to fill potholes and fix broken pipes. The Special Inspector General for Iraq's postmortem on reconstruction concluded, "The deterioration of poorly maintained infrastructure projects after transfer to Iraqi control could end up constituting the largest source of waste in the U.S. reconstruction program."[10]

CIVIL TRAINERS

Another serious problem for technical assistance programs is the inconsistency of aptitude among technical assistance personnel.[11] Given the size of the technical assistance industry and the difficulty of getting the first world's best and brightest to work in impoverished countries, the hiring of a certain number of inept, lethargic, or corrupt individuals is inevitable. Several avoidable decisions have, however, exacerbated the staffing problem. In the aftermath of the Vietnam War, the U.S. Congress decided to slash the staffs of USAID and other U.S. agencies in the foreign assistance business, which necessitated heavy reliance on contractors and NGOs. USAID's personnel strength, which had peaked at 17,500 during the Vietnam era, fell to 1,947 by 2000.[12] The conflicts of the post-9/11 period convinced the U.S. government to expand USAID to a strength of 3,538 in 2011, but some of the additional manpower has been bogged down in the swamp of oversight and regulation, which is much larger and deeper now than it was a generation earlier, and the rest has been used to meet the high demand for civilian personnel in Iraq and Afghanistan.[13]

Contractors and NGO personnel are not necessarily less capable or desirable than government employees. In some instances, they are a better option, as they can provide a short-term surge capacity that is too costly for the government to maintain permanently, and they are much easier to fire for poor performance than government employees. Contracting companies and NGOs, moreover, can put people into austere or dangerous locations much longer than civilian governmental agencies can. But effective use of contractors and NGOs requires extensive supervision, and the civil agencies have been very weak in this regard, because they do not have enough contracting officers and do not generally staff those positions with highly capable people.[14]

One of the most prominent cases of ineffectual contract management in recent history came to light during the Kabul Bank scandal in 2010, a case of epic fraud in which insider loans robbed Afghanistan's national bank of $900 million, nearly 5 percent of Afghanistan's gross domestic product. A U.S. Senate committee report laid much of the blame for the loss of funds on USAID's insufficient supervision of a $92 million contract under which the accounting firm Deloitte had provided technical assistance to the bank. USAID had left the task of supervision to a single person, who was a junior officer with little knowledge of the banking industry, because USAID had been unable to entice one of its senior technical experts into the position. Owing to inexperience and lack of familiarity with banking, this individual failed to ascertain problems at the bank that had long been apparent to more seasoned experts, allowing losses to pile much higher than would otherwise have occurred.[15]

Inadequate contract supervision bedeviled the U.S. State Department's efforts to train police in Afghanistan and Iraq. In the aftermath of regime change in those two countries, the State Department's Bureau of International Narcotics and Law Enforcement contracted the training of new police forces to a few large American companies. The Americans whom the companies hired delivered short, standardized courses that imparted only the most basic knowledge to the Afghan and Iraqi trainees and did little to affect their motivation. The trainers neglected the development of leaders, the sine qua non of any security forces.

During visits to Afghan police facilities in early 2010, I encountered a dismal state of affairs among the contractors who were supposed to be training the Afghans. Instead of working with their Afghan counterparts to make sure that the trainees were actually learning, some spent their time surfing the internet in their offices or relaxing at their living quarters. The egregiously rude behavior of two contractors toward the Afghans would have earned them immediate removal from their jobs had a conscientious supervisor been present. But the State Department contracting officer responsible for these training facilities had shown up only a handful of times over the past year, and only for ceremonial events. No one should have been surprised that the training sites produced policemen who caused more injury to the population than to the insurgents.[16]

The United States could learn some valuable personnel lessons by looking back in history, to the centuries of European imperialism. Although the European powers dispatched their share of misfits and criminals to train indigenous personnel for governmental service, on the whole they allocated better people to the task than the United States is allocating today. European colonial offices kept individuals in the same country or region throughout their careers, based on the premise that deep cultural understanding was vital to successful activity in a foreign culture. Suspicious of universal generalizations, they put local facts before theories.

"Colonial administrations may have been racist and exploitative, but they did at least work seriously at the business of understanding the people they were governing," notes Rory Stewart, a brilliant British politician who rose to prominence as a trekker in Afghanistan and a deputy governor in Iraq. "They recruited people prepared to spend their entire careers in dangerous provinces of a single alien nation. They invested in teaching administrators and military officers the local language. They established effective departments of state, trained a local elite, and conducted countless academic studies of their subjects through institutes and museums, royal geographical societies, and royal botanical gardens."

Stewart laments that the imperial commitment to cultural understanding has been replaced by facile theories about governance and development that purport to apply to all countries and hence validate the current practice of rotating personnel frequently from one country to the next. He recalls a meeting in Kabul at which Mary Robinson, the UN High Commissioner for Human Rights, asserted that Afghanistan's woes were purely a matter of human rights, as presumably they were in every country. "Afghans have been fighting for their human rights for twenty-five years," she explained. The head of an agency that supplied food to the poor retorted, "Villagers are not interested in human rights. They are like poor people all over the world. All they think about is where the next meal is coming from." The head of an NGO that provided psychological counseling interjected, "The only thing to know about these people is that they are suffering from PTSD."[17]

POLITICAL ELITES AND CIVIL TRAINING

Much of the recent research on technical assistance cites the interference of indigenous political leaders as a leading obstacle to success. Carol Lancaster, the dean of the Georgetown School of Foreign Service, notes that numerous attempts to save struggling foreign governments have run aground because of unanticipated resistance from political elites whose interests were at stake. During the reign of Liberian President Samuel Doe, she observes, the United States sent a team of foreign fiscal experts to control governmental revenues and expenditures without considering how Doe would react, despite his well-deserved reputation for misappropriation of state funds. When the team arrived, Doe obstructed them at every turn, rendering their exertions futile. After six months without the slightest of successes, they packed their belongings and flew home.[18]

Political leaders have also been known to obstruct success by marginalizing trainees within their own government. The 2,000 Zambians who received foreign training as preparation for service in the finance ministry learned this truth when they were sidelined by the government's top leaders, who recognized the threat that financial experts posed to their misuse of state resources.[19] In other cases, government leaders have nullified the effects of training by refusing to incorporate essential elements into the government's everyday activities. During an assessment of recent British technical assistance in Africa, Oxford Policy Management found that systems and procedures introduced by foreign experts failed to achieve the intended improvements because of a lack of "government commitment to the use of these systems and procedures."[20]

The political elites of the most corrupt countries divert the government's bureaucracies away from their ostensible purposes to such a degree that the bureaucrats have no interest in the training that foreigners have to offer. "Public service delivery may not be the top priority of government employees where, for example, government positions are used for patronage or are sold or leased," says Melissa Thomas, associate professor of international development at Johns Hopkins University. "Advancement in the civil service may not be tied to performance or merit. In those circumstances, government employees have little use for the type of training that is routinely offered by donors, or they may lack the educational background to benefit from training."[21]

When the trainees are disinterested or illiterate, as they often are in countries with dysfunctional governments, they can easily be subjected to PowerPoint slides or lectures on good governance without learning anything from them. "The participants come to collect money and do not pay attention to the topics," Anaclet Hakizimana wrote of the training administered to civil servants in Madagascar, which is known for poor governance although it is, sadly, far from the most poorly governed country on the planet.[22]

In much of the third world, the indifference of governmental personnel to civil training is so high that securing their attendance requires providing lavish "per diems" or "allowances" that cover a good deal more than the expenses of attending. "You can't expect people to come to training with nothing," said a district official in Malawi in explaining why school training programs disintegrated after training participants stopped receiving allowances.[23] The foreign organizations that pay out the money justify the practice by arguing that government workers are underpaid, which is often true. But if that is an overwhelming problem, it would be better to supplement salaries than to pay for specific tasks, as the latter develops an unhealthy entitlement mentality that causes even the most conscientious workers to expect payment for routine work.

By contrast, good indigenous political leaders most often facilitate and enhance technical assistance. They make life easy for the expatriate helpers, and they order subordinates to implement what they have learned in training. By attracting capable individuals into the government and rewarding superior performers, they keep the government stocked with the human capital required to absorb foreign training and put it to good use.[24]

The presence of smart, energetic, and highly motivated leaders in the Brazilian government has enabled the country to take advantage of a host of U.S. technical assistance programs. One of the largest countries making the transition from third world to first, Brazil no longer has a need for foreign instruction on basic governance, development, or security, but it does still require U.S. help with certain advanced technical skills. Some of those skills help Brazilians accomplish tasks that directly benefit American security, such as intercepting terrorist suspects at airports and keeping transnational drug traffickers in jail.

In countries that were hitherto poorly governed, the arrival of good national leadership is the ideal time to ramp up technical assistance, of both the performance and the training varieties. Past misrule has left these countries deficient in human capital at the middle and lower levels of the civil service, so foreign expertise is required to implement the reforms proposed by the new leaders, as well as to cultivate better civil servants. But aid agencies rarely increase technical assistance to countries at times of turnaround, less because of lack of funds than because of bureaucratic inertia that keeps the same numbers of people in the same countries year after year.[25]

MOTIVATIONAL IMPACT OF CIVIL TRAINING

Technical assistance researchers have largely overlooked one of the biggest reasons behind the disappointing results of technical assistance, the failure to influence the motivational side of human capital. Western technical assistance practitioners have at times been reluctant to delve into the motivational arena because they view it as culturally insensitive, if not imperialistic, or because they fear the wrath of colleagues who think that way. More often they avoid it simply because they are too focused on performing tasks themselves or teaching technical skills, both of which are easier than changing a person's work ethic or proclivity toward corruption.

Prolonged technical training can influence the motives of the recipient, because the culture of the trainer can rub off on the trainee over time, especially if the trainer has a dynamic personality. Most of the civil training these days, however, is too short in duration to have such an effect. Whereas an expatriate in past decades might have spent several years inside a government ministry providing training, most of today's expatriates spend only a few days or weeks with a given civil trainee, as training sessions typically consist of day-long or week-long events.

"Short-term training is important in transferring technical knowledge and skills," concluded a study on USAID in Africa, "but only through long-term training can developing-country professionals absorb the research skills, modified work attitudes, and improved critical thinking that are prerequisites for making a measurable difference in their home countries."[26] Similar comments can be heard from Americans involved in training around the world. "A one-week course is probably not going to change the moral fabric that has been built up in someone over decades," Tyler Truby, the program manager of the U.S. police advisory mission in the Philippines, remarked. "You can change the fabric, but it requires mentoring them on a daily basis for months and years."[27] Colonel Dennis E. Keller, a retired U.S. Army Foreign Area Officer with several decades of experience with Latin American military and police forces, observed, "Only the embedded advisor, one who has gained sufficient trust with a unit to move beyond the mere teaching and coaching role to the macro advisory role, has any hope of influencing the organizational culture, which is the most difficult challenge for any advisor."[28]

CIVIL BRAIN DRAIN

A final cause of the ineffectiveness of civil training is the departure of trained personnel from the recipient government. Civil servants who acquire new skills from foreign experts can and sometimes do leverage those skills to obtain jobs outside of the government, either in their country or in a wealthier one. Some choose to leave because of frustration with corruption, ineptitude, or other symptoms of bad leadership within the government. "Competent professionals and managers often shun a public service environment where the principles of meritocracy are routinely ignored," states a World Bank publication on Africa.[29]

Others are lured away from governmental service by higher salaries. In the third world, as in the first, government employees at the lower end of the pay scale often earn more than their counterparts in the private sector, but at the higher end of the pay scale, where the most capable individuals are located, at least in theory, private enterprise normally provides higher compensation than the public sector. Foreign aid organizations and the web of nonprofit and for-profit organizations that they fund also draw human capital away from third world governments through higher salaries. Because of criticisms of foreign technical assistance programs for their reliance on expatriates, donors have deliberately hired large numbers of locals for their own staffs, awarded more work to local NGOs and contractors, and encouraged foreign-based NGOs and contractors to rely more heavily on local manpower.[30] These well-intentioned efforts have raised living standards for the best and brightest, but at the cost of draining the government's pool of human capital, since in most of the third world the public sector is a leading source of people with the education and interests needed for aid-related work.[31] "All the best talent in Mozambique and Uganda is tied up in 'the aid industry,'" says Arvind Subramanian of the International Monetary Fund.[32] A senior adviser to the Ethiopian government explained, "Aid agencies and their contractors and NGOs have sucked the best people out of the government, leaving the government only with the people whom no one else wants to hire."[33]

At the peak of foreign involvement in Afghanistan, 50,000 Afghans worked in aid-related jobs outside of the Afghan government, pulled there by salaries as high as $1,000 per month, as compared with the average salary of $50 per month for the nation's 280,000 civil servants.[34] Salary disparities of this magnitude ensured that the quality of human capital among the 50,000 was much higher than among the 280,000. Although the 50,000 contributed in important ways to development, they could not achieve transformational change because they were not inside the government. When the number of jobs shrank, some rejoined the government, but most did not want to work for such low salaries and instead sought employment with other foreign organizations or moved abroad.

The aid industry is well aware of the problems caused by its poaching of human capital from poor governments. The more conscientious leaders in the aid community make a concerted effort to avoid hiring the best and brightest away from governments. In some countries, senior government officials who apply for top jobs at the World Bank or United Nations will be disqualified simply because they are widely viewed as indispensable to the government. Ideally, any foreign organization seeking to hire indigenous personnel should perform a human capital impact assessment, which weighs the costs to the indigenous public and private sectors against the benefits to the hiring organization, and it should keep salaries at or below those for comparable positions within the indigenous government.

Unfortunately, such rules cannot be imposed on the entire aid community, consisting as it does of a diverse array of organizations and nations that do not bend to the will of a single authority. Compliance depends upon persuasion rather than coercion, which is unlikely to work with every organization in the aid arena, given how often certain organizations have been willing to siphon off public sector human capital in the past. Every organization likes to think that its mission is especially important, and hence deserving of top-notch talent, which can be secured only by offering high salaries.

MILITARY TRAINING

During the Cold War, the U.S. military trained personnel from the majority of the world's countries at one time or another, and since the collapse of the Soviet Union the list of recipients of U.S. military training has increased to encompass most of the world's armed forces. Unbeknown to most American taxpayers, this training has profoundly altered the human capital of foreign militaries, yielding improvements on a much larger scale than U.S. training on the civil side. In most third world countries, the military stands at or near the top of the list of the most respected institutions. Educated citizens as well as foreign observers usually deem the armed forces more effective and less corrupt than the civil political leadership and the civil service, and the military is invariably viewed as superior to the police.[35]

One reason for the civil-military disparity is a greater emphasis by the U.S. military leadership on developing foreign individuals and organizations. Because of the hierarchical structure of military organizations, the labor-intensive nature of military activities, and the types of personalities that predominate among military officers, military leaders generally attach greater weight to leadership than governmental civilians do. Military officers are more likely than their civilian counterparts to attribute failures to an individual than to factors beyond an individual's control. They are more likely to punish underperforming officers at lower echelons, both for that reason and for the reason that the price of underperformance is so high. The infantry captain who waits too long to send a relief platoon will get people killed, whereas the diplomat who adopts a poor negotiating position or the development official who fails to monitor a project merely wastes money that came from faceless taxpayers thousands of miles away.

As a result of differences in philosophy and resources, the U.S. armed forces devote more time and effort to leadership development and technical training of their foreign partner organizations than do America's civil agencies. Dr. Laura Cleary, the head of the United Kingdom's Centre for International Security and Resilience, ably spelled out this point and its implications in a recent article. Third world military officers differ fundamentally in outlook and ability from their civil counterparts, she explains, because first world militaries invest heavily in the development of those officers, whereas "at no point is the same level of organized or targeted investment being made in the civilian authority structures."[36]

SPEED AND EFFICIENCY OF MILITARY TRAINING

The U.S. military can afford to spend more of its time than its civil counterparts on training because it faces less pressure for short-term results from Congress and the public. Americans generally trust the U.S. military to spend their money wisely, on account of their high regard for the military as an institution. Surveys consistently indicate that the military is the most respected institution in the United States, enjoying the confidence of close to 80 percent of Americans.[37] The fact that much of that spending goes to American individuals and companies in all fifty states helps too.

MILITARY TRAINERS

In general, the personnel employed by the U.S. military in training and advising are better suited to those tasks than their civilian equivalents. The military usually assigns this work to uniformed personnel who have spent a substantial fraction of their careers training or advising other Americans, whether as commanding officers, staff officers, noncommissioned officers, or instructors at military schools. When the U.S. military chooses to hire contractors for training purposes, it usually selects people who are good at training because it recognizes the need for such people and is adept at identifying them. The contractors and NGO personnel employed in civilian technical assistance, on the other hand, are more frequently selected on their ability to perform tasks rather than their ability to train.

POLITICAL ELITES AND MILITARY TRAINING

Military training, like civil training, can be undermined by interference from civilian political leaders. Fear of a military coup has caused more than a few third world politicians to oppose the development of strong armed forces or to stack the leadership ranks with the officers who are most loyal rather than those who are most competent. Generally speaking, though, militaries suffer less from political interference than do civilian organizations. Politicians tend to be less involved with the day-to-day business of the military than with that of the ministry of finance or the ministry of trade. And oftentimes they want a highly competent military because they deem it vital to protecting their government from enemies, foreign or domestic.

MOTIVATIONAL IMPACT OF MILITARY TRAINING

Military trainers also differ from their civilian opposite numbers in their willingness to pursue cultural change. U.S. military officers are considerably less likely than Americans on the civil side of government to doubt the legitimacy or effectiveness of transferring positive cultural attributes to foreigners. When asked if they think the United States should try to change the culture of a foreign military organization, the typical response from a U.S. military officer is, "Of course. How else can we get them to clean their weapons or show up for operations before the enemy gets away?"[38]

Military officers tend to come from communities that have fewer doubts about the soundness of American culture, and they often have personalities conducive to imposing their will on others. The military's institutional culture reinforces these tendencies. Cultural change is a central component of the training that American military personnel administer to one another, which gives the military a wealth of experience in cultural change that is lacking on the civilian side. At Fort Benning, Parris Island, and hundreds of other military installations across the United States, the armed forces inculcate in their personnel a culture that differs from American civilian culture in essential respects. Trainees are isolated from their families for months at a time and are given few opportunities to engage in activities of their own choosing. They are obligated to wear uniforms and receive regulation haircuts, and can be kicked out for lying or cheating. These impositions, together with recurrent pep rallying and the ministrations of chaplains from a variety of faiths, help cultivate a greater allegiance to the organization and the state while weakening the self-serving impulses that lead to corruption and other vices. Some of the instruments of cultural change are relaxed when training ends and graduates are inserted into operational units, but many remain in place throughout the military career.

Contributing to the success of the U.S. military in changing foreign cultures is the depth of its involvement in training. In addition to allocating a larger fraction of its personnel to training than civilian organizations do, the military is more likely to take on a large role in shaping and running foreign training institutions. The content of training at military training institutions from Senegal to Sri Lanka bears striking resemblance to the content at the equivalent facilities in the United States.

In contrast to the civil U.S. agencies that provide training, the U.S. Department of Defense conducts much of its training of foreign personnel in the United States, where it has complete control over training content. Over the past fifty years, the U.S. government has paid for 500,000 foreigners to attend military institutions on American soil. In addition, a number of foreign governments have used their own money to put individuals through military training programs in the United States, which is a good indicator of the value that foreign nations attach to American military training.[39] Some of the recipients come for short courses, but many others attend year-long courses, in which they receive instruction every day, all day long, a setting highly conducive to transmission of culture.

American military trainers influence the culture of foreign trainees in many of the same ways that they influence American trainees. Demonstrating little concern for possible affronts to cultural sensitivities, they demand adherence to American standards of discipline and honesty, punishing those who do not conform. They teach the systematic planning methods that U.S. military units use for their operations and require trainees to use American techniques and procedures in month-long exercises. They call upon the trainees to think independently and make decisions using formal logic as American officers do, which for many non-Western officers is very different from how they are accustomed to thinking and making decisions.[40] My own experiences teaching foreign military students in the United States, and the experiences of many others, indicate that instruction at U.S. institutions has indeed transformed how foreign officers process and use information.[41]

U.S. military training has altered not only how foreign officers think, but what they think, especially with respect to professional and ethical questions. The practice of U.S. military officers of working long hours and demanding the same from subordinates has led foreign trainees to lengthen their work days. Foreign officers who used to stay put in their offices and issue orders by telephone or radio have followed the example of American commanders of visiting the field frequently, even in the face of great danger. Instead of eating like kings while the enlisted soldiers munch on stale bread, they put the needs of their troops on a par with their own. They have become intolerant of dishonesty and corruption – which at times has led them to oust dishonest and corrupt political leaders.[42]

"The most important thing that Colombia gained from U.S. military assistance was the transfer of culture," said General Carlos Ospina, the former commander of Colombia's armed forces, which have by all accounts profited heavily from U.S. assistance. "The Americans served as our role models. We watched their behavior, their discipline, their humility, and their commitment to their country, and tried to emulate them."[43]

For decades, U.S. military personnel have influenced foreign military cultures through human rights training. When training officers from countries where the armed forces have a propensity for torturing or killing civilians, they have emphasized that brutalizing civilians, even those suspected of abetting subversives, is not only morally wrong but also practically unwise because it alienates potential friends and creates new enemies. As members of the world's most respected military organization, the American trainers enjoy greater credibility with their audiences than civilians, even civilians from the indigenous government.[44]

American military training has led to significant reductions in human rights violations in a variety of countries. A top leader of the Salvadoran Insurgency of the 1980s, for instance, asserted that the worst thing that ever happened to the insurgency was the arrival of U.S. military trainers, because they convinced the Salvadoran armed forces to treat the population better and thereby reduced the population's willingness to join the insurgency.[45] In the past few years, the exhortations of U.S. special operations forces troops have curbed the Ugandan army's beating, raping, and murdering of civilians, according to Ugandan civilians interviewed by the foreign press.[46]

In some of the countries where the U.S. military has contributed to declines in human rights abuses, religion has played a role. Unlike its civilian counterparts, the U.S. military is not afraid to encourage or at least condone the use of religion and religious-based ethics training in the instruction of foreign personnel. Military organizations around the world, representing a diversity of faiths, encourage or even require their personnel to participate in religious services, and some organize ethics programs conducted by outside religious groups, such as Campus Crusade for Christ and La Red Business Network. Many military officers, both American and foreign, have told me that religion and associated ethics programs have been a potent weapon against human rights abuses and other bad behaviors such as corruption.

Not every foreigner who has gone through American military training has behaved better as a consequence. Some have been guilty of corruption, sloth, or criminality. But such cases do not diminish the importance of military training. A certain number of Americans who have gone through American military training have subsequently perpetrated misdeeds, as any American battalion commander can relate. It must also be borne in mind that the number of foreign officers receiving American training and the duration of that training are not always sufficient in magnitude to achieve sweeping changes across a nation's armed forces, and without such changes, old habits and cultures are certain to retain influence even over those who received some American training.

U.S. special operations forces, which in many countries constitute most or all of the American troops engaged in training partner-nation personnel, have of late revised their training model to increase duration and enhance continuity. In the past, trainers often rotated in and out of countries in six-week Joint Combined Exchange Training events, with most recipient units undergoing only a few of the events in a year. Experience demonstrated that this intermittent training failed to instill key skills or remove cultural impediments to effective performance. Simon J. Powelson, an American Special Forces officer involved in training Mali's armed forces before the disastrous coup of March 2012, noted that most training did not improve Mali's forces because its episodic nature prevented it from altering a military culture that was "overrun by apathy." As a consequence of this culture, Malian soldiers avoided taking the initiative, and Malian officers did not conduct daily training. The only Malian unit to receive sustained American training performed far better than others, an outcome that has led special operations detachments in other countries to shift from intermittent training to sustained training.[47]

Although the U.S. military's willingness to push foreigners to become more like Americans has generally yielded positive results, the military has at times been too dismissive of indigenous cultural factors that could be enlisted in the service of cultural change. When seeking to encourage positive cultural change in people from other civilizations, invoking examples from their own civilizations is almost always better than citing Western examples, for people prefer role models who speak their language, share their ancestry, and inhabit the same lands. A Muslim is more likely to be persuaded on the need to combat corruption by referring to the record of Sheikh Hamad bin Khalifa Al-Thani, whose Qatari government ranked ahead of the United States and France in Transparency International's Corruption Perceptions Index in 2011, than by recounting the exploits of Eliot Ness or Aleksander Kwaśniewski.

MILITARY BRAIN DRAIN

The military side enjoys inherent advantages over the civil side in terms of personnel retention. An employee in the finance ministry can use accounting skills recently acquired from foreign civil training programs to obtain a job at a bank, but a military officer cannot find a job elsewhere using his artillery skills. In addition, military officers are often reluctant to leave the military because of the difficulty or impossibility of rejoining the military after departing it, whereas most civilians can move back and forth between the public sector and private sector without adverse career consequences.

CONCLUSION

Pressure for rapid and efficient achievement of results is crippling American efforts to train civilians in foreign governments. The U.S. Congress and other big donors should reduce their demands for short-term results and shift emphasis to human capital development in the interest of promoting self-sufficiency and sustainability. It will yield less impressive outcomes in the short term, but will be far more valuable and far less costly in the long term.

The obstruction of technical assistance by malign political leaders serves as another reminder of the importance of human capital at the top of governments. It also tells us that donor nations can get more out of their training expenditures in countries with cooperative and capable leadership than in other countries. They should therefore curtail training in nations where bad leadership prevents it from having an impact, and they should surge training and other forms of technical assistance to nations when new and improved leadership arrives on the scene.[48]

Current civil training programs are also hobbled by their inability to influence the culture of recipient individuals and institutions. Too few personnel are involved in the prolonged training required for cultural change, and those who are often lack the desire or capabilities to inculcate such change. Allocating additional personnel to long-term training will solve the first problem. Solving the second problem will require hiring people who want to promote cultural change and possess the personality and skills required for the task. Likely candidates would be individuals with experience in the military or in missionary work. Civil agencies of the U.S. government can also get more involved in cultural change by taking on a larger role in civil service training institutions and by bringing talented foreign civil servants to the United States for lengthy periods of training in the American way of governance, be it classroom instruction at training institutions or on-the-job training at governmental offices.

The hemorrhaging of public sector human capital can be staunched to some degree through conscious efforts to restrict salaries in aid organizations and avoid the poaching of the government's top talent. The aid industry should employ expatriates, expensive though they are, when the sole alternative is to hire people away from the government. Those expatriates need to focus on training government officials, rather than on doing work in their place, so as to develop indigenous human capital. Concentrating aid on training, education, and other programs dedicated to the betterment of governmental personnel will necessarily reduce aid for traditional economic and social development programs such as building schools and providing social services – which will reduce the amount of indigenous manpower hired by contractors and NGOs.

The U.S. military has demonstrated a greater interest and aptitude than civil organizations in training foreigners and has already surmounted most of the aforementioned obstacles. The gap between civil and military organizations in training prowess can and should be narrowed by reforming the civil side, with the help of techniques that have worked well on the military side. But that gap will never disappear entirely, owing to the military's inherent advantages in resources and organizational culture. The gap's current size and the impossibility of eliminating it completely have profound implications for the division of labor between military and civilian organizations. Those implications are taken up in the next chapter.

7

Militarization

Because civil agencies are not as good as the military at achieving cultural change through training and never can be, the advisability of involving the military in training beyond the purely military sphere deserves consideration. Such involvement could include the training of military forces in law enforcement or other operations normally considered civil in nature. It could include the training of law enforcement organizations that fall under military or civil authority, or the training of governmental organizations of a strictly civil character. While the expansion of the military's writ is sometimes viewed as a formula for oppression, in reality it is more likely to reduce oppression and enhance the well-being of the civilian population.

MILITARIES IN INTERNAL AFFAIRS

Unlike the U.S. armed forces, numerous third world militaries routinely conduct security, governance, and development activities inside their own countries. At times, the U.S. government has encouraged foreign military organizations to engage in these activities and has provided resources to that end. At other times, American policymakers have taken the position that such problems should be handled exclusively by civil authorities, arguing that involving the military in domestic affairs will result in human rights abuses by soldiers and domination of the government by generals.[1] "If you let the military get involved in internal affairs, you'll soon have a military dictatorship," is an oft-heard refrain.

In truth, exclusive reliance on civil agencies to handle internal problems is a luxury that few poor countries can afford. The police and other law enforcement agencies in the third world are often too weak to deal with dire threats to security like organized crime and violent extremism. Private security firms, which have proliferated in the third world as the result of police ineffectiveness, have seldom been more effective than the police in dealing with major threats to the government or the general population, even if they may make life reasonably safe for the affluent.[2] When the police cannot keep drug traffickers from leaving headless corpses along the roadside or ethnic militias from raping and torturing members of rival ethnic groups, governments must turn to the military for help.

In a number of critical cases where the United States steered its aid to the police and other civil organizations and away from the military, it opened the door to well-armed enemies of the state and necessitated a belated American shift to military assistance. The view that the military should stay out of internal affairs caused the United States to concentrate assistance to South Vietnam in the late 1950s on lightly armed police, whose pistols and night sticks proved no match for the AK-47s of the Viet Cong when the insurgency erupted in 1960. By the time the United States infused the South Vietnamese military and paramilitary forces with additional resources and advisers, the Viet Cong had seized control of large swathes of the countryside.[3]

During the 1990s, the United States focused its security aid to Colombia on the civilian police rather than the military. But the Colombian police kept getting steamrolled by narcotics traffickers and insurgents, losing territory along with the confidence of the population. The security situation deteriorated so badly by the late 1990s that the United States finally agreed to provide funding, equipment, and military advisers to the Colombian military for internal security purposes and acceded to the subordination of Colombia's National Police to the Ministry of Defense. The military ultimately succeeded where the police had failed.[4]

A similar situation prevailed in Mexico during the 1990s. In 1995, the Mexican government decided to insert the military into the drug war because the police forces were manifestly incapable of handling the drug trafficking organizations. Dispersed and lightly armed, the police were no match for the large and skilled paramilitary forces of these organizations. The Mexican military, especially the Mexican Marines, proved much more effective than the police at combating these enemies of the state.[5]

Superior firepower and mobility are not the only advantages that military forces possess over police forces in combating internal enemies. In most of the third world, the military is less prone to abuses of power than the police. This reality is widely appreciated by residents of third world countries, as shown by the much higher public approval ratings for the military than for the police in nearly all third world countries. It is unfortunately not understood by Western opponents of militarizing domestic affairs, who are prone to gross exaggerations of military foibles and to similar exaggerations of enlightenment and selflessness on the civil side of government. Even Paul Collier, one of the most knowledgeable economists on security issues, has fallen victim to such inaccurate caricatures. Relying on the account of one African civilian, he explains in his book *The Bottom Billion* that the stupid school room bullies of the third world go on to become military officers while the smart boys whom they pushed around choose to enter the civil service. The dastardly military leaders, Collier asserts, engage in "looting the public sector" and replacing smart and honest civil servants with their "dumb and corrupt" pals.[6]

In the third world, military forces are less likely to commit human rights abuses than the police, on account of differences in the motives of their leaders. Third world militaries tend to attract more idealistic people than their police counterparts because militaries cultivate an ethos of self-sacrifice and military service typically offers fewer opportunities for graft than police duty. American and other foreign training of military forces usually reduces human rights abuses to a greater extent than the training offered by foreign civil agencies to police forces, because the military training is generally more intensive and more effective in altering cultural norms. "You helped us with our military," one exasperated Honduran general told me after detailing the misdeeds of the Honduran police. "Why couldn't you do it with the police?"[7]

Military forces typically succumb less often than the police to bribery and intimidation by their enemies, for the foregoing reasons and for several others. Operating in larger groups and with heavier weapons, they are harder to bully. In much of the third world, military families live in protected areas, preventing mobsters and terrorists from subverting military officers with threats against their wives and children.

Across Africa and Latin America, rampant abuses of power by police forces have generated popular clamoring for military intervention in domestic affairs. Most of Guatemala's citizens, for instance, view the military as the best solution to the predation and collusion with drug traffickers that are endemic within the police, even though the military was known to have committed numerous war crimes in years past. A poll taken in Guatemala a few years ago found that a majority of respondents favored a military coup to rescue the country from its abysmal conditions.[8] In Honduras, human rights activists who had previously denounced the Honduran military for human rights violations have come around to the view that the military is a good alternative to the malign police for domestic security. During November 2011, some of them backed a decision by Honduran legislators to authorize greater military involvement in internal security.[9]

Many third world militaries are also deeply involved in basic activities of governance and development, because the civil administration either lacks the required human and material resources or is incapable of using its resources because of insecurity. In Senegal, the military has routinely worked in the areas of health, infrastructure development, agriculture, education, and border control.[10] For most of Pakistan's history as a nation, the military has run the civil administration, with current and retired military officers holding top civil positions.[11] The Egyptian military owns and operates an economic empire with holdings in construction, tourism, maritime transport, petrochemicals, household appliances, food, and pharmaceuticals, the profits from which go into the military's budget.[12]

Shortages of civil assets have caused many Latin American governments to send the military into distant, sparsely populated areas to serve as the sole implementers of all governmental programs. Even in Brazil, where the police and civil administration rank among the most capable in Latin America, the military provides all governmental services in the least populated regions. "As the Brazilians put it, the military serves as the nation's capillaries," says Colonel Samuel Prugh, the head of the U.S. Defense Attaché Office in Brasilia. "The government and police are present in all the population centers, but only the military reaches into the remote sections. If the police or civil officials need to go into the most remote places, the military provides the transportation and facilities."[13]

Of the scores of countries that have employed their militaries in internal security, governance, or development in recent decades, very few have seen the military usurp civil authority. Military participation in internal matters has caused the military leadership to pay greater attention to domestic problems and, in some cases, to criticize political leaders for poor performance, but in the few countries that have endured military coups, the situation was sufficiently grave that the military might well have intervened even had it not been engaged in domestic operations. In most of those countries, moreover, the military sought to replace a bad civil government with a good one, not to install military rule on a permanent basis.[14]

The few military organizations that have undertaken prolonged management of civil governance in recent decades have usually done so because the nation's civilian human capital was woefully inadequate, not because the military had a strong appetite for civil administration. The Pakistani military chose to govern Pakistan for long periods out of dissatisfaction with the appalling ineffectiveness and corruption of Pakistan's civilian governments. On several occasions, the Pakistani military has voluntarily handed power over to a civil government, including the current democratic government, and on each occasion the civilians have proven unequal to the task.

While Pakistan's military governments have been far from perfect, most Pakistanis are convinced that those governments have been more effective and less corrupt than the country's civil governments. In April 2013, the British Council published a survey of Pakistanis aged eighteen to twenty-nine that revealed massive discontent with civil governance, together with strong admiration for the military institutions that had governed Pakistan a few years earlier. Just 14 percent of those surveyed expressed approval of the current civil democratic government. By contrast, 77 percent approved of the military. Ninety-four percent said that the country was heading in the wrong direction under the current civil democratic government; in 2007, under the last military government, only half of Pakistanis had believed the country to be going the wrong way. More of these young Pakistanis, 32 percent, expressed a preference for military rule than for democracy, which was favored by only 29 percent, while another 38 percent said they wanted an authoritarian government based on Islamic law.[15]

Indonesia's military dominated the civil government and economy from 1966 to 1998, because the civil servants whom the military ousted in 1966 were incompetent and, in many cases, supportive of Communism. When Indonesia's military withdrew from governance and commerce in 1998 and permitted democratic elections, advocates of democratization declared that the new civil government would sweep away the corruption of military rule and modernize the state. But, as in Pakistan, civil rule did not live up to expectations. Corrupt practices intensified, as the military officers and bureaucrats who had run the government gave way to business elites who were even more intent on manipulating the government in the service of personal wealth. Co-opting the major political parties and taking senior positions within the government, these elites directed state funds to patronage networks and awarded state contracts to themselves.[16] Vedi R. Hadiz of the National University of Singapore and Richard Robison of the Institute of Social Studies in the Netherlands have observed that these new political parties "constitute tactical alliances that are largely concerned with new ways of organizing control of and access to the spoils of state power."[17]

Nigeria's transition from military rule to civil democracy in 1999 was similarly disappointing. The Nigerian armed forces suffered from considerable corruption, but the civilians who held power from 1999 onwards were at least as corrupt. "Whether military or civilian," writes Ohio State Professor Kelechi A. Kalu, Nigeria's leaders "have shown interest only in private accumulation [of wealth] and have therefore not made any efforts to produce both a state and government in Nigeria capable of serving the national interest."[18]

The problem with the corrupt Nigerian military officers who have participated in governance was not that they were military in character, as has sometimes been assumed, but rather that they were not military enough in character. They had received considerably less U.S. training and education than many other foreign forces, because the U.S. government had repeatedly suspended military assistance programs on account of the military's involvement in politics and its alleged human rights violations.[19] Without the salutary cultural effects of such external assistance, the Nigerian armed forces were afflicted with the same cultural maladies as the rest of Nigerian society. The Nigerian scholars Osuma Oarhe and Iro Aghedo note that Nigeria's security forces have been corrupt because they "largely mirror the image of the society in which they work," a society that "is egregiously low on morality, ethical standards, and spiritual values."[20]

Too often Americans forget that the United States has in its own past relied upon the military to handle internal security and governance. After the Civil War, the U.S. Army occupied the former states of the Confederacy, governed them directly, and supervised the creation of civil governments led by Northern "Carpetbaggers," Southern "Scalawags," and former slaves. The Posse Comitatus Act of 1878, which sharply constrained the use of U.S. military forces inside the nation's borders, has often been misconstrued as a reaction to abuses by the U.S. military against the civilian population during the Reconstruction period of 1865 to 1877, and hence as evidence of the general inadvisability of using military forces for domestic tasks. In actuality, the U.S. military governed reasonably well during Reconstruction; it was the new civil governments that raised hackles, through their poor governance as well as their commitment to a racial equality that the majority of white Southerners opposed.[21]

Congress passed the Posse Comitatus Act as part of a political deal between Southern whites and Northern whites, in which the Southerners let the Republican Rutherford B. Hayes win a disputed presidential election in return for the removal from the South of remaining federal military forces, the sole guarantors of the beleaguered civil governments. The departure of the U.S. military forces led to the collapse of egalitarian governance in the Southern states and was followed by decades of legalized racial segregation. Ending segregation in the South would require the reintroduction of U.S. Army forces into the South in 1957.

THE U.S. MILITARY AND CIVIL OPERATIONS SINCE 9/11

In the past decade, the U.S. Department of Defense has become heavily engaged in performing nonmilitary activities in the third world. The bulk of this engagement has occurred in Afghanistan and Iraq, where U.S. military units of all shapes and sizes have been given responsibility for governance and development. Men and women in uniform have drilled wells, issued arrest warrants, and operated power plants. Their performance of governance and development has also led, by choice or by default, to their participation in training locals in these activities.

Civil agency personnel, NGO employees, and human rights activists, among others, have called for an end to U.S. military involvement in governance and development. Inserting American troops into these sectors, they contend, alienates the numerous foreign peoples that are said to be fearful of the U.S. military.[22] They believe, in addition, that the military lacks the necessary technical, cultural, and linguistic expertise to be effective in civil activities.[23] While conceding that civil agencies have fallen short in generating governance and development capabilities, they assert that the solution is not to give up on those agencies but to bolster them, if necessary by taking resources from the military.[24]

The merits of their argument have been severely weakened by the persistent failure of the U.S. civil agencies to conduct governance and development activities abroad. The sources of this failure are deep-seated and resistant to correction. One is resource constraints. U.S. civil agencies are small, especially in relation to the U.S. military, and they do not have the administrative capabilities, infrastructure, or managerial experience to facilitate rapid, large-scale deployment of personnel overseas.

Lacking the manpower to protect their own people in conflict zones, the civil agencies hire private companies to provide security, a practice that is enormously expensive. Those companies have also created new problems for the

U.S. government, some of which have caused damage of strategic proportions. The most famous of these companies has become enmeshed in so much controversy that it has changed its name twice, from Blackwater to Xe in 2009 and then from Xe to Academi in 2011. In Iraq, the company's employees were involved in several violent incidents that became political and public-relations nightmares for the U.S. government. The killing and mutilation of four Blackwater contractors in the Iraqi city of Fallujah precipitated an international crisis that led to the largest battles of the Iraq War.

At one point, the State Department attempted to curb its reliance on private security firms by developing an in-house security capability. Governmental regulations prevented the department from offering salaries on par with those of private companies, which proved a fatal stumbling block in attracting individuals to work in conflict zones. When the first recruiting campaign induced only four individuals to sign up for the State Department's security organization, administrators decided to terminate the program.[25]

Civil agency participation in dangerous countries has also been small because most of these agencies have not wanted to participate on a large scale. In Afghanistan and Iraq, the size of the U.S. military gave the Department of Defense the dominant voice in interagency matters, an arrangement unwelcome to civil agencies habitually averse to taking direction from other agencies. The civil agency chiefs feared, moreover, that collaboration with the military would undermine their credibility with the indigenous population and make them targets of insurgents.

During the first year of the Iraqi occupation, risk aversion and disenchantment with the Department of Defense's control over the interim Coalition Provisional Authority (CPA) led U.S. civil agencies to send far fewer personnel to Iraq than promised. CPA was supposed to fill roughly half of its authorized positions with civilians, requiring a total of 1,086 personnel, but the agencies most relevant to the functioning of an interim government – State and AID – provided only ninety-one people, and other civil agencies added just sixty-four. "The Coalition nations have millions of the most talented individuals in the world," said Rear Admiral David Oliver, the former CPA Director for Management and Budget. "We needed, and did not have, several thousand of them."[26] Green twenty-three-year-olds arrived to fill some of the holes in CPA, but their enthusiasm could not compensate for their lack of experience and skills. Officers from the U.S. military who had expected to work with CPA in filling the governance void quipped that the organization's initials stood for "Can't Provide Anything."

This initial lack of civilian participation set the tone for the remainder of the Iraq War. As the insurgency intensified, the military invited civilians to work on interagency Provincial Reconstruction Teams, but the agencies remained miserly in their contributions. In 2005, as the head of a new course on interagency operations at the U.S. Marine Corps University, I sent a request through official channels to find out how many people from each of the civil agencies were working in Anbar province, where the U.S. Marines had thirty thousand troops. The university was seeking to identify the agencies that would be most deserving of inclusion in its curriculum. We expected to hear that ten or more agencies were active, as has often been the case in overseas U.S. operations. The answer we received back was that only two agencies were working in Anbar, and that they had a grand total of three employees present for duty – one from the State Department, one from USAID, and one from a private company under contract with USAID.

The exceptional perils of combat zones have also affected the willingness of civil agencies to deploy their personnel. Numerous civilians have volunteered to serve in Iraq, Afghanistan, and other conflict-ridden countries despite the dangers and the austere living conditions. Among some agencies, especially USAID, individuals anticipated repeated deployments to trying environments when they joined, and hence a request to deploy to Iraq or Afghanistan did not cause a drastic shock. But other U.S. civil agency personnel found compulsory deployments to war zones objectionable and opposed efforts to require individuals to deploy. Outside of the Department of Defense, civilian personnel often do not view themselves as arms of U.S. national security and hence believe that the government should not have authority to put their lives at risk in support of national security objectives against their will, even in cases of war. According to *Wall Street Journal* reporter Nathan Hodge, USAID personnel in Afghanistan objected to their agency's involvement in the Provincial Reconstruction Team program because the teams focused on securing the policy objectives of the U.S. government, rather than on providing assistance in a purely altruistic manner.[27]

Unlike the military, whose members must go wherever the Pentagon directs them, the civil agencies are constrained in their overseas personnel deployments by unions and congressional committees with high degrees of risk aversion. The Foreign Service Association, which serves as the union of the Foreign Service Officers in the State Department and USAID, has strenuously resisted the exposure of civil agency personnel to harm in Iraq, Afghanistan, and other conflict areas. Congressional oversight committees have reinforced that resistance. As a consequence, civilians in these countries have been hunkered down in heavily protected buildings in major population centers, which automatically excludes them from most activities in the governance and development sectors.[28]

During 2007, in response to White House demands that civil agencies stop dragging their feet on sending qualified personnel to Iraq, the Foreign Service's director general notified the Foreign Service Officer community that unless forty-eight of them volunteered to fill vacant positions in Iraq, some individuals would be compelled to go. No U.S. diplomats had been killed in Iraq, but news reports of a precarious security environment in Iraq had stirred up fears among the diplomatic corps. In response to the announcement, a number of Foreign Service Officers made known to higher officials their opposition to forced deployments into a country where mortars and rockets rained down daily.

Because of the grumbling, the State Department convened a town hall meeting at which Foreign Service Officers could air their views. An Associated Press correspondent who attended the meeting reported that many attendees "expressed serious concern about the ethics of sending diplomats against their will to work in a war zone." Jack Croddy, a senior Foreign Service Officer, stood up and said into the microphone, "It's one thing if someone believes in what's going on over there and volunteers, but it's another thing to send someone over there on a forced assignment. I'm sorry, but basically that's a potential death sentence and you know it. Who will raise our children if we are dead or seriously wounded?" According to the Associated Press account, "Croddy's remarks were met with loud and sustained applause from the estimated 300 people at the meeting."[29] Because of widespread opposition from Foreign Service Officers, the State Department aborted its plans for compulsory deployments to Iraq.[30]

The diminutive contributions of the U.S. civil agencies during the early years of the wars in Afghanistan and Iraq compelled the Department of Defense to shoulder the burden of most of the governance and development activities. U.S. battalion commanders served as the principal American liaisons with town mayors and the principal disbursers of U.S. aid. Military reservists filled specialist positions in everything from agriculture to municipal management to business development.[31] On November 28, 2005, the Department of Defense codified its role in governance and development with a directive declaring that stability operations – a term encompassing governance and development – were "a core U.S. military mission" to which the Department of Defense would assign "priority comparable to combat operations." The directive's authors acknowledged that many aspects of stability operations could be performed better by civilian experts, but asserted that the military had to be prepared to do everything because civilians were not always present.[32]

The military had not been eager to take on these nonmilitary duties. Many military officers looked down upon nonmilitary activities as second-rate work, the performance of which would look unimpressive on their personnel records when they came up for promotion in competition with officers possessing combat experience. They had joined the military to kick down doors and brave the demons of mortal combat, not to attend city council meetings or hand out soccer balls to teenagers. In their opinion, civilian officials ought to be taking care of such affairs.

It was common during this period to hear American military officers criticize civil agencies for refusing to require their governance and development specialists to serve in dangerous countries. The risk aversion of the civilians offended them both because it violated the spirit of selfless service to the country and because it compelled the military to pick up the slack. Eventually, even Admiral Mike Mullen, chairman of the Joint Chiefs of Staff, would take the civil agencies to task. "In future struggles of the asymmetric, counterinsurgent variety," Mullen said, "we ought to make a pre-condition of committing our troops that we will do so only if and when the other instruments of national power are ready to engage as well."[33]

During his second term, President George W. Bush sought to fix the problem of civilian nonparticipation by creating a new organization within the State Department dedicated to U.S. stability operations. Dubbed the Office of the Coordinator for Reconstruction and Stabilization (S/CRS), it was given charge of a Civilian Response Corps, which would provide expeditionary civilian personnel to conduct governance and development activities in conflict and postconflict situations. The Corps had an initial target of 250 active duty personnel and a two thousand–strong standby component that could deploy within thirty days.[34] S/CRS also was given the mission of integrating all U.S. stability operations.

S/CRS flopped, for lack of support within Washington. Apathy on the part of Congressional and State Department leaders prevented it from receiving the funding necessary to build up the Civilian Response Corps. Resistance from various agencies kept it from coordinating interagency operations.[35] When President Obama took office, he vowed to overcome this resistance, but like Bush he did not invest the time, effort, and political capital required to surmount the legislative and bureaucratic barriers.

The Obama administration pursued a different route to lessen the imbalance between military and civilian capabilities in Afghanistan, which by the time Obama took office had eclipsed Iraq as the epicenter of stability operations. On the advice of Secretary of State Hillary Clinton, Obama increased the number of State and AID personnel in Afghanistan from 531 in 2009 to thirteen hundred in 2011. But the aversion to casualties among civilian bureaucracies again intervened. Of the thirteen hundred American civilians who filled those positions in 2011, 920 remained in Kabul, and many of the others stayed at regional or provincial headquarters, from which they seldom ventured because of stringent security guidelines or personal preference.[36]

In an effort to increase the power of the State Department and other civil agencies in Afghanistan, the Obama administration created new "senior civilian representatives" who received large budgets for governance and development as well as authority to "coordinate and supervise" all U.S. civilian personnel in their regions. The State Department contended that the new arrangement would "improve unity of government."[37] In actuality, it had the effect of dividing government, since the senior civil representatives had a chain of command separate from that of the military and they did not always see eye-to-eye with their military counterparts. The fact that few civilians journeyed outside the big base areas also reduced the ability of the senior civilian representatives to obtain their own information, and it undermined their prestige in the eyes of military officers who risked their lives every day by going outside the wire.

RESPONSIBILITY FOR GOVERNANCE

The Department of Defense is indisputably the primary U.S. agency for security in foreign countries. In all but the most dangerous of countries, USAID is clearly the primary U.S. agency for development. No agency, however, can be said to be the primary agency for governance. No agency claims governance assistance as its raison d'être, and the U.S. government's experts in governance are spread thinly across multiple agencies. When traveling to countries where the United States is deeply committed to building local capabilities, one often hears the complaint that "the United States has provided people to train soldiers, policemen, and health workers, but what is lacking are the people to train governors and civil servants."

Two U.S. civil agencies aspire to provide full-spectrum assistance in governance – USAID and its larger parent organization, the State Department.[38] Neither, however, has yet to come close to meeting this aspiration. USAID has the largest dedicated capability, with entire embassy sections focused on governance. The agency's core competencies, however, are social and economic development and humanitarian relief, as they have been from the organization's founding. USAID senior management prioritizes material and human resources accordingly. In FY 2010 and the first half of FY 2011, USAID obligated approximately $6 billion for health, $4 billion for other economic and social development initiatives, and $3 billion for humanitarian assistance, against just $1 billion for governance and governance-related sectors. A sizable portion of that $1 billion, moreover, went to activities closer in nature to social development than to governance.[39]

USAID gives short shrift to governance for cultural and philosophical reasons. Accustomed to viewing themselves as humanitarians who advance the social and economic welfare of the host nation's population, much of the USAID leadership looks down on governance as a venue where crass politicians pursue power selfishly and unscrupulously.[40] Some USAID personnel are unwilling to accept the argument that governance is a prerequisite of development, out of either intellectual conviction or the recognition that insistence on good governance can reduce the amount of development work that USAID can support.

The State Department's core competency is diplomacy. The need for governance assistance in Afghanistan and Iraq led Secretaries of State Colin Powell, Condoleezza Rice, and Hillary Clinton to seek a leading role for the State Department in governance assistance, and consequently the State Department acquired greater responsibility for assisting Afghan and Iraqi civil administrations. The State Department has not, however, acquired the capabilities necessary to meet those responsibilities, in these countries or any other. The Foreign Service Association has thwarted attempts to train and educate Foreign Service Officers in governance, owing to the membership's preference for traditional diplomatic activities like policy analysis, cable writing, and negotiation.[41] Today's diplomats gained entrance into the State Department because they, like the people who interviewed them, could discuss intelligently the most recent *New York Times* articles on diplomacy and had served as captains of their college debating teams. When they joined, they had little to no experience in managing programs or helping others accomplish tasks of a nonacademic nature, and today they generally lack interest in doing either. The applicants to the Foreign Service who had those skills were rejected because their grades were not as high, or because they did not know the answers to interview questions about the latest G-20 summit.[42]

For several years now, the Washington, DC think-tank circuit has been entertaining proposals to change the Foreign Service hiring criteria to bring in people who would make good advisers or program managers. They have been stymied by the brick wall of the Foreign Service Association, which opposes the fundamental changes to organizational mission and culture that would ensue. Even if hiring practices do somehow undergo dramatic modification any time soon, they will need a decade or more to have a real impact.

A better solution is to let the development experts stick to development, let the diplomats stick to diplomacy, and entrust governance assistance to a different group of people. When two tasks require very different skill sets and personality types, as they do in this case, creating two different groups to execute them generally works better than asking the experts in one task to become experts in the other, particularly if those experts have no desire to expand their expertise. Consumer products companies that hire introverted computer science geniuses as computer programmers do not call upon those same individuals to manage relationships with the firms' customers. Instead, they employ a different set of people to handle those relationships, whom they hire by interviewing extroverts who in college belonged to fraternities or sororities and spent their summers selling mobile phones or managing painting crews.

Given that USAID and the State Department's diplomatic corps have shown neither the capability nor the desire to engage seriously in governance assistance, it would make sense to create a new civil organization dedicated exclusively to governance assistance. It could fall under the State Department in a manner similar to USAID, or it could fall under the Defense Department. This new organization would recruit its personnel from external sources, since the required skills and the willingness to deploy to unpleasant places are not presently abundant in any one agency. If and when such a scenario comes into existence, the organization will need years to acquire and develop its human capital before it can become highly effective, which means that the U.S. government must find other implements of governance assistance in the interim.

CIVIL AFFAIRS

The one other element of the U.S. government that has been heavily engaged in governance assistance during the twenty-first century is the U.S. military. Iraq and Afghanistan forced the general-purpose forces of the U.S. Army and Marine Corps to participate in governance, but in the rest of the world governance has mainly been the business of specialized Civil Affairs units. Parceled out in small detachments to the military's combatant commands and their combat units, Civil Affairs personnel have of late been concentrated in Iraq and

Afghanistan, while they have been active on a smaller scale in most of the world's other unstable regions.

U.S. Army doctrine assigns the Army's Civil Affairs units responsibility for maintaining the full range of civilian professional skills required by a national government.[43] Supporters as well as detractors agree that Civil Affairs units do not, in reality, possess all of those skills. The most pronounced shortfalls are in specialties requiring both advanced education and prolonged experience, such as monetary policy, judicial reform, or cybercrime, which are important mainly when providing assistance at the national level.[44] Civil agencies such as USAID and the Departments of Treasury and Justice are best suited to providing this high-end expertise. In addition, Civil Affairs teams are often a random admixture of individuals whose expertise may lie in governance or development, so that some teams are much stronger in development than governance and almost none have expertise in a broad range of governance activities.

Civil Affairs, nevertheless, are the only component of the U.S. government that presently possesses the skills, authorities, and manpower to assist in local governance on a global scale. In contrast to the governance and development arms of the civil agencies, the military's Civil Affairs units have large numbers of personnel who can readily be deployed overseas, with nine Army brigades and two Marine Corps groups. Whereas the unions of the civil agencies can block compulsory deployments and exposure to danger, the military has no union, and it can send Civil Affairs troops to any place in the world on short notice. Civil Affairs personnel also carry weapons for their own protection, which reduces if not eliminates the need for additional expenditures on their security.

The governors in impoverished rural districts need help in managing civil servants and preparing budgets, not in establishing money laundering protocols or setting policy on nuclear energy, and those are tasks that Civil Affairs personnel have performed ably, particularly in Afghanistan and Iraq.[45] Although levels of expertise have varied substantially from unit to unit, numerous Civil Affairs personnel have brought with them experience as town mayors, city managers, police officers, or civil engineers, in addition to training and education in governance provided by the Civil Affairs establishment. Because of the wars in Afghanistan and Iraq, most Civil Affairs personnel now have extensive experience in governance under the most trying of circumstances.[46]

Another reason to focus Civil Affairs units on governance assistance is that they are better suited to that mission than to development – despite the fact that many Civil Affairs units have spent much more time on development than governance. Civil Affairs personnel rotate much more frequently than USAID personnel do, so when they concentrate on development they tend to devote their energies and resources to short-term projects like building schools or administering health care, in which Americans do most of the work, rather than longer-term development projects of the sort that USAID undertakes, which, at least in theory, involve greater emphasis on human capital development. Time pressures do not have comparable adverse effects on the training of officials in governance. In addition, the contractors and NGOs whom USAID employs have much more expertise in development than in governance. Thus, the optimal solution is to leave the bulk of development work to USAID and its contractors and NGOs except in highly insecure environments, where the political benefits of short-term stabilization projects are often more valuable and necessary than the long-term benefits of regular development work.[47]

The wars in Afghanistan and Iraq have highlighted the reality that much of the U.S. military's best talent for governance assistance lies outside of Civil Affairs. Numerous commanders and staff officers in combat units spent much of their time advising and assisting Afghan and Iraqi mayors, governors, and ministers on matters of governance, and many of them did it well.[48] One reason for the intrusion of combat officers onto the turf of Civil Affairs officers was the recognition that governance and security were intertwined. Another was the scarcity of experts in governance among civil agencies and Civil Affairs units. Civil agencies could bring few people to the job site, while Civil Affairs personnel, although more numerous, frequently knew only basic developmental skills such as construction or sanitation and preferred sticking to those skills. Helping an inexperienced government address large and complex problems, like building a governmental ministry or managing the competing demands of tribes and their legislative representatives for governmental resources, required smart and driven individuals eager to take on such challenges. In the U.S. military, that description most often fit infantry battalion commanders, division operations officers, special operations detachment commanders, and the like.

"Combat units are dominated by type-A personalities, many of whom possess strong critical thinking skills," observed Adam Strickland, a U.S. Marine Corps lieutenant colonel who was deeply involved in governance and development in Iraq and Afghanistan. "They want to get things done, and have little patience for people who are ineffective. So in Iraq and Afghanistan, they took charge of governance and development. People from Civil Affairs and the civil agencies worked with them if they could keep up."[49]

The officers in Civil Affairs units should, in theory, be as capable as those in combat units. Unfortunately, the armed services have not done enough to attract high-quality officers into Civil Affairs. Across the services, Civil Affairs officers have low rates of promotion, which discourages successful and ambitious officers from selecting it as their area of specialization. The U.S. Army Civil Affairs community did not have a single active-duty general officer until 2011.[50]

To be sure, the U.S. military does possess some highly skilled and dedicated Civil Affairs personnel, who chose that branch because of the nature of the work rather than the likelihood of career advancement. Still, measures can and should be taken to bolster the human capital of Civil Affairs. The career path for Civil Affairs officers needs to be made more attractive. Training and education of Civil Affairs officers should be retooled to develop critical thinking skills and deepen comprehension of governance and development.[51]

It would be a mistake, though, to stop there, for even with greater high-level emphasis on Civil Affairs, the combat forces will always be the primary repository of the top talent in the Army and Marine Corps, at least so long as the military is an all-volunteer force. Most members of today's officer corps entered the military to serve in combat units, and those who make a career of the military more often than not wish to stay in combat units because of personal preference and the prospects for promotion to the top ranks. The culture of the armed services prizes combat above all else, which should not be surprising given that combat is their primary purpose, and this culture cannot be changed short of draconian actions that would strip the military of its vitality. Thus, in addition to encouraging individuals to become Civil Affairs officers, the Department of Defense should seek ways to increase the involvement of combat officers in the activities traditionally associated with Civil Affairs. When combat units are not deployed to combat zones or preparing to deploy to them, which is likely to mean most of the time for the foreseeable future, a fraction of their officers can be deployed for a year or two to countries in need of governance assistance. They could work with an ally's civil affairs units, regular military units involved in internal affairs, or civil ministries. They would be particularly valuable in countries with security problems, since their presence would build U.S. expertise in countries where a larger U.S. footprint might one day be required.

The oft-heard claim that U.S. military involvement in governance alienates the population has been borne out neither in Afghanistan nor in Iraq, nor in a great many other countries. The civil authorities in Afghanistan and Iraq have usually welcomed the involvement of U.S. Civil Affairs and other U.S. military branches in governance as well as development. Military personnel generally like to teach them and are good teachers. In addition, local government officials welcome the layer of protection that U.S. military forces provide to local governmental personnel and operations.

The ultimate results of the U.S. military's governance training in Afghanistan and Iraq may be clouded by the departure of the United States and the intrusion of external actors from the likes of Pakistan and Iran. Afghan and Iraqi officials who received training from U.S. forces may be relieved of duty, forced into exile, or killed. Nonetheless the U.S. military can point to a variety of unequivocal successes in building viable, pro-American governments, such as the Philippines at the dawn of the twentieth century; Germany, Japan, and Italy after World War II; and Bosnia during the late 1990s.[52]

In a few countries, such as Pakistan and Mexico, the presence of uniformed U.S. military personnel is liable to stimulate popular hostility. In such cases, it may be wise to keep U.S. military personnel out, or at least to keep them in civilian clothing as has been done from time to time. In most of the world, however, cultural predispositions do not pose such obstacles, which is a very good thing, for meeting the challenges of governance assistance around the world will require large-scale participation from Civil Affairs and other components of the U.S. military as long as the civil agencies lack a comparable capability.

POLICE TRAINING

Responsibility for the training of foreign police forces has also been a highly contentious and problematic issue for the U.S. government and other international donors. In the international development and human rights communities, numerous voices oppose any international support to police organizations, on the grounds that it constitutes the politicization of aid and could lead to empowerment of oppressive police organizations. This reasoning has prevented the World Bank from assisting police and other law enforcement organizations in most countries.[53]

Some human rights experts as well as many police experts and U.S. government officials favor the involvement of U.S. civil agencies in training foreign police but oppose any participation by the U.S. military. They contend that ill-intentioned militarists would take advantage of such involvement to subvert the police. They argue, further, that military personnel are unqualified to train police because they lack the necessary skills and are predisposed to use brute force rather than the more tactful methods of professional police.[54]

A small group of experts has disputed the view that military forces are inherently ill-suited to police duty. Militarization of police training and police operations has not generally led to wanton abuse and bloodshed, they observe, and has in fact reduced abuses in some cases. Barnard College professor of political science Kimberly Zisk Marten has found much evidence to support this argument in the history of the modern European empires. The British, owners of the most expansive empire, relied especially heavily on soldiers to police their colonial possessions, and their soldiers almost always demonstrated skill and restraint.[55]

The U.S. government, in contrast to some European governments, lacks a national police force and thus has never had ready recourse to what would be an obvious civil candidate for training foreign police. In the first decades of the Cold War, the USAID Office of Public Safety was the principal U.S. agency for training foreign police forces, but it lost that distinction in 1975 when Congress banned all U.S. involvement in overseas police training on account of reported human rights abuses by U.S.-trained Latin American policemen. Aversion to police training eased in the 1980s, enabling the executive branch to obtain waivers to the training ban, but the ban itself still remains in place, and its ongoing presence has prevented the emergence of a single agency responsible for foreign police training.[56]

USAID never resumed its police training activities after 1975. Since that time, the Justice and State Departments have been the civil agencies most heavily involved in the training of foreign law enforcement organizations. The Justice Department's programs are well conceived, with significant attention to human capital improvements in all sectors of criminal justice, but they are constrained by low resources. In terms of building foreign criminal justice capabilities, the most significant Justice Department program is the International Criminal Investigative Training Assistance Program (ICITAP), which helps develop foreign police forces and other institutions of law enforcement. In select countries, ICITAP has made highly valuable contributions, but it is spread very thin and has no presence at all in some third world countries. Its staff totals 431, of whom sixty-seven are federal employees, and its annual budget is roughly $70 million, a paltry sum in comparison with what is needed to assist the struggling police forces of the world.[57]

When I visited the Philippines in the fall of 2012, ICITAP had just five Americans working with the Philippine National Police, an organization with a personnel strength in excess of 100,000. Tyler Truby, the acting ICITAP program manager, remarked that ICITAP was seeking to increase the number to nine, though they needed at least fifty to have a large impact.[58] By comparison, the U.S. special operations task force in the Philippines, which counted police training as one of several missions, had between five hundred and six hundred people.[59]

The State Department's Bureau of International Narcotics and Law Enforcement Affairs (INL) has a much larger budget for police training than the Justice Department's divisions, amounting to fourteen times the police training budgets of all the other civil agencies combined.[60] But the State Department leadership does not view police training as one of its core competencies and does not assign much of its core staff to the mission. INL relies heavily on contractors to provide training, and its staff are stretched too thin to ensure that companies hire qualified personnel and perform up to standards.

The civil agencies have also proven deficient at providing the paramilitary training needed by the police in conflict-ridden countries. They and their contractors typically hire retired American policemen who can teach police recruits how to direct traffic or serve an eviction notice, but not how to fight an enemy that can conduct complex ambushes with fifty heavily armed men. Police chiefs and ministers of interior in a host of third world capitals complain that the Americans are teaching their policemen civil policing skills but not the paramilitary skills they need to survive long enough to engage in civil policing.

Prior to 9/11, the U.S. military's participation in police training was limited to a few countries of high strategic importance where U.S. military police or special operations forces trained foreign police under special authorization from the State Department.[61] Some of these countries, like Colombia, had stable, pro-American governments. Others had nascent governments that were struggling to restore order after a traumatic conflict, as in the cases of Panama and Kosovo.

When the United States deposed Panama's Manuel Noriega in 1989, Panamanian police forces disintegrated and the country descended into wanton criminality. The U.S. government hoped to use civilian U.S. law enforcement personnel to reconstitute Panama's police forces and criminal justice system, but the small contingent of U.S. civilians sent for the mission proved incapable of surmounting the difficulties of reestablishing law and order after it had broken down completely. The mission was soon handed over to a U.S. military task force composed of Civil Affairs and Military Police units and other elements from Special Operations Command and Southern Command. Some members of the task force patrolled the streets while others screened Panamanians for police duty and trained them. Once the task force had trained enough Panamanians to form police units, those units patrolled jointly with U.S. troops. American military personnel took charge of Panama's prison system, and a U.S. Army lawyer assumed responsibility for getting the courts back in operation. Six months after the fall of Noriega, ICITAP assembled enough people in Panama to take over police training, but long thereafter the U.S. military continued its combined patrolling with the Panamanian police, in addition to providing most of the logistical support for ICITAP.[62]

When the Western powers arrived on the ground in Kosovo in 1999, American and European civil agencies and the United Nations did not have the capabilities to take charge of the security situation, so U.S. Military Police and a U.S. combat brigade assumed responsibility for policing and other law enforcement tasks. They patrolled the streets, arrested troublemakers, stopped looting, and ran detention facilities. At times, they operated alongside Kosovar policemen and provided on-the-job training and mentoring. U.S. troops declined in number over time, as the establishment of a secure environment permitted the State Department's INL to bring in contractors, but they did not disappear.[63]

In both Afghanistan and Iraq, INL led police training during the early stages, but the repeated trouncing of the police forces by heavily armed insurgents led U.S. policymakers to transfer police training to the Department of Defense and give the recruits heavy doses of paramilitary training. As soon as the U.S. military took control of police training, the quality of instruction shot up. Relying heavily on its own manpower and the manpower of allied militaries, the U.S. military was able to confer paramilitary skills, instill discipline, cultivate leadership, and promote ethical behavior, none of which the State Department's civilian contractors had been able to do. U.S. soldiers and Marines taught policing skills they had learned in combating the insurgents, such as collecting evidence and questioning witnesses.[64] Having also taken on the mission of working with police units in the field, the military did a much better job than its civilian predecessors of identifying underperforming indigenous police commanders and convincing the government to replace them. Sweeping leadership changes in the Iraqi police during 2007 were instrumental in halting police participation in sectarian murders and reversing the momentum of the war.[65]

After the Obama administration came to office, the U.S. State Department issued a Quadrennial Diplomacy and Development Review that recommended allocating Justice, State, and other civil agencies more resources for police training as the solution to ineffectual police training by civilian personnel.[66] With the U.S. military reducing its presence in Iraq, the Obama administration decided to return Iraqi police training to the State Department. According to the administration's plan, INL was to maintain 350 civilian police advisers in Iraq from 2012 onward. By the time January 2012 arrived, however, problems of resources and logistics had caused the State Department to reduce the number of advisors from 350 to ninety-one. In July 2012, the number was further reduced to thirty-six, almost all of whom were contractors.[67] The State Department's risk aversion and the withdrawal of U.S. military forces from Iraq, moreover, led to a curtailment of travel for those individuals. Despite heavy expenditures on private security firms and a relatively low level of violence, State's trainers stopped traveling to Iraqi facilities that the U.S. military's police trainers had routinely visited at times of much higher insurgent violence.[68]

CONSTABULARY TRAINING

In third world countries beset by well-armed guerrillas or criminals, the ideal security solution is a police force with paramilitary capabilities, along the lines of the French *gendarmerie* and the Italian *carabinieri*. Such forces, commonly termed constabularies, combine the police's law enforcement authorities and proximity to the population with the military's combat power and esprit de corps. Constabularies usually fall within a military chain of command, though they are generally seen as less threatening to civil authorities and the population than the regular military.

Unfortunately, the United States does not have such a force of its own from which experts could be deployed abroad for training foreign constabularies. The United States can rely to some extent on its European allies to provide constabulary training, and has done so at times, but the Europeans are often reluctant to send their personnel into dangerous places, and they do not have enough manpower to cover large numbers of countries. Even in the case of the former Yugoslavia, a top geopolitical concern for Europe's other nations, most European countries with constabularies have repeatedly balked at requests to contribute constabulary forces for peacekeeping and training.[69]

As in the case of governance assistance and police training, the U.S. government does not have an agency with a clear mandate and robust resources for training constabularies. INL is a poor candidate to take on the mission, given its poor track record in police training and its longstanding aversion to paramilitary training, while the Justice Department's programs are too small. The only U.S. organization currently capable of providing effective assistance to foreign constabularies is the Department of Defense, which has already demonstrated its ability to train massive numbers of paramilitary policemen in Afghanistan and Iraq. Consequently, the military needs to get more involved in assisting foreign constabularies as well as police forces.[70]

DEVELOPING U.S. MILITARY CAPABILITIES FOR POLICE
AND CONSTABULARY TRAINING

The general-purpose forces of the U.S. Army and U.S. Marine Corps were heavily involved in police and constabulary training in Afghanistan and Iraq. They mainly trained Afghans and Iraqis in the basic skills required to survive in a war of insurgency. In the event of another such war, the general-purpose forces will again be asked to undertake this type of training. But in the meantime, most will go back to more conventional military activities or will help train the military forces of partner nations. U.S. special operations forces, which worked intensively with the paramilitary Afghan Local Police, are also moving away from training police and constabulary forces and toward training of special operations and other military forces.

The Department of Defense has, however, sought to maintain a sizable police training capability beyond Iraq and Afghanistan through the formation of specialized military police units. The training of foreign police forces is a major departure for U.S. military police units, which traditionally have focused on base security, detentions, and other activities involving little interaction with foreign personnel. Nevertheless, the mission is well within the capability of Army and Marine military police forces and is deserving of further encouragement.

The U.S. Army's Military Police Corps is in the midst of a gradual shift from traditional military police functions to civilian law enforcement functions, including the training of foreign forces in law enforcement. In the 1990s, the Army started using Military Police units in law enforcement and constabulary missions, and the number of units conducting those missions soared as Military Police personnel went to Iraq and Afghanistan to train police forces.[71] Deploying Military Police troops to Afghanistan and Iraq to conduct training has been an easy matter because the U.S. military took over the police training missions in those countries and needed skilled police trainers in large numbers. In the rest of the world, however, their employment in police training has been sharply constrained by the reluctance of the State Department to authorize military participation in law enforcement matters of any type.

The Marine Corps was slower to begin this shift, but once the Marine headquarters gave the order, the change was more rapid and thorough. In the summer of 2012, based on the belief that security assistance would be a top Marine Corps priority in the coming years, the Marines consolidated their military police forces into three law enforcement battalions for overseas deployment. The missions of the new law enforcement battalions include training foreign military and police forces in policing skills and assisting local law enforcement authorities in investigations, forensics, and detainee processing.[72] As in the case of the Army's Military Police, State Department concerns about militarization of police forces have impeded attempts to use the Marine law enforcement battalions in training police forces beyond Afghanistan.

CONCLUSION

The U.S. government should provide all necessary training and other assistance to third world militaries involved in internal affairs. Aid to foreign militaries is usually more effective and efficient than aid to police forces and other civil governmental entities because military organizations are more susceptible to the cultural influences of American trainers, and hence easier to improve in competence and integrity. When the United States has used its power to make aid recipients rely solely on police forces for internal security, it has frequently paved the way for the success of armed rebels.

The United States should create a new civil organization dedicated to governance assistance, with a new staff tailored to the mission. The lack of such an agency has badly hindered the training of foreign governments. Existing civil organizations have been given many opportunities to solve the problem, and they have consistently failed.

The U.S. military should become more involved in training foreign personnel in governance. While Civil Affairs and the other components of the military do not have all the high-end skills that are needed at the national level, they have a strong record of providing basic governance assistance on a large scale. Their ability to deploy quickly to dangerous places and their ability to defend themselves make them an especially attractive option in war zones. The governance capabilities of Civil Affairs must be maintained for use in troubled third world countries now and possible contingency operations in the future. U.S. officers from combat arms branches should be deployed as necessary to assist struggling nations with governance at all levels.

U.S military forces should increase their involvement in police and constabulary training, with the U.S. Army's Military Police brigades and the U.S. Marine Corps' law enforcement battalions bearing the largest share of the burden. U.S. civil agencies have been unable to provide adequate police training – in most countries because of inadequate funding and staffing, in a handful of top-priority countries because acute shortages of in-house expertise necessitated employment of contractors who proved unsatisfactory. Focused solely on training police for peacetime in modern societies, the civil agencies cannot provide the paramilitary training required by police and constabulary forces in insecure environments.

8

Education in the Third World

Over the course of world history, the largest changes to the cultures of peoples have come from either brutal conquest, education, or a combination thereof. As the Hoover Institution's Thomas Sowell showed in his book *Conquests and Cultures,* conquests that result in cultural change have typically involved the violent overthrow of the existing ruling class, the forceful imposition of the conquerors' culture on the vanquished, and prolonged military occupation of the conquered land. Such was the methodology of the Normans in England, the Ottomans in the Balkans, and the Spanish in the Americas.

In its recent occupations of Afghanistan and Iraq, the United States used violence to remove the ruling class from power but did not hold the new rulers or their peoples at gunpoint while demanding conformance to American cultural norms. The draconian techniques of Hannibal and Cortes have never been especially popular in the United States. The pressures of omnipresent media and international opinion have, in any case, made them inconceivable as options for the U.S. government.

Some of the Americans responsible for planning the military expeditions to Afghanistan and Iraq hoped to transform these countries into liberal democracies in a few years through the installation of democratic institutions and free market capitalism. But this kinder, gentler form of conquest did not yield the cultural changes required for liberal democracy. The Americans did not impose severe punishments on Afghan and Iraqi leaders every time they resisted elements of liberal democracy that clashed with their traditional cultures. When Hamid Karzai ignored American advice to award key jobs based on merit, or when Iraqi Prime Minister Nouri al-Maliki seized control of governmental entities intended to limit executive authority, the Americans did not hang them, or even cut off funding to their governments.

The presence of American forces did compel Karzai and Maliki to heed some American demands, but that advantage dissipated as the American forces departed. American politicians chose not to maintain a large military presence in either country for the long term, as had been done in Germany and Japan after World War II and in South Korea after the Korean War. In those countries, half a century of American occupation had provided security, political guidance, and cultural influence in enough depth to ensure permanence. A single decade of occupation, on the other hand, has been unable to prevent reversion to the old ways as the Americans departed.

Afghanistan and Iraq soured the American body politic on military occupation of any sort. Even if a cataclysmic event causes the United States to invade and occupy another country in the future, chances are good that the United States will avoid maintaining a multi-decade military presence. In the years ahead, therefore, its principal instrument for promoting broad cultural change will likely be educational assistance, administered only when willingly accepted by foreign governments and peoples.

PRIMARY EDUCATION

For several decades, all major foreign aid donors have allocated most of their third world education funding to primary education. Low rates of literacy in the third world and natural affection for small children have always made primary education attractive to foreign donors, but it did not come to dominate the education sector until the 1990s, when World Bank economists published cost-benefit analyses showing that a dollar spent on primary and secondary education yielded more in personal incomes and tax revenues than a dollar spent on higher education. Because the World Bank has long been considered the world's most prestigious source of development research, other donors and third world governments followed its lead in shifting resources from higher education to primary education and, to a lesser extent, secondary education.[1] Primary education received another boost in 2000 from the call for universal literacy in the UN's Millennium Development Goals.[2]

The surge in foreign funding for primary education that began in the 1990s yielded dramatic increases in the numbers of primary schools, primary school teachers, and primary school students in the third world. Expectations for rapid poverty reduction and economic growth rose in proportion. During the ensuing years, however, primary education failed to meet those expectations in most of the countries where expenditures had multiplied. The view that spending on primary education is a highly efficient use of development money has therefore come under fire in recent years, though it has retained powerful defenders, as we shall see.[3]

As the World Bank highlighted in a 2012 study, large numbers of the students undergoing primary schooling are not becoming literate or acquiring other basic skills.[4] One reason for the poor outcomes is the inconsistency of student attendance in much of the third world. The demands of the family farm, the dangers of traveling through crime-ridden slums, the disinterest of parents in education, and other factors cause students to stay home for substantial numbers of school days. Another factor is the inconsistency of teacher attendance, as with the previously mentioned Indian teachers who did not show up for work or read the newspaper in their offices instead of teaching their classes. In some countries, especially those that have undertaken swift expansions of public education, large percentages of the teachers are not well educated themselves.[5] Lastly, endemic corruption and mismanagement oftentimes deprive students of classrooms and books. "We are short on schools because the money for new schools goes into the pockets of government officials," the head of the UN Development Program in one Latin American country told me. "We have school children who don't have classrooms but instead listen to their teacher while sitting outside on concrete blocks."[6]

SECONDARY EDUCATION

Secondary education comes in second place in terms of foreign funding of education. Like the primary schools that feed into them, the secondary schools of the third world often fail to educate students. The inability of secondary schools to impart problem solving skills and other intermediate cognitive skills prevent individuals from performing skilled work or going on to college, much to the detriment of individual and national prosperity.[7]

CULTURE AND EDUCATION

Most of the contemporary research on primary and secondary education in the third world concentrates on the teaching of knowledge and skills, above all literacy and numeracy. Most U.S. assistance programs in the education field are focused on achievements in these areas. Researchers and practitioners give short shrift to the instilling of cultural traits and values, owing mainly to reluctance to accept cultural explanations for third world blight. Another reason for the inattention to cultural attributes, though, is a practical one – the absence of valid quantitative measures. No one has developed standardized tests for work ethic or patriotism, whereas literacy tests can be found everywhere and the results immediately quantified.

American education pioneers of the nineteenth century like Horace Mann viewed the cultural power of primary and secondary schools as their single greatest asset. Teachers and school books, they asserted, should emphasize virtues like honesty, hard work, patriotism, and kindness. The proliferation of values education in American schools during the second half of the nineteenth century contributed heavily to the emergence of the United States as a global economic and military power, regardless of the fact that the contributions could not be quantified. When intellectual fads caused American primary and secondary schools to drift away from teaching culture and values in the 1960s and 1970s, student performance declined and student misbehavior increased, prompting a return to the earlier ways during the 1990s.[8] Unfortunately, the lessons of America's own educational development have not been heeded by American development experts.

The importance of child acculturation in third world schools is better understood today among the education experts of the third world than the development experts of the first. Luis Diego Herrera Amighetti, a prominent Costa Rican educational reformer who specializes in child psychiatry, advocates cultural change through schooling as a means of remedying Latin America's most debilitating maladies, especially bad governance. Education, he says, should be used to eradicate destructive cultural behaviors and values, such as procrastination and chronic absenteeism, that schools and parents too often tolerate. At present, he says, "Children learn that if they have not planned their tasks and done their homework or chores, they may give perfunctory excuses, or simply do nothing, and the system will not consistently respond with negative consequences."[9]

Other third world education experts stress the use of primary and secondary education as incubators of patriotism and national identity, in the interest of enhancing cooperation, alleviating internal conflict, and reducing governmental corruption and sloth. This practice has been very effective when national leaders have implemented it with the requisite vigor. Sukarno of Indonesia and Julius Nyerere of Tanzania made excellent use of schools in campaigns to promote national identity in their diverse nations.[10] During the economic climbs of the East Asian Tigers in the second half of the twentieth century, fostering national identity and patriotism ranked among the top educational goals and achievements of their educational systems.[11]

Experience has also shown that diverse countries risk exacerbating internal divisions if they educate children without promoting patriotism and national identity. When teachers are indifferent to national identity or advance ethnic, religious, or regional identities in its stead, they set the conditions for favoritism in governance and for civil war. In Africa, where the arbitrary drawing of national borders during colonial days has left many nations home to dissimilar ethnic groups, educators have often used the classroom to promote ethnic separatism. One survey of Africans in nine nations found that the most educated people identified themselves most closely with their ethnicity.[12]

FAITH-BASED EDUCATION

Foreign missionaries and indigenous religious organizations have spread faith-based primary and secondary education across much of the third world. Education researchers who have compared schools in particular countries or regions of the third world have found that faith-based schools generally outperform their secular competitors in both academic proficiency and positive acculturation. One oft-cited reason for the disparity is teacher quality. A World Bank analysis of faith-based primary and secondary schools in Sierra Leone determined that religious faith gave the teachers higher levels of motivation than teachers at secular schools.[13] Religious inspiration is one of several factors that have been identified as causes of superior teacher performance at Fe y Alegría, a network of Jesuit primary and secondary schools spanning fifteen Latin American countries and covering 1.2 million pupils of poor socioeconomic backgrounds. Other factors cited in the case of Fe y Alegría include better training of teachers, emphasis on values in the classroom, and the absence of the teacher unions that prevent the public schools from firing bad teachers. Salary is not a factor – Fe y Alegría's teachers are actually paid less than public school teachers.[14]

In addition to receiving donations from foreign religious charities, faith-based schools often receive subsidies from their national governments, some of which are linked directly to religious institutions. Faith-based schools have faced considerably larger challenges in obtaining funding from U.S. foreign assistance programs. Some American aid officials have preferred to support only secular education, because of either personal conviction that government funds should not support religious organizations, or the judgment of certain legal experts that the U.S. Constitution's First Amendment bars such support. Other American officials have funded faith-based education on the basis of opinions from legal experts who argue that the Constitution is inapplicable in foreign countries.[15]

The 9/11 attacks brought the issues of faith-based education to the fore. Research on Islamic education conducted in the aftermath of 9/11 determined that madrassas in Pakistan and other Islamic countries were producing many of the extremists engaged in insurgency and international terrorism around the world. Indoctrinating boys from an early age, these madrassas instilled contempt for other religions and cultures and awe for religiously inspired violence. Western experts concluded that countering these extremist views required use of moderate Islam in primary and secondary public schools. Purely secular education was not a viable antidote, because secularism was so unpopular in the Islamic world that promoting it would merely drive up enrollment at madrassas and other private religious schools.

In 2004, the growing U.S. awareness of education's role in terrorism led the Bush administration to authorize funding of foreign faith-based organizations when it was "necessary to further the national security or foreign policy interests of the United States." Since that time, the U.S. government has spent large sums on faith-based primary and secondary education programs in countries where the threat of Islamic extremism is high, principally Pakistan, Iraq, and Afghanistan.[16] USAID has funded textbooks containing moderate religious messages, in partnership with local Islamic educators, and has supported Islamic schools that are supervised by local communities. This American support of education has been reasonably effective in promoting moderate Islam in publicly funded schools as a counterweight to the immoderate Islam taught in madrassas.[17]

The United States has not, however, been able to affect what goes on inside the madrassas. The government of Pakistan, the country where the most dangerous of the madrassas are located, has turned a deaf ear to American requests to exert a moderating influence on the madrassas. Although Pakistani officials tell the Americans that they do not act because of respect for the private status of the madrassas, a more important reason for their inaction is Pakistani foreign policy. The individuals radicalized at these schools provide much of the manpower for militant organizations in India and Afghanistan that enjoy the quiet support of the Pakistani government.[18]

HIGHER EDUCATION

In the colonial era, European governments and missionary organizations built new universities in most every region where a colonial flag flew. One of the principal purposes of these institutions was to prepare students for careers in public service, and therefore course offerings were plentiful in fields such as public administration, law enforcement, education, diplomacy, and medicine. These universities tended to be small, allowing them to be highly selective in faculty recruitment and student admissions.

Following the global wave of decolonization in the mid-twentieth century, socialism and populism led many newly independent third world nations to abolish tuition and allow all citizens to attend college. These changes precipitated explosive growth in the size of student bodies at existing universities and led to the founding of many new universities. Egalitarianism discouraged concentration of resources in elite institutions, diluting the quality of faculty at the original universities and provoking top professors to go to elite universities in the Western world.[19] Huge numbers of students proved incapable of university-level work, and they dragged down the quality of education for the rest. Some countries eventually saw the folly in their ways and curtailed university admissions, but others continued to admit enormous numbers of ill-qualified students. Today, many third world universities still have more students than the largest U.S. universities, with the majority of their students unable ever to graduate.[20]

During the early decades of the Cold War, the U.S. government poured money into universities in the third world and funded bilateral partnerships connecting those universities to American universities. Between 1952 and 1980, USAID provided a total of $1 billion to 117 universities.[21] Private U.S. foundations also became heavily involved in third world higher education, led by the Ford Foundation, which allocated three-fourths of all its third world assistance to the higher education sector.[22] The U.S. government and the foundations channeled a large fraction of the funding to schools of public administration and other schools and departments that prepared individuals for governmental service, on the theory that good public sector human capital was essential to good governance and development.

The American higher education initiatives of the 1950s and 1960s received widespread plaudits for cultivating indigenous human capital. In the 1970s, however, they came under fire from development experts and intellectuals who argued that higher education benefited only privileged elites, leaving the poor behind.[23] In their view, poverty should be eliminated by taking wealth from elites and redistributing it to the poor, and thus public monies spent on universities ought to be redirected to primary education for those living in poverty. Redistribution was, moreover, easier to sell to members of Congress because it produced immediate and quantifiable results, whereas higher education's results were slow to materialize and impossible to quantify with any accuracy.

This critique spurred a sharp decline in U.S. public and private assistance to foreign higher education in the late 1970s.[24] Funding was to slide further in the 1990s as a result of the increased spending on primary education stemming from the World Bank's research, and again in 2000 with the Millennium Development Goals. The World Bank's lending for higher education fell from 29 percent of its education portfolio between 1996 and 2000 to 14.3 percent between 2006 and 2010.[25]

In the early 2000s, a team of Harvard scholars led by David E. Bloom and Henry Rosovsky assailed the World Bank research of the 1990s that had touted the superiority of spending on primary education. They faulted the World Bank's analysts for disregarding the benefits of higher education for the public sector and for society more broadly. The World Bank's statistical analysis, they asserted, "neglects the broader benefits of advanced education manifested through entrepreneurship, job creation, good economic and political governance, and the effect of a highly educated cadre of workers on a nation's health and social fabric." If one considered those broader benefits, the case for funding higher education became appreciably stronger. New research, moreover, showed a strong correlation between higher education levels and economic growth.[26]

Interest in the funding of higher education rebounded in certain circles, particularly in the United Kingdom. In 2005, British prime minister Tony Blair established the Commission for Africa, which called on the international community to invest $5 billion over ten years in African higher education to produce "the doctors, nurses, teachers, police officers, lawyers, and government workers of tomorrow."[27] The leaders of the G8 promised to use Blair's report as the blueprint for future assistance to Africa.

The supporters of primary education stood their ground, however, and they were able to hold on to most of the education pie. An investigation by the Commission for Africa in 2010 found that international donors had put little new money toward higher education since the G8's promise to Blair in 2005.[28] The USAID Education Strategy for 2011–2015 apportioned most educational aid to primary education, on the grounds that spending on higher education could not be productive until the entire population possessed basic education.[29]

"All bilateral and multilateral donors in the Philippines currently support basic education and vocational training programs," noted one USAID official in Manila. "None of them are involved in higher education." After a lengthy absence from the higher education sector in the Philippines, USAID has made plans to support science and technology at Philippine universities, which is a positive development in that it represents greater receptivity to higher education. But its benefits will largely be confined to economic development, so it will do little to alleviate the more pressing problems of governance and security.

While first world donors regularly pull out their checkbooks when they hear about an innovative new primary school, they pay little heed to comparable institutions of higher education. In Ghana, for instance, foreign donors have refrained from funding Ashesi University, a private university founded by the Ghanaian Patrick Awuah with the help of some colleagues at Microsoft. A graduate of Swarthmore College, Awuah has sought to give Ashesi's students an education that combines liberal arts with computer science, business, ethics, and leadership. The university provides free tuition to poor students, who make up half the entering class, while the wealthier students pay $4,000 per year in tuition.[30] "Africa can only be transformed by enlightened leaders," Awuah contends. "Leaders have to be trained and educated right . . . and they are not. There is very little emphasis on ethics."[31] Instead of giving Ashesi or other Ghanaian universities funds to bring in more students, the U.S. mission in Ghana concentrates its aid on primary education and other traditional poverty-reduction staples like health, agriculture, and transportation infrastructure.[32]

While primary and secondary education are undeniably important to the well-being of a modern government and economy, bringing countries out of the third world also requires higher education. A successful government ministry must have people with advanced education in finance and information technology to ensure that proper procedures are instituted, data are processed efficiently, and employees do not siphon off funds for their personal use. It must have college-educated technical specialists to organize complex tasks and college-educated managers to oversee the entire enterprise. The creation and management of the private sector businesses required for economic growth likewise depend on individuals with advanced educations. The critical high-end skills cannot be conferred merely by training high school graduates; experience has shown that individuals with no education beyond a third world high school can seldom master skills that are taught in the West at the graduate school level. For these reasons, the mass redirection of resources from higher education to primary and secondary education has harmed both the elites, who have failed to receive higher education of good quality, and the poor, whose fates are dependent on the capabilities and motives of elites.

"The skills required for management and leadership do not come about in the absence of a first-rate system of higher education," note Ashraf Ghani and Clare Lockhart, the founders and directors of the Institute for State Effectiveness, which advises donors and weak governments on how to build states. Ghani, the former chancellor of Kabul University who was elected Afghanistan's president in 2014, and Lockhart, a former World Bank and UN governance specialist, have been the most prominent critics of the development community's withdrawal from the higher education sector. "If a country does not train its children beyond the age of eleven," they ask, "where are its managers, doctors, engineers, and teachers going to come from?"[33]

Ghani and Lockhart point out that the lack of funding for higher education leaves foreign donors with high and endless bills for skilled expatriates who perform the tasks for which indigenous human capital is lacking. After the fall of the Taliban, note Ghani and Lockhart, the World Bank and UN refused to fund higher education in Afghanistan and insisted that the Afghan government not fund it either, on the grounds that the Millennium Development Goals demanded a focus on primary education. As a consequence, the West is now stuck shelling out massive sums for technical assistance in Afghanistan.[34]

High spending on higher education has been a key plot line in most third world success stories. Especially effective have been those countries that have dedicated disproportionate human and material resources to elite institutions. Indian Prime Minister Jawaharlal Nehru, a Cambridge graduate, invested profusely in the elite Indian Institutes of Technology (IITs) during the 1950s, in disregard of widespread jeers that he was wasting money on social elites who already enjoyed too many privileges. His willingness to pony up India's money inspired donors from around the world to chip in. By concentrating funds, talented faculty, and the nation's brightest students at a few places, the IITs developed the human capital that made possible India's recent economic takeoff.[35]

Funding for higher education has also been a valuable means of curbing brain drain. Kuzvinetsa Peter Dzvimbo, a World Bank researcher who has taught at universities in Sierra Leone, Nigeria, Zimbabwe, South Africa, and Mozambique, stresses that promising African youth who want a university education will study in their home country if the local universities are well funded, but will go abroad and perhaps never return if the local universities are too poor to provide a decent learning environment. Well-educated professors will stay in their countries of birth if local universities can afford to pay them good salaries but will seek jobs in other countries if local universities can pay professors no more than clerks, as is true in much of the third world.[36]

In a world of scarce resources, an increase in expenditures on higher education may require a decrease in expenditures on primary and secondary education. Primary and secondary school enrollment rates, and possibly also literacy rates, could stagnate or decline. But such drawbacks will be only short-term problems if spending on higher education fuels long-term improvements in governance and development, as it has in so many countries. Given the hierarchical nature of human activity, it is more important to have a substantial minority with a college education than a large majority with a primary school education.

"The shortage of educated and technically trained cadres of nationals who can devise effective national strategies and policies is a far greater constraint to the alleviation of rural poverty than is the illiteracy or lack of receptivity of the rural population," the World Bank's Uma Lele wrote in an essay on rural Africa.[37] She penned those words in the early 1980s, when African higher education received considerably more funding and African illiteracy rates were considerably higher than today. The subsequent defunding of higher education and rise of literacy has made a shift in emphasis to higher education all the more worthwhile.

Historically, Americans have had few philosophical qualms about the income inequality that is the inevitable result of educating some members of society more than others and allowing the free market to determine salaries. Thomas Jefferson proposed the replacement of hereditary aristocracy with an aristocracy of virtues and talents, a proposition that Americans by and large embraced for the next 150 years. Few Americans begrudged those who earned more than others, convinced that talent and hard work accounted for their higher incomes. They strove to earn more themselves, not to take money away from those who had more.

Only in the twentieth century did significant elements of the American population decide that inequality of outcomes was inherently problematic and worthy of governmental intervention. A disproportionate percentage of those Americans gravitated to the international development world during the late twentieth century, and they retain a large presence in the early twenty-first. Their sentiments are shared by many development officials from other nations, especially European nations with traditions of strong state intervention in economic matters. Pronouncements on the need to redistribute wealth that one would not find in mainstream American politics are commonplace in the world of international development. "Inequality per se is an obstacle on the road to human development," stated a 2010 report by the UN Development Program. "The reduction of inequality should form an explicit part of the public agenda."[38]

Critics of Jefferson's aristocracy of virtues and talents assert that it is premised on an ideal of equal opportunity that no society has fully realized in practice. In the case of higher education, they point out, the children of socioeconomic elites are disproportionately represented at institutions of higher education, most markedly in the third world but also in highly advanced democracies. Elite parents have money and connections that give their children large advantages over other children in gaining entrance to universities.[39] For radical egalitarians, the solution is to eliminate, or at least reduce, the disparities in educational opportunities available to the rich and the poor, through regulations that make it easier for the poor to gain admission to universities and through funding of their education with state revenues or tuition paid by wealthy students.

There is no denying that the children of poor families the world over are less likely to attend college than the children of elites. But that fact cannot be altered without discarding the principle that virtue and talent should be rewarded, a principle that most Americans still wish to retain. In liberal democracies, social and economic elites generally possess above-average intelligence, for superior intelligence is required to obtain most of the high-paying jobs. These elites transmit their superior intelligence to their children genetically, ensuring that those children will have a higher probability than other children of gaining admittance to colleges.[40]

Thus, if a government or university wishes to boost the enrollment of the lower socioeconomic classes it will have to give them highly preferential treatment in admissions or eliminate selective admissions altogether. Either of those methods will not only lower the quality of the educational environment but also induce the elites to send their children elsewhere for higher education, quite possibly to another country from which they will never return. A massive, wealthy country like the United States can withstand a certain amount of this social engineering, but for a poor country the results can spell devastation for human capital development.

This is not to say that no efforts should be made to facilitate higher education for students from low-income families. Scholarships for virtuous and talented students are an excellent means of expanding a nation's pool of human capital, as the contributions of millions of American scholarship recipients to the public and private sectors attest. In countries where cultural attitudes or lack of funds have prevented their use in the past, scholarships offer prime opportunities for foreign donors seeking to make a difference. Scholarships for the poor to attend college are especially valuable in countries with disfranchised ethnic minorities or insurgent groups that need to be reconciled with the mainstream society, as they can move human capital toward the government side and away from sources of instability.

The case against income inequality has been dealt mortal injuries by the recent economic successes of China and other rising economic powers like India, Chile, and Brazil. As the elites have gained in skills and wealth, their countries have experienced economic growth as well as higher incomes for all social strata. Rapid economic growth has lifted all boats, to use John F. Kennedy's phrase, even if the big boats have usually been lifted higher than the small ones.

These recent economic triumphs have shown that governmental efforts to eliminate inequality are often a greater impediment to general prosperity than inequality is. China's economy stagnated from 1949 to 1978 under Communist economic policies that prevented individuals from accumulating large amounts of personal wealth, leaving China an economic weakling with a GNP smaller than Spain's. After Deng Xiaoping's introduction of capitalist reforms in 1978, Chinese private investment soared and so did income for the most capable members of the work force, both of which caused spectacular economic growth and rising income inequality. China's per capita GDP annualized growth rate increased from 2.23 percent in the Maoist era to 6.57 percent during the next twenty-five years.[41]

India, which after independence from Britain languished for several decades under the egalitarian policies of high taxation on the wealthy and state control of industry, has experienced a similar boom since the abandonment of statist economic egalitarianism in the 1980s. During the first decades of independence, per capita GDP grew at a rate of 1.4 percent per year, whereas in the twenty-five years following the economic liberalization of the early 1980s, it grew at an annualized rate of 3.6 percent.[42]

These developments have also shattered a longstanding belief in the development community that poverty alleviation does not require economic growth. According to World Bank estimates, the economic growth in China and India after 1980 cut the percentage of the world population living in extreme poverty from 40 percent to 20 percent.[43] The leading development experts at all points on the political spectrum now accept that any country wishing to raise the living standards of its entire society must experience robust economic growth.[44] They are also in general agreement that economic growth requires capitalism – which leads inescapably to the conclusion that poverty alleviation requires capitalism and the inequality that goes with it.

FAITH AND HIGHER EDUCATION

Faith-based colleges and universities rank among the most prestigious institutions of higher learning in many third world countries. Owing to their overarching moral mission, faith-based colleges and universities spend more time than their secular counterparts on the moral education of students. In countries rife with corruption or violence, these institutions may be the best places to cultivate leaders who can remove political and cultural toxins from society. Kenya's Daystar University, a nondenominational Christian university with 4,400 students, is one of many African Christian universities that aspire to fulfill this purpose. Daystar strives to "educate Christ-centered servant leaders to transform Africa," according to its mission statement, which is similar to those of most of its peer institutions. Daniel Wesonga, the former Vice-Chancellor of Daystar, explains that Africans must make moral development central to higher education if they wish to avoid the morass of corruption. "Education without character does not produce a leader in Africa," Wesonga asserts. "It is like educating a thief, which only makes one an educated thief."[45]

Very similar comments can be heard from African Muslims. "Reliance on the provision of only secular education will not do," says Amadou Cissé, former prime minister of Niger. "It needs to be combined with religious education aimed at raising the moral caliber of the people." Cissé asserts that religious education is required to increase "honesty, integrity, fulfillment of promises and contracts, punctuality, and conscientiousness," and to improve work ethic, the lack of which has impeded economic production in Niger and other Islamic countries.[46]

Western support to faith-based higher education in the non-Western world has a long and distinguished history. Most of the American assistance to faith-based colleges and universities has come from private religious organizations rather than the U.S. government. American missionaries have participated in the founding of a host of Christian universities in the third world, such as the American University in Cairo, the American University of Beirut, Universidad Mariano Gálvez de Guatemala, Fu Jen University, Yonsei University, and Cuttington University.[47] USAID and other governmental donors have provided some assistance to these universities, but since the late 1970s the low prioritization of higher education has rendered the amounts exceedingly small.

Another valuable faith-based means of bolstering higher education, at both religious and secular institutions, is the support of religious student organizations. The YMCA, YWCA, and American churches supported student groups that helped develop pro-American, prodemocratic, and anti-Communist leaders during the Cold War. In the 1950s and 1960s, their financial and educational assistance bolstered South Korean Christian student organizations that became major participants in the democracy movement that ultimately democratized South Korea. These student organizations also spurred South Korea's wave of Christian conversion, which increased the number of South Korean Christians from three hundred thousand in 1945 to 4.3 million in 1974.[48]

EXTREMISM AND HIGHER EDUCATION

One of the most interesting findings of the recent research on extremism is the remarkable similarity of educational backgrounds among Islamic terrorists. Most of the 9/11 hijackers and most of the other leading figures of Islamic terrorism attended universities in their home countries or in the West, and nearly all studied engineering or other scientific fields. A large fraction underwent radicalization during their university experience, under the guidance of Muslim student organizations.

Why are science majors much more likely to become extremists than other students? One reason, most experts agree, is that individuals who opt for the sciences have a strong preference for black-and-white answers over ambiguity. That preference receives reinforcement when higher education is restricted to the study of universal laws of nature and quantitative problem solving, as is the case at the numerous non-Western universities where liberal arts courses are purely optional, if they exist at all. Those third world universities that do require science majors to take liberal arts courses or other courses of a non-scientific nature often teach the material in a dogmatic fashion that requires only recitation of what the teacher said rather than the independent analysis of competing ideas characteristic of traditional Western education. In the past few decades, moreover, Islamists have gained influence at the universities of countries such as Egypt, Algeria, and Sudan, and have used their clout to stifle free inquiry and debate in the name of religious purity.[49]

"Engineers don't exercise their fantasy and imagination," observes Khalid Duran, a Pakistani expert in Islamic law. "Everything is precise and mathematical. They don't study what we call 'the humanities.' Consequently, when it comes to issues that involve religion and personal emotion, they tend to see things in very stark terms." Duran points out that the Muslim Brotherhood's efforts to recruit students in the humanities have been abject failures. "Having an education in literature or politics or sociology seems to inoculate you against the appeals of fundamentalism," he concludes.[50]

When taught in the pluralistic manner of the Western tradition, courses in the humanities show that religious and political matters do not lend themselves to the easy certitude of scientific analysis. They can dispel hostile caricatures of foreign civilizations by providing exposure to the best achievements that those civilizations have to offer. Abdurrahman Wahid, the first democratically elected president of Indonesia, was attracted to the writings of the radical Islamist Said Qutb as a youth, but he was drawn in a very different direction by reading Aristotle. "If I hadn't read the Nichomachean Ethics as a young man, I might have joined the Muslim Brotherhood," he remembered. As Indonesia's president, Wahid promoted religious tolerance and denounced militant Islamists in his country who sought to fan the fires of religious conflict.[51]

Scholars such as Kumar Ramakrishna and Malise Ruthven have advocated compulsory courses in the liberal arts for students concentrating in the sciences, which seems a highly sensible remedy.[52] USAID and other international development actors, however, have made no effort to promote that outcome. Nor have they pursued other measures in third world higher education that could curb extremism, such as supporting faculty, academic centers, and student groups that offer moderate religious or ideological alternatives. Of the scant foreign assistance that has been provided for higher education reform during the past decade, most has been dedicated to science, technology, and other areas that are relevant primarily to the private sector.[53]

Supporting moderates at universities is a valuable measure that can and should be employed not just in Islamic countries but across the globe, for various forms of extremism still prevail at universities throughout the world. Many third world universities are replete with Marxism-Leninism, dependency theory, and other forms of anticapitalist and anti-Western radicalism that are inimical to development and good governance. "Visiting a Latin American university campus is like traveling to the past, to an era in which the Berlin Wall had yet to fall and Russia and China had yet to embrace capitalism," Oscar Arias, the former president of Costa Rica, remarked in 2011. "Instead of giving students practical tools – such as technological and language skills – to help them succeed in a globalized world, many schools devote themselves to teaching authors no one reads and repeating doctrines in which no one believes."[54]

MILITARY AND POLICE ACADEMIES

Most of the third world's armed forces and police forces have academies where they educate some or all of their officers. Because these schools bring together future national leaders at a formative age, they can have an extraordinary long-term impact on the culture and capabilities of the security forces and the government more broadly. Yet in practice the academies often fail to capitalize on this advantage, and their foreign friends sometimes do too little assist them, especially in the case of police academies.

El Salvador's military academy was in a sorry state when the Salvadoran insurgency erupted in 1980. Dubbed the Captain General Gerardo Barrios Military School after a Salvadoran officer who had ousted the American adventurer William Walker from Nicaragua's presidency in 1857, the academy was housed in a few old cement buildings that could have been mistaken for industrial warehouses. The academy's instructors taught mainly by reciting facts for the cadets to memorize and regurgitate. Physical fitness received priority over fitness of the mind; cadets who struggled with squat jumps flunked out, whereas those who struggled with arithmetic stayed in. The academy taught cadets to be loyal to the officer corps above all else, perpetuating an organizational culture in which officers avoided change to prevent conflict with the fathers of the status quo, and refrained from punishing one another for crimes all the way up to murder. Not surprisingly, the officers who graduated from the academy fared very poorly when thrust onto the battlefield against cunning insurgent leaders who had learned to think for themselves at El Salvador's civilian universities.

The American advisory mission in El Salvador identified the inferior educational practices at the Captain General Gerardo Barrios Military School as a major reason for the pathetic condition of the Salvadoran armed forces. At the time, concerns about getting sucked into another Vietnam restricted the number of U.S. military advisers in the country to fifty-five, severely constraining their ability to change educational programs inside the country. The U.S. Department of Defense therefore decided to send Salvadoran cadets to Fort Benning, Georgia, where they could receive education from unlimited numbers of American officers at either the School of the Americas or the U.S. Army Infantry School. By stressing independent thinking instead of rote memorization, and by explaining the hows and whys of U.S. military leadership, the American instructors transformed the minds of an entire generation of Salvadoran officers. By the end of the decade, the graduates of Fort Benning were the driving force on the ground as the Salvadoran security forces reversed the momentum of the insurgency.[55]

Another solution that the United States has employed to overcome inferior military and police academies in the third world is to educate and train security forces on the job. In the Philippines, the U.S. government has been trying for years to provide instruction at the Philippine National Police Academy, but has found minimal receptivity to its offers of help. In 2012, the Justice Department's International Criminal Investigative Training Assistance Program (ICITAP) received permission for the first time to teach a course to the cadets, but it was just a one-day course. To get around this problem, ICITAP has focused its efforts on education and training for police officers after they graduate, since ICITAP does not face significant constraints in working with police officers once they have been assigned to duty in the field.

The best solution, possible in the select cases where large numbers of foreign advisers are available and the indigenous government tolerates heavy foreign involvement, is to improve the quality of the academies within the third world.

In some countries, it has involved building new academies from the ground up. During the past twenty-five years, the United States has established and, for at least a few years, managed police academies in Panama, Haiti, Bosnia, and Kosovo. The introduction of American trainers and American curricula did much to professionalize the police and curb abuses of power.[56]

Among the most impressive of the academies developed with extensive American participation is the National Military Academy of Afghanistan. Assisted by West Point professors, the academy adopted an admissions process comparable in rigor to those employed at the U.S. military academies. With huge numbers of Afghan high school students applying each year, the academy has been able to select an extraordinarily talented cohort of cadets. The curriculum has also been patterned after U.S. academies and is taught by a combination of American and Afghan faculty. Graduates from the military academy became a prized commodity across the Afghan government, deemed much more capable than civil servants and older military officers.[57]

CONCLUSION

Assistance to higher education is among the most valuable forms of assistance that the first world can provide to the third world. It is especially advantageous in poorly governed states, for corrupt governments typically find it harder to steal from universities, even public ones, than from most public treasure chests. In such nations, moreover, universities can serve as safe havens for virtuous political elites who may one day find their way into the government.

Having underestimated the importance of elites to development, governance, and security, the U.S. government and other foreign donors committed a huge error in slashing support to higher education in the late 1970s and have yet to mend their ways. The United States should restore support to third world higher education to the levels of the 1950s and 1960s, with priority given to elite universities and specific programs of direct relevance to governance. Money will not solve all the problems, but it can attract better faculty and students and enable professors to devote all their energies to teaching instead of moonlighting as bartenders or car salesmen. In the security sector, the United States needs to boost support to police and military academies in needy countries.

Involvement in faith-based education is, at all levels, important not only to build human capital but also to combat extremism. Faith-based schools are usually more efficient than public schools, because their teachers generally do more for less and their finances are most often beyond the reach of venal politicians. The United States should continue its existing funding for faith-based education in the third world and pursue new opportunities to support faith-based schools. It should also promote the teaching of the liberal arts and courses on religious moderation to all students, to weaken support for extremism in the sciences.

9

Education in the United States

Nearly all citizens of third world countries attend primary and secondary schools in their country of birth. A substantial minority of them, however, go on to attend institutions of higher learning in the first world for undergraduate or graduate studies. Since colonial times, educational odysseys to Western universities have profoundly influenced non-Western societies. Education at first world universities has often imparted valuable practical knowledge, but its most momentous effects, in centuries past as well as the current century, have been felt in the realm of civilization.

THE EUROPEAN EXPERIENCE

A historical examination of most any Asian or African nation will reveal that some of its elites underwent Westernization during the age of European imperialism. It will also show that during the same period, the nation's elites engaged in protracted debates over the extent to which they should Westernize. The fact of conquest itself contributed to desires to Westernize; with so many nations having been vanquished by European imperialists, it was natural for the conquered, and for bystanders in countries that escaped colonization like Thailand and Japan, to seek understanding into why the West had become so powerful and how others could acquire that same power. Training and education provided by Westerners in the colonies did much to encourage Westernization, for the reasons described in the two preceding chapters. The most potent instrument of Westernization, though, was the education of indigenous elites at Western universities.

During the age of empire, Oxford, the École Normale Supérieure, and the University of Amsterdam admitted students from the colonies and provided them the same education as English, French, and Dutch youth. European governments and universities often provided scholarships to those students. Like most of the colonial activities of European empires, these initiatives arose from a mixture of motives. Some European imperialists were concerned exclusively with extracting resources from colonies, whether for military or economic reasons, and viewed inculcation of Western work habits and admiration for the West into indigenous governing classes as an efficient means of facilitating the extraction. When the people of Senegal or Java submitted to European authority, Senegalese or Javanese administrators were cheaper to sustain than European ones, and were less likely to perish from local diseases. Other European imperialists were deeply concerned about bettering the material and moral conditions of the indigenous populations, and viewed the Westernization of the elites as central to that mission. Recipients of European educations, it was believed, could provide the political and economic leadership required for material progress, and some of them could become preachers of the Christian faith.

As it turned out, the education of colonized peoples succeeded in Westernizing individuals and elite societies with a potency that surprised even diehard cultural imperialists. Scions of Kenya, Indochina, the West Indies, and a great many other countries discarded traditional ideas and embraced Western individualism and rationalism. Taking up interest in Shakespeare and Rousseau, they often came to see their own societies as culturally backward. Students from colonies whose societies did not firmly oppose religious proselytization converted to Christianity with considerable frequency. Those from Hindu societies, where conversion to Christianity usually resulted in social ostracization, and those from Muslim societies, where conversion could be punishable by death, were a good deal less likely to convert, though some still did. In addition, a number of students embraced the secular cosmopolitanism of liberal European peers, becoming what Samuel Huntington later called "Davos Men," after the annual gathering of the World Economic Forum in the alpine resort of Davos – individuals who dismissed civilization and nationality as passé and occupied themselves mainly with the cosmopolitan classes of other nations.

While some of the students embraced Western ways wholeheartedly, others absorbed selected elements of Western civilization, such as its scientific methods and its system of law, while retaining core cultural or religious elements of their own civilization. These individuals were to provide much of the leadership for the independence movements of the twentieth century. By embracing major parts of their native civilization, they were able to mobilize their countrymen more effectively than those who had shed their civilization completely.

By the design of the imperialists, a large number of the third world natives who attended European universities entered the civil services in their native country after graduation. Over time, European education gave most colonies a cadre of efficient and skilled civil servants who could administer the major cities and strategic infrastructure, though not usually the whole national territory. Only a minority of the colonies, such as India and Mauritius, were able to maintain professional civil services on their own after independence. In the postcolonial era, the most farsighted of the former colonies, like Malaysia,

Oman, and Botswana, recognized the value of European tutelage and continued the education of their governing classes by Europeans, either in Europe or in their home country, much to their advantage. Those that repudiated Europe and the members of their own societies who had been educated in Europe usually ended up with bad governance and economic stagnation.

POSTCOLONIAL WESTERNIZATION

After the ropes of imperialism were severed in the mid-twentieth century, the upper classes of many third world countries continued to send their children to Western universities. A smaller number of children from the third world went to the Soviet Union or Eastern Europe for higher education during the decades of Marxist-Leninist dictatorship. After the collapse of Soviet Communism, Eastern Europeans and their former third world allies joined the rest of the world in sending students to Princeton and Cambridge.

In the postcolonial era, the education of third world elites in the first world has continued to shape courthouses, medical facilities, and engineering firms in Dar es Salaam, Dhaka, Asunción, and countless other cities. Westernized elites in a few postcolonial countries have pursued sweeping cultural changes, derived heavily from Western models. The most successful have been those who held dictatorial powers and used them to overcome resistance from tradition-minded elites, such as in Singapore, which has remained autocratic, and Chile, which has evolved into a democracy. Others have provided enlightened leadership that has held society's worst tendencies in check. King Abdullah II of Jordan, a product of Deerfield Academy, Sandhurst, Oxford, and Georgetown, has managed to keep a lid on the virulently anti-American and anti-Israeli sentiments of his subjects, the majority of whom are Palestinian refugees or their descendants.

As in colonial times, many of the Western-educated elites in the postcolonial third world do not accept Western civilization in its totality. In India, democracy and capitalism have thrived among an elite class that has embraced some of the ways of the West but has retained the Hindu religion and core cultural elements of Hindu civilization. In Taiwan, the recent adoption of capitalism, democracy, and Christianity has not displaced the cultural preferences for the community over the individual. In a number of countries, elites with degrees from top Western universities have chosen to cling to harmful cultural traditions, such as the overwhelming fealty to family that caused Western-educated leaders like Pakistan's Benazir Bhutto, Mexico's Carlos Salinas, and Kenya's Mwai Kibaki to indulge in massive embezzlement of public funds.

THIRD WORLD STUDENTS IN THE UNITED STATES

Since the dawning of the Cold War, the United States has been by far the most popular destination for third world students seeking to study abroad. The total number of foreign students attending American colleges and universities reached 723,277 in 2011, representing an increase of 32 percent from just a decade earlier.[1] The foremost reason for the gravitation of students to American universities is quality. Of the two main global rankings of higher education, one includes thirty-eight American universities in the world's top fifty universities, and the other includes twenty-one.[2]

Resource advantages contribute heavily to the superiority of American colleges and universities. In the United States, higher education receives a total of 3.3 percent of GDP from all sources, public and private, whereas America's nearest competitor, the European Union, allocates only 1.3 percent of GDP to higher education. U.S. spending comes out to $54,000 per student, versus $13,500 in the European Union.[3]

The United States also owes some of its edge to the concentration of human and material resources at elite institutions. During the Cold War, egalitarian politicians in continental Europe obstructed such concentrations, prohibiting selective admissions policies and higher faculty salaries for top researchers. They turned formerly great universities like Göttingen and L'Université de Paris into mediocrities. Although some European governments have recently begun initiatives to restore their elite universities by apportioning them high shares of talent and funds, the most renowned universities of continental Europe remain uncompetitive with the likes of Yale and Duke.

From the 1950s to the 1980s, American universities accumulated an impressive record of transforming foreign elites who went on to implement dramatic cultural and political change in their home countries. The conversion of Chile's economy from stagnant statism to flourishing capitalism during the Presidency of Augusto Pinochet was inspired by the so-called "Chicago Boys," economists at the Catholic University of Chile who had been educated by Milton Friedman and other free-market thinkers at the University of Chicago through an interuniversity partnership arranged by the U.S. government in the 1950s. After Pinochet overthrew the Marxist government of Salvador Allende in 1973, he appointed the Chicago Boys to top positions in the Chilean government, where they used their free-market ideas to craft new policies. They privatized state-owned enterprises, cut onerous governmental regulations, provided financial incentives to entrepreneurs, and curtailed the privileges of organized labor. Within the halls of the Catholic University, the Chicago Boys educated a new entrepreneurial class, which provided the private sector human capital required for rapid economic growth.[4]

During the 1970s, Taiwanese with degrees from prestigious American universities led a reform movement that pressured Taiwan's government into economic liberalization and merit-based human resource practices.[5] They also had a large hand in the economic advances and democratization of the 1980s and early 1990s. When the Cold War ended, American-educated technocrats made up twelve of the twenty-one ministers in the Taiwanese cabinet.[6]

A study of USAID scholarship programs for African students from 1963 to 2003 concluded that cultural transformation was the most significant result of the programs. Based on survey responses from 203 African scholarship recipients who had studied in the United States during the period, the authors observed that "participants pointed to changes in their ability to think critically, design research projects correctly, and analyze objectively as more than or as important as the specific technical knowledge they gained in the United States." Respondents asserted, in addition, that their educational experiences in the United States revolutionized their work ethic. "Many participants developed a strong commitment for their work during their graduate studies and credit this aspect as key to their ability to implement change," the authors reported. Some respondents remarked that their time in the United States improved their management abilities, even though most of them did not receive any formal instruction in management.[7]

SCHOLARSHIPS

During the Cold War, USAID scholarship programs brought close to twenty thousand foreign students to American universities each year. Most of the recipients were government employees who attended graduate school in fields related to their career specialization, while a smaller number were up-and-coming academics who pursued advanced studies in subjects of relevance to governance or development, which they would then teach at universities in their native countries. Individual U.S. universities often had special relationships with particular foreign countries or universities, admitting large numbers of students from that country or university and sending their faculties in the summer to provide additional instruction.

Numerous USAID officers were to conclude that these scholarship programs were the most effective programs in the history of USAID. Surveys of recipients determined that most deemed their education in the United States highly valuable, and that upon returning home most of them applied what they had learned and taught it to others.[8] Substantial numbers of recipients eventually became senior leaders in the government. In 2006, for example, close to 40 percent of Indonesia's cabinet ministers held degrees from U.S. universities because of USAID scholarships received in the 1970s and 1980s.[9]

During the last two decades of the twentieth century, the number of USAID scholarship recipients plummeted, falling below one thousand in the early twenty-first century, where it has since languished. The development community's general loss of interest in higher education stood among of the leading causes of the decline. The White House Office of Management and Budget used its influence to help sink the program based on its view that the program took too long to achieve results and that those results could not be plugged into cost-benefit analyses because they could not be put into dollars.[10] The perception that scholarship recipients were mainly the children of foreign elites also contributed to the drop in support, even though most recipients actually came from the middle class, which accounted for the bulk of government bureaucrats in nearly all recipient countries.

Another erroneous claim that led to the defunding of scholarships held that many recipients did not become leaders in their native countries but instead ended up working at NGOs or private firms in the United States. This idea arose from the conflation of foreigners who came to the United States on USAID scholarships with the rest of the foreign student population. Most recipients of USAID scholarships actually did return home and serve in the government of their native country. USAID awarded most scholarships to individuals who had already served in government for several years, thereby demonstrating their capabilities and their commitment to public service. In addition, the U.S. government pressed the governments of scholarship recipients to ensure that they provided appropriate jobs to returning graduates, knowing that the few scholarship recipients who did not return home were motivated mainly by the lack of a job in their home government.[11]

The severe contraction of the USAID scholarship programs never drew much attention in the United States, but for American development experts and foreign governments it has been heart rending. Several years ago, at a U.S. Senate hearing on overseas operations, Senator Robert F. Bennett of Utah recounted the despair of a foreign finance minister, whose country he did not name because of political sensitivities, at the disappearance of the scholarships.

"What do you need the most?" Bennett had asked the finance minister over dinner.

"I need 15 people I can trust," replied the minister, who was an economist with a Ph.D. from one of America's top universities. "I preside over a bureaucracy that has about 50,000 people. And this is a country where the government is the employer of last resort. I could fire every one of them if I had 15 people I could trust and I keep trying to get AID to pay for scholarships." All his requests to USAID to fund scholarships had been rebuffed. "If I could get 15 young people to come back with Ph.D.s from legitimate American universities," the minister said ruefully, "I could run my whole bureaucracy and fire the other 50,000."[12]

The Ford Foundation, the Rockefeller Foundation, and other U.S. foundations also downsized their scholarship programs in the last decades of the twentieth century. In 2001, the Ford Foundation started a new international scholarship program, but one that differed in key respects from earlier programs. Aimed at members of racial and ethnic minorities and other marginalized populations, it sought to prepare recipients for furthering the cause of "social justice," a term connoting egalitarian political activities that can undermine economic growth when taken too far. The Ford Foundation's website stated that "80% of alumni report positive social justice impacts from their work" and that the alumni "remain committed to social justice causes in areas such as education, community development, environmental issues and children, youth and family." The program was terminated after its initial ten-year funding package expired, and no scholarship program took its place.[13]

The divestiture of USAID and the big foundations from the scholarship business has left the Fulbright program as the principal U.S. program for funding study by foreigners at American universities. In 2010, the Fulbright program provided scholarships to 3,763 foreign students, 962 foreign scholars, and 203 foreign professionals. Although the program purports to develop future leaders, its scholarships are not targeted specifically at individuals with governmental experience or aspirations as USAID's scholarships were. The Fulbright program's 2011 annual report is instructive, highlighting numerous recipients whose interests and specializations had little or nothing to do with public-sector leadership. Among them were a South African singer, an astronomer from Chile, and a doctoral student who was writing his dissertation on juvenile southern right whales in Patagonia. Even among the 203 professionals, who were supposed to be selected from fields "critical to U.S. relations with developing and transitioning countries," some did not appear to be budding governmental leaders. The list of professionals included a Chinese geriatric physician and a Panamanian conservationist.[14]

VISA POLICIES

Foreigners seeking to study in the United States by means other than a U.S. government scholarship must apply for a visa. Once relatively routine, education visas came under enormous scrutiny following the 9/11 attacks. Concerns about terrorist infiltration, particularly from countries with histories of producing Islamic terrorists, resulted in long waiting periods and low acceptance rates, keeping away large numbers of students who would otherwise have studied in the United States.

In the atmosphere of fear that prevailed after 9/11, the government's exceptional caution was understandable, and to some extent warranted. Many of the 9/11 hijackers had studied in the West, and a terrorist organization seeking to hijack more aircraft would be hard pressed to find a better recruit than a smart eighteen-year-old male with a visa for entering the United States. Nevertheless, the diminution in the number of students coming to the United States had costs that may have outweighed the benefits in the end. Instead of studying in the United States, where they would quite possibly have become strongly pro-American, young Saudis and Pakistanis went to universities near their homes where they were likely to receive highly negative depictions of the United States from anti-American professors and students.

The visa rejection rate diminished toward the end of the Bush presidency. Saudi Arabia, which had experienced an especially sharp drop after 9/11, convinced the Bush administration to grant more visas to Saudis than ever before. In 2005, Saudi King Abdullah began paying for huge numbers of Saudis to study in the United States and other Western countries, in the belief that his people needed education in the West to prepare for the day when they could no longer live on oil revenues. By 2012, Saudi Arabia was sending sixty-six thousand students to American universities per year, four times the pre-9/11 total.[15] Chances are good that some of them will be Saudi cabinet ministers in the 2040s, which should work to the advantage of Saudi Arabia, the United States, and most of the world's other nations.

RETURNING HOME

The successes of USAID's scholarships notwithstanding, large numbers of foreign students who come to the United States on other scholarships or pay their own way choose to stay in the United States after completing their studies, and their choices have serious adverse consequences for a great many other people. The U.S. government is a major contributor to the problem, because it gives foreign graduates of American universities preference in residency requests, via the annual distribution of 140,000 green cards to individuals based on educational attainment and job skills.[16] Proponents of this green card program argue that the immigration of skilled foreign workers is crucial to American prosperity, as evidenced by the contributions of highly skilled foreigners at American universities and private companies.[17]

Providing green cards for skilled workers might seem a good way to help people of other nations, but it is a distinctly bad way when it comes to all the people of other nations. The biochemists and lawyers from poor countries who stay in Boston and San Francisco after receiving American degrees will benefit personally from their decisions to stay, but they will harm most of the people in their native societies, namely, those lacking the means to study in the United States and obtain one of the 140,000 green cards. When the best and brightest depart, third world countries are robbed of the people who would make good legislators, engineers, and cabinet ministers. For this reason, development experts of a multitude of political persuasions have taken a dim view of human capital migrations from the third world to the first. "By draining these countries of their talent," writes Paul Collier, "migration is more likely to make it harder for these nations to decisively escape the trap of bad policy and governance."[18] Joan Dassin of the Ford Foundation notes that the emigration of educated elites deprives poor countries of "citizens who otherwise might play key roles in developing responsive governments and organizing civil society, often resulting in political instability and regional conflict."[19]

By allowing high-quality human capital from third world countries to stay in the United States, Americans imperil those countries and, as Chapter 5 showed, themselves. The United States should therefore curtail the number of green cards awarded to highly educated individuals from struggling countries. By asking them to return home, is the United States compelling them to go somewhere with fewer economic opportunities, fewer political rights, and less personal security? The answer, in many cases, is yes. But the United States does not have a moral obligation to grant them citizenship or permanent residency, except in the small number of cases where their return would result in certain death or in severe retribution for prior assistance to the United States.

Foreign elites, on the other hand, do have a moral obligation to help their own countrymen, even if it may involve hardship and peril. George Washington, Alexander Hamilton, and James Monroe did not flee to France in the 1770s when the British made their lives uncomfortable and dangerous, but instead struggled to bring a better government to their birthplace. The peoples of the third world are justified in demanding the same from their elites.

Supporters of liberal green card distribution contend that the United States will suffer economically if it retains fewer of the foreign physicists, engineers, and medical researchers who are educated at American universities.[20] A reduction in the number of highly capable people in the United States will have some type of economic impact, but it will be very small, especially in comparison with the costs and risks to the United States resulting from human capital deficiencies in foreign countries. A nation of more than 300 million people, many of them highly educated, the United States has enough native-born talent to overcome even a large decline in the importation of foreign human capital. With plentiful opportunities for the talented to acquire critical job skills, America has not suffered from crippling shortages of skilled workers in the past and does not face shortages now, contrary to a recent spate of warnings about worker shortfalls in "STEM" – science, technology, engineering, and mathematics. "The alarms about widespread shortages or shortfalls in the number of U.S. scientists and engineers are quite inconsistent with nearly all available evidence," notes Michael S. Teitelbaum, author of a recent book on the subject of human capital in scientific fields.[21]

Counting upon less wealthy countries to provide the U.S. economy with skilled workers also has serious disadvantages for the U.S. work force. Large increases in the number of foreign STEM workers has led to a lowering of wages in those fields, which in turn has caused native-born Americans to turn away from STEM occupations and instead seek careers in fields with higher wages, such as law and finance. Norman Matloff, a professor of Computer Science at the University of California, Davis, observes, "The stagnant salaries caused by the foreign influx discourage young people from pursuing a career in STEM." Matloff adds that "this internal brain drain might have been justified if the foreign workers were of higher caliber than the Americans," but "this is not the case."[22]

The reduction in the number of U.S. citizens working in STEM fields poses special problems for America's defense industries, for much of their advanced research is classified and thus participation is restricted by law to U.S. citizens. Research directors have often run into trouble while assembling research teams because of shortages of U.S. citizens in certain STEM disciplines. The U.S. government has refused requests to waive the citizenship requirements for classified projects, based on fears that foreign intelligence agencies will use graduate students and postdoctoral researchers to steal American military technology and other national security secrets. China, which sent 76,830 graduate students to U.S. universities in 2010, and Iran, which sent 4,696, are considered to be the most active in exploiting such opportunities.

Despite the quite valid national security concerns, some American professors and administrators have characterized the prohibitions as pernicious intrusion into the business of universities that pride themselves on free inquiry and equal treatment of all students. Several universities, including the University of California and Stanford, have on these grounds refused to accept governmental contracts that limit participation to U.S. citizens. Research that "would restrict access on the part of certain students should not be conducted at universities where our mission is to educate students and disseminate knowledge," explained a Stanford spokeswoman.[23]

At universities that have accepted U.S.-only contracts, the difficulty of finding enough U.S. citizens for projects has led some professors to ignore the rules and administrators to look the other way. Professors have been prosecuted for violation of the rules only in a few egregious cases, like that of University of Tennessee professor J. Reece Roth, who went to prison for using unlicensed students from China and Iran on an Air Force project involving plasma actuators for unmanned aircraft. University officials contacted federal authorities only after Roth disregarded warnings from the university's export control officer and traveled to China with a laptop containing restricted information, some of which he e-mailed to a Chinese student.[24] If American universities cannot be trusted to keep Chinese and Iranian students out of classified high-tech research, then the U.S. government needs to keep Chinese and Iranian students out of high-tech research graduate programs at American universities.

U.S. MILITARY HIGHER EDUCATION

Small numbers of foreign students attend the U.S. Military Academy at West Point, the U.S. Naval Academy, and the U.S. Air Force Academy, receiving bachelor's degrees after four years like the American graduates. Combining the acculturating regimentation of military training with the mind-broadening inquiry of traditional Western education, the academies excel at transforming raw youth into highly capable and motivated leaders. Several foreign graduates of these institutions have become world leaders, including Philippine President Fidel Ramos, Nicaraguan President Anastasio Somoza Debayle, and Costa Rican President José María Figueres. Further evidence of the value of Western military academies can be found in the alumni register of the British military academy at Sandhurst, which includes three of the ablest leaders in the Arab world – Sultan Qaboos bin Said of Oman, Sheikh Hamad bin Khalifa Al-Thani of Qatar, and King Abdullah II of Jordan.

Despite these impressive results, the United States does not admit foreigners into its academies in large numbers. At present, each of the U.S. academies admits approximately fifteen students per year, amounting to just 1 percent of the student body. By comparison, foreign students make up 10 percent of the freshman class at Harvard and 14 percent at Oxford. Increasing the number of foreign students at U.S. military academies would be a very effective and inexpensive way to bolster and influence the leadership of foreign nations.

Most of the foreign military personnel who receive education in the United States attend the professional military schools that American officers attend at various points during their careers. At these schools, international students often make up 10 percent or more of the class. Foreign militaries recognize that these schools provide high-quality instruction and help build relationships with the mighty U.S. military, so they usually send officers who have stood out among their peers and are likely to receive promotions in the future. Not surprisingly, many foreign attendees of America's professional military schools have gone on to hold top positions in their militaries and other parts of their governments.[25] Thirty-five foreign graduates of the U.S. Army War College, for example, have become the chiefs of their armies.[26]

During their military education and training in the United States, foreign officers build friendships with American military officers of similar age and rank, establishing communication links that can be maintained when these officers ascend the organizational ladder. For each country that receives U.S. military training or education, the U.S. embassy produces an annual "Positions of Prominence Report" listing past recipients of U.S. military training or education who are currently in important positions in their country. The report is a valuable map for engaging foreign governments on day-to-day business or, especially, in emergency situations.[27] During the Arab Spring, for instance, links between U.S. military officers and Arab military officers provided critical channels of communication and influence.[28]

The U.S. professional military schools most frequently attended by foreign officers typically offer a mixture of training and education, the latter including everything from history lectures to ethics seminars to meetings with U.S. government leaders. These schools also require foreign students to participate in social and cultural events, some of them organized by exchange program administrators, others arranged informally by U.S. students enrolled in the same educational programs. These educational and social experiences have contributed to the changes in thoughts and values cited in Chapter 6.

Foreign attendance of these schools has helped, as well, to change individual views on political and cultural questions. Carol Atkinson, a retired U.S. Air Force officer who teaches political science at Vanderbilt University, and Derek S. Reveron, a professor at the U.S. Naval War College, have shown that foreign recipients of American professional military education often come away with a much more favorable view of America's democratic political principles. Atkinson and Reveron note that many of these recipients have injected democratic principles into their own political systems after returning home.[29]

In the numerous third world countries where military organizations wield formidable political and cultural influence, military officers who studied in the United States have frequently been lead actors in democratization. In analyzing the impact of U.S. aid to the third world during the Cold War, the British researchers R. D. McKinlay and A. Mughan discovered that the extent of U.S. military aid correlated closely with the advance of liberal democratization in the recipient countries. By contrast, they observed, U.S. economic aid showed little correlation with democratization.[30] Preoccupied with quantitative analysis, McKinlay and Mughan did not delve into the complexities of individual countries and thus did not attempt to answer the question of whether the correlation between military education and democratization was the result of causation. But one need not look far to find numerous examples of foreign military officers who received education in the United States and subsequently became the vanguard of liberal democratization in their countries. Examples include El Salvador's officer corps, which pushed the country's political classes into accepting liberal democracy in the 1980s; the Indonesian generals who enforced democratization following the resignation of Suharto in 1998; and the Arab military leaders who backed democratic movements during the Arab Spring.

The education of foreign military officers in the United States has also improved their perceptions of American culture and society, a particularly valuable achievement in the case of officers whose governments routinely choose whether or not to impose restraints on large anti-Western elements, such as Egypt, Pakistan, and Jordan. A survey of foreign officers who received military education in the United States found that 84 percent reported that the experiences changed their views of the United States, in most cases for the better.[31] Another study showed that first hand exposure to the United States disabused numerous foreign officers of negative impressions of American culture that were widespread in their countries. A military officer from the Middle East recalled that before coming to the United States, he had regarded Americans as lonely and selfish, but his time at an American professional military school convinced him that Americans were "very friendly and open minded to other people and respectful to other attitudes." For another foreign officer, the educational experience in the United States had negated the impression he had received from American movies that "the US was about shooting people in the streets and sex." An Asian military officer who had arrived believing that Americans were arrogant, superficial, materialistic, and exceedingly open about sex came away believing that Americans were patriotic, civic-minded, sincere, and "mostly conservative about sex, especially those who have a daughter."[32]

All of these benefits come at a cost that is miniscule in comparison with the U.S. defense budget. The annual expenses incurred by the United States to put students from 107 nations through the entire International Military Education and Training (IMET) program total less than $100 million per year.[33] That sum is less than the cost of the single American F-15 aircraft that crashed during the bombing of Libya – not to mention a tiny fraction of the costs that Americans have paid at the gas pump because of political instability and insecurity in oil-producing countries, or the costs they have incurred because of the insecurity in Latin America that permits cocaine to pour across the Mexican border.

U.S. CIVIL INSTITUTIONS

While civil agencies cannot change culture through training to the same extent that militaries do, they can come close to the military when it comes to education, for education at the military's professional schools is not fundamentally different from civilian education. Unfortunately, the civil agencies of the U.S. government are not providing education to foreigners in any significant numbers. They do not possess equivalents of the Department of Defense's professional schools, to which foreign leaders could be brought for extended periods of education. Unlike many countries with highly centralized governments, the United States lacks a national civil service school and a national police academy, two types of institutions that would be ideally suited to the purpose. The State Department's main professional school, the Foreign Service Institute, is focused on preparing Americans for diplomatic service abroad – it can teach Foreign Service Officers how to negotiate with a foreign diplomat or how to handle a sexual harassment complaint, but not how to run a governmental ministry or prosecute a corrupt police chief. The senior State Department leadership does not value the Foreign Service Institute as highly as the military leadership values its institutions of training and education, and consequently the school does not receive the human and material resources that it deserves.[34]

An alternative concept for building America's educational capacity for civil governance surfaced in 2007, when a bipartisan movement came to Capitol Hill with a plan to create a civilian equivalent of West Point. Like the military academies, it would employ a rigorous screening process to pick an elite cadre of students and would provide four years of free education in return for a commitment to serve in government for at least five years, with graduates choosing to serve at the national, state, or local level. The school would offer courses on traditional liberal arts subjects as well as civic education, foreign languages, foreign cultures, and communications.[35]

The proposal obtained the backing of prominent individuals across the political spectrum, from Sandra Day O'Connor and Mike Huckabee to Madeleine Albright and Hillary Clinton. A bill to create the academy received 123 cosponsors in the House and twenty-four cosponsors in the Senate.[36] The recession of 2008, however, led to its shelving, and as yet it has not been taken back off the shelf.

THE DECLINING CORE

The intellectual trends of the past five decades have diluted the export value of American higher education, even at military and religious universities that are commonly believed to be bedrocks of Western tradition. Fifty years ago, most American universities required all undergraduates to take a course in the history of Western civilization or familiarized them with Western civilization through other mandatory courses. Graduate students in the humanities and social sciences received large doses of Western civilization through their sem-inars and research projects. Consequently, foreigners who came to study in the United States were certain to receive education in subjects of central importance to culture and politics, like the Western tradition of law, the philosophical origins of individualism, and the U.S. Constitution. They returned home carry-ing new ideas and techniques, which they often applied in their own countries.

Today almost no U.S. universities require students to take courses on the basics of Western civilization. Some do not even offer them. The inclusion of American history and civic education in the list of graduation requirements has also fallen by the wayside in much of the academic world. America's recent college graduates fare very poorly on tests on the basics of Western civilization and American history, their knowledge barely exceeding that of Americans who never attended college.[37]

At present, most U.S. universities require that students take a certain number of courses in the humanities and social sciences, but they give them a broad array of options, many of which have nothing to do with the West. As the American Council of Trustees and Alumni has documented, it is quite easy for a student to meet all of the humanities and social science requirements without exposure to any of the core principles of Western civilization or its American embodiment. At Yale, for instance, students can fulfill the humanities require-ment with nearly three hundred different classes, including "Mold Making and Casting" and "New York Mambo." At Emory University, 470 different courses satisfy the "History, Society, Cultures" core requirement, including "Gynecology in the Ancient World."[38]

The National Association of Scholars, a Manhattan-based organization that promotes the restoration of traditional principles to American higher educa-tion, chronicled the degeneration of American university curricula in a 2011 report entitled "The Vanishing West." The report attributed the disap-pearance of mandatory courses on Western civilization to both multicultural-ism and the preference of professors to teach the specialized subjects of greatest interest to them.[39] Leading members of the educational establishment accepted the report's identification of multiculturalism and faculty preferences as the principal causes of de-Westernization, but unlike the association they viewed the causes and their effects as positives.[40]

By failing to explain its core principles at its universities, the United States allows pop culture to serve as its spokesperson. For this reason, many of today's foreign exchange students are more likely to equate the West with Hollywood and Lady Gaga than with the Federalist Papers and René Descartes. Foreign students, especially science majors who hail from Muslim countries, are liable to come away from American universities convinced that the West is morally and culturally depraved.

Some university faculty further encourage students to draw negative conclu-sions by criticizing and misrepresenting Western and American traditions. Denunciations of capitalism and the U.S. government incite contempt and deprive students of useful knowledge that can be applied in the real world. While criticism is an essential component of a high-quality education, the one-sided criticism found in some classrooms is detrimental, to foreign and domestic students alike.

The current flaws in American higher education, considerable though they are, are not so potent as to negate all the advantages of bringing foreigners to U.S. universities. Most universities do require students to take some humanities courses of one sort or another, which is considerably better than providing no humanities courses at all, as is the case at some foreign institutions. Oftentimes these courses will provide at least a smattering of classic Western texts. In addition, prolonged exposure to faculty and students, inside and outside the classroom, stands a good chance of engendering respect for the West and sparking cultural borrowing.

CONCLUSION

Education of foreigners in the United States is the most potent weapon in the American arsenal of cultural transformation. All who study in the United States are deeply affected by the experience in one way or another, although not necessarily for the good. Some become thoroughly Westernized, others become partially Westernized and gain respect for the West, while a select element, consisting mainly of science majors who see only the superficial and degenerate aspects of American culture and society, grow in hostility toward the West.

Scholarships for foreign government personnel rank among the most effect-ive foreign assistance programs ever implemented by the U.S. government. Restoring funding for these scholarships should be a top priority. The costs per individual will be high, but the total costs will be very low relative to other line items in the U.S. national security budget, and the return on investment will be enormous. Many of the recipients will go on to serve in high positions in government or disseminate what they have learned to hundreds of others through education, training, and publication. A few of them will end up working at investment banks in New York or at NGOs in London, but we should no more be dissuaded by the certainty of a few misses than the CEO of IBM is dissuaded from developing managerial talent because of the know-ledge that a few mangers will leave the company earlier than the company would like.

Unlike USAID scholarship recipients, the general population of foreign students in the United States has a considerable propensity to stay in the United States after graduation. The U.S. government's willingness to give green cards to large numbers of them yields some short-term benefits for the U.S. economy but is risky to America's economic prosperity and national security in the long term, above all because it robs third world countries of the human capital required to solve grave problems affecting the whole world. The number of green cards for the highly educated should be reduced, with the biggest cuts targeting residents of the third world and scientists from dangerous countries like China and Iran.

The U.S. military should increase the intake of foreign students at West Point, the Naval Academy, and the Air Force Academy, in order to multiply the successes that the U.S. military has already achieved in educating foreign officers. To replicate the military's achievements on the civil side, the Foreign Service Institute should be given additional resources to recruit permanent faculty with expertise in governance, development, and security and to bring foreign civil officials to the school for year-long courses. A civil version of West Point should be created, to educate the future governors and presidents of other countries, as well as future governors and presidents of the United States.

In light of the low costs and high benefits of the International Military Education and Training program, the United States ought to step up the annual throughput. Presently, a collection of high-priority countries receive sufficient slots to ensure major long-term improvements to their military organizations, but many others have only modest numbers of recipients, which may not be enough to effect such changes. As the preposterous Malian coup of March 2012 showed, U.S. interests can sustain a severe setback when a third world military receives too little human capital assistance from the first world.

To convey positive impressions of the West and promote cultural transfer, American colleges and universities should reinstate mandatory courses on core subjects like Western civilization and U.S. history. Groups like the National Association of Scholars and the American Council of Trustees and Alumni have worked with donors to establish new academic centers or departments focused on these subjects, but every private attempt has met fierce resistance from faculty, and consequently their impact has been severely constrained.[41] Governmental action is, therefore, necessary. A few states, including Virginia and Texas, have passed legislation requiring that all students at public universities take American history survey courses. Similar legislation should be enacted to mandate courses in Western Civilization. Given the difficulties and variability at the state level, action at the federal level will likely be required to achieve broad change.[42]

IO

Support

Funding for training and education represents the best use of foreign aid dollars, since they are the most important activities in human capital development. Aid can, however, be used in other ways that bolster the human capital of recipient nations, as this chapter will show. Some are targeted specifically at human capital, while others affect it indirectly. Their effectiveness varies greatly and is heavily dependent on local conditions.

FUNDS TRANSFERS

Donor nations can transfer funds to third world governments through a wide range of financial vehicles, which are distinguished most significantly by their degree of conditionality. Donors impose the fewest conditions on recipients with what the development community calls "budget support" – the depositing of funds directly into the bank accounts of governments for use as those governments see fit. The recent emphasis of development agencies on "local ownership" has increased the amount of aid provided in this manner. But budget support continues to run up against the problem of bad governance. Governmental leaders, as the keepers of the national treasuries, can all too easily divert state monies to palaces, offshore bank accounts, or patronage networks.[1]

Even where theft of public funds is not rampant, the chances of unshackled foreign assistance funds reaching human capital development programs may be low. Human capital is not a high priority for many third world governments, which after all is a leading reason why they are third world governments. Spending on human capital development takes a long time to produce results and is not easy for politicians to advertise in an election season, unlike, say, building health clinics or handing out welfare checks.

In most countries, therefore, foreign donors who wish to ensure that their donations support human capital development must condition the transfer of funds on the allocation of those funds to specific programs. They must be prepared, in addition, to resort to the "tough love" approach of withdrawing funding commitments if the money is not used for the promised purpose. Past corruption scandals have, in fact, convinced many donors to withdraw funds in response to misuse.

Donors face the difficult task of imposing enough restrictions on the use of funds to prevent misuse while leaving enough latitude for the recipient government to take initiative and make adjustments based on its understanding of local conditions, which is almost always better than that of foreign donors. Considerable skill is also required to mitigate the resentment naturally engendered by the use of money to compel changes in someone's behavior. Gifted diplomats, for example, can soften the blow of aid compulsion by using the money primarily as an afterthought to an act of persuasion.

SALARY SUPPORT

Donors have sought to bolster governmental human capital by earmarking aid for the salaries of government employees. Salary increases can help attract and retain talent, particularly in countries where private sector and NGO salaries are much higher than those available in the government. It can also reduce corruption, since the ordinary salaries of government employees in some countries are so low that they have to engage in corruption if they are to feed their families.

Increasing salaries is, however, far from guaranteed to achieve these positive outcomes, and it can lead to negative ones. The public sector employees in some countries are already paid significantly higher than their counterparts in the private sector, except at the top end of the pay scale, and in such countries additional monetary inputs have typically had little impact on personnel quality or behavior. As the case of faith-based schools suggests, getting better results from adequately paid employees in public service jobs may require reliance on appeals to a cause higher than money. In addition, public employee unions that have been effective in acquiring higher salaries for their members have often been just as effective at blocking reforms that would improve performance, such as firing ineffectual personnel or tying salaries to individual performance. From 1990 to 2007, for instance, organized labor convinced the Honduran government to ramp up its spending on the salaries of teachers and administrators, causing education spending to increase from 5 to 8.6 percent of GDP, yet teacher quality and student test scores did not improve, a result that World Bank analysts blamed on union blockage of merit-based reforms.[2]

In other cases, salary support funds have been used mainly to increase the quantity of governmental personnel, oftentimes for the purpose of giving jobs to friends, family, or political supporters of the government's leaders. The third world, indeed, is replete with governments that have diminished governance quality by hiring large numbers of unqualified people for such reasons. Civil service reformers have spent enormous amounts of time trying to cut the dead wood from these patronage-laden bureaucracies, butting up repeatedly against political leaders who have no desire to unclutter the system.[3]

Nor are higher salaries certain to decrease corruption. In some countries, leading public officials are intent on amassing wealth in amounts far beyond the earnings of the most generously paid civil servant, having gone into government to attain the lifestyles of the most well heeled in their societies. In Afghanistan, provincial governors and police chiefs do not aspire to a three-bedroom house and a Honda Civic, but rather to a stucco mansion with marble flooring and stainless steel appliances, a fleet of sport utility vehicles, and a retinue of servants and bodyguards.

Salary support has negative consequences that can and sometimes do outweigh the benefits conferred. Large-scale increases in public sector income spur inflation and reduce the purchasing power of those not fortunate enough to be public-sector employees.[4] Salary subsidization creates a dangerous dependency, exposing the recipient government to the risk of having to slash salaries and lose top workers to the private sector if the foreign support dries up.

To mitigate these problems, salaries have in some instances been supplemented on a more limited scale, with the beneficiaries restricted to the high achievers who are most valuable to the government and most likely to receive large salary offers from outside the government. This approach, however, can sow dissension within the government by arousing envy and scorn among the lower-paid members of the government. Some experts have concluded that selective salary support should be avoided altogether because of such adverse consequences.[5] While the possibility of engendering jealously should be taken into consideration, allowing it to override all else would be unwise. Western governments and commercial enterprises are full of people who are jealous of the higher salaries collected by coworkers and yet the governments and companies still function effectively.

AID CONDITIONALITY

A less direct way of using aid funds to promote human capital development is to condition their disbursement on good governance, writ large. Since the turn of the twenty-first century, first world countries and the World Bank have made many of their grants and loans conditional on good governance in recipient countries, in belated recognition of the importance of governance to development. Since good governance requires good human capital, improvements in governance resulting from external pressure should involve a certain amount of improvement in human capital.[6]

At first, donors made the provision of aid conditional on promises of good governance in the future. They found to their regret that the recipients' readiness to take their money was not matched by preparedness to meet the promises of reform. Nonetheless, donors only infrequently stopped the flow of aid, because of an overriding desire to spend aid or the conviction that withholding aid would hurt the poor in the recipient country.[7]

After the conditioning of aid on future behavior failed a sufficient number of times, donors shifted to aid preconditionality, insisting that recipients fulfill the governance conditions prior to receiving the aid. This principle undergirded the Millennium Challenge Corporation (MCC), which President George W. Bush proposed in 2002 and the U.S. Congress passed into law in 2004. Separated bureaucratically from the State Department and USAID, the MCC distributes five-year grants to countries that have already met specific conditions, most of which concern governance. As of the end of 2010, $2.9 billion had been spent through the program, mostly on high-priority areas in development or governance.[8] Countries that are close to meeting the MCC's conditions but have not fully met them can receive "threshold" grants that provide funding for a few years to improve governance, a feature that has been successful in gaining support for governance reforms from chiefs of state eager to obtain full-blown MCC grants.

Unsurprisingly, conditioning aid on actual improvements has done more to promote good governance than conditioning it on promises of improvements. But aid preconditionality has also had its share of difficulties. Determining whether the recipient has sufficiently improved the quality of governance is a difficult business, since it requires qualitative judgments and is based on information that is far from complete, especially where corruption is concerned.[9] Nations may make impressive improvements in governance without reaching the levels that ensure effective use of development aid. The recipients of MCC grants include a large number of countries that still have very high levels of governmental corruption and other serious governance problems, such as Benin, Honduras, Moldova, Mongolia, Nicaragua, Senegal, and Uganda. Most of the grants to these countries have been targeted at economic development, when the money most likely would have been better spent on governance programs.

While development aid is the type of foreign assistance most commonly conditioned upon good governance, military aid has at times been conditioned on good governance as well, particularly by the United States. Stereotypes of military organizations as chronic sources of human rights abuses, political mischief, and international conflict make military aid particularly attractive as an item to be withheld from uncooperative governments.[10] On occasion, the entire military assistance program has been canceled, though more commonly only certain types of aid have been cut – typically weapons or other implements of violence, rather than "nonlethal" items like communications gear and medical supplies.

Of particular note for the United States is the practice of withholding assistance to specific military units based on past human rights violations. In 1997, the U.S. Congress passed the Leahy Law, which prohibits U.S. funding of any foreign military unit for which there exists "credible evidence that such unit has committed gross violations of human rights." The law's provisions can be waived if the Secretary of State can confirm that the government of the country in question is "taking effective measures to bring the responsible persons to justice."[11] In addition, some types of counterterrorism training are exempt from the Leahy Law's requirements, permitting the U.S. military to continue training in certain countries with poor human rights records.[12]

Despite the exemptions, the Leahy Law has seriously diluted U.S. security assistance programs in a host of countries. Leahy vetters in the State Department, some of whom are predisposed to view third world militaries as predators rather than protectors, have frequently relied on unverified internet accusations as evidence of wrongdoing. The vetting process can take months, delaying assistance programs and increasing the resentment of foreign military officers, who naturally recoil at the thought of awaiting judgment before American bureaucrats in Washington who might know nothing about their country or show no comparable interest in human rights violations by the insurgents or drug traffickers whom they are fighting.

At times, Leahy vetters apply the term "human rights violation" unambiguously to actions that are often morally ambiguous or morally justifiable when viewed in context. They apply human rights standards intended for highly advanced, peaceful societies to third world countries beset by warfare or by criminal violence that approaches guerrilla warfare in intensity. Hence, soldiers who employ lethal force against a drug trafficker's SUV without pulling it over and asking to see a driver's license are considered guilty of a human rights violation, even if the SUV was found to contain six loaded assault rifles and five kilograms of cocaine, and even if eight soldiers were killed the previous month while attempting to pull vehicles over. Policemen who kill an insurgent prisoner are put into the same human rights violator bucket as child rapists, even if that prisoner had murdered the families of police officers and had bribed his way out of jail the last three times he was arrested. As one congressional staffer involved in the vetting process put it, the Leahy Law takes "an axe to complicated situations that should be handled with laser eye surgery detail."[13]

The Leahy Law's critics also decry as counterproductive the withholding of assistance from entire units based on the bad behavior of a single individual. In some cases, that bad behavior occurred years or decades earlier. Such long-term stigmatization can keep large sections of a nation's security forces off limits to U.S. trainers, in addition to exacerbating partner-nation loathing for Leahy vetting. An American military officer responsible for security assistance in much of Africa explained, "In some countries, the Leahy vetting process has disqualified so many units and people that American military advisers have trouble finding anyone to train."[14]

The consequences of collective punishment of units can readily be seen in Guatemala, where the United States badly needs local partners in fighting Mexican drug traffickers and their Guatemalan allies. At present, the U.S. Congress prohibits Guatemala from receiving most types of military aid, including funding to bring foreign military officers to the United States for training and education, on account of human rights violations dating back to the 1970s. This stance allows American Congressmen to congratulate themselves and to claim innocence whenever a Guatemalan soldier misbehaves, but it is bad for the interests of the United States, not to mention those of the Guatemalan people. The training that the Guatemalan military officers would have received in the United States emphasizes respect for human rights, and it has, in general, increased the willingness of foreign officers to heed American recommendations.

Ambassador David Passage, the State Department's Director for Andean Affairs at the dawn of the twenty-first century, stressed the self-defeating nature of the Leahy Law during debates over U.S. assistance to Colombia's armed forces. "Congress still prohibits U.S. assistance and training programs to Colombian police and military units guilty of human rights violations in the past or with human rights violators still in their ranks," Passage asserted in 2000. "A better and more productive approach might be for the United States to insist on training precisely these units. Certainly the response to human rights abuses committed by American police forces (Los Angeles, Chicago, New York City, Washington, DC) has not been to cut off federal training programs and funds but, rather, to increase them."[15] In the case of Colombia, the perceived severity of the threat and the exhortations of individuals like Ambassador Passage led ultimately to some waivers of the Leahy Law, but Colombia has been the exception in this regard rather than the rule.

During Congressional hearings in March 2013, U.S. Special Operations Command commander Admiral William H. McRaven asserted that the Leahy Law was preventing U.S. special operations forces from working with the foreign units that most needed help. "We're getting forced out at a time when we probably need to engage them more than ever before," Admiral McRaven told the House Armed Services Committee.[16] Adam Smith, the committee's ranking Democrat, expressed agreement with the admiral. "The irony of the Leahy amendment," said Smith, was that it barred McRaven's trainers "when you're needed most."[17]

The withholding of military aid has been more effective when it has been based solely on the behavior of a unit's current leader. During the Iraq War, General David Petraeus and Ambassador Ryan Crocker identified Iraqi police units that were complicit in sectarian murders and, if the Iraqi national leadership refused to relieve their commanders, cut off assistance to those units until new commanders were appointed. By this means, Petraeus and Crocker cleaned out numerous malign elements from the police, which contributed greatly to a steep decline in sectarian killings and to the suppression of Iraqi insurgents.[18]

Conditioning aid on specific personnel decisions has also achieved some major successes at the uppermost levels of government, on both the civil and military sides. In 1950, the United States notified Philippine President Elpidio Quirino that he would receive large amounts of aid to fend off the Communist Hukbalahap insurgency if he would replace his uninspired secretary of national defense with a dynamic young Philippine Congressman named

Ramon Magsaysay. Quirino agreed to the deal, forever changing the course of Philippine history. Within a matter of months, Magsaysay's vigorous leadership and purging of weak commanders turned the tide against the insurgency. Magsaysay went on to win election as president of the Philippines.[19]

ANTICORRUPTION PROGRAMS

The rising interest in good governance among first world donors at the start of the twenty-first century led to a profusion of funding for anticorruption initiatives. Some of these initiatives have resided within governments, such as anticorruption commissions and judicial reform programs. Others have been run by "civil society" organizations independent of the government.

The current generation of anticorruption programs has been heavily influenced by the view of Western economists that stopping corruption is a matter of "incentivization." Transplanting concepts from the economic marketplace into the world of governance, these economists contend that government leaders engage in corrupt practices because the benefits exceeds the costs. Therefore, it will cease as soon as detection and punishment of corruption are effective enough to drive the costs higher than the benefits.[20]

Efforts to increase the costs of corruption have achieved some localized successes in curbing corrupt behavior, but by and large the results have been disappointing. The most important reason behind the failure of anticorruption programs based on "incentivization" is the opposition of political leaders. Nearly all anticorruption researchers and practitioners agree that anticorruption efforts, whether inside or outside the government, have consistently failed when they lack the support of the national leadership.[21]

GOVERNMENTAL ANTICORRUPTION PROGRAMS

Anticorruption programs that are established within governments are almost always subject to the influence of top national leaders. When national leaders set up or permit others to set up anticorruption programs, they create the impression that the programs have the power to alter the incentives targeted by economists. Professing to be opponents of corruption, these leaders vow to use the new programs to clean up problems at lower levels of government. Experience has shown, however, that many of these leaders have accepted these programs merely to evade accusations of corruption against their governments and themselves, and have worked feverishly behind the scenes to prevent them from fulfilling their ostensible tasks.

National political leaders have multiple means of obstructing internal anticorruption programs and preventing them from modifying the incentives of government employees. They can block the access of independent auditors to information. Using official or unofficial authority over the judicial system, they can thwart court proceedings against those accused of corruption. In Nigeria, for example, the Economic and Financial Crimes Commission, Nigeria's top anticorruption body, has charged many of the Niger Delta's governors with corruption, but the top political elites have blocked all but a few efforts to convict the accused.[22]

In Afghanistan, President Hamid Karzai repeatedly set up anticorruption commissions under foreign pressure, then put straitjackets on each one. The Anticorruption Unit that he authorized in 2009 investigated two thousand cases, yet every single case against Karzai's close acquaintances was shut down, and only twenty-eight people were convicted in all. Attorneys who vigorously pursued the prosecution of Karzai's friends were taken off the cases and demoted or sent to remote provinces. In response to Karzai's political meddling, the U.S. State Department suspended its training of the Anticorruption Unit and announced that the training program would not resume until anticorruption "is taken seriously" by the Karzai government.[23]

The international community ran into similar frustrations when it urged Karzai to institute meritocracy in governmental hiring. Karzai agreed to use standardized tests to determine job eligibility, but then allowed his relatives, tribesmen, political supporters, and other preferred candidates to receive the test answers in advance. At foreign insistence, Karzai established personnel boards that were supposed to make appointments by consensus agreement, but then he restricted the frequency of their meetings and made numerous appointments of personnel without going through the boards.[24]

The internal anticorruption programs that have achieved success invariably enjoyed the support of the national leadership, and in most cases they needed very strong and active support to overcome the resistance of bureaucrats or local officials who were profiting from the corruption. An excellent example of top-level support for anticorruption initiatives comes from the International Commission against Impunity in Guatemala (Comision Internacional contra la Impunidad en Guatemala, or CICIG). Assisted by experts from twenty-five foreign countries, the CICIG is home to highly motivated Guatemalan law enforcement officials who have been trained in wiretapping, polygraphing, and other state-of-the-art techniques. Its policemen have gathered information on important governmental figures suspected of corruption and placed them under arrest after amassing sufficient evidence. Its prosecutors have taken the accused to court, breaking a long tradition in which the powerful had ridden roughshod over the rest of society with impunity. Crucial to the CICIG's success has been the honest and aggressive leadership of attorney general Claudia Paz y Paz and the backing she received from President Otto Perez Molina.[25]

Numerous financial management reforms supported by the Millennium Challenge Corporation, USAID, World Bank, and International Monetary Fund have helped stem corruption in countries where the political leadership has stood behind them. A case in point is the Philippines, where Benigno Aquino III has worked closely with foreign partners to implement anticorruption measures since his election in 2010. Aquino's insistence that subordinates abide by the reforms and his willingness to punish even high-level officials for noncompliance have permitted changes to bureaucracies that had clung to the status quo for decades.[26]

Merit-based human resources programs have likewise worked well where the political leadership has backed them. The support of the national leadership for meritocracy in governmental hiring has, indeed, been a central feature of most third world success stories, such as Botswana, Singapore, South Korea, and Chile. In a telling remark on Botswana's public-sector personnel practices, one governance expert observed, "Botswana is the only country in the world where the ablest 20 people are in the 20 most important jobs."[27]

POLYGRAPHING

In countries where the political leadership is amenable, the polygraph machine has served as a highly effective weapon against corruption. During the past decade, the U.S. government has pioneered the use of the polygraph in third world governments, helping form special units whose personnel are administered polygraph tests periodically to check for complicity in bribery, embezzlement, and other forms of corruption and criminality. Known as "vetted units," they include elite police forces, investigative bureaus, judicial organizations, and counternarcotics units, and they have been used in a variety of Latin American countries, Afghanistan, Thailand, and Uzbekistan.[28]

U.S. personnel have been embedded in some of the vetted units to provide managerial and technical advice. In vetted units supported by the Drug Enforcement Administration, for example, one American is present for every fifteen individuals from the host government. Americans provide vetted unit members with special training in their home countries and in the United States, on such topics as interrogation, investigative techniques, recruitment of information sources, and development of criminal cases.[29]

Polygraphing has made the vetted units the most trustworthy organizations in governments that have been corrupted from within or by external forces and hence they are the preferred choice of U.S. agencies seeking collaboration with the government. In Colombia, the DEA has given vetted units advanced technologies and wiretapping information that it is unwilling to entrust to other governmental organizations. "The ability to share some of the relevant technology with vetted/trusted Colombian police has led to successful operations," asserts a study published by the U.S. Army's Strategic Studies Institute. "The vetted units and the law enforcement measures that are currently being used and expanded have provided the Colombians with a vastly expanded set of tools to target the FARC and other criminals."[30]

Vetted units have also been valuable producers of information for both their own governments and for the U.S. government. They have identified and prosecuted numerous criminals, including criminals in the upper tiers of their own governments. Evidence collected by vetted units has been used to convict suspects in the United States, where third world kingpins are often brought to trial because of the U.S. judicial system's imperviousness to bribery. Vetted units enjoy strong support from the U.S. Congress, which recognizes their value and has pushed for their expansion into additional countries.[31]

The number of Americans participating in vetted unit programs has been small, which has usually prevented them from becoming large enough to transform governance and security beyond a few islands of excellence at the national level. Spreading the benefits of polygraphing requires that the indigenous government take charge of administering the polygraph tests itself. One place where the mass polygraphing of government officials and security forces is already well along is Mexico, because of the efforts of President Felipe Calderón. Soon after he took office in 2006, Calderón used polygraphs to purge bribe takers from law enforcement agencies that had been infested with drug-related corruption. When he created new federal police forces, he directed that all applicants undergo polygraph screening before they could be hired.[32] Calderón also gave funds to local communities for use in polygraphing and drug testing of the police.[33]

The successes achieved in Mexico have encouraged other Latin American nations to implement polygraphing on a large scale. In 2011, for example, boisterous public criticism of police corruption caused the Ecuadorian government to institute polygraph examinations for all forty-two thousand members of the police.[34] To promote this trend, the United States has expanded its training of foreign governments in the use of polygraphs. In Bolivia, where corruption within the government's counternarcotics organizations led the national leadership to administer polygraph tests to all counternarcotics personnel, the United States now provides a Polygraph Examiner Certification Training course.[35]

Latin America is even experimenting with the polygraph as a means of screening out dishonest politicians. During Costa Rica's 2010 presidential campaign, candidate Otto Guevara sought to capitalize on voter suspicions about corruption by submitting himself to a polygraph test on national television. While strapped to the machine, the former legislator was asked, "Have you profited in any way while carrying out your duties for which you could be legally charged?" No, he replied, at which point a green light went on to signify a truthful answer. His leading rival, Laura Chinchilla, refused his challenge to undergo the same test.[36]

The display of honesty was not enough to win Guevara the election. But subsequent events have caused Costa Rican voters to reconsider whether they should have elected the polygraphed candidate. Upon taking office, Laura Chinchilla filled the position of chief of tax administration with Francisco Villalobos, who vowed to get tough on tax cheats but then had to resign when the press revealed that he had failed to pay a portion of his own tax bill. The new finance minister, Fernando Herrero, and Chinchilla's own brother were implicated in a scandal in which the state-owned Costa Rican National Oil

Refinery awarded a contract to a company owned by Herrero and his wife. Herrero had to step down when this violation of contracting rules came to light. The president's brother suffered only public ignominy, having not held a governmental office.[37]

CIVIL SOCIETY

Frustration with governments whose leaders prevent real improvements in governance has caused foreign donors to redirect large sums of aid to nongovernmental entities known as "civil society" organizations. Ranging from community committees to trade associations to professionally staffed national watchdog agencies, civil society organizations address all types of public problems, of which combating corruption is presently among the most popular. Most of USAID's "governance programs" actually support civil society organizations, rather than the government itself.[38]

The civil society organizations that receive U.S. funding for anticorruption programs are typically led by passionate individuals who are well educated and speak English. The majority of these leaders view their government as an adversary and seek to change it through pressure tactics. They attempt to uncover governmental misdeeds and publicize them to stimulate corrective action by voters, governmental agencies, or foreign governments. Although they may recognize that the government contains some "good guys" who can assist in anticorruption efforts, they often see these helpful persons merely as curious aberrations who fortuitously ventured across their path, rather than as proof that government employees are not innately corrupt, and consequently they do not attempt to cultivate more such individuals in the government.

These civil society organizations have achieved many small victories, particularly at the local level. Seldom, however, have they achieved major change across a nation. After an initial outpouring of development community excitement about "civil society" organizations at the start of this century, enthusiasm has been on the wane for several years, even though donor spending has remained high.[39] Many civil society organizations are short on members because of cultural indifference to this type of civic participation or because the organizations are dismissed by the populace as pawns of foreign donors. Some ostensible civil society organizations are in the pocket of the political elites whom they are supposed to be reforming. The eagerness of donors to spend large amounts on civil society organizations, especially in Iraq and Afghanistan, has necessitated a reduction in the standards demanded of civil society organizations, so that persons of modest abilities, with half-baked ideas, can get grants.

In September 2010, USAID funded a festival in Kabul organized by just such individuals. Tasked with generating popular backing for a more effective Afghan judiciary in the face of President Karzai's disregard of the law, the organizers purchased a thousand kites emblazoned with slogans on the "rule of law" and women's rights, which they planned to distribute to children on the day of the event. The festival's promotional materials explained that "the mere portrait of 500 kites soaring in the winds, against a backdrop of beautiful mountain ranges, is enough to instill hope in even the most disheartened observer of the war-torn country."

The kite distribution went amiss as soon as it began. Afghan policemen who were supposed to provide security pilfered dozens of the kites and stashed them in their vehicles for safe keeping. Rod Nordland of the *New York Times* reported that when a police major was asked why one of his men was loading kites into his truck, he replied, "It's okay, he's not just a policeman, he's my bodyguard."

Women's rights fared no better than the rule of law. Parents made sure that all the kites went to the boys, who by Afghan custom were deemed more worthy than girls of privileges like kite flying. One organizer, particularly troubled by the lack of girls flying the gender-equality kites, handed a kite to an enthusiastic ten-year-old girl. The girl took the kite to her father, who promptly gave it to the boy standing next to him. "He is my son and he should get the kite," the father said.[40]

Much of the anticorruption work undertaken by civil society organizations is based on the premise that once the general population learns about corruption, it will vote the scoundrels out of office or, in autocratic states, raise voices in protest. The world's preeminent anticorruption organization, Transparency International, gets its name from the idea that public access to information is the key to defeating corruption.[41] But publics in many countries have not proven willing to hold the government accountable when presented with evidence of corruption. One reason is that some of what Westerners call corruption has been accepted practice in many societies for centuries or millennia. The central government's funneling of money to local elites in return for their support has been viewed by the population as a legitimate instrument of governance and security, not as a form of corruption as Westerners typically see it. In countries where government employees earn very little, the populace often expects that those employees will require small payments, which may be called "gifts" rather than bribes, in exchange for services.[42]

No societies are completely tolerant of what Westerners call corruption. All abhor and stigmatize highly avaricious or oppressive acts. Yet even the most despised actions do not necessarily provoke a public outcry. In some democratic states, large segments of the population benefit from corruption, for governmental leaders allow some of the corrupt funds to trickle down to supporters or their identity groups. In some countries with authoritarian traditions, the people do not spend time protesting against the government because the government's past torturing and murdering of protesters has left them with a culture of passive acceptance. The citizens in these countries, and in some democratic ones, know that any information they provide on corruption could wind up in the hands of the corrupt, who would then initiate reprisals against them.[43] Escaping from this sort of quagmire most likely requires fundamental changes to the political leadership, changes that lie beyond the powers of civil society organizations.

The biggest limitation of civil society organizations is the sheer fact that they are outside the government. No matter how much one might wish otherwise, the quality of governance depends ultimately on the people inside the government. As one Brazilian civil society expert put it, "Civil society organizations try to achieve change by standing outside the building and raising a lot of complaints, but they aren't succeeding because they are not having much effect on what goes on inside the building."[44]

INCENTIVIZATION OF NATIONAL LEADERS

The successes of national leaders in thwarting changes to incentives within a government have made clear the inadequacy of anticorruption efforts that are not targeted at the national leadership. Consequently, some corruption fighters have turned their attention to changing the incentives of national leaders. In theory, foreign donors can convince national leaders to desist by giving them annual stipends that exceed their earnings from corruption, in exchange for discontinuing their corrupt practices. But many national leaders rake in tens or hundreds of millions of dollars each year from corruption, and no foreign donors are willing to pay such sums into the pockets of corrupt national leaders simply to get them to stop stealing public money.

The incentivization of national leaders to refrain from corruption has been cited as a rationale for conditioning aid on good governance. In truth, however, aid conditionality provides only modest incentives. If national leaders meet the governance conditions required to receive aid, they stand to add little to their personal wealth and must forswear actions that would increase their wealth by much larger amounts. Self-serving leaders would rather maintain their ability to steal $20 million a year from the national treasury than secure a $100 million grant for the nation's schools from which they can pilfer no more than a few hundred thousand dollars.

Punishment of national leaders has seldom been a viable means of increasing the costs of corruption to the degree required to alter behavior. Severe punishments, such as economic sanctions, require an international consensus that can seldom be mustered. Punishing every corrupt leader as a routine policy is impractical and strategically unpalatable, because three-quarters of the world's countries fall into the category of very corrupt and many of these are strategic U.S. allies whom the United States can ill afford to alienate.

Furthermore, cutting off U.S. aid to a country as punishment for corruption would seldom cause grievous harm to the pocketbooks of the ruling elites, for they have access to plenty of opportunities for corruption besides those afforded by U.S. assistance programs. China, Russia, and other countries that do not share the West's anticorruption zeal are always willing to bribe corrupt leaders or let them keep some aid in exchange for help of one type or another.

Third world leaders can also profit greatly from bribes offered by private sector firms seeking governmental contracts or regulatory changes. The United States and Western Europe have tried to halt corporate corruption by outlawing bribes and prosecuting companies under their jurisdiction for noncompliance, but the main result has been to deprive American and Western European firms of contracts that are now being fulfilled by Chinese, Russian, Indian, or South Korean firms, whose governments are glad to see them get a leg up on their Western competitors.[45]

MORAL CHANGE

The only sure way to change corruption at the top of a government is to change the moral character of individuals. The individual leader may undergo this change as a moral choice, but those outside the government seeking to alter the moral character of a government's leadership usually attempt to influence the ethical culture of the political elite more broadly, because the single individual comes and goes and is influenced by the other political elites. "We must develop a culture of intolerance for corruption," asserts Oliva Z. Domingo, professor at the National College of Public Administration and Governance of the University of the Philippines. The only viable solution to corruption, she says, is to develop a culture where "we ostracize the corrupt rather than envy or even idolize their ill-gotten wealth; where we do not partake of the fruits of corruption but rather shun these as reprehensible products of one's depravity."[46]

David Nussbaum, the chief executive of Transparency International from 2002 to 2007, has criticized much of the international community's anticorruption work for ignoring the centrality of morality and ethics. Nussbaum argues that the preoccupation with "incentives" among the economists, political scientists, and lawyers active in the anticorruption field has obscured the fact that corruption is a matter of ethical choice for governmental leaders and hence can be combated effectively only by influencing ethical values. "In the case of values-based decisions like whether or not to bribe or accept a bribe," Nussbaum has asserted, "values will be a fundamental guide."[47]

The linking of morality and ethics to corruption has met fierce resistance not only from economists but also from multiculturalists. To adherents of multiculturalism, the connection is unacceptable because it opens the door to unpleasant cross-cultural comparisons. With corruption generally lower in Western countries than in non-Western countries, the casting of corruption as a moral choice would necessarily mean that Westerners make better moral decisions than others, and would lend support to the view that Western culture and religion are morally superior. Multiculturalist criticisms of moral, ethical, cultural, and religious explanations of corruption have been so sharp-edged as to discourage anticorruption researchers and practitioners from accepting and acting upon them.[48]

At the 15th International Anti-Corruption Conference, a four-day gathering in November 2012 that drew eight thousand attendees to Brazil, almost all of the event's panelists focused on the symptoms of corruption and the treatment of the symptoms, and steered clear of the root causes of corruption other than to say that "political will" was a critical factor. The words morality, ethics, culture, and religion were rarely uttered.

While attending the event, I queried various anticorruption activists, aid experts, and government officials about these omissions. They explained that people in the anticorruption field steered clear of morality and culture because they thought that any mention of the subjects would offend people from poor countries and elicit accusations of bigotry from multiculturalists of all nationalities. They surmised that religion did not come up because of the lack of religious belief among Europeans and the cosmopolitan elites of other countries. It was like talking about the symptoms and treatments of obesity without any mention of overeating because it was considered too hurtful a topic.

A surprisingly large number of the conference attendees were willing to say in private that avoidance of ethical, cultural, and religious factors had undermined the anticorruption discourse. My visits to the front lines of foreign assistance also indicate that a significant number of the people engaged in fighting corruption are still willing to treat corruption as a moral and ethical problem.[49] Some anticorruption programs include ethics training for participants and require that they sign "integrity pledges." Some promote ethical development through persuasion of the leadership and support to reform-minded officials. Transparency International's Defence and Security Programme, for instance, engages recently retired officers to help gain access to open-minded security force leaders, for whom they then provide training on ethics as well as anticorruption procedures.[50]

Considerably fewer anticorruption reformers mention religion. The discounting of morality is one reason. Lack of religious belief among some of the reformers, especially those from the first world, is another. Secular anticorruption fighters have deliberately sought to marginalize religion, as Katherine Marshall and Marisa Van Saanen deftly described in their 2007 World Bank report *Development and Faith: Where Mind, Heart, and Soul Work Together,* one of the only World Bank publications to address religious antidotes to corruption. Marshall and Van Saanen explained that secularists sought to separate religion from ethics by characterizing integrity as a universal value, common to all religions and secular traditions and hence the special preserve of none.[51] This invocation of universal values, Marshall observed, also served the ulterior purpose of "countering arguments that have arisen in widely different settings, that cultures and religions have different approaches to issues such as public service standards, gifts and sharing of benefits."[52]

As stated in Chapter 3, religious belief has been a cause, and the only possible cause in some minds, of respect for all human beings and other values underlying good governance. Most of the world's religions invoke divine authority in their moral injunctions against selfishness, which is the fundamental cause of most corrupt practices. Secular ideologies, on the other hand, have no recourse to the power of divinity. Unlike religious teaching, the writings of

humanist philosophers and proclamations of the United Nations do not per-
suade many people to treat strangers as they would treat their own family,
tribe, or ethnic group.

Eighty-eight percent of the world's people adhere to a religion, while only
2 percent consider themselves atheists.[53] Although atheists comprise a larger
percentage in elite circles, especially in the West, religion remains the dominant
force in the ethics of nearly all societies, and it is still widely accepted as a
positive factor in promoting good governance. Marshall notes that "there is a
broad public expectation that faith leaders and institutions should go beyond
their traditional focus on personal and community values to play more active
roles in alliances against corrupt behaviour – whether at the community,
national or global level."[54] One African legislator who has championed anticorruption measures in his country explained it thus: "Africans recognize that
the churches must take on a leadership role in fighting corruption, because only
religion will be able to change the moral character of Africa's leaders."[55]

Some of the governments that have been most successful in combating
corruption have profited from their encouragement of the nation's clergy to
preach against corruption. A good example is Ugandan President Yoweri
Museveni, for whom the enlisting of religious authorities has been a central
part of one of Africa's most effective anticorruption campaigns. "The government cannot fight corruption to its end," Museveni has said. "The Church has a
better platform to do that."[56]

A small number of faith-based NGOs have used lay believers to provide faith-
based ethics training to third world governments. During an unscheduled visit to
the national headquarters of one Latin American army, I was startled to see ethics
training materials produced by La Red Business Network sitting on the desks of
several officers. A nondenominational Christian organization headquartered in
Ohio, La Red Business Network provides ethics booklets and videos, conducts
training, and organizes discussion groups for civil and military leaders in a variety
of countries. The organization's contributions touch the vital moral core of
military and governmental leaders, and yet the organization is known to very
few people in the aid world and the media, in contrast to some of the NGOs that
concentrate their energies on public agitation against governments.

The U.S. government and other donors have been somewhat more receptive to
secular ethics programs, having from time to time funded programs of a non-
religious character for the purpose of instilling ethical values in youth. A few
years ago, American NGOs teamed with Participatión Ciudadana, a secular
Ecuadoran civil society organization, to promote a national campaign for punctuality. Ecuadorans, like people in many other poor countries, pay little attention
to clocks and are notoriously tardy. The worst offenders are government, military, and business leaders, who deliberately show up late to demonstrate how
valuable their time is. This lack of punctuality has a highly detrimental effect on
economic productivity; according to one study, tardiness costs Ecuador's economy $2.5 billion per year, close to 10 percent of the country's GDP.

The country's president, Lucio Gutiérrez, agreed to participate in the campaign, though the aide he dispatched to announce his participation arrived at the studio well after the appointed hour. The group also brought in the country's only Olympic gold medalist, the race-walker Jefferson Pérez, as a spokesman. Participatión Ciudadana coated cities and villages with posters bearing slogans like "Inject yourself each morning with a dose of responsibility, respect, and discipline." At the suggestion of campaign organizers, companies started meetings on time and prevented latecomers from joining.

Ultimately, however, the campaign sputtered out and most Ecuadorians reverted to their belated ways. Independent analysts attributed the campaign's failure to a lack of reinforcement from other institutions with access to the masses like the schools and the media.[57] One also suspects that the campaign would have fared better had it invoked Ecuador's cultural and religious traditions.

Octavio Mavila, a champion motorcyclist in his youth, was the Honda distributor in Peru from the 1960s to the 1990s, during which time he made several trips to Japan and came away convinced that Japan's sole advantage over Peru was the culture of its people. "Japan has only water and Japanese people," Mavila commented. "Peru has a rich endowment of natural resources. Japan dedicated itself to the development of its people. Peru fooled itself with the idea that it was rich because of its natural resources." In 1990, Mavila founded the Institute of Human Development (INDEHU) to promote what he considered to be the ten cultural values most responsible for Japan's success: order, cleanliness, punctuality, responsibility, achievement, honesty, respect for the rights of others, respect for the law, work ethic, and frugality. His goal was to impart these ten values to half of Peru's population of 25 million by the year 2000.

Mavila obtained the support of private businessmen and three private universities. The international development community, however, did not provide funding because of its aversion to promotion of cultural change. Over the course of nearly a decade, more than two million Peruvians took INDEHU classes. The program faded after 1998, however, owing to an economic downturn that dried up the institute's sources of funding. Its lasting effects exceeded those of Ecuador's punctuality campaign because of its scope and duration, but its impact was sharply constrained by the same lack of reinforcement from other sectors.[58]

CONCLUSION

Certain types of U.S. support can bolster foreign human capital development, under the right conditions. Salary support for government workers can help attract and retain high-quality human capital, but its negative economic consequences recommend that it be limited to key leadership and technical positions. Although the practice of conditioning aid on good governance has compelled some governments to work harder to develop human capital and appoint the best people to the most important positions, it has done little to sway highly corrupt national leaders.

More surgical attempts to condition aid have a mixed record of success. The Leahy Law, conceived in exceeding ambition and implemented with insufficient care, has led to unwarranted and unnecessary withholding of aid to military forces. Its sweeping cuts to American training and education have taken away the best available means for fixing the deficiencies of foreign security forces. The suspension of military aid has been much more productive when it has been restricted to the here and now, penalizing only the misbehavior of current leaders.

Programs aimed directly at combating corruption within a government are worthy of foreign aid, but only in countries where the political leadership supports them. Anticorruption commissions, fiscal controls, and merit-based human resources programs can achieve a great deal with top-level backing and very little without it. Polygraphing has worked especially well and is worthy of adoption or expansion in additional countries.

Fundamentally a problem of ethics, systemic corruption must be addressed by changing the moral decisions of top governmental leaders. Anticorruption programs need to shift focus from the largely ineffectual pressuring of governments from the outside to the transformation of cultural values on the inside, such that rulers decide on moral grounds to stop trampling the public good in the service of their own families, tribes, or ethnic groups. Civil society groups should spend more time on ethics training and education for governmental employees. Religion can play an important role in effecting these changes, since the large majority of the world's population adheres to a religion and all the world's major religions oppose selfishness. Standalone values-education programs of a secular nature have been disappointing, indicating that ethics are best taught at schools, universities, training grounds, and places of worship, in addition to the home.

11

Measurement

The issue of measurement hangs over all U.S. foreign assistance programs of the present era. Many aid officials and many of their overseers in the executive and legislative branches deem quantitative measurement essential to the assessment of effectiveness, the management of aid programs, and the allocation of aid dollars. Quantitative data can indeed contribute much in all these respects. The concern over measurement of results has, moreover, been helpful in correcting past tendencies to assume that programs were effective simply because they conformed to preconceived notions about aid, such as the notion that giving money to the poor necessarily improves their lives, or the notion that handing out pamphlets on female empowerment is certain to promote gender equality. But measurement, especially that of a quantitative nature, has received so much emphasis, and has been advanced in so dogmatic a manner, that it now undermines the very activities it is supposed to be helping.

THE RISE OF MEASUREMENT

Much of the American public is skeptical about foreign aid because of past instances of corruption, the persistence of third world dysfunction after decades of aid, and the perception that foreign aid accounts for a huge chunk of spending by first world governments. The first two concerns are thoroughly justified, as the preceding chapters attest. The third is not: The average American believes that foreign aid constitutes 10 percent of the federal budget, when in reality it accounts for approximately 1 percent.[1] Even if this misperception were corrected, however, the public would still have ample reason for skepticism. Because of foreign aid's shoddy track record, voters and their elected representatives now feel compelled to demand that aid organizations show measurable results and show them quickly if they wish to survive, much as investors would demand of the management of a company that has been underperforming for years.

U.S. governmental agencies also receive demands for measurements from an ever-expanding group of oversight and regulatory agencies, which includes the Office of Management and Budget, the Government Accountability Office, various inspectors-general, and a multitude of congressional committees. The accountants, economists, procurement officers, and legislative staffers who run these organizations bear the stamp of professors in public administration, business administration, or economics who overemphasized quantification in educating them. These agencies are themselves subjected to pressure for numbers from Congress and the White House.

The externally imposed requirements for data have encouraged the federal bureaucracies to hire staff to generate statistics. As these staff have increased in number and influence, they have convinced management to impose new requirements for statistical reporting, many of which are a shocking waste of people's time. They have also converted some senior leaders to their view that quantitative measurement is the key to success, causing those leaders to change how they dispense aid and manage aid programs.

Academic economists and political scientists of numerical predisposition have furthered the quantitative measurement trend through their production of strategies and assessment methods for aid organizations. Leading the charge is the "randomnista" school of economists, which advocates statistical "randomized controlled trials" as the gold standard of assessment. Used routinely in the medical world, randomized controlled trials assess the effectiveness of a treatment by comparing the results of a "trial" group that received the treatment against the results of a "control" group that received a placebo. If we can gauge a cholesterol drug by comparing cholesterol scores of drug recipients against those of placebo recipients, contend the randomnistas, then we can determine the impact of distributing malarial bed nets or textbooks to indigent populations by comparing rates of bed net usage or literacy with equivalent trial and control groups.

THE IMPRECISION OF QUANTITATIVE ANALYSIS

Quantitative analysis is extremely impressive in the abstract, where one can create an elegant hypothetical case and assume away thorny complications. In the real world, however, a great many problems chip away at the validity of the analysis, often with such force as to preclude precision of any degree. The accuracy of statistics pertaining to foreign assistance programs is often questionable or worse. First world researchers need large amounts of data to perform their calculations, which usually necessitates obtaining data through indigenous personnel, such as government officials or research staff hired for the project. In cultures where people have few qualms about misappropriating funds, they have just as few qualms about misrepresenting information, particularly if they stand to benefit from the misrepresentation.

Randomized controlled trials and other quantitative analytical methods depend on simple cause-and-effect relationships between a few discrete and measurable variables, when in practice the relationships are often complex and the variables confound the reductionist aspirations of statistical analysis. Administration of a "treatment" can have a profusion of unintended and unperceived effects on other variables, in which case its actual merits are likely to be quite different from those shown in a statistical report. A program to distribute medicines for free may reduce the prevalence of disease, but may also lead to corruption or undermine indigenous human capital development, both of which likely lie outside of the researcher's original scope and are impossible to quantify.

For the sake of illustration, let us say that Sally and Bob wish to conduct a randomized controlled trial to determine the impact of an anticorruption program in Kenya. They intend to ask Kenyan citizens how often civil servants demand bribes in trial areas where the program is implemented and in control areas where it is not. Unable to find a Kenyan survey firm that they trust, Sally and Bob hire an American surveying firm that has conducted surveys around the world. This company identifies four districts where the anticorruption campaign will be implemented, and four where it will not be implemented, making sure to select districts with similar ethnic compositions, income levels, and population densities. The American project manager hires Kenyans from the capital city of Nairobi to travel to these districts, survey the residents, and write down their responses. A few months later, the Kenyans submit stacks of interview data, which are input into spreadsheets by a start-up in India and then crunched by Sally and Bob at their offices in suburban Maryland. The process is repeated a year later, following the implementation of the anticorruption program.

Once all the numbers have been tabulated and analyzed, Sally and Bob issue a thick report containing the final results. The report states that in the districts where the anticorruption program was instituted, the percentage of Kenyans reporting solicitation of bribes by government officials in the past month decreased from 21 percent before the program to 8 percent after the program. In the other districts, where the program was not instituted, the percentage ticked up slightly in the same period, from 20 percent to 21 percent. The donors and the Kenyan government publicize the survey results as proof that their anticorruption campaign has succeeded. When foreign auditors review the anticorruption program, they declare that definitive evidence of the program's success has been found by means of randomized controlled trial. Everyone is a winner.

Except, perhaps, the people of Kenya. There are a great many means by which these numbers could have been corrupted along the way. The Kenyans who were hired to do the surveys may not actually have interviewed the people whom they were supposed to have interviewed, because they preferred to spend the time visiting their native villages or were scared off by reports of insecurity in the districts they were scheduled to visit. They could easily have filled out the survey forms with bogus data and would most likely not have been caught unless they did something extraordinarily foolish like filling in the same answers for every respondent. The Americans who hired them might not have been inclined to question their honesty, owing to naïveté or the fear of being accused of cultural imperialism or racism.

Another possibility is that the surveyors notified their friends in the government about the survey, and those friends told the officials working in the four districts targeted for implementation to shift their extortion to different villages after the initial surveys were conducted. Alternatively, the government could have paid the surveyors to fill out the surveys in such a way as to show better results in the districts where the program was implemented, knowing that evidence of the program's effectiveness would cause donors to release funds that had been withheld over corruption concerns. Or, if the surveyors actually reached the districts, the respondents might have suspected them to be spies for the government or a subversive group and thus told them only what they believed the listeners wished to hear.

Although the foregoing case is fictionalized, it reflects problems encountered in Kenya and many other countries. Charles Hornsby, one of the foremost experts on Kenyan politics and culture, cited many of these problems in a sobering report on surveying in Kenya. The interviewing of individuals in Kenya, Hornsby observed, was subject to the following limitations: "hidden biases amongst interviewers in their random selections; difficulties in supervision of staff at a distance; the huge logistical problem of the semi-arid areas; the problems of language, cultural and gender differences between interviewers and interviewees; fear of retribution if people answer truthfully; and supervision, even harassment from local chiefs and district officials." Hornsby added that the problems inherent in surveying are worse in most African countries than they are in Kenya.[2]

DISTORTING THE FOREIGN ASSISTANCE AGENDA

Previous chapters demonstrated some of the ways in which demands for quantitative measurement have negatively influenced American foreign aid programs. The inability to measure acculturation in schools quantitatively has encouraged primary education programs to disregard cultural instruction and concentrate on quantifiable outcomes, such as enrollment and literacy. The White House Office of Management and Budget helped gut the USAID scholarship program on the grounds that the benefits of scholarships could not be put into dollars and thus the U.S. government could not know whether the benefits exceeded the costs.

The number of ways by which quantitative measurement has undermined U.S. aid programs is regrettably large. Andrew Natsios, who headed USAID from 2001 to 2006, wrote recently of broad harm resulting from demands for quantitative measures by U.S. oversight and regulatory organizations. The employees of these organizations, Natsios observed, had "become infected with a very bad case of Obsessive Measurement Disorder, an intellectual dysfunction rooted in the notion that counting everything in government programs will produce better policy choices and improved management." According to Natsios, their insistence on quantification has compelled USAID to focus almost entirely on delivery of services through foreign contractors and NGOs, because services like health and primary education yield results that are easy to quantify and good results are easy to achieve when foreign experts perform the work.

The overwhelming emphasis on quantifiable results has severely undermined efforts to build local capabilities, Natsios believes. The quality of the human capital of a civil service or a judicial system cannot be quantified with anything approaching scientific precision, and improving it is difficult and time-consuming. The victims of Obsessive Measurement Disorder, Natsios concludes, ignore "a central principle of development theory – that those development programs that are most precisely and easily measured are the least transformational, and those programs that are most transformational are the least measurable."[3]

Although the Millennium Challenge Corporation is seen as more innovative and less burdened by bureaucratic rigidities than USAID, it too is shackled by statistics. The organization's administrators determine which projects to fund based on a weighing of the estimated dollars spent on a project against the estimated increase in dollars earned by low-income citizens. While conscientious officials strive to include considerations of human capital development in project selection and management, the focus on numerical cost-benefit analysis ensures that those considerations will be a secondary priority at best.

Claims from randomnistas that randomized controlled trials have a monopoly on accurate assessment have led substantial numbers of donors to focus their spending on the types of projects for which randomized control trials seem to work best, and to ignore projects for which they are clearly unfeasible. Human capital development has been one of the leading casualties of this randomnista-driven exclusion. The fact that the quality of human capital cannot be quantified, other than by a subjective rating system that does not translate into dollars or other indubitable units of measurement, is an instant turnoff for randomnistas. Problems of time and space are also extremely daunting. Researchers would need to observe large numbers of people for decades to determine how educational programs affected the quality of a nation's senior leaders, a task beyond the capacity of most research initiatives. During those decades, moreover, large numbers of the original control and trial groups might leave government for jobs where their quality could no longer be assessed, rendering the research less valid or completely meaningless.[4]

PERVERTING PERFORMANCE

The purported superiority of quantitative measurement causes the multitudinous evaluators of U.S. foreign assistance programs to undervalue quality. To take one example, a recent analysis of USAID educational management assistance in Indonesia deemed the program a success based on the following statistics: 96 percent of the schools in question produced plans that met at least twenty-five of the criteria on a thirty-two–item checklist for good planning, 79 percent of programs in the plans were being executed, and more than 50 percent of schools disseminated financial reports in two or more venues. The report's 187 pages were full of numbers and words, but very few of them shed light on crucial qualitative issues such as the character and quality of training, the impact of training on human motivation, or the amounts and types of work performed by foreign experts because of a lack of domestic capabilities.[5]

In explaining the program's success, moreover, the report did not cite changes in student learning, which would have been the most valuable quantitative measurement. As it turned out, student learning did not increase appreciably during the project implementation period, a fact that the report mentioned only in passing. It is, indeed, quite common for reports that are supposed to measure output quantitatively to fall back instead on measuring input quantitatively, either because the output cannot easily be quantified or because the program is clearly ineffective but needs to be portrayed as successful for bureaucratic or political reasons.

In the case of programs that are intended specifically to develop indigenous human capital and institutions, the unquantifiability of the output has led quantitative analysts to focus almost entirely on input. The available statistics on input, moreover, usually reflect only the quantity of the input, not its quality. "No one has come up with a valid way to quantify the effectiveness of capacity building activities," remarked one USAID official. "So instead of focusing on effectiveness in reporting, USAID focuses on what can be measured, such as the number of workshops held or the number of people who have participated in training."[6]

The disinterest of evaluators in quality is easily discerned by those being evaluated, and it causes the less principled among them to lose interest in quality and focus instead on the quantifiable. If an aid official believes that the keys to a good evaluation are producing plans that satisfy a checklist and providing evidence that plans are being implemented, then that individual might focus overwhelmingly on producing conforming plans and ensuring that school staff are doing something that can be described as implementation. They would thereby neglect more valuable tasks like providing high-quality training, promoting better human resource practices, and encouraging staff to strive for excellence rather than adequacy.

An incisive 2009 study by the Global Health Technical Assistance Project noted that the provision of much-needed leadership training for health professionals in the third world has been undermined by the quest for quantitative measures. According to study authors Donna R. Dinkin and Robert J. Taylor, "the inherent difficulty in measuring and evaluating the impact of leadership and management interventions" has diverted attention to activities that are less important but more easily quantified. "To evaluate the success or value of a program," wrote Dinkin and Taylor, "funders and program staff often select and monitor metrics that are easy to count, but are poor markers of success." For instance, USAID officials concentrated on the numbers of patients treated, which said nothing about the quality of treatment or the capacity of health systems. "Some quantitative measures may be appropriate for measuring short-term process goals, but in general, a solely quantitative approach to measuring the impact of a complex, multilevel capacity-building initiative is misguided," concluded Dinkin and Taylor. To assess such initiatives, they recommended use of qualitative data from sources such as interviews, focus groups, and case studies, and called for special attention to changes in beliefs and behaviors.[7]

Baleful consequences of this sort are also to be found in the security sector. During 2009, American eagerness to build Afghan security forces that could take the place of American military units led to Congressional demands to accelerate the expansion of the Afghan army and police.[8] Despite an influx of additional trainers at that time, achieving expansion to the desired level required shortening the training for all new Afghan soldiers and policemen. Junior officers received only half of the training that experienced American advisers recommended. In 2012, with elections looming, American and Afghan politicians touted the success in training the Afghan security forces by pointing out how many Afghans had been trained. Close examination of the Afghan security forces in 2012, however, revealed that the quality of the Afghan security forces had been badly compromised by the haste in developing their human capital, leaving Afghanistan's future in grave doubt.[9]

Amid the Defense Department bureaucracies responsible for managing the wars in Iraq and Afghanistan could be found a plethora of statisticians who were convinced that the key to victory was identifying the right set of statistical measures. Most of these individuals knew little about what was actually happening politically or militarily in these countries, but believed that their statistical models captured broad trends that transcended particular events or people. Some believed that individuals who had spent years working in a country or studying it were less reliable than statisticians because the former had only subjective impressions whereas the latter employed "rigorous" quantitative modeling and their minds had not been clouded by untidy particularities. Their contentions often convinced unsuspecting military leaders to send out demands for more data to officers in the field, who then had to divert energies from productive action to useless data collection.

In Iraq and Afghanistan, statistics could not capture essential factors like leadership quality, and collecting more data could help little in addressing overriding problems like dysfunctional national governance. Statistical correlations frequently caused Americans to jump to mistaken conclusions about causation. For instance, declining levels of violence in Iraqi neighborhoods were widely cited as evidence that the Iraqi security forces were performing better in those neighborhoods. When American forces arrived, however, they frequently learned from interviews and hostile attacks that these neighborhoods were actually insurgent hotbeds, the violence having subsided only because Iraqi police commanders had allowed the insurgents to recruit and move supplies in return for a reduction in insurgent violence.

The statistician's typical response to such critiques was that the United States simply had not done a good enough job of identifying the proper metrics. With some additional effort by pioneering researchers, we would soon find the set of metrics that would at last provide an accurate understanding of the war. Few knew that the same things had been said five and ten years earlier.

A RETURN TO THE QUALITATIVE

If quantitative metrics alone cannot reveal which programs, departments, and people are performing well, how can managers determine what needs to be fixed, replaced, or reinforced? The answer is that they most often can obtain the best picture possible by analyzing qualitative and quantitative data in their proper context and drawing qualitative conclusions therefrom. The Emperor Augustus did not require statisticians to determine which of his provinces were being governed well and which needed help. General George S. Patton did not rely on regression analysis in determining which of his divisions ought to be sent to seize critical bridges. They, like innumerable other effective executives in history, collected a broad range of information, both qualitative and quantitative, and used intuitive, spatial, and analytical reasoning to reach decisions.

Effective assessment and decision making of this sort demand the complex problem-solving skills of the historian or the geologist more than the linear thinking of the social scientist or the engineer.[10] A relatively small number of individuals are rich in those skills. Only 25 percent of the U.S. population relies primarily on intuition in perceiving the world, which is among the best indicators of individual aptitude in complex problem solving.[11] The other 75 percent of the population, which perceives the world primarily with the five senses, prefer straightforward certitude – such as statistics provide – and is disinclined to "think outside the box." The linear quantitative analysis to which they are drawn can work relatively well in areas of foreign assistance like primary education where outcomes are easily quantified and cause-and-effect relationships are simple. But, unless they are very careful, they will run into trouble by trying to apply the same way of thinking in more complex situations.[12]

People who prefer the five senses are especially prevalent in governmental bureaucracies, because the structure and standardization of governmental service attracts them in great numbers. Highly intuitive individuals are less likely to gravitate to government bureaucracies, and those who join are more likely than their coworkers to quit, which they usually do out of frustration with excessive rules, risk aversion, hostility to innovation, and the other negative characteristics associated with the term "bureaucratic." Because of the shortage of highly intuitive individuals in government, effective qualitative assessment may require external assistance.

Academics, think tank analysts, government contractors, and journalists have, to varying degrees, provided independent analyses of foreign assistance programs. These groups tend, however, to concentrate around high-profile countries and programs, and some of them are as wedded to numbers as any governmental bureaucrat. Therefore, the government must work harder to seek out individuals and organizations with high proficiency in qualitative analysis if it wishes to obtain truly insightful evaluations of its programs.

Perhaps the most difficult problem in demonstrating the effectiveness of foreign assistance programs is convincing a skeptical Congress and public that qualitative assessment is often better than quantitative assessment. While Americans may at times invoke the phrase that there are "lies, damned lies, and statistics," they can easily be mesmerized by the seeming precision of statistics. Because qualitative assessments leave more room for individual judgment than statistics do, Americans often see them as more susceptible to manipulation by self-serving politicians, government officials, or polemicists.

Persuading the American public and Congress to move away from preoccupation with statistical measurement requires educating them on a number of key points. Given the political culture of the United States, the task will require a high-level public relations campaign, which could well be rolled into the sales pitch for higher U.S. government funding for training and educating foreigners. First, the people and Congress need to be educated on the unintended consequences of quantitative measurement, using examples like those cited earlier in this chapter. Second, they must be disabused of the idea that numbers are inherently more accurate than qualitative data. Third, they need to be shown the value of foreign assistance programs that defy accurate quantitative measurement, particularly those in the realm of human capital assistance. Evidence can be summoned from the early Cold War, when the receptivity of the government to nonquantifiable, long-term human capital development led to many of the greatest successes in the history of U.S. foreign assistance.[13] Finally, they must receive assurances that the government will employ evaluators who have unfettered access to information and are not susceptible to the influence of the people whose work they are evaluating.

CONCLUSION

The obsession with quantitative measurement of foreign assistance programs has done little to improve understanding, and it has consumed huge amounts of labor hours – those of the individuals dedicated to processing statistics and those of the otherwise productive workers who must divert time to satisfying the voracious appetites of the statisticians. It has caused the U.S. government and other donors to concentrate foreign aid on the activities that are easiest to measure instead of those that are most important, human capital development in particular. Program managers have given top priority to performing the most quantifiable tasks instead of the most important ones.

To alleviate these problems, quantitative analysis must be downgraded and qualitative analysis upgraded, especially in human capital development and other activities where numerical precision is impossible. Instead of placing confidence in a rigid set of quantitative measures, aid administrators and evaluators should rely on a plurality of quantitative and qualitative information, which in aggregate will be more accurate even if it may appear to be less precise. The American public and Congress need to be educated on the perils of quantification, in conjunction with education on the value of programs with nonquantifiable results like training and education. Aid donors and aid recipients cannot afford to let the keepers of the purse strings remain under the spell of statistical absolutists any longer.

12

Conclusion: A New Foreign Assistance Strategy

After 9/11, the United States did not need long to adopt a grand strategy better suited to impeding international terrorism, in which the bolstering of third world governments occupied a central role. Ever since, the obvious importance building of partner-nation capacity has ensured that Americans of all political persuasions support a certain amount of assistance to third world partners. But building partner-nation capacity has been much easier said than done, and realization of that truth is eroding the will of the United States to fund it. Today, the United States still lacks a foreign assistance strategy that can produce the desired improvements to the capabilities of third world nations. This chapter outlines a strategy that can achieve the optimal improvements, drawing together the findings of the preceding chapters.

Much of the blame for the ineffectiveness of America's foreign assistance can be traced to misapprehension of the dynamics of human societies. Convinced that the economic and social development of poor nations should be promoted first and foremost, American development thinkers have given too little attention to governance and security, the essential prerequisites for development. Investing in development in the absence of good governance and security is counterproductive, for officials focus on siphoning off aid instead of governing, and enemies of the state steal or destroy the seeds and fruits of development work. But achieving good governance and security requires resources, which are difficult for economically underdeveloped nations to accumulate, so foreign aid can make a real difference when reoriented toward good governance and security.

Recent theorizing on nation building has focused on impersonal institutions and policies as the main drivers of good governance. Just as inordinate preoccupation with sins may divert attention from the people who commit those sins, so has the single-minded concern with institutions and policies obscured the government leaders who guide those institutions and policies. Consequently, foreign assistance programs have often sought to achieve results by other, less productive routes than human capital development.

Multiculturalism has hidden the truth that civilization and its main components, culture and religion, exert enormous influence over the quality of human capital, especially in terms of human motivation. The United States can readily contribute to foreign human capital development by providing skills and experience, but achieving transformational change requires the changing of motives, which is much more difficult because it requires alteration of culture or religion. This type of change is, nevertheless, within the capabilities of the United States so long as its people reject the multiculturalist prescription that they should avoid imparting elements of their civilization to others.

A large fraction of the dire threats to America's national security in the twenty-first century – from terrorism and insurgency to narcotics and disruption of commerce – are the result of human capital deficiencies in the third world. Focusing foreign aid on human capital development is the most effective way to combat these threats, as can be seen from the subsiding of threats in countries where foreign assistance has improved the government's human capital. It is also the most cost-efficient, a particularly important consideration today in light of the economic troubles in the United States and the accompanying aversion to high foreign aid expenditures.

The needs of the United States for military bases, overflight permissions, trade concessions, and many other geopolitical assets give some third world partners significant bargaining power in foreign aid negotiations. When a foreign chief of state demands combat aircraft or the construction of a paved road from the capital to his summer chalet, the United States might have to grant the chief of state's wishes, rather than provide aid focused directly on human capital. Even in these cases, however, the United States can still promote human capital development by inserting provisions on the use of the aid, such as earmarking funds for aircraft pilots to attend training and education in the United States or including local companies in road construction.

The proposed strategy is comprised of five pillars, each one covering a major functional area within foreign assistance.

PILLAR I: TRAINING

The training of foreign personnel ranks among the most important means by which the U.S. government can strengthen human capital in the third world. In recent times, pressures for rapid social and economic gains, emanating from inside and outside the U.S. government, have undercut training by driving first world donors to rely on expatriates for task performance. The United States must take a longer-term perspective and shift resources from short-term performance to the training of indigenous personnel. To alleviate the pressure for short-term results, it must do away with the Millennium Development Goals and similar performance targets.

Training has a much higher impact when a nation's leadership is willing to put its best people into training programs and to assign training recipients to important leadership or technical positions. Hence, the U.S. government should concentrate training resources in countries where such national leadership exists. Resources should be infused into countries when their top-level leadership improves, and withdrawn when it deteriorates.

The United States should fund more long-term training programs and fewer of the day-long and week-long training events that are the norm today in civil training, for prolonged exposure is required to effect cultural change. In hiring the additional trainers required for this shift, U.S. agencies should select candidates based not only on technical competence but also on their willingness and capability to promote cultural change. Such people can be found in sufficient numbers only by seeking applicants from outside the traditional aid world, with particular attention to groups possessing relevant skills and experiences, such as military veterans and missionaries. U.S. civil agencies should take on a larger role in the institutions where third world governments train civil servants, in order to promote cultural change as well as to bolster technical training. They should, in addition, bring foreign civil servants to the United States for extended training, whether at training institutions or at governmental offices where they can see how the U.S. government works first hand.

PILLAR 2: MILITARIZATION

The U.S. military has been much more effective than the civil agencies in training foreigners, because of greater resources, greater interest in achieving cultural change, and the nature of military training. Although the foregoing reforms will improve civil training, they will not eliminate the disparity between military and civil training because of the military's inherent advantages. As a consequence, the military should become more involved in training on several fronts.

Most third world militaries conduct military and nonmilitary operations in their own countries, usually because civil agencies are incapable of performing all the necessary governance, development, and security tasks. The U.S. government has refused time and again to train foreign militaries because of reservations about military involvement in internal affairs, reservations that are based mainly on a misreading of history. Insisting that third world militaries restrict themselves to external problems has repeatedly put the hands of internal security in the hands of police forces that proved unable to handle the threats. In countries of particular importance and suitability, the U.S. military should step up its training of military forces that conduct extensive domestic operations.

The United States needs primary agencies for the principal areas of overseas assistance – governance, development, and security – but it has them for only the second and the third, USAID and the Department of Defense, respectively. Past attempts by civil agencies to make governance assistance a core competency have failed, because those agencies were focused on other missions and were reluctant to embrace a new one. The best solution is to create a new civil organization with governance assistance as its primary mission, under either the State Department or the Defense Department.

In the meantime, only the U.S. military is capable of fulfilling the mission of governance assistance on a substantial scale. Civil Affairs units and other branches of the U.S. military should be employed more often in that mission, both in war zones and in other imperiled countries with ineffectual governance. The U.S. government should make Civil Affairs more attractive as a military career track and should ensure that Civil Affairs units retain expertise in governance assistance so that in the future they can fulfill this role broadly and provide a surge capability in the event of unforeseen conflicts. Officers from combat arms branches, having demonstrated their ability to tackle governance problems in Afghanistan and Iraq, should be deployed to provide advice on governance in other unstable countries.

The civil agencies of the U.S. government have provided training to police forces in a multitude of third world countries, but they have seldom been able to train large numbers of policemen effectively. Chronic deficiencies in funding and staffing have characterized their participation in most places. In a few countries, the U.S. government has allocated large sums of money to police training because of an active conflict of strategic interest, but the lack of staff compelled civil agencies to rely on contractors who were not up to the task. Civil agencies, moreover, lack the ability to provide paramilitary training to police and constabulary forces, which is essential for survival when combating insurgents, organized criminals, or other internal menaces.

The U.S. military, on the other hand, has shown itself capable of training police forces in massive quantities without sacrificing quality. Its trainers are thoroughly versed in paramilitary skills, and some have expertise in police skills, particularly those from Army Military Police brigades and Marine Corps law enforcement battalions. In countries with woefully inadequate police forces, U.S. military participation in police training should receive serious consideration.

PILLAR 3: EDUCATION IN THE THIRD WORLD

Of all the foreign assistance sectors, higher education is the most effective in shaping the capabilities and motives of a society's elites. Since the late 1970s, the U.S. government's support for higher education in the third world has been very small in comparison with its support for primary and secondary education, owing to the mistaken belief that the benefits of higher education accrue exclusively to a society's elites. Experience has shown that concentrating resources in primary and secondary education cannot provide the managers, technicians, police chiefs, and teachers required for an effective government and a growing economy.

The United States should make higher education a top foreign assistance priority, just as it did in the 1950s and 1960s. Aid should be concentrated on elite institutions as well as academic programs directly related to governance, in order to attract talent into the pool of public sector human capital and develop that talent into the political elites of tomorrow. In addition, the U.S. government should increase support to police and military academies in countries where those institutions are short on resources.

The United States should support faith-based education at all levels, maintaining existing funding streams and pursuing new funding opportunities. Generally speaking, faith-based schools achieve better results with fewer resources than public schools and are less vulnerable to the predations of corrupt governments. They can, moreover, be highly valuable in combating religious extremism, particularly in Islamic countries where extremism is inculcated in youths at an early age. By underwriting university courses on religious moderation and other courses in the liberal arts, the United States can broaden the minds of the science students who are most susceptible to radicalism.

PILLAR 4: EDUCATION IN THE UNITED STATES

The education of foreigners at American universities has influenced the culture of foreign peoples more than anything else the United States has done aside from long-term occupation. Unfortunately, the United States has of late squandered numerous opportunities to acculturate the foreigners studying at its universities. The removal of mandatory courses on Western civilization and American history has deprived foreign students of exposure to the best the West has to offer. Hence, those students are more likely to receive reinforcement in negative stereotypes of American culture and society, which is particularly dangerous with students from Muslim countries who come to study the sciences. To reverse this negative trend, the federal government and state governments must restore mandatory university courses on America's traditions.

In terms of direct foreign assistance, the most important contribution that the U.S. government can make is to revive its scholarship program for foreign governmental personnel. During the early decades of the Cold War, the U.S. government awarded tens of thousands of scholarships per year to promising foreigners working in the public sector, many of whom became national leaders. Most of the scholarship recipients returned to their home countries and worked in government because they had already begun careers in public service and had been screened for their long-term commitment to public service before receiving the scholarships.

Residents of the third world who come to the United States for higher education without scholarships from the U.S. government are considerably more likely to remain in the United States after completing their studies. The U.S. government has encouraged them to stay by handing out green cards based on education and job skills, in the belief that their presence assists U.S. private enterprises.

But allowing students from the third world to stay in the United States deprives their native countries of the human capital required to solve their grave problems. In addition, retaining large numbers of graduates in scientific fields undermines production of home-grown talent in the sciences, which weakens the talent available for the defense-related research that has so greatly benefited American security and technological advancement in the past. The number of green cards for educated and skilled workers must therefore be cut sharply, particularly for individuals from countries in the third world and for scientists from countries that are or could become adversaries, such as Iran and China.

The U.S. military has achieved impressive human capital improvements by bringing foreign officers to study at its professional schools, but it can and should bring more of them. The academies of the Army, Navy, and Air Force, which have admitted only small numbers of foreigners, should undertake the largest increases, with special preference given to students from third world countries of strategic importance. The civil side of the U.S. government lacks educational institutions comparable to those of the military, a deficiency that ought to be corrected in order to permit human capital gains in civil governance. The State Department should transform the Foreign Service Institute into a world-class educational institution, with permanent faculty and sufficient resources to bring foreign governmental personnel for year-long courses on governance, development, and security. In addition, the U.S. government should create a civil equivalent of its military academies to educate the future civil leaders of both foreign countries and the United States.

PILLAR 5: SUPPORT

Various support programs and policies can contribute substantially to human capital development, especially in the area of ethics. The United States needs to allocate additional resources to the most promising of them, while cutting resources to others that are ineffective or counterproductive. Supplementing the salaries of government officials can help attract and retain the best and the brightest, but it must be limited to small numbers of jobs to avoid inflation and massive funding commitments of indefinite duration. The conditioning of aid on good governance has led to some progress on the human capital front, but it is insufficient to alter the behavior of very corrupt leaders, since their personal bank accounts stand to benefit more from preserving the status quo than from governing virtuously and receiving foreign aid that is difficult to steal. The blanket withholding of aid to foreign military units under the Leahy Law has done more harm than good to human capital because it has denied valuable U.S. training and education to countries that badly need it. Cutting off aid to specific units for recent abuses, on the other hand, has been effective in compelling governments to remove bad leaders.

Targeted anticorruption programs are deserving of U.S. funding in countries where the national political leadership supports them. They should not receive funding in other countries, for the best conceived of anticorruption initiatives will fail when the political leaders do not wish for them to succeed. The programs with the best track records include governmental anticorruption commissions, reforms to financial management, and institution of merit-based human resources practices. Within the past decade, polygraphing has emerged as a highly effective tool for combating corruption, one that the United States should help other countries institute on a nationwide scale.

The view of economists that fighting corruption is merely a matter of incentivizing good behavior has not held up in a world where foreign powers have little control over the incentives of the top leaders of foreign governments, who are the ultimate arbiters of corruption. Changing the behavior of national leaders requires changing their ethical culture, such that they decide for moral reasons to stop putting their families, tribes, or ethnic groups ahead of everyone else. This type of moral transformation is seldom achieved through exposure of misdeeds or shrill denunciation. Most often it comes from prolonged training and education during youth and early adulthood and usually includes religious instruction of some type. Therefore, the U.S. government should increase support to faith-based organizations and other civil society organizations that teach ethics to public sector employees, in addition to other training and educational programs that address ethics.

MEASUREMENT

U.S. foreign assistance must be freed from the shackles of quantitative measurement. The pressure on governmental agencies to show quantifiable results has led their leaders to concentrate on achieving what can most easily be quantified, which is often not what is most important. Deemphasizing statistics and increasing reliance on gifted qualitative analysts will negate this problem and increase the accuracy of assessments. Creating the political conditions necessary for this reorientation will require educating the American public and Congress on the problems created by the obsession with statistics.

BLENDING THE OLD AND THE NEW

As stated at the beginning of this book, those seeking answers to the world's problems must explore history to see what has been tried and must also conceive new solutions to newly arisen challenges, in both cases evaluating options in the context of circumstances prevailing today. Many of the above recommendations came from analyses of U.S. foreign assistance programs of the 1950s and 1960s that determined those programs to have been effective then and similarly meritorious now. The concentration of resources on elite education in foreign countries, the awarding of scholarships for study in the United States, and the reliance on qualitative, long-term assessment come straight from the playbook of 1955.

Other recommendations reflect a finding that the prevailing wisdom of the 1950s and 1960s was not entirely correct. The proponents of modernization during that period underestimated the power of indigenous cultures and religions and hence made the error of dismissing them as unnecessary relics. As more recent events have confirmed, efforts to Westernize non-Western peoples completely have been frustrated by the forces of culture and religion and have at times generated backlashes that hurt the West. A sounder approach is to convince non-Western peoples to borrow elements of Western Civilization for the betterment of their civilizations, thereby harnessing the power of culture and religion to promote stability and to suppress religious and secular extremism.

The tactics of foreign assistance must constantly be reassessed and adjusted. Some elements of the foregoing foreign assistance strategy are targeted at problems that have come into existence in recent times. For instance, reducing the number of educated foreigners permitted to stay in the United States has become necessary because of increases in the number of highly educated workers seeking residence in the United States and changes to U.S. green card policies.

By contrast, the nature of foreign assistance—the set of fundamental realities that constrains and sways interactions between donors and recipients—is enduring. Awareness of its nature, which the thinkers of the 1950s and 1960s largely possessed, will ensure that the tactics are not too far from the mark. Ignorance or misapprehension of its nature, which has characterized most of the theorizing in the United States since the 1960s, will yield tactics incapable of achieving the intended results. Success in foreign assistance programs of the past, present, and future hinges on understanding the relationships among governance, development, and security and recognizing the importance of human capital development. It requires, above all, the ability to apply this awareness in the many nations upon whose stability the world's security depends.

Notes

PATHWAYS TO DEVELOPMENT

1   The descriptions of the coup and the surrounding events are derived from the following sources: Serge Daniel, "Mali Soldiers Attack Presidency in Apparent Coup Bid," Agence France Presse, March 21, 2012; David Lewis, "Mali Seals Presidency as Gunfire Heard in Capital," Reuters, March 21, 2012; "Renegade Mali Soldiers Announce Takeover," BBC, March 22, 2012; "Soldiers Loot Mali Presidential Palace after Ousting Leader," Associated Press, March 22, 2012; Thomas Fessy, "Gaddafi's Influence in Mali's Coup," BBC News, March 22, 2012; James Schneider, "Mali's CNRDR: An Accidental Coup?" *Think Africa Press,* March 22, 2012, http://thinka fricapress.com/mali/how-cnrdr-took-control; David Lewis and Tiemoko Diallo, "Mali Soldiers Attack Palace in Coup Bid," Reuters, March 22, 2012; Rukmini Callimachi, "Amadou Haya Sanogo, Mali Coup Leader, Derails 20 Years of Democracy," Associated Press, July 7, 2012; Rukmini Callimachi, "Mali's Accidental Coup," Associated Press, July 28, 2012; J. Peter Pham, "The Mess in Mali," *New Atlanticist,* April 2, 2012, www.acus.org/new_atlanticist/mess-mali.
2   Callimachi, "Amadou Haya Sanogo, Mali Coup Leader, Derails 20 Years of Democracy."
3   Human Rights Watch, "Mali: War Crimes by Northern Rebels," April 30, 2012; J. Peter Pham, "The Mess in Mali," *New Atlanticist,* April 2, 2012, www.acus.org/ new_atlanticist/mess-mali; Adam Nossiter, "Islamists in North Mali Stone Couple to Death," July 30, 2012; Robbie Corey-Boulet, "West Africa Leader Urges Mali Intervention," Associated Press, September 17, 2012; John Irish, "U.N. Members Divided over Response to Mali Crisis," Reuters, September 26, 2012.
4   Drew Hinshaw, "Clinton, in Africa, Hails 'Resilience of Democracy,'" *Wall Street Journal,* August 1, 2012; Adam Nossiter, "Burkina Faso Official Goes to Islamist-Held Northern Mali in Effort to Avert War," *New York Times,* August 8, 2012.
5   Testimony of Ambassador Johnnie Carson, "The Tuareg Revolt and the Mali Coup," House Foreign Affairs Committee Subcommittee on African Affairs, June 29, 2012.

6 John Irish, "U.N. Members Divided over Response to Mali Crisis," Reuters, September 26, 2012.

7 Steven Lee Myers, "Clinton Suggests Link to Qaeda Offshoot in Deadly Libya Attack," *New York Times,* September 26, 2012.

8 Scott Stearns, "US Backs African Intervention Force in Mali," Voice of America, October 1, 2012.

9 No one has produced clear and accurate definitions of these terms as they pertain to foreign assistance. The definitions presented here are derived from the most common usages of the terms in the practice of foreign assistance.

10 The spending figures in this and subsequent paragraphs can be found at Mali Fiscal Year 2011 Disbursements, *foreignassistance.gov,* http://foreignassistance.gov/OU. aspx?OUID=209&FY=2011&AgencyID=0&budTab=tab_Bud_Spent&tabID= tab_sct_Peace_Disbs; U.S. Department of State, "International Military Education and Training Account Summary," www.state.gov/t/pm/ppa/sat/c14562.htm; U.S. Department of State, Foreign Military Financing Account Summary, www.state. gov/t/pm/ppa/sat/c14560.htm; Millennium Challenge Corporation, "Quarterly Status Report, Mali Compact," March 2012, www.mcc.gov/documents/reports/ qsr-2012002103102-mali.pdf.

11 On the AQIM presence, see U.S. Department of State, "Country Reports on Terrorism 2010," August 2010, www.state.gov/documents/organization/170479. pdf, 19–20. The figure of $4 million is the published figure. The entire amount spent may include some additional items, but it was still far smaller than what was spent on development.

12 USAID, Mali Overview, www1.usaid.gov/locations/sub-saharan_africa/countries/ mali/.

13 U.S. Senate Committee on Foreign Relations, Subcommittee on African Affairs, "Assessing Developments in Mali: Restoring Democracy and Reclaiming the North," December 5, 2012, www.foreign.senate.gov/hearings/assessing-develop ments-in-mali-restoring-democracy-and-reclaiming-the-north.

14 David Pugliese, "African Special Forces Improve but Lack Gear," *Defense News,* March 14, 2011, 22. See also United Nations Security Council Report S/2012/894, "Report of the Secretary-General on the Situation in Mali," November 29, 2012, 4.

15 A highly respected measure of corruption, the Corruption Perceptions Index is based upon the perceptions of governance and business experts. The data cited can be found at http://cpi.transparency.org/cpi2011/results/. An International Monetary Fund report from January 2012 stated that the principal impediment to higher economic growth was a business environment that discouraged private investment, and it blamed the sorry state of the business environment on factors that included "shallow financial intermediation, a persistently high incidence of corruption and a feeble judicial system." International Monetary Fund, "Mali: Seventh Review under the Extended Credit Facility and Request for a New Three-Year Arrangement under the Extended Credit Facility," January 2012.

16 Neil MacFarquhar, "Mali Tackles Al Qaeda and Drug Traffic," *New York Times,* January 1, 2011; interviews with U.S. government personnel, December 2014.

17 Nina Munk, *The Idealist: Jeffrey Sachs and the Quest to End Poverty* (New York: Doubleday, 2013), 225.

18 Jared Diamond, *Guns, Germs, and Steel: The Fates of Human Societies* (New York: W. W. Norton, 1997); Jeffrey D. Sachs, *The End of Poverty: Economic Possibilities*

for Our Time (New York: Penguin, 2005). For a more recent exposition of the *Annaliste* position, see Ian Morris, *Why the West Rules – For Now* (New York: Farrar, Straus and Giroux, 2010).

19 Sachs, *The End of Poverty*, 56–57, 73.

20 Thomas P. Barnett, *The Pentagon's New Map* (New York: Putnam, 2004). See also Thomas L. Friedman, *The World Is Flat: A Brief History of the Twenty-First Century* (New York: Farrar, Straus and Giroux, 2005).

21 Sachs, *The End of Poverty*, 190–209. See also United Nations Research Institute for Social Development, *Combating Poverty and Inequality: Structural Change, Social Policy and Politics* (Geneva: United Nations, 2010).

22 On the disparities of economic performance among groups in the same society, see Thomas Sowell, *Migrations and Culture: A World View* (New York: Basic Books, 1996).

23 Organisation for Economic Co-operation and Development/Development Assistance Committee (OECD/DAC), "Concepts and Dilemmas of State Building in Fragile Situations: From Fragility to Resilience," 2008, www.oecd.org/dataoecd/59/51/41100930.pdf; Johann Graf Lambsdorff, *The Institutional Economics of Corruption and Reform: Theory, Evidence and Policy* (Cambridge: Cambridge University Press, 2007); USAID, "Fragile States Strategy," January 2005, www.usaid.gov/policy/2005_fragile_states_strategy.pdf; Edwina Thompson, Report on Wilton Park Conference 1022, April 1, 2010, www.wiltonpark.org.uk/resources/en/pdf/22290903/22291297/wp1022-report; Standing Senate Committee on Foreign Affairs and International Trade, "Overcoming 40 Years of Failure: A New Roadmap for Sub-Saharan Africa," February 2007, www.parl.gc.ca/Content/SEN/Committee/391/fore/rep/repafrifeb07-e.pdf; William Easterly, *The White Man's Burden: Why the West's Efforts to Aid the Rest Have Done So Much Ill and So Little Good* (Penguin, 2006); Dambisa Moyo, *Dead Aid: Why Aid Is Not Working and How There Is a Better Way for Africa* (Farrar, Straus and Giroux, 2009).

24 Daniel F. Runde, Sadika Hameed, and Jeremiah Magpile, "The Costs of Corruption: Strategies for Ending a Tax on Private-Sector Growth," Center for Strategic and International Studies, February 2014.

25 World Governance Indicators 2013, Country Reports, http://info.worldbank.org/governance/wgi/index.aspx#countryReports.

26 Paul Collier, *The Bottom Billion: Why the Poorest Countries Are Failing and What Can Be Done about It* (New York: Oxford University Press, 2006), 66.

27 Democracy International, "Ghana Democracy and Governance Assessment," August 2011, www.democracyinternational.com/sites/default/files/Ghana%20DG%20Assessment.pdf.

28 Management Systems International, "Corruption Assessment: Senegal," August 31, 2007, http://pdf.usaid.gov/pdf_docs/PNADK548.pdf.

29 USAID official, interview with author, 2012.

30 Nazmul Chaudhury et al., "Missing in Action: Teacher and Health Worker Absence in Developing Countries," *Journal of Economic Perspectives*, vol. 20, no. 1, 91–116; Barbara Burns et al., *Making Schools Work: New Evidence on Accountability Reforms* (Washington, DC: World Bank Publications, 2011); Abhijit Banerjee and Esther Duflo Benerjee and Duflo, *Poor Economics: A Radical Rethinking of the Way to Fight Global Poverty* (New York: PublicAffairs, 2011), 74–75. For another

example, from the health care sector, see Abhijit Banerjee, Rachel Glennerster, and Esther Duflo, "Putting a Band-Aid on a Corpse: Incentives for Nurses in the Indian Public Health Care System," *Journal of the European Economic Association*, vol. 6, no. 2–3 (April–May 2008), 487–500.

31 The emphasis on governance can be found not only at the top, but also at the country level, as I found during discussions with World Bank officials in a variety of countries.

32 For the evolution of World Bank thinking on governance, see Praveen Kulshreshtha, "Public Sector Governance Reform: The World Bank's Framework," *International Journal of Public Sector Management*, vol. 21, no. 5 (2008), 556–567; World Bank Independent Evaluation Group, "Public Sector Reform: What Works and Why?" (Washington, DC: World Bank, 2008).

33 Robert B. Zoellick, speech at the International Institute for Strategic Studies, September 12, 2008, http://web.worldbank.org/WBSITE/EXTERNAL/NEWS/0, contentMDK:21898896~pagePK:34370~piPK:42770~theSitePK:4607,00.html#_edn4.

34 See, for example, Paul Collier, *Wars, Guns, and Votes: Democracy in Dangerous Places* (New York: Harper, 2009).

35 Zoellick, speech at the International Institute for Strategic Studies.

36 A few development experts have emphasized the point that development requires security. See Department for International Development, "Eliminating World Poverty: Making Governance Work for the Poor," July 2006, www.gov.uk/government/uploads/system/uploads/attachment_data/file/272330/6876.pdf; World Bank, *World Development Report 2011: Conflict, Security, and Development* (Washington, DC: World Bank Publications, 2011); Gary A. Haugen and Victor Boutros, *The Lotus Effect: Why the End of Poverty Requires the End of Violence* (New York: Oxford University Press, 2014).

37 "Peace Corps Reviews Operations in Honduras," December 21, 2011, www.peacecorps.gov/index.cfm?shell=resources.media.press.view&news_id=1932.

38 UN Special Representative for Children and Armed Conflict, "Visit of the Special Representative for Children & Armed Conflict to Afghanistan," www.un.org/children/conflict/_documents/countryvisits/afghanistan.pdf.

39 Stephen Grey, "Cracking on in Helmand," *Prospect*, August 27, 2009.

40 Mark Moyar, "The Third Way of COIN: Defeating the Taliban in Sangin," Orbis Operations, July 2011, http://smallwarsjournal.com/documents/moyar-3rdway_in_sangin_jul2011.pdf. The District Stabilization Framework, which the USAID Office of Military Affairs developed in 2010 for use in Afghanistan, rejected the widespread notion that development fosters stability and instead focused on solving root problems of instability, principally political conflict and bad governance. For an overview of the District Stabilization Framework, see James W. Derleth and Jason S. Alexander, "Stability Operations: From Policy to Practice," *Prism*, vol. 2, no. 3 (June 2011), 125–136.

41 Vanda Felbab-Brown et al., "Assessment of the Implementation of the United States Government's Support for Plan Colombia's Illicit Crop Reduction Components," April 17, 2009, http://pdf.usaid.gov/pdf_docs/PDACN233.pdf, 26.

42 Peter DeShazo et al., "Countering Threats to Security and Stability in a Failing State," Center for Strategic and International Studies, September 2009, http://csis.org/files/publication/090930_DeShazo_CounteringThreats_Web.pdf, 58.

43 U.S. Government Accountability Office, "Plan Colombia: Drug Reduction Goals Were Not Fully Met, But Security Has Improved," October 2008, www.gao.gov/products/GAO-09-71, 46–49.

44 David Spencer et al., *Colombia's Road to Recovery: Security and Governance 1982–2010* (Washington, DC: Center for Hemispheric Defense Studies, 2011), 62–63.

45 DeShazo et al., "Countering Threats to Security and Stability in a Failing State," 50.

46 For recent expositions of the view that foreign assistance for security tends to undermine governance and development, see Gordon Adams and Rebecca Williams, "A New Way Forward: Rebalancing Security Assistance Programs and Authorities," Henry L. Stimson Center, March 2011, www.stimson.org/images/uploads/A_New_Way_Forward_Final.pdf; Yahia H. Zoubir, "The United States and Maghreb-Sahel Security," *International Affairs*, vol. 85, no. 5 (2009), 977–995.

47 See Dominique Djindjéré, "A New Governance of Africa's Security Sector," November 2010, Africa Center for Strategic Studies, http://africacenter.org/2010/11/sbo8/; Dennis C. Blair, "Military Support for Democracy," *Prism*, vol. 3, no. 3 (June 2012), 3–16.

48 International Crisis Group, "Guatemala: Squeezed between Crime and Impunity," June 22, 2010, www.crisisgroup.org/en/regions/latin-america-caribbean/guatemala/033-guatemala-squeezed-between-crime-and-impunity.aspx. See also Ralph Espach et al., "Criminal Organizations and Illicit Trafficking in Guatemala's Border Communities," Center for Naval Analysis, December 2011.

49 Eastern Congo Initiative et al., "The Democratic Republic of Congo: Taking a Stand on Security Sector Reform," April 16, 2012, www.enoughproject.org/files/DRC_SSR-Report_2012_0.pdf, 9.

50 See, for instance, International Crisis Group, "Guatemala: Squeezed between Crime and Impunity," 7–8.

51 Amitai Etzioni, *Security First: For a Muscular, Moral Foreign Policy* (New Haven: Yale University Press, 2007).

HOW GOVERNMENTS WORK

1 UN Millennium Project, "A Q&A on the Millennium Project and the Millennium Development Goals," December 2006, www.unmillenniumproject.org/documents/UNMP-QandA-E.pdf.

2 For a discussion of the competing views on good governance, see Roger C. Riddell, *Does Foreign Aid Really Work?* (Oxford: Oxford University Press, 2007), 372–377.

3 Daron Acemoglu and James A. Robinson, *Why Nations Fail: The Origins of Power, Prosperity, and Poverty* (New York: Crown Business, 2012).

4 Douglass C. North, John Joseph Wallace, and Barry R. Weingast, *Violence and Social Orders: A Conceptual Framework for Interpreting Recorded Human History* (New York: Cambridge University Press, 2009); Morton H. Halperin, Joseph T. Siegle, and Michael M. Weinstein, *The Democracy Advantage: How Democracies Promote Prosperity and Peace* (New York: Routledge, 2005); Amartya Sen, *Development as Freedom* (New York: Knopf, 1999); Stephen D. Krasner and Carlos Pascual, "Addressing State Failure," *Foreign Affairs*, vol. 84, no. 4 (July/August 2005), 153–163.

5 Steven Radelet, *Emerging Africa: How 17 Countries Are Leading the Way* (Washington, DC: Center for Global Development, 2010); Halperin, Siegle, and Weinstein, *The Democracy Advantage.*

6 For a good overview of poor democratic governance, see Fareed Zakaria, *The Future of Freedom: Illiberal Democracy at Home and Abroad* (New York: W. W. Norton, 2003). See also Frances Fukuyama, *State-Building: Governance and World Order in the 21st Century* (Ithaca: Cornell University Press, 2005), 26–29.

7 For evidence of discontent with democracy in Latin America, see Juan Forero, "Latin America Graft and Poverty Trying Patience with Democracy," *New York Times*, June 24, 2004. Although that survey was conducted in 2004, the same poor conditions and the same disillusionment remain prevalent in much of Latin America today, as I have found during recent visits. See also Oscar Arias, "Culture Matters: The Real Obstacles to Latin American Development," *Foreign Affairs*, vol. 90, no. 1 (January/February 2011), 5–6. For democratic disillusionment in Pakistan, see Alex Rodriguez, "Survey: Young Pakistanis Harbor Doubts about Future, Democracy," *Los Angeles Times*, April 3, 2013.

8 Zbigniew Brzezinski, *Strategic Vision: America and the Crisis of Global Power* (New York: Basic Books, 2012), 31–32; Lisa Anderson, "Demystifying the Arab Spring: Parsing the Differences between Tunisia, Egypt, and Libya," *Foreign Affairs*, vol. 90, no. 3 (May/June 2011), 2–7.

9 Robert Lustig, "Have Oman and Qatar Escaped the Arab Revolts?" *BBC News*, 20 April 2011.

10 Some of these autocrats benefited from massive oil wealth, which enabled them to placate protesters with cash, jobs, or services. But that achievement should not be dismissed lightly; many authoritarian leaders have chosen to keep oil wealth to themselves rather than distribute its benefits widely. In addition, some of the countries that weathered the Arab Spring – Jordan and Morocco, in particular – do not have the benefit of massive oil revenues.

11 Fergus Nicoll, "Oman: Sultan Qaboos Still Popular Despite Discontent," *BBC News*, March 3, 2011.

12 Collier, *Wars, Guns, and Votes*, 65.

13 John Pimlott, "The British Army: The Dhofar Campaign, 1970–1975," in Ian F. W. Beckett and John Pimlott, ed., Armed Forces & Modern Counter-Insurgency (Kent, UK: Croom Helm, 1985), pp. 25–43; John Akehurst, *We Won a War: The Campaign in Oman 1965–1975* (Wilton, UK: Michael Russell, 1984).

14 Robert Kaplan, *Monsoon: The Indian Ocean and the Future of American Power* (New York: Random House, 2010), 34–46.

15 UNDP, "Five Arab Countries among Top Leaders in Long-Term Development Gains," November 4, 2010, http://hdr.undp.org/en/mediacentre/news/announce ments/title,21573,en.html.

16 Inder Sud, "Poverty: A Development Perspective," in Joanna Spear and Paul D. Williams, eds., *Security and Development in Global Politics: A Critical Comparison* (Washington, DC: Georgetown University Press, 2012), 220. Some advocates of development through democracy have contended that authoritarian rule has rarely led to economic and political development except in Asia and Europe. Halperin, Siegle, and Weinstein, *The Democracy Advantage*; Radelet, *Emerging Africa*. But the number of success stories outside of Asia and Europe belies that claim. Among them

are Chile, the foregoing examples from the Arab world, and several countries in sub-Saharan Africa. Of the twenty non-oil-exporting countries in sub-Saharan Africa that experienced high growth rates from 1996 to 2008, only six (Botswana, Cape Verde, Lesotho, Mauritius, Namibia, and South Africa) were classified as democracies on the *Economist*'s Democracy Index. Two (Burkina Faso and Rwanda) were classified as authoritarian, and nine more (Ethiopia, Ghana, Liberia, Kenya, Mali, Mozambique, Sierra Leone, Tanzania, and Uganda) were designated "hybrid." São Tomé and Principe and the Seychelles were not included in the index. The *Economist* Intelligence Unit, Index of Democracy 2008, http://graphics.eiu.com/PDF/Democracy%20Index%202008.pdf. According to the Polity IV classification system, nine of these countries (Botswana, Ghana, Kenya, Lesotho, Liberia, Mali, Mauritius, Mozambique, Namibia, Sierra Leone, and South Africa) were classified as democracies, and five (Burkina Faso, Ethiopia, Rwanda, Tanzania, and Uganda) were ranked in the range of "anocracies," which were defined as "mixed, or incoherent, authority regimes." Radelet, *Emerging Africa*, xvi, 65. Ethiopia, one of Africa's most powerful and prosperous countries, has moved further toward authoritarianism since 2008, becoming an "authoritarian" state on the *Economist*'s Democracy Index in 2010.

17 Acemoglu and Robinson, *Why Nations Fail;* North, Wallace, and Weingast, *Violence and Social Orders.*

18 See, for instance, OECD, "The Challenge of Capacity Development: Working towards Good Practice," 2006, www.oecd.org/dataoecd/4/36/36326495.pdf.

19 DFID, "The Politics of Poverty: Elites, Citizens and States: A Synthesis Paper Findings from Ten Years of DFID-Funded Research on Governance and Fragile States 2001–2010," June 1, 2010, www.dfid.gov.uk/Documents/publications1/evaluation/plcy-pltcs-dfid-rsch-synth-ppr.pdf, 15.

20 OECD, "The Challenge of Capacity Development."

21 See Sue Unsworth and Mick Moore, "Societies, States and Citizens: A Policy-maker's Guide to the Research," Centre for the Future State, July 2010, www2.ids.ac.uk/futurestate/pdfs/Future%20State%20DRC%20Policy%20Briefing%20SSC10.pdf.

22 Influential expositions include Christopher Paul et al., *Victory Has a Thousand Fathers: Detailed Counterinsurgency Case Studies* (Santa Monica: RAND, 2010); Rupert Smith, *The Utility of Force: The Art of War in the Modern World* (New York: Knopf, 2007); Timothy J. Lomperis, *From People's War to People's Rule: Insurgency, Intervention, and the Lessons of Vietnam* (Chapel Hill: University of North Carolina Press, 1996); Anthony James Joes, *Resisting Rebellion: The History and Politics of Counterinsurgency* (Lexington: University Press of Kentucky, 2004); Andrew Krepinevich, *The Army in Vietnam* (Baltimore: Johns Hopkins University Press, 1986); U.S. Army Field Manual 3–24/Marine Corps Warfighting Publication 3–33.5, *Counterinsurgency.*

23 The most prominent of recent examples are Banerjee and Duglo, *Poor Economics;* Philippe Aghion and Peter Howitt, *The Economics of Growth* (Cambridge, MA: MIT Press, 2009).

24 Matthew Devlin and Sebastian Chaskel, "Organizing the Return of Government to Conflict Zones: Colombia, 2004–2009," *Innovations for Successful Societies,* Princeton University, http://www.princeton.edu/successfulsocieties.

25 Two of the most acclaimed works of the period were Chester Barnard, *The Functions of the Executive* (Cambridge, MA: Harvard University Press, 1938); Philip Selznick, *Leadership in Administration: A Sociological Interpretation* (New York: Harper & Row, 1957). One exception to the current trend comes from Robert I. Rotberg, former director of the Program on Intrastate Conflict and Conflict Resolution at Harvard's John F. Kennedy School of Government. Robert I. Rotberg, *Transformative Political Leadership: Making a Difference in the Developing World* (Chicago: University of Chicago Press, 2012).

26 Thomas C. Schelling, "Command and Control," in James W. McKie, ed., *Social Responsibility and the Business Predicament* (Washington, DC: Brookings Institution, 1974), 83–84. On Schelling's influence on U.S. strategy during the Vietnam War, see Mark Moyar, *Triumph Forsaken: The Vietnam War, 1954–1965* (New York: Cambridge University Press, 2006).

27 For more on the inadequacies of rational choice theory, see John Lewis Gaddis, *The Landscape of History: How Historians Map the Past* (New York: Oxford University Press, 2002).

28 Lanre Olu-Adeyemi, "The Challenges of Democratic Governance in Nigeria," *International Journal of Business and Social Science*, vol. 3, no. 5 (March 2012), 167–171.

29 In Afghanistan, which is sometimes believed to have a weak central government because of the prevalence of insurgency, President Hamid Karzai actually dominates local governments because he appoints the governors and police chiefs. He appears weak merely because his appointees have often failed to wield power effectively outside of the district and provincial capitals.

30 Martin Meredith, one of the most trenchant analysts of recent African history, has observed that Africa's fundamental problem is that most of its leaders have opted to subordinate public welfare to the perpetuation of their power "for the purpose of self-enrichment." Martin Meredith, *The Fate of Africa: A History of the Continent since Independence* (New York: PublicAffairs, 2011), 697–698. The Canadian Senate's Foreign Affairs Committee, in a study of forty years of largely unproductive Western assistance to sub-Saharan Africa, put it bluntly: "By far the biggest obstacle to achieving growth and stability in sub-Saharan Africa has been poor government and poor leadership within Africa itself." Standing Senate Committee on Foreign Affairs and International Trade, "Overcoming 40 Years of Failure: A New Roadmap for Sub-Saharan Africa," February 2007, www.parl.gc.ca/Content/SEN/Committee/391/fore/rep/repafrifeb07-e.pdf.

31 John McMillan, and Pablo Zoido, "How to Subvert Democracy: Montesinos in Peru," *Journal of Economic Perspectives*, vol. 18, no. 4: 69–92.

32 Former World Bank researcher William Easterly has aptly noted that the international aid community's obsession with producing grand policy plans often obscures the importance of having the right people to lead the implementation of policy. William J. Easterly, *The White Man's Burden: Why the West's Efforts to Aid the Rest Have Done So Much Ill and So Little Good* (New York: Penguin, 2006).

33 Radelet, *Emerging Africa*, 138.

34 Marek Jan Chodakiewicz, "Kwasniewski's Chekist Service Killed His Chance to Head UN," November 16, 2006, www.iwp.edu/news_publications/detail/dr-c-kwasniewskis-chekist-service-killed-his-chance-to-head-un.

35 Transparency International, annual reports, http://archive.transparency.org/publica tions/annual_report.

36 "Horse Power to Horsepower," *The Economist,* January 28, 2010.

37 Barbara K. Bodine, "Yemen: Primer and Prescriptions," *Prism,* vol. 1, no. 3 (June 2010), 52.

38 Mark Moyar, *A Question of Command: Counterinsurgency from the Civil War to Iraq* (New Haven: Yale University Press, 2009).

39 Honduran development executive, interview with author, 2012.

CIVILIZATION

1 Lawrence E. Harrison, *The Central Liberal Truth: How Politics Can Change a Culture and Save It from Itself* (New York: Oxford University Press, 2006), 1.

2 The West has traditionally been defined as Western Europe and its offshoot societies in North America and Australasia. Some scholars of Western Civilization, however, have argued in favor of including additional countries on the list. Latin America was shaped by European colonizers much as the United States and Canada were, but it differed from its northern neighbors in that it was shielded from the Protestant Reformation and its lands were owned by much smaller segments of society, both of which inhibited the growth of representative bodies and broad civic participation. Consequently, the societies of Latin America have for most of their history been ruled by governments that were more autocratic and predatory than most Western governments. More recently, democracy has proliferated in Latin America, and middle classes have begun to emerge, but corruption and disregard for the law remain endemic in many places. Latin America is at present among the most receptive areas of the world to Western- ization, on account of its Christian and European roots, its extensive interaction with the United States and Europe, and its growing Protestant populations. It also stands to benefit greatly from further Westernization. Consequently, the region receives exten- sive treatment in this book. Orthodox Christendom, comprising Russia and most of the smaller countries of Eastern Europe, shares the Christianity and classical heritage of Western Europe but differs in its lack of exposure to the Enlightenment, which kept it from absorbing the Enlightenment's individualism and rationalism. Because the Orthodox countries are relatively advanced in terms of development and governance, they are not covered in this book.

3 See, for instance, Sachs, *The End of Poverty,* 39.

4 The products of the Culture Matters Research Project include Lawrence E. Harrison and Samuel P. Huntington, eds., *Culture Matters: How Values Shape Human Pro- gress* (New York: Basic Books, 2000), 69–70; Lawrence E. Harrison and Peter L. Berger, *Developing Cultures: Case Studies* (New York: Routledge, 2006); Lawrence E. Harrison and Jerome Kagan, eds., *Developing Cultures: Essays on Cultural Change* (New York: Routledge, 2006); Harrison, *The Central Liberal Truth.* Another highly important book on culture from this period is Thomas Sowell, *Conquests and Cultures: An International History* (New York: Basic Books, 1998).

5 Niall Ferguson, *Civilization: The West and the Rest* (New York: Penguin, 2011).

6 The Catholic theologian Philip Jenkins notes, "Since the 1940s, most European countries have consciously tried to move away from national identification and to encourage a new European consciousness, largely leaving the potent symbols of patriotism to the lower

classes, or the far right." Philip Jenkins, *God's Continent: Christianity, Islam, and Europe's Religious Crisis* (Oxford: Oxford University Press, 2007), 246.

7   The best recent history of the fall of the Roman Empire, which convincingly refutes scholarship that attributes Rome's demise exclusively to external factors, is Adrian Goldsworthy, *How Rome Fell: Death of a Superpower* (New Haven: Yale University Press, 2009).

8   Recent historical works have shown that France experienced a resurgence in patriotism as war neared and have emphasized the importance of such factors as poor French intelligence on the location of the main German thrust and Hitler's cunning in anticipating the French reaction to that thrust. For an overview of scholarship on the conflict, see Douglas Porch, "Military Culture and the 'Fall' of France," *International Security*, vol. 4, no. 4 (Spring 2000), 157–180.

9   Encapsulating the linkage of pacifism to antipatriotism, the acclaimed French novelist Jean Giono remarked, "There is no glory in being French, there is only one glory: to be alive." Julian Jackson, *The Fall of France: The Nazi Invasion of 1940* (New York: Oxford University Press, 2003), 147. George Soulès, a left-wing technocrat who later joined the right-wing Pétain government, recounted that in his working-class Toulouse neighborhood, "the war, its massacres, it scandals, had ruined a certain sentimental idea of the fatherland." The people "looked on patriotism as an absolute evil." Eugen Weber, *The Hollow Years: France in the 1930s* (New York: W. W. Norton, 1994), 18. For Frenchmen who were more favorably disposed to patriotism and the military, the widespread contempt for patriotic duty engendered disgust and raised doubts about whether the French nation was still worthy of patriotic affection and self-sacrifice.

10 Jackson notes, "Many men whose level of education would normally have led them to be officers served only as common soldiers because, owing to the anti-militarism prevalent among intellectuals and *instituteurs*, they had refused to perform their PMS." Jackson, *The Fall of France,* 158–159.

11 Eugenia C. Kiesling, *Arming against Hitler: France and the Limits of Military Planning* (Lawrence: University Press of Kansas, 1996).

12 Williamson C. Murray, "Armored Warfare: The British, French, and German Experiences," in Williamson C. Murray and Allan R. Millett, eds., *Military Innovation in the Interwar Period* (New York: Cambridge University Press, 1998), 6–49.

13 Ernest R. May, *Strange Victory: Hitler's Conquest of France* (New York: Hill and Wang, 2000), 448–449.

14 Ferguson, *Civilization,* 262–264; David Landes, *The Wealth and Poverty of Nations: Why Some Are So Rich and Some So Poor* (W. W. Norton, 1998), 174–179.

15 Ronald Inglehart, *Culture Shift in Advanced Industrial Society* (Princeton: Princeton University Press, 1990), 49–60. Some Catholic countries reduced the economic gap in the second half of the twentieth century, but the gap has remained large. The per capita GDP of the average first world Protestant country at the start of the twenty-first century was $30,062, versus $22,890 for the average first world Catholic country. Harrison, *The Central Liberal Truth,* 88–89.

16 Bernard Ellis Lewis and Buntzie Ellis Churchill, *Islam: The Religion and the People* (Upper Saddle River, NJ: Pearson Prentice Hall, 2009), 102–104.

17 Charles A. Kupchan, *No One's World: The West, The Rising Rest, and the Coming Global Turn* (New York: Oxford University Press, 2012), 47–58.

18   Landes, *The Wealth and Poverty of Nations*, 335–349.

19   See, for instance, Phil Zuckerman, *Society without God: What the Least Religious Nations Can Tell Us about Contentment* (New York: New York University Press, 2008); Patricia S. Churchland, *Braintrust: What Neuroscience Tells Us about Morality* (Princeton: Princeton University Press, 2011).

20   The decline in European Christianity was the result of a larger process of decline in belief and rise in hedonism among Europeans, stemming from the scapegoating of nationalism for the world wars, a process spurred on by the radicalism of the 1960s. See George Weigel, *The Cube and the Cathedral: Europe, America, and Politics without God* (New York: Basic Books, 2005); Jenkins, *God's Continent*.

.21   Some have blamed corruption in the third world upon Western imperialism, asserting that the imperialists imposed governments that existed only to protect imperial interests and those of their indigenous allies. Haugen and Boutros, *The Locust Effect*, 172–181. It is true that colonial institutions and their elitist tendencies often persisted after independence, but those tendencies were not peculiarly European. Governmental favoritism toward elites existed in most of the world before the spread of Europe's empires, and it has been present in modern times in places that largely or entirely escaped colonization, such as Thailand, Ethiopia, and Japan.

22   T. S. Eliot, *Christianity and Culture* (New York: Harcourt, Brace, Jovanovich, 1940), 200.

23   Samuel P. Huntington, *The Clash of Civilizations and the Remaking of World Order* (Simon & Schuster, 1996), 305. Some religious experts, in fact, contend that Church rituals have lost their popularity in Scandinavia because the exceptionally thorough infusion of Christian principles into state and society has rendered the Church superfluous. Jenkins, *God's Continent*, 65. This observation likely contains some truth, although it does not adequately take into account how the loss of religious conviction has encouraged hedonism and other ills.

24   http://stats.oecd.org/index.aspx.

25   Charles Murray, *In Our Hands: A Plan to Replace the Welfare State* (Washington, DC: AEI Press, 2006).

26   Ferguson, *Civilization,* 266. For the linking of European work habits to culture more generally, see Walter Laqueur, *The Last Days of Europe: Epitaph for an Old Continent* (New York: Thomas Dunne Books, 2007).

27   For comparisons of European political culture with American political culture, see Zoltan J. Acs, *Why Philanthropy Matters: How the Wealthy Give, and What It Means for Our Economic Well-being* (Princeton: Princeton University Press, 2013); Murray, *In Our Hands*.

28   Arthur C. Brooks, *Who Really Cares: The Surprising Truth about Compassionate Conservatism* (New York: Basic Books, 2006).

29   For recent analysis of the connections between religion, patriotism, and foreign policy, see Mary N. Hampton, *A Thorn in Transatlantic Relations: American and European Perceptions of Threat and Security* (New York: Palgrave Macmillan, 2013); Erin K. Wilson, *After Secularism: Rethinking Religion in Global Politics* (New York: Palgrave Macmillan, 2012). What economists term "free riding" on American protection is a conceivable alternative explanation for the decline of European defense spending and military activity, but it is not a compelling one. In the early Cold War, when religious and patriotic belief were still relatively strong in Europe, European defense spending

levels were high, and European countries fought repeatedly in overseas conflicts, despite the availability of the U.S. nuclear umbrella. The major downward trend in European military spending did not begin until the 1970s, at the same time that secularism was overtaking religion and patriotism. The large expenditures of European welfare states on shrinking and aging populations have contributed to the decline in military spending, but they did not cause it, as military spending was already declining before demographic shifts put intense pressure on European budgets.

30 Josef Joffe, "The Demons of Europe," *Commentary,* January 2004.

31 Steven Erlanger, "Shrinking Europe Military Spending Stirs Concern," *New York Times,* April 22, 2013.

32 Landes, *The Wealth of Nations;* Sowell, *Conquests and Cultures.*

33 Joy Kooi-Chin Tong, *Overseas Chinese Christian Entrepreneurs in Modern China: A Case Study of the Influence of Christian Ethics on Business Life* (London: Anthem, 2012); Nanlai Cao, *Constructing China's Jerusalem: Christians, Power, and Place in Contemporary Wenzhou* (Palo Alto: Stanford University Press, 2010); Francis Khek Gee Lim, ed., *Christianity in Contemporary China: Socio-cultural Perspectives* (London: Routledge, 2012); David Aikman, *Jesus in Beijing: How Christianity Is Transforming China and Changing the Global Balance of Power* (Washington, DC: Regnery, 2006).

34 Ferguson, *Civilization,* 277–288. Quote is on 287.

35 Lawrence E. Harrison, *Who Prospers? How Cultural Values Shape Economic and Political Success* (New York: Basic Books, 1992), 2–3, 39–40, 56.

36 Nina Munk, *The Idealist: Jeffrey Sachs and the Quest to End Poverty* (New York: Doubleday, 2013), 162.

37 Joe Nocera, "Fighting Poverty, and Critics," *New York Times,* September 2, 2013.

38 Munk, *The Idealist,* 49, 160–161, 193–194.

39 Barack Obama, *Dreams from My Father: A Story of Race and Inheritance* (New York: Times Books, 1995), 417.

40 Daniel Etounga-Manguelle, "Does Africa Need a Cultural Adjustment Program?" in Harrison and Huntington, eds., *Culture Matters,* 69–70.

41 Huntington, *The Clash of Civilizations and the Remaking of World Order,* 56–101, 308–312.

42 David D. Kirkpatrick of the *New York Times* reported from Cairo, "The vast majority of liberals, leftists and intellectuals in Egypt have joined in the jubilation at the defeat of the Muslim Brotherhood." David D. Kirkpatrick, "Egyptian Liberals Embrace the Military, Brooking No Dissent," *New York Times,* July 16, 2013.

43 Jeffrey Herbst, *States and Power in Africa: Comparative Lessons in Authority and Control* (Princeton: Princeton University Press, 2000), 159–161.

44 For more on the relationship between economic modernization and democratization, see Adam Przeworski et al., *Democracy and Development: Political Institutions and Well-being in the World, 1950–1990* (New York: Cambridge University Press, 2000); Stephen D. Krasner, "International Support for State-Building: Flawed Consensus," *Prism,* vol. 2, no. 3 (June 2011), 65–74.

45 Charles Tilly, *Coercion, Capital, and European States, AD 990–1990* (Hoboken, NJ: Basil Blackwell, 1990); Robert Bates, *Prosperity and Violence: The Political Economy of Development* (New York: W. W. Norton, 2001).

46 Acemoglu and Robinson, *Why Nations Fail,* 57–58, 70–76, 83–87, 93.

47 For a comparison of the founding of the two Koreas, see Sung Chul Yang, *The North and South Korean Political Systems: A Comparative Analysis* (Boulder: Westview Press, 1994).

48 John Kie-Chiang Oh, *Korean Politics: The Quest for Democratization and Economic Development* (Ithaca: Cornell University Press, 1999), 60–97; San-Jin Han, "Modernization and the Rise of Civil Society: The Role of the 'Middling Grassroots' for Democratization in Korea," *Human Studies*, vol. 24, no. 1/2 (2001), 113–132; Gregg A. Brazinsky, *Nation Building in South Korea: Koreans, Americans, and the Making of a Democracy* (Chapel Hill: University of North Carolina Press, 2009), 189–250.

49 Chong-Min Park and Doh Chull Shin, "Do Asian Values Deter Popular Support for Democracy in South Korea?" *Asian Survey*, vol. 46, no. 3 (May/June 2006), 341–361.

50 Acemoglu and Robinson, *Why Nations Fail*, 7–9, 57.

51 Tim Johnson, "Mexico's Subpar Schools Put Shackles on Its Future," *McClatchy*, June 17, 2012.

52 David Agren, "Education System Holding Mexico Back, Critics Say," *USA Today*, March 30, 2012.

53 For two excellent recent studies on Mexican culture and politics, see Jorge G. Castañeda, *Mañana Forever? Mexico and the Mexicans* (New York: Alfred A. Knopf, 2011); Roderic Ai Camp, *Mexico: What Everyone Needs to Know* (New York: Oxford University Press, 2011). On the rise of liberal democracy in the Mexican middle class, see Shannon O'Neil, "The Real War in Mexico: How Democracy Can Defeat the Drug Cartels," *Foreign Affairs*, vol. 88, no. 4 (July/August 2009), 64–77; Ioan Grillo, *El Narco: Inside Mexico's Criminal Insurgency* (New York: Bloomsbury, 2011).

54 Some within the institutional school concede that culture is critical to the functioning of liberal institutions, but contend that the requisite culture is the product of social and economic incentives, as opposed to civilization, religion, or intellectual currents. See, for instance, Avner Greif, *Institutions and the Path to the Modern Economy: Lessons from Medieval Trade* (Cambridge: Cambridge University Press, 2006). Douglass C. North, John Joseph Wallace, and Barry R. Weingast go so far as to acknowledge that the cultural beliefs required for successful institutions originate with "larger cultural, educational, and religious organizations." North, Wallace, and Weingast, *Violence and Social Orders*, 29.

55 The Turkmenistan Constitution, www.turkmenistanembassy.org/turkmen/business/consta.html.

56 http://graphics.eiu.com/PDF/Democracy_Index_2010_web.pdf.

57 "Berdymukhamedov Wins Turkmenistan Election in Landslide," *BBC News*, www.bbc.co.uk/news/world-asia-17009053.

58 "The Personality Cult of Turkmenbashi," *The Guardian*, www.guardian.co.uk/world/2006/dec/21/1.

59 Oliva M. Domingo, "Chronicling Corruption in the Philippines, 2005–2011: The Road to Perdition…?" in Leonor M. Briones, et al., *Pinoy Solutions to Corruption* (Manila: USAID, 2012).

60 North, Wallace, and Weingast, *Violence and Social Orders*.

61 Martin Paldam, "Corruption and Religion: Adding to the Economic Model," *Kyklos*, vol. 54, no. 2–3 (2001), 383–414; S. Douglas Beets, "International

Corruption and Religion: An Empirical Examination, *Journal of Global Ethics*, vol. 3, no. 1 (April 2007), 69–85; Daniel Treisman, "The Causes of Corruption: A Cross-national Study," *Journal of Public Economics*, vol. 76, no. 3 (June 2000), 399–457.

62 For Ramon Magsaysay, see Robert Aura Smith, *Philippine Freedom, 1946–1958* (New York: Columbia University Press, 1958); for Kim Young Sam, see Michael Breen, *The Koreans: America's Troubled Relations with North and South Korea* (New York: Thomas Dunne, 1998); for Ngo Dinh Diem, see Moyar, *Triumph Forsaken;* for Chiang Kai-shek, see Jay Taylor, *The Generalissimo: Chiang Kai-shek and the Struggle for Modern China* (Cambridge, MA: Belknap, 2009).

63 On Christianity's contributions to ethical behavior in contemporary Africa, see Collier, *Wars, Guns, and Votes,* 54; Ritva Reinikka and Jakob Svensson, "Working for God? Evidence from a Change in Financing of Not-For-Profit Health Care Providers in Uganda," *Journal of the European Economic Association*, vol. 8, no. 6 (December 2010), 1159–1178.

64 Taryn Vian et al., "Perceptions of Per Diems in the Health Sector: Evidence and Implications," *U4 Issue*, no. 6 (June 2011), 23.

65 David McKittrick, "Doctor Maria Santos Gorrostieta: Politician Murdered for Her Fight against Drug Cartels," *The Independent,* November 28, 2012.

66 Jun Medina, "COA Exec Bares More Fund Scams," *Philippine Daily Inquirer,* April 30, 2011.

67 Transparency International, Corruption Perceptions Index, 2011, http://cpi.trans parency.org/cpi2011/results/.

68 Katherine Marshall, "Ancient and Contemporary Wisdom and Practice on Governance as Religious Leaders Engage in International Development," *Journal of Global Ethics*, vol. 4, no. 3 (December 2008), 217.

69 Amy L. Sherman, *The Soul of Development: Biblical Christianity and Economic Transformation in Guatemala* (New York: Oxford University Press, 1997).

HUMAN CAPITAL DEVELOPMENT

1 James S. Coleman and David Court, *University Development in the Third World: The Rockefeller Foundation Experience* (Oxford: Pergamon, 1993); Nils Gilman, *Mandarins of the Future: Modernization Theory in Cold War America* (Baltimore: Johns Hopkins University Press, 2003). The concentration of assistance on the poor at the local level was not an entirely new concept, as it reflected the philosophy of some development champions of the first half of the twentieth century and had been a guiding principle of the Peace Corps from its foundation in 1961. David Ekbladh, *The Great American Mission: Modernization and the Construction of an American World Order* (Princeton: Princeton University Press, 2009); Nick Cullather, *The Hungry World: America's Cold War Battle against Poverty in Asia* (Cambridge, MA: Harvard University Press, 2010).

2 Ashraf Ghani and Clare Lockhart, *Fixing Failed States: A Framework for Rebuilding a Fractured World;* Sowell, *Migrations and Cultures;* Sowell, *Conquests and Cultures.*

3 For a detailed treatment of social capital, see Francis Fukuyama, *Trust: The Social Virtues and the Creation of Prosperity* (New York: Free Press, 1995).

4 For Lee Kuan Yew, who transformed Singapore into one of the best-governed and most prosperous countries in the world, instilling competence and moral virtues in the government was a single enterprise, not two separate tasks. "The quality of a people determines the outcome of a nation," he observed, including both capabilities and motives in his definition of quality. "It is how you select your people, how you train them, how you organize them and ultimately how you manage them that makes the difference." Edgar H. Schein, *Strategic Pragmatism: The Culture of Singapore's Economic Development Board* (Cambridge, MA: MIT Press, 1996), 29.

5 USAID and most other development agencies currently allocate most of their governance funding to NGOs and community organizations, especially in the most impoverished communities, rather than to the government itself, and are focused primarily at the local rather than the national level. This approach reflects official USAID policy, as articulated in the USAID Policy Framework 2011–2015, http://transition.usaid.gov/policy/USAID_PolicyFramework.PDF, and USAID Policy, "The Development Response to Violent Extremism and Insurgency," September 2011, http://pdf.usaid.gov/pdf_docs/PDACS400.pdf.

6 On the measurement of talent, see Nik Kinley and Shlomo Ben-Hur, *Talent Intelligence: What You Need to Know to Identify and Measure Talent* (San Francisco: Jossey-Bass, 2013); Gene Pease, Boyce Byerly, and Jac Fitz-enz, *Human Capital Analytics: How to Harness the Potential of Your Organization's Greatest Asset* (Hoboken, NJ: Wiley, 2012).

7 For different interpretations of charisma, see Olivia Fox Cabane, *The Charisma Myth: How Anyone Can Master the Art and Science of Personal Magnetism* (New York: Portfolio, 2012); Kurt W. Mortensen, *The Laws of Charisma: How to Captivate, Inspire, and Influence for Maximum Success* (New York: Amacom, 2011); Joseph S. Nye, *The Powers to Lead* (New York: Oxford University Press, 2008).

8 Benedict Brogan, "Mugabe Stripped of His Knighthood after Queen Gives Her Backing and Brown Calls on Businesses to Pull Out of Zimbabwe," *Daily Mail*, June 26, 2008.

9 Mary Anne Weaver, *Pakistan: In the Shadow of Jihad and Afghanistan* (New York: Farrar, Straus, and Giroux, 2002), 193.

10 Innumerable books have been written on development of interpersonal skills, but none has surpassed Dale Carnegie, *How to Win Friends and Influence People* (New York: Simon and Schuster, 1936).

11 The classic text on investment in human capital is Gary Becker, *Human Capital* (New York: National Bureau of Economic Research), 1964.

12 On the value of experience, see Thomas O. Davenport, *Human Capital: What It Is and Why People Invest It* (San Francisco: Jossey-Bass, 1999); Joan E. Pynes, *Human Resources Management for Public and Nonprofit Organizations*, 2nd ed. (San Francisco: Jossey Bass, 2004); Cynthia D. McCauley and D. Scott Derue, *Experience-Driven Leader Development: Models, Tools, Best Practices, and Advice for On-the-Job Development*, 3rd ed. (San Francisco: Wiley, 2013).

13 Moyar, *A Question of Command*, 169–182.

14 Greg Jaffe, "Army Worries about 'Toxic Leaders' in Ranks," *Washington Post*, June 25, 2011.

15 Clare Ribando Seelke and Kristin M. Finklea, "U.S.-Mexican Security Cooperation: The Mérida Initiative and Beyond," *Congressional Research Service Report*, August 15, 2011, 4, 21–23; Daniel Sabiet, "Police Reform in Mexico: Advances and Persistent Obstacles," in Eric L. Olson et al., eds., *Shared Responsibility: U.S. Mexico Policy Options for Confronting Organized Crime* (Washington, DC: Woodrow Wilson Center, 2010), 251–252; George W. Grayson, "Threat Posed by Mounting Vigilantism in Mexico," Strategic Studies Institute, September 2011, www.strategicstudiesinstitute.army.mil/pubs/display.cfm?pubID=1082, 15–16; Luis Astorga and David A. Shirk, "Drug Trafficking Organizations and Counter-Drug Strategies in the U.S.-Mexican Context," in Olson et al., eds., *Shared Responsibility*, 50; Sylvia Longmire, *Cartel: The Coming Invasion of Mexico's Drug Wars* (New York: Palgrave Macmillan), 179.

16 For historical analyses of the theory and practice of U.S. nation building, see Jeremi Suri, *Liberty's Surest Guardian: Rebuilding Nations after War from the Founders to Obama* (New York: Free Press, 2011); James Dobbins et al., *America's Role in Nation-Building from Germany to Iraq* (Santa Monica: RAND, 2003).

17 This book will follow the popular convention of referring to expenditures on human capital as "investments in human capital." Businessmen who are unfamiliar with this convention will find the phraseology confusing, since they do not invest in capital but rather invest capital in assets or companies. For those who are disconcerted by this semantic infelicity, the term "human assets" may be substituted wherever "human capital" appears.

18 For analyses of human capital's impact on private sector development, see Becker, *Human Capital*; Jacob Mincer, *Schooling, Experience, and Earnings* (New York: Columbia University Press, 1974); Alan Burton-Jones and J. C. Spender, eds. *The Oxford Handbook of Human Capital* (Oxford: Oxford University Press, 2011).

HUMAN CAPITAL AND NATIONAL SECURITY

1 Frances Fukuyama, *The End of History and the Last Man* (New York: Free Press, 1992). Quote is from p. 51.

2 Fouad Ajami, "The Summoning," *Foreign Affairs,* vol. 72, no. 4 (September/October 1993), 5.

3 On the quest for a unified paradigm, see Huntington, *The Clash of Civilizations and the Remaking of World Order,* 29–31.

4 Huntington, *The Clash of Civilizations and the Remaking of World Order;* Robert D. Kaplan, *The Coming Anarchy: Shattering the Dreams of the Post Cold War* (New York: Random House, 2000).

5 For critiques, see Jack F. Matlock, Jr., "Can Civilizations Clash?" *Proceedings of the American Philosophical Society,* vol. 143, no. 3 (September 1999), 428–439; Robert Holton, "Globalization's Cultural Consequences," *Annals of the American Academy of Political and Social Science,* vol. 570 (July 2000), 140–152; Bruce M. Russett, John R. Oneal, and Michaelene Cox, "Clash of Civilizations, or Realism and Liberalism Déjà Vu? Some Evidence," *Journal of Peace Research,* vol. 37, no. 5 (2000): 583–608; Errol A. Henderson and Richard Tucker, "Clear and Present Strangers: The Clash of Civilizations and International Conflict," *International Studies Quarterly,* vol. 45, no. 2 (June 2001), 317–338; Maurice Keens-Soper, *Europe in the World: Persistence of Power Politics* (New York: Palgrave Macmillan, 1998).

6 David Frum and Richard Perle, *An End to Evil: How to Win the War on Terror* (New York: Random House, 2003).

7 Even Fukuyama came to acknowledge that solving the third world's maladies had become "the central project of contemporary international politics." Fukuyama, *State-Building,* 99.

8 Some problems fall into a gray area between those that are entirely amenable to human capital solutions and those that are not at all amenable. Such problems are especially prevalent in countries in the process of making the transition from third world to first world, since their governments contain a mixture of human capital-rich organizations and human capital-poor ones. In addition, some behaviors are difficult to classify into the buckets of bad conduct and service of state interests. For instance, the willingness of South Korean officials or businessmen to bribe foreign officials in return for preferential treatment of South Korean businesses could be considered a human capital problem; if these South Koreans had been educated at Yale or the Sorbonne, they might have been dissuaded from engaging in such bribery. On the other hand, it could be argued that the South Koreans were sufficiently educated and were merely engaged in Machiavellian pursuit of their national interests. Owing to the deep ambiguities of such cases, this chapter avoids most of the gray areas and concentrates on the cases where human capital solutions are most likely to be useful.

9 Paul Cruickshank, "The Militant Pipeline: Between the Afghanistan-Pakistan Border Region and the West," New America Foundation, July 2011; Jeffrey Dressler, "The Haqqani Network: A Strategic Threat," Institute for the Study of War, March 2012, www.understandingwar.org/sites/default/files/Haqqani_Strategic Threatweb_29MAR_o.pdf; Matthew Rosenberg and Julian E. Barnes, "Al Qaeda Makes Afghan Comeback," *Wall Street Journal,* April 6, 2011; Zia Ur Rehman, "Taliban Recruiting and Fundraising in Karachi," *CTC Sentinel,* vol. 5, no. 7 (July 2012), 9–11; Tom Hussain, "U.S. Pullback in Lahore Another Sign of Growing Al Qaida Violence in Pakistan," *McClatchy,* August 9, 2013.

10 Bruce Hoffman, "Why al Qaeda Will Survive," *Daily Beast,* September 30, 2011; Jonathan Masters, "Al-Qaeda in the Arabian Peninsula," Council on Foreign Relations, May 24, 2012, www.cfr.org/yemen/al-qaeda-arabian-peninsula-aqap/ p9369; Julian E. Barnes, "Gates Makes Recommendations in Ft. Hood Shooting Case," *Wall Street Journal,* January 15, 2010.

11 Michael S. Schmidt and Eric Schmitt, "Syria Militants Said to Recruit Visiting Americans to Attack U.S.," *New York Times,* January 9, 2014.

12 Spencer Ackerman, "Al-Qaida Faction in Syria Contemplating US Attack, Intelligence Officials Warn," *The Guardian,* January 29, 2014.

13 Najib Sharifi, "ISIS Makes Inroads in Afghanistan, Pakistan," *Foreign Policy,* October 1, 2014; Khalil al-Anani "ISIS Enters Egypt: How Washington Must Respond," *Foreign Affairs,* December 4, 2014; Paul D. Shinkman, "War against ISIS Becoming Blurrier," *U.S. News and World Report,* December 5, 2014; Nani Afrida, "Alarming Rise in IS Support," *Jakarta Post,* December 8, 2014; Carlotta Gall, "Tunisia: ISIS Fighters Claim 2 Killings," *New York Times,* December 18, 2014; Sami Yousafzai and Christopher Dickey, "ISIS Targets Afghanistan Just as the U.S. Quits," *Daily Beast,* December 19, 2014.

14 U.S. Department of Defense, "Unclassified Report on the Military Power of Iran," April 2010, www.fas.org/man/eprint/dod_iran_2010.pdf.

15 Jeremy M. Sharp, "U.S. Foreign Aid to Israel," Congressional Research Service, March 12, 2012, 15.

16 John Mueller, *Overblown: How Politicians and the Terrorism Industry Inflate National Security Threats, and Why We Believe Them* (New York: Free Press, 2006); Fareed Zakaria, *The Post-American World* (New York: W. W. Norton, 2008).

17 Jonathan Alter, *The Promise: President Obama, Year One* (New York: Simon and Schuster, 2010), 374.

18 Jamie Crawford, "Syria, al Qaeda: U.S. Officials Offer Grim Assessment," *cnn.com*, February 11, 2014.

19 World Bank President James Wolfensohn, for instance, urged the first world to double its foreign aid to the third world with the assertion that "the war against terrorism will be won by eliminating poverty." Bernard Harborne, "Aid: A Security Perspective," in Spear and Williams, eds., *Security and Development in Global Politics*, 41. Jared Diamond has called for "combating the forces of poverty and hopelessness on which international terrorism feeds," with extensive first world spending aimed at "providing basic health care, supporting family planning and addressing such widespread environmental problems as deforestation." Jared Diamond, "Why We Must Feed the Hands That Could Bite Us," *Washington Post*, January 13, 2002. See also Sachs, *The End of Poverty*, 215–221.

20 Daniel Pipes, "God and Mammon: Does Poverty Cause Militant Islam?" *National Interest*, no. 66 (Winter 2001/2002), 14–21. Some individuals become rank and file members of terrorist organizations because they need a paycheck, but that is true of any organization that pays its armed forces.

21 Thomas Sowell developed the concept of negative human capital in the economic realm, describing how higher education can promote attitudes that undermine economic productivity. Sowell, *Conquests and Cultures*. In this book, the same concept is expanded to cover attitudes that are politically or socially damaging. The distinction between positive and negative human capital is admittedly not always clear-cut, as sensible individuals often disagree over the definition of positive political and social outcomes. But it is useful in extreme cases, where there is broad agreement over the negative character of certain motives, which is true of the motives of most violent extremist organizations.

22 Huntington, *Clash of Civilizations and the Remaking of World Order*, 109–121, 209–218.

23 Dinesh D'Souza, *The Enemy at Home: The Cultural Left and Its Responsibility for 9/11* (New York: Doubleday, 2007).

24 John J. Mearsheimer and Stephen M. Walt, *The Israel Lobby and U.S. Foreign Policy* (New York: Farrar, Straus and Giroux, 2007); Rashid Khalidi, *Resurrecting Empire: Western Footprints and America's Perilous Path in the Middle East* (Boston: Beacon Press, 2004).

25 Bassam Tibi, *Islam between Culture and Politics* (New York: Palgrave Macmillan, 2005); Pipes, "God and Mammon"; Malise Ruthven, *A Fury for God: The Islamist Attack on America*, 2nd ed. (London: Granta Publications, 2004). See also Alan B. Krueger, *What Makes a Terrorist: Economics and the Roots of Terrorism*

(Princeton: Princeton University Press, 2007); Mary Habeck, *Knowing the Enemy: Jihadist Ideology and the War on Terror* (New Haven: Yale University Press, 2006).

26 Pakistan, which provides various types of assistance to some of the world's most notorious terrorist organizations, presents a more complicated case than most of the state sponsors of terrorism. Pakistan, moreover, appears to be less zealous than other states in employing terrorist organizations, relying on them with Machiavellian cunning to hurt India and prevent the emergence of a strong, hostile state in Afghanistan. See Bruce O. Riedel, *Deadly Embrace: Pakistan, America, and the Future of the Global Jihad* (Washington, DC: Brookings Institution Press, 2011).

27 Concerning Ahmadinejad's halo, see Philippe Naughton, "Mahmoud Ahmadinejad Mocked for UN 'Halo'," *Times*, June 8 2009. That the policies of Sudan and Iran toward terrorism are driven by the thinking of the leaders rather than impersonal geopolitical forces can be seen in the opposition to Islamist terrorists of earlier regimes. The Shah of Iran, it may be recalled, staunchly opposed the extremists in his country until his abdication in 1979, which the administration of Jimmy Carter helped engineer in the mistaken belief that it would bring enlightened liberals to power.

28 For more on the likelihood of failed or failing states to play host to international terrorists, see James A. Piazza, "Incubators of Terror: Do Failed and Failing States Promote Transnational Terrorism?" *International Studies Quarterly*, vol. 53, no. 3 (September 2008), 469–488.

29 Daily Mail, "Whipped for Wearing a 'Deceptive' Bra: Hardline Islamists in Somalia Publicly Flog Women in Sharia Crackdown," October 16, 2009.

30 Total spending from 1991 to 2011 was $13 billion in humanitarian and development aid, and $7.3 billion for security. John Norris and Bronwyn Bruton, "Twenty Years of Collapse and Counting: The Cost of Failure in Somalia," September 2011, Center for American Progress, www.americanprogress.org/issues/2011/09/pdf/somalia.pdf.

31 Ted Dagne, "Somalia: Current Conditions and Prospects for a Lasting Peace," Congressional Research Service, August 31, 2011.

32 Michelle Nichols, "U.N. Security Council Approves Boost to Somalia Peacekeepers," *Reuters*, November 12, 2013; Peter Clottey, "Troop Surge Could End Al-Shabab Insurgency, Says AU Official," *Voice of America*, November 14, 2013.

33 Kenneth F. McKenzie, Jr. and Elizabeth C. Packard, "Enduring Interests and Partnerships: Military-to-Military Relationships in the Arab Spring," *Prism*, vol. 3, no. 1 (December 2011), 105; F. S. Aijazuddin, "Two Halves Did Not Make A Whole: Pakistan Before and After Bangladesh," in Lawrence E. Harrison and Peter L. Berger, *Developing Cultures: Case Studies* (New York: Routledge, 2006), 207; Seth G. Jones and C. Christine Fair, *Counterinsurgency in Pakistan* (Santa Monica: RAND, 2010), 135–136.

34 For descriptions of the twenty-six conflicts, see J. Joseph Hewitt et al., *Peace and Conflict 2012* (Boulder: Paradigm Publishers, 2012), 121–141. See also Andrej Tusicisny, "Civilizational Conflicts: More Frequent, Longer, and Bloodier?" *Journal of Peace Research*, vol. 41 no. 4 (July 2004), 485–498; World Bank, *World Development Report 2011*, 52. The scarcity of interstate conflicts within a given year, it should be noted, provides a somewhat distorted view of the overall prevalence of interstate conflict, because in general interstate conflicts are considerably shorter than intrastate conflicts and thus show up less frequently on single-year

snapshots. The war between Russia and Georgia over South Ossetia in 2008 lasted scarcely more than one week but witnessed more casualties than many intrastate conflicts see in an entire year. The war between Libya and NATO, which racked up a higher death toll than most intrastate conflicts do in their lifetimes, started and ended within the same year.

35 Collier, *The Bottom Billion*, 32; World Bank, *World Development Report 2011*, 5–6.
36 Countries with low incomes have shown a higher tendency toward insurgency and civil war. Collier, *The Bottom Billion*, 18–22. But it does not necessarily follow that lower incomes cause war. Rather, low income and internal conflict occur frequently together because both are the product of bad governance and bad leadership.
37 For the views of the Obama administration, see White House Office of the Press Secretary, "Remarks by the President on a New Strategy for Afghanistan and Pakistan," March 27, 2009; Bob Woodward, *Obama's Wars* (New York: Simon and Schuster, 2010), 134; Susan E. Rice, "Poverty Breeds Insecurity," in Lael Brainard and Derek Chollet, eds., *Too Poor for Peace? Global Poverty, Conflict, and Security in the 21st Century* (Washington, DC: Brookings Institution Press, 2007), 31–49.
38 Case studies that support this interpretation can be found in Moyar, *A Question of Command*. This interpretation has recently gained acceptance among some social scientists and aid professionals; see World Bank, *World Development Report 2011*, 73–89; USAID Policy, "The Development Response to Violent Extremism and Insurgency," September 2011, http://pdf.usaid.gov/pdf_docs/PDACS400.pdf, 3–15.
39 Testimony of Andrew Wilder, Hearing on U.S. Aid to Pakistan: Planning and Accountability, House Committee on Oversight and Government Reform, Subcommittee on National Security and Foreign Affairs, December 9, 2009, www.hks. harvard.edu/cchrp/sbhrap/news/Wilder_PakistanAidTestimony_12_9_09.pdf. For more detailed analyses, see Andrew Wilder, "Losing Hearts and Minds in Afghanistan," Middle East Institute, December 2009; Mark Moyar, "Development in Afghanistan's Counterinsurgency: A New Guide," Orbis Operations, March 2011, http://smallwarsjournal.com/documents/development-in-afghanistan-coin-moyar.pdf; Thompson, Report on Wilton Park Conference 1022; Hassan Abbas and Shehzad H. Qazi, "Rebellion, Development and Security in Pakistan's Tribal Areas," *CTC Sentinel*, vol. 6, no. 6 (June 2013), 23–26.
40 Katarina Gospic et al., "Limbic Justice – Amygdala Involvement in Immediate Rejection in the Ultimatum Game," *PLoS Biology*, 2011; 9 (5): e1001054; Jerome Kagan, *The Nature of the Child* (New York: Basic Books, 1994). More controversial than the question of whether moral judgment is prewired is the question of who did the prewiring. Evolutionary biologists view the human capacity for moral reasoning as the result of its effectiveness in promoting human survivability. Through genetic mutation, a number of early humans developed the capacity for differentiating between right and wrong and consequently took actions that increased their likelihood of survival. They gave the next generation the genes that had made them moral, while those without moral scruples were, over generations, killed off by other cave men or gobbled up by wild beasts. The most famous exposition of this position is Edward O. Wilson, *On Human Nature* (Cambridge, MA: Harvard University Press, 1979). A much longer and deeper tradition of thought has sought to explain the human capacity for moral reasoning in theological or philosophical terms. Buddhist,

Christian, Jewish, and Islamic doctrine view the ability of humans to tell right from wrong as a fundamental, if not the most fundamental, proof that a higher being or law exists. Metaphysical philosophers from Aristotle to Kant have found in the human conscience a force that transcends human flesh, while materialist philosophers from Epicurus to Marx have expended equal effort in explaining how the conscience is rooted in the body and nothing more.

41 For more on the relationship between security and political rebellion, see Etzioni, *Security First.*

42 David Kilcullen, *The Accidental Guerilla: Fighting Small Wars in the Midst of a Big One* (New York: Oxford University Press, 2009), 60.

43 Moyar, *A Question of Command.* The ensuing paragraphs on Afghanistan and Iraq are taken from pages 213–258.

44 Halperin, Siegle, and Weinstein, *The Democracy Advantage*; Larry Diamond, *The Spirit of Democracy: The Struggle to Build Free Societies throughout the World* (New York: Henry Holt, 2008); Radelet, *Emerging Africa*; Sen, *Development a Freedom.*

45 Edward D. Mansfield and Jack Snyder, *Electing to Fight: Why Emerging Democracies Go to War* (Cambridge, MA: MIT Press, 2005). See also Collier, *Wars, Guns, and Votes,* 20–21.

46 Paul Lewis, "Kosovo PM Is Head of Human Organ and Arms Ring, Council of Europe Reports," *The Guardian,* 14 December 2010.

47 Carol Cratty, "Three Men Sentenced in North Carolina Terrorist Ring," *cnn.com,* January 13, 2012.

48 Filip Reyntjens, "The Proof of the Pudding Is in the Eating: The June 1993 Elections in Burundi," *Journal of Modern African Studies,* vol. 31, no. 4 (December 1993), 563–583; Léonce Ndikumana, "Institutional Failure and Ethnic Conflicts in Burundi," *African Studies Review,* vol. 41, no. 1 (April 1998), 29–47; International Commission of Inquiry for Burundi, Final Report, January 13, 2004, www.usip. org/files/file/resources/collections/commissions/Burundi-Report.pdf.

49 Abdelaziz Barrouhi, "Le Général Ammar, L'homme Qui a Dit Non," *Jeune Afrique,* 7 February 2011.

50 Definitive evidence on the motives of the Egyptian military in February 2011 is not available, but several well-placed observers have cited American military assistance as a key factor in the military's behavior and as a facilitator of communication between the United States and the Egyptian military. See Jeffrey D. Feltman's testimony in "Assessing U.S. Foreign Policy Priorities and Needs Amidst Economic Challenges in the Middle East," Subcommittee on the Middle East and South Asia, House Foreign Affairs Committee, March 10, 2011, www.gpo.gov/fdsys/pkg/CHRG-112hhrg65055/pdf/CHRG-112hhrg65055.pdf; Nelly Lahoud et al., "The 'Arab Spring': Investing in Durable Peace," Combating Terrorism Center, June 29, 2011, www.ctc.usma.edu/wp-content/uploads/2011/09/White-Paper-Final.pdf; Tara McKelvey, "U.S.-Funded Democracy Crushers?" *Daily Beast,* October 13, 2011.

51 Egypt's liberal democrats, recognizing their impotence once the Egyptian population had overwhelmingly rejected their worldview at the ballot box, threw their support behind the military as the best protection against Islamist domination. Matt Bradley, "Egypt's Military Seeks to Preserve Powers," *Wall Street Journal,* May 19, 2012.

52 Chris Newsom, "Conflict in the Niger Delta: More than a Local Affair," United States Institute of Peace, June 2011.

53 UNDP Nigeria, "Niger Human Development Report," 2006, http://hdr.undp.org/en/reports/national/africa/nigeria/nigeria_hdr_report.pdf.

54 Newsom, "Conflict in the Niger Delta."

55 Ibid. John Campbell, the U.S. Ambassador to Nigeria from 2004 to 2007, commented in 2012, "Nigeria's fundamental problem is a system of institutionalized corruption that channels public money into the pockets of a few Nigerian 'big men.'" John Campbell, "Nigeria's Battle for Stability," *National Interest,* March–April 2012.

56 UPI, "Troubled Nigeria's Oil Output under Threat," March 23, 2012.

57 Peter M. Lewis, "Nigeria: Assessing the Risks to Stability," CSIS, June 2011, http://csis.org/files/publication/110623_Lewis_Nigeria_Web.pdf.

58 David C. Becker, "Gangs, Netwar, and 'Community Counterinsurgency' in Haiti," *Prism,* vol. 2, no. 3 (June 2011), 137–154.

59 Christopher Roads, "Peacekeepers at War," *Wall Street Journal,* June 23, 2012.

60 "Who Will Watch the Watchmen?" *The Economist,* May 29, 2008.

61 OECD, "Aid to Health," www.oecd.org/dataoecd/26/39/49907438.pdf.

62 Laurie Garrett, "The Challenge of Global Health," *Foreign Affairs,* vol. 86, no. 1 (January/February 2007), 26.

63 Roger Bate, "Fighting the Major Diseases of Africa: Sustaining the Gains of the Last Decade," American Enterprise Institute, February 2012, www.aei.org/files/2012/02/07/-fighting-the-major-diseases-of-africa-sustaining-the-gains-of-the-last-decade_100846573844.pdf; Brian Senoga Kimuli, "Global Fund Cuts AIDS Cash to Uganda," *Daily Monitor,* February 12, 2012; "Zambia: Corruption Scandal Rocks ARV Programme," *Plusnews,* March 14, 2011, www.irinnews.org/Report/92191/ZAMBIA-Corruption-scandal-rocks-ARV-programme;Nandini   Oomman et al., "Zeroing in: AIDS Donors and Africa's Health Workforce," Center for Global Development, 2010, www.cgdev.org/files/1424385_file_CGD_Health_Workforce_FINAL.pdf; Donald G. McNeil, "At Front Lines, AIDS War Is Falling Apart," *New York Times,* May 9, 2010.

64 An estimated thirty million donated malaria treatments are stolen each year, for instance. Roger Bate, "Africa's Epidemic of Disappearing Medicine," *Foreign Policy,* January 11, 2011. In 2011, an internal audit of the Global Fund to Fight AIDS, Tuberculosis, and Malaria uncovered widespread theft in Africa, including at least $2.5 million of antimalarial drugs that disappeared from its warehouses in thirteen countries and were sold on the black market. An estimated 70 percent of the theft was perpetrated by security personnel, warehouse managers, or doctors at government-operated warehouses. This organization had been more trusting of recipient governments than other aid organizations at the insistence of Jeffrey Sachs, who was its intellectual founding father, but these revelations led to the withdrawal of aid from certain countries and more stringent oversight of recipient governments in the others. Maria Cheng, "Millions in Malaria Drugs Stolen," *Boston Globe,* April 20, 2011; Sarah Boseley, "Global Fund Verdict Could Be Devastating for the Fight against Aids," *The Guardian,* September 19, 2011. In Ghana, one of Jeffrey Sachs's "relatively well-governed" African countries, a World Bank study found that corruption diverted 80 percent of nonsalary health resources from their

intended purposes. World Bank, "Africa Development Indicators 2010," http://siteresources.worldbank.org/AFRICAEXT/Resources/english_essay_adi2010.pdf, 11.

65 Garrett, "The Challenge of Global Health," 26.

66 Executive Office of the President, Office of National Drug Control Policy, "National Drug Control Budget – FY 2012 Funding Highlights," www.whitehouse.gov/sites/default/files/ondcp/policy-and-research/fy12highlight_exec_sum.pdf; David A. Shirk, "The Drug War in Mexico: Confronting a Shared Threat," vii.

67 National Drug Intelligence Center, "National Threat Assessment: The Economic Impact of Illicit Drug Use on American Society," May 2011, www.justice.gov/ndic/pubs44/44731/44731p.pdf.

68 U.S. Department of Health and Human Services, "Results from the 2009 National Survey on Drug Use and Health," September 2009, www.oas.samhsa.gov/NSDUH/2k9NSDUH/2k9ResultsP.pdf; ONDCP, "How Illicit Drug Use Affects Business and the Economy," http://www.whitehouse.gov/sites/default/files/ondcp/Fact_Sheets/effects_of_drugs_on_economy_jw_5-24-11_0.pdf.

69 Gretchen Peters, *Seeds of Terror: How Heroin Is Bankrolling the Taliban and al Qaeda* (New York: Thomas Dunne, 2009).

70 DeShazo et al., "Countering Threats to Security and Stability in a Failing State," 8–9.

71 U.S. Government Accountability Office, "Plan Colombia: Drug Reduction Goals Were Not Fully Met, But Security Has Improved," October 2008, www.gao.gov/products/GAO-09-71, 11–15; DeShazo et al., "Countering Threats to Security and Stability in a Failing State," 5–16.

72 Thomas Pickering, "Anatomy of Plan Columbia," *The American Interest*, November/December 2009, 75–76.

73 Felbab-Brown et al., "Assessment of the Implementation of the United States Government's Support for Plan Colombia's Illicit Crop Reduction Components"; Peter DeShazo et al., "Countering Threats to Security and Stability in a Failing State," 23–24.

74 Felbab-Brown et al., "Assessment of the Implementation of the United States Government's Support for Plan Colombia's Illicit Crop Reduction Components," 11; United States Department of State and the Broadcasting Board of Governors, Office of Inspector General, "Inspection of Embassy Bogotá," June 2011, 15.

75 Clare Ribando Seelke et al., "Latin America and the Caribbean: Illicit Drug Trafficking and U.S. Counterdrug Programs," Congressional Research Service, May 12, 2011, 14.

76 Jack Martin and Eric A. Ruark, "The Fiscal Burden of Illegal Immigration on United States Taxpayers," Federation for American Immigration Reform, Washington, DC, July 2010. Critics have attempted to cast doubt on the study by noting that its sponsoring organization has been active in opposing illegal immigration. A recent report without partisan sponsorship would be ideal, but no such report exists, and no critiques have identified severe flaws in the work of Martin and Ruark, leaving their study as the best source presently available. For an analysis of this and other studies on the topic, see William A. Kandel, "Fiscal Impacts of the Foreign-Born Population," Congressional Research Service, October 19, 2011.

77 John Simanski and Lesley M. Sapp, "Immigration Enforcement Actions: 2011," Department of Homeland Security, http://www.dhs.gov/sites/default/files/publications/immigration-statistics/enforcement_ar_2011.pdf.

78 Associated Press, "Feds Estimate Deportation Costs $12,500 Per Person," January 26, 2011.

79 Anna Bowden, "The Economic Costs of Somali Piracy 2011," One Earth Future Foundation, http://oceansbeyondpiracy.org/sites/default/files/economic_cost_of_piracy_2011.pdf.

80 Christopher Alessi and Stephanie Hanson, "Combating Maritime Piracy," Council on Foreign Relations, March 23, 2012, www.cfr.org/france/combating-maritime-piracy/p18376.

81 National Intellectual Property Rights Coordination Center, "Intellectual Property Rights Violations: A Report on Threats to United States Interests at Home and Abroad," November 2011, www.iprcenter.gov/reports/ipr-center-reports/IPR%20Center%20Threat%20Report%20and%20Survey.pdf/view.

82 National Intellectual Property Rights Coordination Center, "Intellectual Property Rights Violations: A Report on Threats to United States Interests at Home and Abroad," November 2011, www.iprcenter.gov/reports/ipr-center-reports/IPR%20Center%20Threat%20Report%20and%20Survey.pdf/view.

83 Center for Strategic and International Studies, "The Economic Impact of Cybercrime and Cyber Espionage," July 2013, http://csis.org/files/publication/60396rpt_cybercrime-cost_0713_ph4_0.pdf.

84 www.justice.gov/dea/programs/money.htm.

85 www.unodc.org/unodc/en/frontpage/2012/July/new-unodc-campaign-highlights-transnational-organized-crime-as-an-us-870-billion-a-year-business.html.

86 John Rollins and Liana Sun Wyler, "International Terrorism and Transnational Crime: Security Threats, U.S. Policy, and Considerations for Congress," Congressional Research Service, March 18, 2010.

87 For an analysis of this collaboration, see Bruce E. Bechtol, Jr., *Defiant Failed State: The North Korean Threat to International Security* (Washington, DC: Potomac Books, 2010). The multinational Financial Action Task Force, which has declared Iran and North Korea the two countries of highest priority for anti-money-laundering measures, has emphasized the risks that money laundered by these two countries will fall into the hands of terrorists. Financial Action Task Force, Public Statement, 22 June 2012, www.fatf-gafi.org/topics/high-riskandnon-cooperativejurisdictions/documents/fatfpublicstatement-22june2012.html.

88 S. S. Dudley, "Central America Besieged: Cartels and Maras Country Threat Analysis," *Small Wars & Insurgencies*, vol. 22, no. 5 (December 2011), 907–908.

TRAINING

1 Some experts use the term technical assistance to refer exclusively to the use of expatriates to provide project or program support, but this book will employ the broader definition, which includes training.

2 Ghani and Lockhart, *Fixing Failed States*, 101–102; Riddell, *Does Foreign Aid Really Work?*, 203; OECD, "The Challenge of Capacity Development."

3 Riddell, *Does Foreign Aid Really Work?*, 205.

4 B. J. Ndulu, "Human Capital Flight: Stratification, Globalization and the Challenges to Tertiary Education in Africa," *JHEA/RESA,* vol. 2, no. 1 (2004), 70.

5 Riddell, *Does Foreign Aid Really Work?,* 32–47; Dewan, "Humanitarian Assistance: A Development Perspective," in Spear and Williams, eds., *Security and Development in Global Politics,* 106; Nathan Hodge, *Armed Humanitarians: The Rise of the Nation Builders* (New York: Bloomsbury, 2011), 75–76.

6 Garrett, "The Challenge of Global Health," 17–20.

7 Andrew Natsios, "The Clash of the Counter-Bureaucracy and Development," Center for Global Development, July 13, 2010, www.cgdev.org/files/1424271_file_Natsios_Counterbureaucracy.pdf. Recently, foreign donors have increased spending on the training of native workers in combating HIV/AIDS, but most recipients of the training were already working in the general health care sector, and their transfer to HIV/AIDS has degraded the quality of general care, as occurred previously in Botswana. Oomman et al., "Zeroing in."

8 Laurie Garrett, "Money or Die: A Watershed Moment for Global Public Health," *Foreign Affairs,* March 6, 2012.

9 Ghani and Lockhart, *Fixing Failed States,* 218.

10 Special Inspector General for Iraq Reconstruction, *Hard Lessons: The Iraq Reconstruction Experience* (Washington, DC: Government Printing Office, 2009), 332.

11 A study by Oxford Policy Management of British technical assistance programs in Africa from 1999 to 2004, for instance, attributed numerous failures to the inferior skills, both technical and interpersonal, of the people providing the technical assistance. Oxford Policy Management, "Developing Capacity? An Evaluation of DFID-Funded Technical Co-Operation for Economic Management in Sub-Saharan Africa, Synthesis Report," June 2006, www.dfid.gov.uk/Documents/publications1/evaluation/ev667.pdf.

12 Allison Stanger, *One Nation under Contract: The Outsourcing of American Power and the Future of Foreign Policy* (New Haven: Yale University Press, 2009), 119.

13 U.S. Department of State, "Congressional Budget Justification, Volume 2: Foreign Operations, Fiscal Year 2013," http://transition.usaid.gov/performance/cbj/185014.pdf, 63.

14 Noam Unger et al., "Capacity for Change: Reforming U.S. Assistance Efforts in Poor and Fragile Countries," Brookings and CSIS, April 2010, www.brookings.edu/~/media/Files/rc/reports/2010/04_aid_unger/04_aid_unger.pdf; Stanger, *One Nation under Contract.*

15 Committee on Foreign Relations, United States Senate, "Evaluating U.S. Foreign Assistance to Afghanistan," S. Prt. 112–21, 112th Congress, First Session, June 8, 2011, 15–17.

16 Mark Moyar, "Can the Afghans Keep Order?" *The Daily Beast,* February 18, 2010. For more on police training in Iraq and Afghanistan, see Moyar, *A Question of Command,* 195–196, 203–204, 232, 237; David H. Bayley and Robert M. Perito, *The Police in War: Fighting Insurgency, Terrorism, and Violent Crime* (Boulder: Lynne Rienner, 2010), 154–156; Richard Downie and Jennifer G. Cooke, "A More Strategic U.S. Approach to Police Reform in Africa," Center for Strategic and International Studies, 2011, 5–8, 21–22.

17 Rory Stewart, *The Places in Between* (Orlando: Harcourt, 2006), 247. For a detailed treatment of the British colonial services, see Anthony Kirk-Greene, *Britain's Imperial Administrators, 1858–1966* (Houndmills: Macmillan, 2000).

18 Carol Lancaster, "Failing and Failed States: Toward a Framework for U.S. Assistance," in Nancy Birdsall et al., eds., *Short of the Goal: U.S. Policy and Poorly Performing States* (Washington, DC: Center for Global Development, 2006), 296.

19 Riddell, *Does Foreign Aid Really Work?*, 209–210.

20 Oxford Policy Management, "Developing Capacity?." See also World Bank Evaluations Department, "Country Assistance Evaluation Retrospective: An OED Self-Evaluation," 2005, http://lnweb90.worldbank.org/oed/oeddoclib.nsf/DocUNID ViewForJavaSearch/A767522586AFBD1585256FE00051A85A/$file/cae_retros pective.pdf.

21 Melissa Thomas, interview with author, 2012.

22 Anaclet Hakizimana, "La Course au per diem, un sport national ruineux," *Madagascar Tribune,* November 17, 2007. Madagascar ranked thirty-fifth out of fifty-two African countries on the Ibrahim Index of African Governance in 2012. Mo Ibrahim Foundation, "2012 Ibrahim Index of African Governance," October 2012. A report published by the Norwegian Agency for Development Cooperation in 2012 noted that in Tanzania, international civil society organizations "are concerned that some attend seminars only for the sake of obtaining per diem payments, not for the benefit of training itself." Tina Søreide, Arne Tostensen, and Ingvild Aagedal Skage, *Hunting for Per Diem: The Uses and Abuses of Travel Compensation in Three Developing Countries* (Oslo: Norwegian Agency for Development Cooperation, 2012), 31.

23 Tracy Brunette et al., "USAID/Malawi Education Decentralization Support Activity (EDSA) Mid-Term Evaluation," Social Impact, July 2011, http://pdf.usaid.gov/ pdf_docs/PDACT803.pdf. A health officer in Malawi noted that people only attend health care training workshops if they receive allowances. "Mostly during workshops," said the officer, "they tell you logistics on the first day, and if they just tell you that there is no allowance, people would just attend the first session and then when they have a break they will disappear." Vian et al., "Perceptions of Per Diems in the Health Sector," 12. See also Kelly Currie, "Mirage or Reality? Asia's Emerging Human Rights and Democracy Architecture," Project 2049 Institute, 2010, http://project2049.net/documents/mirage_or_reality_asias_emerging_hu man_rights_and_democracy_architecture_currie.pdf, 25.

24 A classic example is the leadership of Botswana in its early years. Harrison, *The Central Liberal Truth,* 181–182.

25 Collier, *The Bottom Billion,* 113–115.

26 Andrew Gilboy et al., "Generations of Quiet Progress: The Development Impact of U.S. Long-Term University Training on Africa from 1963 to 2003," Aguirre International, September 2004, http://pdf.usaid.gov/pdf_docs/PNADB130.pdf, 52.

27 Tyler Truby, interview with author, 2012.

28 Dennis E. Keller, "U.S. Military Forces and Police Assistance In Stability Operations: The Least-Worst Option to Fill the U.S. Capacity Gap," Peacekeeping and Stability Operations Institute, August 2010, 29–30.

29 World Bank Task Force on Capacity Development in Africa, "Building Effective States, Forging Engaged Societies," September 2005, 41–42.

30 Increasing the amount of assistance allocated to local contractors and NGOs has been a principal objective of USAID Forward, the signature initiative of USAID Administrator Rajiv Shah.

31 Riddell, *Does Foreign Aid Really Work?*, 206–207.

32 Garrett, "The Challenge of Global Health," 28–32.

33 Ethiopian senior adviser, interview with author, 2012.

34 Ghani and Lockhart, *Fixing Failed States*, 100.

35 For examples of comparisons, see Carol Atkinson, "Constructivist Implications of Material Power: Military Engagement and the Socialization of States, 1972–2000," *International Studies Quarterly*, vol. 50, no. 3 (September 2006), 509–537; Laura R. Cleary, "Lost in Translation: The Challenge of Exporting Models of Civil-Military Relations," *Prism*, vol. 3, no. 2 (March 2012), 19–36; Robert D. Kaplan, *Imperial Grunts: The American Military on the Ground* (New York: Random House, 2005), 52, 60; Derek S. Reveron, *Exporting Security: International Engagement, Security Cooperation, and the Changing Face of the U.S. Military* (Washington, DC: Georgetown University Press, 2010); International Crisis Group, "Guatemala: Squeezed Between Crime and Impunity," 8.

36 Cleary, "Lost in Translation," 22–23.

37 Jeffrey M. Jones, "Americans Most Confident in Military, Least in Congress," *Gallup*, June 23, 2011, www.gallup.com/poll/148163/Americans-Confident-Military-Least-Congress.aspx; "Distrust, Discontent, Anger and Partisan Rancor," Pew Research Center, April 18, 2010, http://pewresearch.org/pubs/1569/trust-in-government-distrust-discontent-anger-partisan-rancor.

38 This statement is derived from the author's own observations.

39 Thomas C. Bruneau et al., "IMET Assessment Project, 2007–2008," Naval Postgraduate School Center for Civil-Military Relations, 2008, 19–20.

40 Good analyses of how culture affects thinking include Richard Nisbett, *The Geography of Thought: How Asians and Westerners Think Differently … and Why* (New York: Free Press, 2003); Margaret K. Nydell, *Understanding Arabs: A Contemporary Guide to Arab Society*, 5th ed. (Boston: Nicholas Brealey, 2012); Castañeda, *Mañana Forever*.

41 Brazinsky, *Nation Building in South Korea*, 81–99; DeShazo et al, "Countering Threats to Security and Stability in a Failing State," 5; Bruneau et al., "IMET Assessment Project," 46–48; Cleary, "Lost in Translation," 19–36.

42 This paragraph is based primarily on the author's own interactions with foreign militaries. See also Cleary, "Lost in Translation"; Reveron, *Exporting Security*.

43 Carlos Ospina, interview with author, May 2013.

44 On this point, see Kaplan, *Imperial Grunts*, 61–62.

45 Kalev I. Sepp, "The Evolution of United States Military Strategy in Central America, 1979–1991," Ph.D. diss., Harvard University, 2002, 225.

46 Alan Boswell, "Central Africa: For Region, U.S. Troops Seen as 'Saviors'," *McClatchy News Service*, February 14, 2012; Sudarsan Raghavan, "U.S. Troops Moving Slowly against Kony," *Washington Post*, April 17, 2012.

47 Simon J. Powelson, "Enduring Engagement Yes, Episodic Engagement No: Lessons for SOF from Mali," Master's thesis, Naval Postgraduate School, December 2013. Quoted material is on p. 31.

48 Oxford economist Paul Collier advanced this recommendation in 2007, but it has yet to gain traction. Collier, *The Bottom Billion,* 115–117.

MILITARIZATION

1 Adam Isacson and Nicole Ball, "U.S. Military and Police Assistance to Poorly Performing States," in Birdsall et al., eds., *Short of the Goal,* 439–447; Downie and Cooke, "A More Strategic U.S. Approach to Police Reform in Africa."

2 On private security companies, see Haugen and Boutros, *The Locust Effect,* 190–193.

3 Moyar, *Triumph Forsaken,* 67–159.

4 DeShazo et al., "Countering Threats to Security and Stability in a Failing State," 58; U.S. Government Accountability Office, "Plan Colombia," 27, 33; Spencer et al., *Colombia's Road to Recovery,* 66.

5 Inigo Guevara Moyano, "Adapting, Transforming, and Modernizing under Fire: The Mexican Military 2006–11," Strategic Studies Institute, September 2011, 8.

6 Collier, *The Bottom Billion,* 111. See also Halperin, Siegle, and Weinstein, *The Democracy Advantage.*

7 Interview with Honduran military officer, 2012.

8 International Crisis Group, "Guatemala: Squeezed between Crime and Impunity," 8.

9 Mariano Castillo, "Honduras Gives Military New Policing Powers," *cnn.com,* November 30, 2011.

10 Birame Diop, "Sub-Saharan African Military and Development Activities," *Prism,* vol. 3, no. 1 (December 2011), 87–98.

11 Mazhar Aziz, *Military Control in Pakistan: The Parallel State* (New York: Routledge, 2008).

12 Daniel Brumberg and Hesham Sallam, "The Politics of Security Sector Reform in Egypt," U.S. Institute of Peace, October 2012.

13 Samuel Prugh, interview with author, 2012.

14 Blair, "Military Support for Democracy," 3–16.

15 Rodriguez, "Survey: Young Pakistanis Harbor Doubts about Future, Democracy." Today the inferior capabilities of civilian political leaders encourage the Pakistani military to remain involved informally in governance, especially when it comes to foreign policy. "Until Pakistan's civilian leaders demonstrate greater capacity for statesmanship and governance, Washington will be forced to deal with the military," states Daniel S. Markey, a former State Department policy planner for South Asia. "The real way for Pakistan's civilians to assert themselves against the over-dominant military is to demonstrate that they are actually capable of governing in ways that bring tangible benefits to large segments of the population." Daniel S. Markey, *No Exit from Pakistan: America's Tortured Relationship with Islamabad* (New York: Cambridge University Press, 2013), 220, 223.

16 Yuki Fukuoka, "Politics, Business and the State in Post-Soeharto Indonesia," *Contemporary Southeast Asia,* vol. 34, no. 1 (April 2012), 80–100.

17 Vedi Hadiz and Richard Robison, "Neo-Liberal Reforms and Illiberal Consolidations: The Indonesian Paradox," *Journal of Development Studies,* vol. 41, no. 2 (2005), 233.

18 Kelechi A. Kalu, "Nigeria: Learning from the Past to Meet the Challenges of the 21st Century," *Social Research,* vol. 77, no. 4 (winter 2010), 1384.

19 Lauren Ploch, "Nigeria," Congressional Research Service, June 4, 2010; Senate Committee on Foreign Relations Senate Hearing 106–295, "The Nigerian Transition and the Future of U.S. Policy," 106th Cong., 1st Sess., November 4, 1999.

20 Osuma Oarhe and Iro Aghedo, "The Open Sore of a Nation: Corruption Complex and Internal Security in Nigeria," *African Security*, vol. 3, no. 3 (2010), 140.

21 Moyar, *A Question of Command*, 33–61.

22 Paul Folsmbee, "From Pinstripes to Khaki: Governance under Fire," *Foreign Service Journal*, September 2009, 35–39; The United States Commission on Helping to Enhance the Livelihood of People around the Globe, "Beyond Assistance: The HELP Commission Report on Foreign Assistance Reform," December 7, 2007, www.americanprogress.org/issues/2007/12/pdf/beyond_assistence.pdf, 28–29; Senate Foreign Relations Committee Print, "Embassies as Command Posts in the Anti-Terror Campaign," 109th Congress, Second Session, December 15, 2006 (Washington, DC: U.S. Government Printing Office, 2006).

23 Senate Foreign Relations Committee Print, "Embassies as Command Posts in the Anti-Terror Campaign"; Folsmbee, "From Pinstripes to Khaki," 35–39; Hodge, *Armed Humanitarians*, 19; Reveron, *Exporting Security*, 64; Michelle Parker, "The Role of the Department of Defense in Provincial Reconstruction Teams," RAND Corporation, September 2007, www.rand.org/content/dam/rand/pubs/testimonies/2007/RAND_CT290.pdf; J. Brian Atwood, "Elevating Development Assistance," *Prism*, vol. 1, no. 3 (June 2010), 3–12.

24 Kori Schake, "Operationalizing Expeditionary Economics," in *Proceedings from the Summit on Entrepreneurship and Expeditionary Economics*, Kauffman Foundation, January 2011, sites.kauffman.org/eee/resources/ee_summit_proceedings.pdf, 209–210; Gordon Adams and Rebecca Williams, "A New Way Forward: Rebalancing Security Assistance Programs and Authorities," Henry L. Stimson Center, March 2011, www.stimson.org/images/uploads/A_New_Way_Forward_Final.pdf; Folsmbee, "From Pinstripes to Khaki," 35–39; Noam Unger et al., "Capacity for Change: Reforming U.S. Assistance Efforts in Poor and Fragile Countries," Brookings and CSIS, April 2010, www.brookings.edu/~/media/Files/rc/reports/2010/04_aid_unger/04_aid_unger.pdf.

25 Hodge, *Armed Humanitarians*, 294–295.

26 Special Inspector General for Iraq Reconstruction, "Iraq Reconstruction: Lessons in Human Capital Management," January 2006, 23 (quote), 31.

27 Hodge, *Armed Humanitarians*, 93–94. Another objection to participation in conflict environments, raised by some at USAID and other civil agencies, is the difficulty of finding organizations to implement projects and programs. These agencies normally outsource much of their work to NGOs that refuse, on philosophical grounds, to perform work that directly supports U.S. political objectives. Those NGOs have been particularly resistant to work that promotes the interests of one side in an intrastate conflict. But this difficulty should not serve as an excuse for inaction. The U.S. government can and does carry out plenty of development work toward clear policy ends, through the use of government personnel, private contractors, and members of those NGOs that do not object to undertaking work that is aimed at affecting political outcomes. See Robert Maletta with Joanna Spear, "Humanitarian Assistance: A Security Perspective," in Spear and Williams, eds., *Security and Development in Global Politics*, 77–95.

28 Committee on Foreign Relations, U.S. Senate, S. Prt. 109–40, "Iraq: Assessment of Progress in Economic Reconstruction and Governmental Capacity," December 2005; Hodge, *Armed Humanitarians,* 97, 159, 170; Matthew Lee, "Rice Orders Baghdad Embassy Posts Filled," *Associated Press,* June 20, 2007.

29 "Compelled Iraq Duty Angers U.S. Envoys," *Associated Press,* November 1, 2007.

30 Paul Richter, "Diplomats Won't Be Forced to Go to Iraq, for Now," *Los Angeles Times,* November 14, 2007.

31 By 2006, the Department of Defense was delivering 21.7 percent of all U.S. official development assistance, most of it in Iraq and Afghanistan but some of it reaching other insecure countries. Dewan, "Humanitarian Assistance: A Development Perspective," in Spear and Williams, eds., *Security and Development in Global Politics,* 106. See also Senate Foreign Relations Committee Print, "Embassies as Command Posts in the Anti-Terror Campaign"; United States Commission on Helping to Enhance the Livelihood of People Around the Globe, "Beyond Assistance: The HELP Commission Report on Foreign Assistance Reform," December 7, 2007, www.americanprogress.org/issues/2007/12/pdf/beyond_assistence.pdf, 28–29; David M. Satterfield, "On-the-Record Briefing on Provincial Reconstruction Teams (PRTs) in Iraq," February 7, 2007, http://2001–2009.state.gov/p/nea/rls/rm/2007/80216.htm.

32 Gordon England, DoD Directive 3000.05, 28 November 2005, http://fhp.osd.mil/intlhealth/pdfs/DoDD3000.05.pdf. The U.S. Army/Marine Corps counterinsurgency manual of 2006 stated, "Soldiers and Marines should prepare to execute many nonmilitary missions to support COIN efforts. Everyone has a role in nation building, not just Department of State and civil affairs personnel." Field Manual 3–24/Marine Corps Warfighting Publication 3–33.5, Counterinsurgency, 1–27.

33 John J. Kruzel, "Mullen Urges More 'Soft Power' in Afghanistan," American Forces Press Service, March 3, 2010. See also Brian M. Michelson and Captain Sean P. Walsh, "Lopsided Wars of Peace: America's Anemic Ability to Project Civilian Power," *Small Wars Journal,* December 12, 2011.

34 Krasner and Pascual, "Addressing State Failure," 153–163.

35 Nina M. Serafino, "Peacekeeping/Stabilization and Conflict Transitions: Background and Congressional Action on the Civilian Response/Reserve Corps and other Civilian Stabilization and Reconstruction Capabilities," Congressional Research Service January 12, 2012; Special Inspector General for Iraq Reconstruction, "Applying Iraq's Hard Lessons to the Reform of Stabilization and Reconstruction Operations," February 2010.

36 Committee on Foreign Relations, United States Senate, "Evaluating U.S. Foreign Assistance to Afghanistan," S. Prt. 112–21, 112th Congress, First Session, June 8, 2011, 6–8.

37 United States Department of State and the Broadcasting Board of Governors, Office of Inspector General, "Report of Inspection, Embassy Kabul," February 2010, 30–31.

38 Specialized agencies such as the Drug Enforcement Administration and the Justice and Treasury Departments cover components of governance, but not governance writ large. They work mainly with counternarcotics agents, judges, or finance ministers, not governors or civil administrators.

39 USAID, "Top 10 Bureaus That Obligated the Most Program Funds for FY 2010 & FY 2011 thru 3/31," www.usaid.gov/policy/budget/money/. As will be discussed in

Chapter 10, much of USAID's assistance in the governance sphere goes to "civil society" organizations rather than to governments.

40 Derleth and Alexander, "Stability Operations," 126; Atwood, "Elevating Development Assistance," 3–12.

41 Kori Schake, "How State Can Take Back Diplomacy," *Politico.com*, April 5, 2012.

42 On this point, see Patrick M. Cronin and R. Stephen Brent, "Strengthening Development and Reconstruction Assistance," in Hans Binnendijk and Patrick M. Cronin, eds., *Civilian Surge: Key to Complex Operations* (Washington, DC: National Defense University Press, 2009), 132.

43 Headquarters, Department of the Army, FM 3–07, "Stability Operations," October 2008.

44 Dennis Edwards, "Army Civil Affairs Functional Specialists: On the Verge of Extinction," Strategy Research Project, U.S. Army War College, 2012; Frederick W. Little, "Order from Chaos: Restructuring Army Civil Affairs," *Special Warfare*, vol. 26, no. 4 (October-December 2013), 28–31; Brian M. Michelson and Captain Sean P. Walsh, "Lopsided Wars of Peace: America's Anemic Ability to Project Civilian Power," *Small Wars Journal*, December 12, 2011; Mark L. Kimmey, "Transforming Civil Affairs," *Army*, March 2005, 17–25.

45 Civil Affairs also performed these tasks in Haiti during the 1990s. Michael A. Quinn and Douglas W. Daniel, "Civil Affairs Organization in Haiti," *Military Review*, July-August 1998, 3–10.

46 The training and education of Civil Affairs personnel in governance is a topic worthy of further exploration. Several experts have recently proposed reopening a school of military governance, similar to the schools that prepared Americans for the governance of the Axis countries after World War II. Rebecca Patterson, "Revisiting a School of Military Government: How Reanimating a World War II-Era Institution Could Professionalize Military Nation Building," Ewing Marion Kauffman, June 2011, www.kauffman.org/uploadedFiles/EE%20Revisiting%20report-final_withphotos.pdf; Brent C. Bankus and James O. Kievit, "Reopen a Joint School of Military Government and Administration?" *Small Wars & Insurgencies*, vol. 19, no. 1 (2008), 137–143.

47 Concerning military involvement in short-term stabilization projects, see Moyar, "Development in Afghanistan's Counterinsurgency"; Edwina Thompson, Report on Wilton Park Conference 1022, 1 April 2010, www.wiltonpark.org.uk/resources/en/pdf/22290903/22291297/wp1022-report.

48 This conclusion is based on direct observation of the U.S. military in Iraq and Afghanistan and interviews with numerous witnesses.

49 Adam Strickland, interview with author.

50 USASOC PAO, "Civil Affairs Officer to Become Branch's First Active-Duty General," July 14, 2011, http://archive.paraglideonline.net/071411_news1.html.

51 In October 2012, Lieutenant General Charles Cleveland, commander of the U.S. Army Special Operations Command, ordered the creation an Institute for Military Support to Governance, which included training and education in its charter. Michael Warmack, Michael Chagaris, and Tony Vacha, "Closing the Gaps in Governance," *Special Warfare*, vol. 26, no. 4 (October–December 2013), 13.

52 Nadia Schadlow, "War and the Art of Governance," *Parameters*, vol. 33, no. 3 (autumn 2003), 85–94; Kathleen H. Hicks and Christine E. Wormuth, "The Future

of U.S. Civil Affairs Forces," Center for Strategic and International Studies, February 2009.

53 Haugen and Boutros, *The Locust Effect,* 205–207.

54 Bayley and Perito, *The Police in War,* 81; Adams and Williams, "A New Way Forward."

55 Kimberly Zisk Marten, *Enforcing the Peace: Learning from the Imperial Past* (New York: Columbia University Press, 2004).

56 Downie and Cooke, "A More Strategic U.S. Approach to Police Reform in Africa," 4.

57 Ibid., 21–22. The Justice Department's Office of Overseas Prosecutorial Development, Assistance and Training (OPDAT) provides assistant U.S. attorneys as advisers to foreign prosecutors, judges, and other justice sector personnel. It is even smaller, with only fifty-one assistant attorneys deployed. FBI, DEA, ATF, and the U.S. Marshals Service do some training but their main focus is current criminal investigations that pertain to the US.

58 Tyler Truby, interview with author.

59 Thomas Lum, "The Republic of the Philippines and U.S. Interests," Congressional Research Service, January 3, 2011, 16; Fran Beaudette, "JSOTF-P Uses Whole-of-Nation Approach to Bring Stability to the Philippines," *Special Warfare,* July–September 2012.

60 Government Accountability Office, "Foreign Police Assistance: Defined Roles and Improved Information Sharing Could Enhance Interagency Collaboration," May 2012, 8.

61 For an example of the use of U.S. special operations forces to train police forces, see David Spencer et al., *Colombia's Road to Recovery: Security and Governance 1982–2010* (Washington, DC: Center for Hemispheric Defense Studies, 2011), 49.

62 Dilshika Jayamaha et al., *Lessons Learned from U.S. Government Law Enforcement in International Operations* (Carlisle: Strategic Studies Institute, 2010), 19–33.

63 Ibid., 115–118.

64 Dennis E. Keller, "U.S. Military Forces and Police Assistance In Stability Operations: The Least-Worst Option to Fill the U.S. Capacity Gap," Peacekeeping and Stability Operations Institute, August 2010; John B. Alexander, *Convergence: Special Operations Forces and Civilian Law Enforcement* (MacDill Air Force Base: Joint Special Operations University Press, 2010).

65 Moyar, *A Question of Command,* 195–207, 231–251. Because of the shift of police training to the military, the Department of Defense accounted for 73 percent of all U.S. expenditures on police training, versus 25 percent for the Department of State. Government Accountability Office, "Foreign Police Assistance," 8.

66 U.S. Department of State and U.S. Agency for International Development, "Leading through Civilian Power: The First Quadrennial Diplomacy and Development Review, 2010," www.state.gov/documents/organization/153108.pdf.

67 Office of the Special Inspector General for Iraq Reconstruction, "Iraq Police Development Program: Lack of Iraqi Support and Security Problems Raise Questions about the Continued Viability of the Program," July 31, 2012.

68 Special Inspector General for Iraq Reconstruction, "Quarterly Report and Semi-annual Report to the United States Congress," January 30, 2012, 33–34; Office of

the Special Inspector General for Iraq Reconstruction, "Iraq Police Development Program."

69 Perito, *Where Is the Lone Ranger When You Need Him? America's Search for a Postconflict Stability Force* (Washington, DC: U.S. Institute for Peace, 2004), 141–142, 150–151.

70 A 2009 report by a distinguished group of Rand Corporation experts argued in favor of creating a new policing organization under the U.S. Marshals Service. Terrence K. Kelly et al., *A Stability Police Force for the United States: Justification and Options for Creating U.S. Capabilities* (Santa Monica: RAND, 2009). Obtaining funding for such an organization would be very difficult, however, given that the Marshals Service lacks the Congressional backers that the Department of Defense enjoys. Recent changes to the missions of U.S. Army and Marine Corps military police forces have allowed the Department of Defense to get ahead of the civilian agencies to such an extent that a civilian effort could now be seen as unnecessary duplication.

71 Perito, *Where Is the Lone Ranger When You Need Him?*, 79–80, 186; Chad B. McRee, "The Marshall Force: A 21st Century Constabulary for Future Demands," U.S. Army War College, 2009; Jon P. Myers, "The Military Police Brigade, Operational Art, and the Army Operating Concept 2016–2028," School of Advanced Military Studies, 2011; Jesse D. Galvan, "Military Police, The Answer to the Stability Operations Gap," U.S. Army War College, 2012. Current U.S. Army Stability Operations Doctrine calls for the Military Police to train police and corrections officers in postconflict environments and to provide sustained training to foreign military police, though it advises that the military should transfer the police training mission to civilian law enforcement agencies as quickly as possible. Department of the Army, Field Manual 3–07, "Stability Operations," October 2008, 6–18.

72 Julie Watson, "Marine Corps Activates Three Law Enforcement Battalions," Associated Press, July 23, 2012; interviews with U.S. Marine Corps officers.

EDUCATION IN THE THIRD WORLD

1 David E. Bloom et al., "Higher Education and Economic Development in Africa," World Bank, February 2006.

2 International Bank for Reconstruction and Development/World Bank, "Learning for All: Investing in People's Knowledge and Skills to Promote Development," 2011, 48–49.

3 James W. Fox, "Donor Projects and Culture Change: The Case of Costa Rica," in Harrison and Kagan, eds., *Developing Cultures*, 347.

4 Lars Sondergaard et al., *Skills, Not Just Diplomas: Managing Education for Results in Eastern Europe and Central Asia* (Washington, DC: World Bank, 2012).

5 For a detailed case study of teacher quality problems, see U.S. Agency for International Development, "Impact Assessment of USAID's Education Program in Ethiopia, 1994–2009," July 20, 2010.

6 UNDP official, interview with author, 2012. See also William Baah-Boateng, "Human Capital as a Vehicle for Africa's Economic Transformation," Social Science Research Network, April 2009, http://ssrn.com/abstract=1805125.

7 Sondergaard et al., *Skills, Not Just Diplomas,* 5. See also Eric A. Hanushek and Ludger Woessmann, "Do Better Schools Lead to More Growth? Cognitive Skills, Economic Outcomes, and Causation," *Forschunginstitut zur Zukunft der Arbeit,* November 2009, http://ftp.iza.org/dp4575.pdf.

8 Thomas Lickona, "Character Education: Restoring Virtue to the Mission of Schools," in Harrison and Huntington, eds., *Culture Matters,* 58–59.

9 Luis Diego Herrera Amighetti, "Parenting Practices and Governance in Latin America: The Case of Costa Rica," in Harrison and Huntington, eds., *Culture Matters,* 30.

10 Collier, *Wars, Guns, and Votes,* 66–72.

11 Jandhyala B. G. Tilak, "Building Human Capital in East Asia: What Others Can Learn," World Bank, 2002, 11–13; Molly N. N. Lee, "Higher Education in Southeast Asia in the Era of Globalization," in James. J. Forest and Philip G. Altbach, eds., *International Handbook of Higher Education,* vol. 2 (Dordrecht: Springer, 2006), 542.

12 Collier, *Wars, Guns, and Votes,* 178.

13 Quentin Wodon and Yvonne Ying, "Literacy and Numeracy in Faith-Based and Government Schools in Sierra Leone, in Felipe Barrera-Osorio et al., eds., *Emerging Evidence on Vouchers and Faith-Based Providers in Education: Case Studies from Africa, Latin America, and Asia* (Washington, DC: World Bank, 2009), 99–117. See also Prospere Backiny-Yetna and Quentin Wodon, "Comparing the Performance of Faith-Based and Government Schools in the Democratic Republic of Congo," in Barrera-Osorio et al., eds., *Emerging Evidence on Vouchers and Faith-Based Providers in Education,* 119–135.

14 Katherine Marshall and Marisa Van Saanen, *Development and Faith: Where Mind, Heart, and Soul Work Together* (Washington, DC: World Bank, 2007), 78–82; Hunt Allcott and Daniel E. Ortega, "The Performance of Decentralized School Systems: Evidence from Fe Y Alegría in República Bolivariana de Venezuela," in Barrera-Osorio et al., eds., *Emerging Evidence on Vouchers and Faith-Based Providers in Education,* 81–97.

15 Etzioni, *Security First,* 173–178.

16 F .S. Aijazuddin, "Two Halves Did Not Make a Whole: Pakistan Before and After Bangladesh," in Harrison and Berger, *Developing Cultures,* 185; C. Christine Fair, *The Madrassah Challenge: Militancy and Religious Education in Pakistan* (Washington, DC: United States Institute of Peace Press, 2008); Guilain Denoeux and Lynn Carter, "Development Assistance and Counter-Extremism: A Guide to Programming," U.S. Agency for International Development, October 2009, 42–43.

17 Etzioni, *Security First,* 173–192.

18 Fair, *The Madrassah Challenge,* 94–98.

19 See, for example, Peter Materu et al., "The Rise, Fall, and Reemergence of the University of Ibadan, Nigeria," in Philip G. Altbach and Jamil Salmi, eds., *The Road to Academic Excellence: The Making of World-Class Research Universities* (Washington, DC: World Bank, 2011), 195–227.

20 Jamil Salmi, *The Challenge of Establishing World-Class Universities* (Washington, DC: World Bank, 2009), 21; Ana M. Garcia de Fanelli, "Argentina," in Forest and Altbach, eds., *International Handbook of Higher Education,* vol. 2 (Dordrecht: Springer, 2006), 576–579.

21 Coleman and Court, *University Development in the Third World*, 15.

22 Daniel C. Levy, *To Export Progress: The Golden Age of University Assistance in the Americas* (Bloomington: Indiana University Press, 2005), 37–39.

23 For a recent articulation of this view, see Rebecca Winthrop and Corinne Graff, "Beyond Madrasas: Assessing the Links between Education and Militancy in Pakistan," Brookings Institution, June 2010, 23.

24 Coleman and Court, *University Development in the Third World*, 9–10; Levy, *To Export Progress*, 48–49.

25 David E. Bloom et al., "Higher Education and Economic Development in Africa," World Bank, February 2006; International Bank for Reconstruction and Development/World Bank, "Learning for All: Investing in People's Knowledge and Skills to Promote Development," 2011, 48–49.

26 David E. Bloom et al., "Higher Education and Economic Development in Africa," World Bank, February 2006, 17; David E. Bloom and Henry Rosovsky, "Higher Education in Developing Countries," in Forest and Altbach, eds., *International Handbook of Higher Education*, vol. 2, 451.

27 Commission for Africa, "Our Common Interest: Report of the Commission for Africa," March 2005, www.commissionforafrica.info/2005-report. See also OECD, "The Challenge of Capacity Development," 29.

28 Commission for Africa, "Still Our Common Interest."

29 USAID Education Strategy 2011–2015, "Education: Opportunity through Learning," February 2011.

30 Easterly, *The White Man's Burden*, 306–307.

31 Radelet, *Emerging Africa*, 125–126.

32 U.S. Foreign Assistance to Ghana, *foreignassistance.gov*, http://foreignassistance.gov/OU.aspx?OUID=200&FY=2011&AgencyID=0&budTab=tab_Bud_Spent&tabID=tab_sct_Education_Disbs.

33 Ghani and Lockhart, *Fixing Failed States*, 89–90.

34 Ibid., 142.

35 Riddell, *Does Foreign Aid Really Work?*, 204; Ghani and Lockhart, *Fixing Failed States*, 143; Zakaria, *The Post-American World*, 189.

36 Kuzvinetsa Peter Dzvimbo, "The International Migration of Skilled Human Capital from Developing Countries," World Bank, HDNED, 2003, 5.

37 Uma Lele, "Rural Africa: Modernization, Equity, and Long-Term Development," in Carl K. Eicher and John M. Staatz, eds., *Agricultural Development in the Third World* (Baltimore: Johns Hopkins University Press, 1984), 108.

38 *Acting on the Future: Breaking the Intergenerational Transmission of Inequality* (New York: United Nations Development Programme, 2010), 6, 23.

39 For an example of this argument, see Dennis L. Gilbert, *The American Class Structure in an Age of Growing Inequality*, 9th ed. (Los Angeles: Sage, 2014).

40 The most incisive analysis of these realities is Charles Murray, "IQ and Economic Success," *Public Interest*, no. 128 (summer 1997): 21–35.

41 Angus Madisson, *Chinese Economic Performance in the Long Run* (Paris: Organisation for Economic Co-operation and Development, 2007), 100.

42 Arvind Panagariya1, "India in the 1980s and 1990s: A Triumph of Reforms," International Monetary Fund, March 2004; Uma Kapila, ed., *India's Economic Development since 1947* (New Delhi: Academic Foundation, 2008), 64.

43 Robyn Meredith, *The Elephant and the Dragon: The Rise of India and China and What It Means for All of Us* (New York: W. W. Norton, 2007), 107.

44 See, for instance, Commission on Growth and Development, "The Growth Report: Strategies for Sustained Growth and Inclusive Development," http://cgd.s3.amazo naws.com/GrowthReportComplete.pdf; Collier, *The Bottom Billion*; Sachs, *The End of Poverty*.

45 Daniel Wesonga, "Private Provision of Higher Education in Kenya: Trends & Issues in Four Universities," in Douglas Ouma-Odero and Violet Wawire, *Public & Private Universities in Kenya: New Challenges, Issues & Achievements* (New York: Partnership for Higher Education in Africa, 2007), 159; *Habari Daystar*, fall 2012, www.daystarus.org/Newsletters/DaystarFall12Newsletter.pdf.

46 Amadou Cissé, interview with Katherine Marshall, December 2007, http://berkley center.georgetown.edu/interviews/a-discussion-with-amadou-cisse-former-prime-minister-niger.

47 Paul E. Pierson, "The Rise of Christian Mission and Relief Agencies," in Abrams, ed., *The Influence of Faith*, 153–170; Mark R. Amstutz, "Faith-Based NGOs and U.S. Foreign Policy," in Abrams, ed., *The Influence of Faith*, 175–187.

48 Brazinsky, *Nation Building in South Korea*, 205–209; 225.

49 Linda Herrera, "Higher Education in the Arab World," in Forest and Altbach, eds., *International Handbook of Higher Education*, vol. 2, 415.

50 Steven Emerson, *American Jihad: The Terrorists Living among Us* (New York: Free Press, 2002), 173.

51 Paul Wolfowitz, "Wahid and the Voice of Moderate Islam," *Wall Street Journal*, January 6, 2010.

52 Kumar Ramakrishna, "Madrassas, Pesantrens, and the Impact of Education on Support for Radicalism and Terrorism," in Joseph McMillan, ed., *"In the Same Light as Slavery: Building a Global Antiterrorist Consensus* (Washington, DC: National Defense University Press, 2006), 129–150; Ruthven, *A Fury for God*.

53 Examples include Sondergaard et al., *Skills, Not Just Diplomas*; Altbach and Salmi, eds., *The Road to Academic Excellence*.

54 Oscar Arias, "Culture Matters: The Real Obstacles to Latin American Development," *Foreign Affairs*, vol. 90, no. 1 (January/February 2011), 3–4. See also Harrison, *The Central Liberal Truth*, 201.

55 Moyar, *A Question of Command*, 170–176.

56 Robert M. Perito, "U.S. Police in Peace and Stability Operations," U.S. Institute of Peace, August 2007; Keller, "U.S. Military Forces and Police Assistance in Stability Operations."

57 The description of the National Military Academy of Afghanistan is based on the author's visit to the institution in 2010.

EDUCATION IN THE UNITED STATES

1 Ellen Knickmeyer, "Saudi Students Flood in as U.S. Reopens Door," *Wall Street Journal*, July 27, 2012.

2 Zakaria, *The Post-American World*, 190.

3 Salmi, *The Challenge of Establishing World-Class Universities*, 24.

4 Juan Gabriel Valdes, *Pinochet's Economists: The Chicago School in Chile* (Cambridge: Cambridge University Press, 1995); Rachel A. Schurman, "Chile's New Entrepreneurs and the 'Economic Miracle': The Invisible Hand or a Hand from the State?" *Studies in Comparative International Development,* vol. 31, no. 2 (Summer 1996), 83–109.

5 Li Cheng and Lynn White, "Elite Transformation and Modern Change in Mainland China and Taiwan: Empirical Data and the Theory of Technocracy," *China Quarterly,* no. 121 (March 1990), 1–35.

6 Harrison, *Who Prospers,* 91.

7 Gilboy et al., "Generations of Quiet Progress." Quotes on pp. 6 and 7.

8 Andrew S. Natsios, "The Foreign Aid Reform Agenda," *Foreign Service Journal,* December 2008, 37; Gilboy et al., "Generations of Quiet Progress"; Brazinsky, *Nation Building in South Korea,* 67–69.

9 U.S. Senate, Committee on Appropriations, Subcommittee on State, Foreign Operations, and Related Programs, Hearing on Appropriations for Fiscal Year 2006, May 26, 2005.

10 Natsios, "The Clash of the Counter-Bureaucracy and Development," 10.

11 Brazinsky, *Nation Building in South Korea,* 67; Andrew Gilboy et al., "Generations of Quiet Progress," 12–13; Natsios, "The Foreign Aid Reform Agenda," 37.

12 U.S. Senate, Committee on Appropriations, Subcommittee on State, Foreign Operations, and Related Programs, Hearing on Appropriations for Fiscal Year 2006, May 26, 2005.

13 Ford Foundation International Fellows Program, "Outcomes: An Overview," www.fordifp.org/AboutIFP/Outcomes.aspx.

14 J. William Fulbright Foreign Scholarship Board, 2010–2011 Annual Report, http://fulbright.state.gov/uploads/f4/e5/f4e53777be10653b16ffb159bd2a2e0d/FSB-Annual-Report-2010-2011-Final.pdf.

15 Knickmeyer, "Saudi Students Flood in as U.S. Reopens Door."

16 U.S. Citizenship and Immigration Services, www.uscis.gov.

17 Zakaria, *The Post-American World,* 198; Jonathan R. Cole, *The Great American University: Its Rise to Preeminence, Its Indispensable National Role, Why It Must Be Protected* (New York: PublicAffairs, 2010), 40; Ben Wildavsky, *The Great Brain Race: How Global Universities Are Reshaping the World* (Princeton: Princeton University Press, 2010).

18 Collier, *The Bottom Billion,* 94–95.

19 Joan Dassin, "Brain Drain Is Not Inevitable," *Inside Higher Ed,* February 14, 2006. See also Radelet, *Emerging Africa,* 127–129.

20 See, for example, Thomas L. Friedman, "Invent, Invent, Invent," *New York Times,* June 28, 2009; Stuart Anderson, "Keeping Talent in America," National Foundation for American Policy, October 2011, www.nfap.com/pdf/keeping_talent_in_america_nfap_october_2011.pdf.

21 Michael S. Teitelbaum, *Falling Behind?: Boom, Bust, and the Global Race for Scientific Talent* (Princeton: Princeton University Press, 2014).

22 Norman Matloff, "Are Foreign Students the 'Best and the Brightest'?: Data and Implications for Immigration Policy," Economic Policy Institute, February 28, 2013.

23 Daniel Golden, "Military Secrets Leak from U.S. Universities with Rules Flouted," *Bloomberg News,* April 30, 2012.

24 Ibid.
25 Ronald H. Reynolds, "Is Expanded International Military Education and Training Reaching the Right Audience?" *DISAM Journal of International Security Assistance Management,* vol. 25, no. 3 (spring 2003), 93–99.
26 Dennis C. Blair, "Military Support for Democracy," *Prism,* vol. 3, no. 3 (June 2012), 11.
27 Mark Ahles et al., "State Department and DISAM Study on the Effectiveness of the International Military Education and Training (IMET) Program," *DISAM Annual,* vol. 1 (2012), 185.
28 Jeffrey D. Feltman, testimony before the House Foreign Affairs Committee, March 10, 2010, www.hcfa.house.gov/112/65055.pdf.
29 Carol Atkinson, "Constructivist Implications of Material Power: Military Engagement and the Socialization of States, 1972–2000," *International Studies Quarterly,* vol. 50, no. 3 (September 2006), 509–537; Reveron, *Exporting Security.*
30 R. D. McKinlay and A. Mughan, *Aid and Arms to the Third World: An Analysis of the Distribution and Impact of US Official Transfers* (London: Frances Pinter, 1984), 213–246. The authors hypothesized that American preferences for providing military aid to democratic regimes contributed to the correlation between military aid and democratization. But the United States did not demonstrate such a preference until the Carter administration, whereas nearly all of the data in the study predated the Carter administration, concentrated in the years 1950 to 1975.
31 Thomas C. Bruneau et al., "IMET Assessment Project, 2007–2008," Naval Postgraduate School Center for Civil-Military Relations, 2008, 34.
32 Clay Akaishi Benton, "Efficacy of International Officer In-Resident Professional Military Education Attendance on Building Partnerships: A Survey of International Officers Attending Air University PME Programs during Academic Year 2010," *DISAM Annual,* vol. 1 (2012), 170–172.
33 Ahles et al., "State Department and DISAM Study on the Effectiveness of the International Military Education and Training (IMET) Program," 183–184.
34 The comparison of the Foreign Service Institute with the military's institutions is based on the author's experiences teaching courses at the Foreign Service Institute and the military schools as well as conversations with others who have taught at one or both.
35 Brittany Ballenstedt, "Advocates Sketch Plan for Public Service Academy," *Government Executive,* June 4, 2007; Zac Westbrook, "Public Service Academy Fills U.S. Needs," *Albuquerque Journal,* March 1, 2009.
36 Chris Myers Asch, "Capitalize on Inaugural Enthusiasm by Building Public Service Academy," *Tucson Citizen,* February 11, 2009.
37 Intercollegiate Studies Institute, "Our Fading Heritage: Americans Fail a Basic Test on Their History and Institutions," www.americancivicliteracy.org/2008/summary_summary.html.
38 American Council of Trustees and Alumni, "What Will They Learn? 2011–2012: A Survey of Core Requirements at Our Nation's Colleges and Universities," www.goacta.org/publications/downloads/WWTLReport2011–2012LR.pdf, 15.
39 Glenn Ricketts et al., "The Vanishing West, 1964–2010: The Disappearance of Western Civilization from the American Undergraduate Curriculum," National

Association of Scholars, May 2011, www.nas.org/images/documents/TheVanishing West.pdf.

40 In a response to the "The Vanishing West," Dr. James Grossman, the executive director of the American Historical Association stated, "The notion that the cultural traditions of our population reside in Western Civilization is belied by the demographic changes in the American population." It was better to teach world history than the history of Western civilization, he said, because world history "helps give students a more global perspective, which is needed in such a connected world." Princeton University Professor Anthony Grafton, president of the American Historical Association, defended the faculty's avoidance of introductory courses in favor of specialized courses with the argument that "people do the best teaching and studying when they study and teach what they love." Kevin Kiley, "Decline of 'Western Civ'?" *Inside Higher Ed,* May 19, 2011.

41 John J. Miller, "The Death of the Hamilton Center," *National Review,* March 5, 2007; Barbara Moeller, "The Texas Mugging of Western Civ," *Minding the Campus,* July 6, 2009.

42 In January 2012, a blue-ribbon academic commission organized by the Department of Education published a high-profile report on civic education entitled "A Crucible Moment: College Learning and Democracy's Future." It started out in promising fashion, asserting that civic education had to be restored in higher education after decades of neglect. But as soon as it delved into the definition of civic education, the report veered into multiculturalist platitudes. Civics courses, said the authors, should include the experiences of whole world, not just the history and government of the United States. The word "global" appeared 148 times and the word "collective" forty-eight times in the 136-page report, while "patriotism" and "Western civilization" made no appearances. The commission, moreover, advocated civic education as a means of promoting its preferred answers to controversial political questions, a sharp break with traditional civic education, which lauded only the most fundamental principles, such as democracy, liberty, justice, and pluralism. "A Crucible Moment calls for transformations necessary for this generation," read the report. "A daunting one is to eliminate persistent inequalities, especially those in the United States determined by income and race, in order to secure the country's economic and civic future. But the academy must also be a vehicle for tackling other pressing issues – growing global economic inequalities, climate change and environmental degradation, lack of access to quality health care, economic volatility, and more." The National Task Force on Civic Learning and Democratic Engagement, "A Crucible Moment: College Learning and Democracy's Future," Association of American Colleges and Universities, 2012. Useful critiques of this report can be found in *Academic Questions,* vol. 25, no. 3 (fall 2012).

SUPPORT

1 Collier, *The Bottom Billion,* 101–102.

2 World Bank, "Strengthening Performance Accountability in Honduras," March 9, 2009, vol. 1, 27.

3 World Bank Task Force on Capacity Development in Africa, "Building Effective States, Forging Engaged Societies," 41–42, 119; Oxford Policy Management, "Developing Capacity?" 66–67.

4 Garrett, "The Challenge of Global Health," 28–32.

5 Coleman and Court, *University Development in the Third World,* 258.

6 The momentum of governance conditionality has been slowed somewhat by the pressures of the Millennium Development Goals, which discourage withholding of aid for reasons of poor governance because it is likely to reduce the number of AIDS patients treated and school children educated, at least in the short run. Alasdair Bowie, "Governance: A Development Perspective," in Spear and Williams, eds., *Security and Development in Global Politics,* 142.

7 Riddell, *Does Foreign Aid Really Work?,* 236; World Bank Evaluations Department, "Country Assistance Evaluation Retrospective"; Natsios, "The Foreign Aid Reform Agenda," 34–35.

8 www.mcc.gov/pages/results.

9 See Christiane Arndt and Charles Oman, "Uses and Abuses of Governance Indicators," OECD Development Centre, August 2006.

10 One major study blamed U.S. military aid to autocratic governments for the fact that autocratic governments are more likely than democratic governments to engage in armed international conflict, and on this grounds advocated discontinuation of the aid. Halperin, Siegle, and Weinstein, *The Democracy Advantage.* This critique is flawed on several counts. First, while autocratic rule may increase the propensity for international conflict, there is little evidence that foreign military assistance contributes to that increase. Plenty of other factors, such as cultural differences or the absence of accountability to voters, are more likely contributors. Considerable evidence exists, on the other hand, that foreign military assistance, particularly training and education, frequently contributes to good governance and military restraint. Much of the evidence can be found in this book. In addition, lumping all military aid together, as Halperin, Siegle, and Weinstein did, obscures critical variations among the types of military aid received. Providing ammunition that can be sold by corrupt leaders is very different from providing military education that builds up human capital.

11 H.R. 3057 (109th): Foreign Operations, Export Financing, and Related Programs Appropriations Act, 2006, Section 551, www.govtrack.us/congress/bills/109/hr3057.

12 Seth G. Jones et al., *Securing Tyrants or Fostering Reform? U.S. Internal Security Assistance to Repressive and Transitioning Regimes* (Santa Monica: RAND Corporation, 2006), 152.

13 Ibid., 74–76.

14 U.S. military officer assigned to AFRICOM, interview with author, 2012.

15 David Passage, *The United States and Colombia: Untying the Gordian Knot* (Carlisle: Strategic Studies Institute, 2000), 26.

16 Phil Stewart, "U.S. Commander Seeks To Ease Human-Rights Rules That Limit Training," *Reuters,* March 6, 2013.

17 Sydney J. Freedberg, Jr., "Reps. Mac Thornberry, Adam Smith Lead House Push for More Foreign Military Training," *AOL Defense,* March 6, 2013.

18 Moyar, *A Question of Command,* 231–251.

19 Ibid., 98–107.

20 The foremost proponent of this approach to combating corruption is Robert Klitgaard, a former professor of economics at Harvard and Yale. His seminal book is *Controlling Corruption* (Berkeley: University of California Press, 1988). For

critical appraisals of this approach, see World Bank Independent Evaluation Group, "Public Sector Reform: What Works and Why?" World Bank, 2008; Anna Persson et al., "The Failure of Anti-corruption Policies: A Theoretical Mischaracterization of the Problem," Quality of Government Institute Working Papers, June 2010; Jeffrey Race, "Fighting 'Corruption' with What Really Works: Lessons from Today and from History," paper presented January 12, 2012, at the Second Conference on Evidence-Based Anti-Corruption Policies.

21 Alix J. Boucher et al., "Mapping and Fighting Corruption in War-Torn States," Henry L. Stimson Center, March 2007, 23; World Bank Independent Evaluation Group, "Public Sector Reform: What Works and Why?"

22 Newsom, "Conflict in the Niger Delta."

23 Adam Goldman and Heidi Vogt, "Afghanistan Obstructs Graft Probes," Associated Press, October 11, 2011; Special Inspector General for Afghanistan Reconstruction, Quarterly Report to the United States Congress, April 30, 2012, www.sigar.mil/pdf/quarterlyreports/2012-04-30qr.pdf, 106.

24 Moyar, *A Question of Command*, 196, 203–204.

25 Julie Lopez, "Guatemala's Crossroads: The Democratization of Violence and Second Chances," in Cynthia J. Arnson and Eric L. Olson, eds., *Organized Crime in Central America: The Northern Triangle* (Washington, DC: Woodrow Wilson Center for Scholars, 2011), 207–214; Steven S. Dudley, "Drug Trafficking Organizations in Central America: Transportistas, Mexican Cartels, and Maras," in ibid., 50; "Soldiers' Arrest Marks Shift in Guatemala," *Associated Press*, October 21, 2012.

26 James Hookway, "Philippine Leader Touts U.S.'s Asia Role," *Wall Street Journal*, February 13, 2012. A Millennium Challenge Corporation official in the Philippines gave this description of the reforms the MCC has been implementing with Aquino's cooperation: "We are supporting reforms in the Philippine Bureau of Internal Revenue to reduce opportunities for corruption and increase revenue collection by reengineering and computerizing the tax administration system. This will reduce the discretion of revenue agents in their interaction with taxpayers and improve transparency in the calculation and collection of taxes." Millennium Challenge Corporation official, interview with author, 2012.

27 Harrison, *The Central Liberal Truth*, 181–182. Much of the credit for Singapore's stunning drop in corruption goes to Lee Kuan Yew's merit-based recruitment and promotion of leaders, which included a studious refusal to show favoritism toward friends and relatives. Rotberg, *Transformative Political Leadership*, 110–112; Ghani and Lockhart, *Fixing Failed States*, 37.

28 Jones et al., *Securing Tyrants or Fostering Reform?*; U.S. Department of State, Bureau of International Narcotics and Law Enforcement Affairs, "2012 International Narcotics Control Strategy Report," vol. 1, March 2012, www.state.gov/documents/organization/187109.pdf.

29 U.S. Senate Caucus on International Narcotics Control, "Responding to Violence in Central America," 112th Cong., 1st Sess., September 2011, www.grassley.senate.gov/judiciary/upload/Drug-Caucus-09-22-11-Responding-to-Violence-in-Central-America-2011.pdf, 36–37.

30 Jayamaha et al., *Lessons Learned from U.S. Government Law Enforcement in International Operations*, 63.

31   Jones at al., *Securing Tyrants or Fostering Reform?*; U.S. Department of State, Bureau
     of International Narcotics and Law Enforcement Affairs, "2012 International Nar-
     cotics Control Strategy Report," vol. 1, March 2012, www.state.gov/documents/
     organization/187109.pdf; United States Senate Caucus on International Narcotics
     Control, "Responding to Violence in Central America," 112th Cong., 1st Sess.,
     September 2011, www.grassley.senate.gov/judiciary/upload/Drug-Caucus-09-22-
     11-Responding-to-Violence-in-Central-America-2011.pdf.

32   John Bailey, "Combating Organized Crime and Drug Trafficking in Mexico: What
     Are Mexican and U.S. Strategies? Are They Working?" in Olson et al., eds., *Shared
     Responsibility: U.S. Mexico Policy Options for Confronting Organized Crime*, 337;
     Daniel Sabiet, "Police Reform in Mexico: Advances and Persistent Obstacles," in
     Olson et al., eds., *Shared Responsibility: U.S. Mexico Policy Options for Confront-
     ing Organized Crime*, 264.

33   Sabiet, "Police Reform in Mexico: Advances and Persistent Obstacles," 255–256,
     260–261.

34   "Ecuador Police to Take Lie Detector Test," *BBC*, August 16, 2011.

35   U.S. Department of State, Bureau of International Narcotics and Law Enforcement
     Affairs, "2012 International Narcotics Control Strategy Report," vol. 1, March
     2012, www.state.gov/documents/organization/187109.pdf; U.S. Department of
     State, Bureau of International Narcotics and Law Enforcement Affairs, "2009
     End-Use Monitoring Report," September 1, 2010, www.state.gov/j/inl/rls/rpt/eum/
     2009/148247.htm.

36   Alex Leff, "Truth or Dare in Costa Rica's Presidential Campaign," February 1,
     2010, *Americas Quarterly*, www.americasquarterly.org/node/1193/.

37   Matt Levin, "What Else Can Go Wrong for Laura Chinchilla's Government?" *Tico
     Times*, April 13, 2012.

38   USAID policy pronouncements call for supporting governance in this manner.
     USAID Policy, "The Development Response to Violent Extremism and Insurgency,"
     September 2011, http://pdf.usaid.gov/pdf_docs/PDACS400.pdf, 4–5.

39   Sue Unsworth and Mick Moore, "Societies, States and Citizens: A Policymaker's
     Guide to the Research," Centre for the Future State, July 2010, www2.ids.ac.uk/
     futurestate/pdfs/Future%20State%20DRC%20Policy%20Briefing%20SSC10.pdf;
     Boucher et al., "Mapping and Fighting Corruption in War-Torn States," 43; Deven-
     dra Raj Panday, "Technical Cooperation and Institutional Capacity-Building for
     Development: Back to the Basics," in Sakiko Fukudu-Parr et al., eds., *Capacity for
     Development: New Solutions to Old Problems* (London: Earthscan, 2002), 71–72.

40   Rod Nordland, "Afghan Equality and Law, but with Strings Attached," *New York
     Times*, September 24, 2010.

41   An ardent exposition of this approach to corruption can be found in Frank Vogl,
     Waging War on Corruption: Inside the Movement Fighting the Abuse of Power
     (Lanham, MD: Rowman and Littlefield, 2012).

42   For a discussion of this practice in Africa, see J. P. Olivier de Sardan, "A Moral
     Economy of Corruption in Africa?" *Journal of Modern African Studies*, vol. 37,
     no. 1 (March 1999), 25–52.

43   Anna Persson et al., "The Failure of Anti-Corruption Policies: A Theoretical
     Mischaracterization of the Problem," Quality of Government Institute Working
     Papers, June 2010.

44 Brazilian civil society expert, interview with author, 2012.
45 U.S. and international laws have been modified in recent decades because of complaints that anticorruption prosecutions put U.S. and European firms at a competitive disadvantage, but Western firms continue to face much stiffer punishments for bribery than do non-Western firms. Prosecutions under the U.S. Foreign Corrupt Practices Act have mainly targeted U.S. and European firms. Stephen J. Choi and Kevin E. Davis, "Foreign Affairs and Enforcement of the Foreign Corrupt Practices Act," New York University Public Law and Legal Theory Working Papers, Paper 340, 2013, http://lsr.nellco.org/nyu_plltwp/340. The OECD Convention on Combating Bribery of Foreign Public Officials in International Business Transactions, which requires signatories to enact antibribery legislation, has been signed by only thirty-eight countries, most of them located in Europe or the Americas. "OECD Convention on Combating Bribery of Foreign Public Officials in International Business Transactions: Ratification Status as of 8 April 2014," www.oecd.org/daf/anti-bribery/WGBRatificationStatus_April2014.pdf.
46 Domingo, "Chronicling Corruption in the Philippines, 2005–2011."
47 David Nussbaum, "Money versus Morality: Is Corruption Just a Matter of Misaligned Incentives?" London School of Economics, October 18, 2006, www2.lse.ac.uk/PublicEvents/pdf/20061018_Nussbaum.pdf.
48 The University of Birmingham's Heather Marquette has noted, "Moral definitions of corruption have been accused of being Eurocentric, racist even." Heather Marquette, "Whither Morality? 'Finding God' in the Fight against Corruption," Religions and Development Research Programme, 2010, http://eprints.bham.ac.uk/638/1/WP41_complete_for_web.pdf.
49 In 2005, for instance, a World Bank task force praised Tanzania's civil service reform program, which began in 1999, for its emphasis on ethical behavior. Tanzania's political leaders realized that effective reform required "a cultural and behavioral reorientation," in which civil servants adopted "a mindset to serve customers with efficiency, effectiveness, and high standards of courtesy and integrity." World Bank Task Force on Capacity Development in Africa, "Building Effective States, Forging Engaged Societies," September 2005, 41–42.
50 Mark Pyman, "How Can Civil Society Best Tackle Corruption in the Security Services?" presentation at the 15th International Anti-Corruption Conference, Brasilia, November 9, 2012. For a partial description of this approach, see Transparency International Defence and Security Programme's website, www.ti-defence.org/our-work/education-training/nato.
51 As one international anticorruption proclamation put it, "corruption should be condemned and eradicated for the sake of the universally held value of integrity." Marshall and Van Saanen, *Development and Faith*, 233–234.
52 Marshall, "Ancient and Contemporary Wisdom and Practice on Governance as Religious Leaders Engage in International Development," 223.
53 CIA World Factbook, www.cia.gov/library/publications/the-world-factbook/fields/2122.html#xx, accessed April 17, 2014.
54 Marshall, "Ancient and Contemporary Wisdom and Practice on Governance as Religious Leaders Engage in International Development," 217.
55 Zambian anticorruption expert, interview with author, 2012. See also Mvume Dandala, interview with Angela Reitmaier, November 14, 2011, http://berkleycenter.

georgetown.edu/interviews/a-discussion-with-bishop-mvume-dandala; Adam Nossiter, "Church Helps Fill a Void in Africa," *New York Times*, February 23, 2013.

56   Hillary Kiirya and Adam Alagiah, "Uganda: Church Urged on Graft," Allafrica. com, June 4, 2006.

57   Harrison, *The Central Liberal Truth*, 191–192; James Surowiecki, "Punctuality Pays," *The New Yorker*, April 5, 2004.

58   Harrison, *The Central Liberal Truth*, 185–187.

MEASUREMENT

1   "Americans Flunk Budget IQ Test," CNN, http://politicalticker.blogs.cnn.com/2011/ 04/01/cnn-poll-americans-flunk-budget-iq-test/.

2   Charles Hornsby, "The History and Impact of Opinion Polls in Kenya," unpublished paper presented at the ICAD/IRI Seminar on opinion polling, Nairobi, June 2001, www.scribd.com/doc/76538933/Opinion-Polling-in-Kenya-2001. For another good example of the shortcomings of surveys in the third world, see Ryan Grim, "Experts on Afghanistan Doubt Survey on Foreign Occupation: Results Are Impossible," *Huffington Post*, March 18, 2010. The first world has also experienced its share of survey fraud. See Mark Blumenthal, "Daily Kos vs. Research 2000 Lawsuit Settled," *Huffington Post*, May 27, 2011; Elizabeth Douglass, "Edison Is Hit Hard for Fraud on Survey," *Los Angeles Times*, October 2, 2007.

3   Natsios, "The Clash of the Counter-Bureaucracy and Development"; Natsios, "The Foreign Aid Reform Agenda," 35.

4   For critiques of randomized controlled trials in the development world, see World Bank Independent Evaluation Group, "Impact Evaluation: The Experience of the Independent Evaluation Group of the World Bank," 2006; Dani Rodrik, "The New Development Economics: We Shall Experiment, But How Shall We Learn?" July 2008, www. hks.harvard.edu/fs/drodrik/Research%20papers/The%20New%20Development% 20Economics.pdf; Martin Ravallion, "Should the Randomnistas Rule?," *Economists' Voice*, February 2009; Mead Over, "Sachs Not Vindicated," January 18, 2008, http:// blogs.cgdev.org/globalhealth/2008/01/sachs-not-vindicated.php.

5   Research Triangle Institute, "Implementing School-Based Management in Indonesia: The DBE1 Experience, 2005–2010," July 2010, http://pdf.usaid.gov/pdf_docs/ pdacq711.pdf. Other examples of assessments overwhelmed by preoccupation with statistical measures include U.S. Government Accountability Office, "Combating Terrorism: Planning and Documentation of U.S. Development Assistance in Pakistan's Federally Administered Tribal Areas Need to Be Improved," GAO-10–289, April 2010; Government Accountability Office, "Foreign Police Assistance: Defined Roles and Improved Information Sharing Could Enhance Interagency Collaboration," May 2012.

6   USAID official, interview with author, 2012.

7   Donna R. Dinkin and Robert J. Taylor, "Evaluation of the Leadership, Management and Sustainability (LMS) Project," Global Health Technical Assistance Project, September 2009, www.ghtechproject.com/files/LMS_final_508_9-28-09.pdf.

8   See, for example, Carl Levin, Senate Floor Speech, "Surge the Afghan Army," September 11, 2009, www.levin.senate.gov/newsroom/press/release/?id=e88c9643-97d4-4abd-b751-5f6a2f552359.

9   For the adverse consequences of the rushed expansion, see Rajiv Chandrasekaran, "Afghan Security Force's Rapid Expansion Comes at a Cost as Readiness Lags," *Washington Post*, October 20, 2012; James K. Wither, "Challenges of Developing Host Nation Police Capacity," *Prism*, vol. 3, no. 4 (September 2012), 39–53.

10 For a thorough and incisive discussion of the methodologies of academic disciplines, see Gaddis, *The Landscape of History*.

11 Charles R. Martin, *Looking at Type: The Fundamentals* (Gainesville, FL: Center for Applications of Psychological Type, 1997), 49.

12 For individual differences in cognition and decision making, see Stephen A. Stumpf and Roger L. M. Dunbar, "The Effects of Personality Type on Choices Made in Strategic Decision Situations," *Decision Sciences*, vol. 22, no. 5 (November/December 1991), 1047–1072; Allan H. Church and Janine Waclawski, "The Relationship between Individual Personality Orientation and Executive Leadership Behaviour," *Journal of Occupational and Organizational Psychology*, vol. 71, no. 2 (June 1998), 99–125; Reg Lang, "Type Flexibility in Processes of Strategic Planning and Change," in Catherine Fitzgerald and Linda K. Kirby, eds., *Developing Leaders: Research and Applications Psychological Type and Leadership Development* (Palo Alto, CA: Davies Black, 1997), 487–511; John C. Henderson and Paul C. Nutt, "The Influence of Decision Style on Decision Making Behavior," *Management Science*, 26, no. 4 (April 1980), 371–386; W. Scott Sherman et al., "Organizational Morphing: The Challenges of Leading Perpetually Changing Organizations in the Twenty-First Century," in James G. Hunt et al., eds., *Out-of-the-Box Leadership: Transforming the Twenty-First-Century Army and Other Top-Performing Organizations* (Stamford, CT: JAI, 1999), 43–62. Examples of the data collection practices of effective and ineffective leaders can be found in Moyar, *A Question of Command*.

13 On the lack of concern with quantification in the early Cold War, see Coleman and Court, *University Development in the Third World*, 26.

Index

Cameroon, democratization efforts in, 81
capitalism
    free-market, 8
    positive perspectives regarding after Cold
        War, 68
Captain General Gerardo Barrios Military
    School, 149
Carson, Johnnie, 5
Catholic University of Chile, 154–66
Center for Strategic and International Studies,
    19–20, 94
Central Asia, leadership in, 35
Chad, corruption in, 13
change, receptivity to in Western civilization, 40
charisma, 60
cheetah generation, 35
Chiang Kai-shek, 29
"Chicago Boys," 154–66
chiefs of state, as human capital, 59
children. *See* primary education; secondary
    education
Chile, impact of U.S. education on economy of,
    154–66
China
    Christianity's role in economic ascent
        of, 47
    concerns regarding students in the U.S.,
        159–60
    economic growth of, 145
Chinchilla, Laura, 176–7
Christianity
    conversion of students to, 152
    effect on Western civilization, 42–6
    faith-based institutions of higher learning,
        146–7
    relation to corruption, 44, 55–7
    role in Western-inspired economic
        ascents, 47
CICIG (Comision Internacional contra la
    Impunidad en Guatemala [International
    Commission against Impunity in
    Guatemala]), 174
Cissé, Amadou, 146
citizenship requirements for classified projects,
    159–60
civic virtue, in Western civilization, 41
Civil Affairs units, U.S. military, 125–9, 198
civil agencies. *See also specific civil agencies*
    failure of in governance and development,
        119–23
    police training activities by, 129–30, 198
    U.S., education through, 163, 200

civil operations
    involvement of militaries in, 114–19, 197
    by U.S. military since 9/11, 119–23
civil society organizations, support for, 177–9
civil training, 98–9, 112–13. *See also*
    militarization
    brain drain, 106–7
    motivational impact of, 105–6
    personnel, 101–3
    political elites and, 103–5
    speed and efficiency of, 99–101
    in strategy for foreign assistance, 197
civil wars, 77–80. *See also* wars
civilization, 39, 57, 202. *See also* culture
    borrowing of by non-Western nations, 46–50
    Christianity, 42–6
    education at first world universities, 151–3
    forecasting of civilizational conflict, 68
    and governance, 50–7
    and inequality of nations, 39–42
    postcolonial Westernization, 153
    in strategy for foreign assistance, 196
    in U.S. education, 163–6, 199
    waning influence of Western, 46–50
civilizational conflict, forecasting of, 68
civilizational convergence paradigm, 67–9
Clapper, James R., 71
The Clash of Civilizations, 40, 49–50
classified projects, foreign workers on, 159–60
Cleary, Laura, Dr., 108
Clinton, Bill, 45
Clinton, Hillary, 5
Coalition Provisional Authority (CPA), Iraq,
    120
coca elimination program, Colombia, 19–20
Cold War, 66–7
Collier, Paul, 115–16, 158
Colombia
    coca elimination program in, 19–20
    counternarcotics in, 90–2
    DEA vetted units in, 175
    military training in, 110
    role of military in internal affairs, 115
    U.S. military aid conditionality, 172
colonialism, European
    civil training under, 102–3
    education at first world universities, 151–3
    and higher education, 140
combat officers, governance assistance from,
    127–8
combat zones, civil agencies in, 120–3. *See also*
    wars